The Development of autism

of related interest

Children with Autism
Diagnosis and Intervention to Meet Their Needs, 2nd Edition
Colwyn Trevarthen, Kenneth Aitken, Despina Papoudi and Jacqueline Roberts
ISBN 1 85302 555 0

Autism – From Research to Individualized Practice
Edited by Robin L. Gabriels and Dina E. Hill
Foreword by Dr Gary B. Mesibov
ISBN 1 84310 701 5

Understanding Autism Spectrum Disorders
Frequently Asked Questions
Diane Yapko
ISBN 1 84310 756 2

Asperger's Syndrome
A Guide for Parents and Professionals
Tony Attwood
Foreword by Lorna Wing
ISBN 1 85302 577 1

Caring for a Child with Autism
A Practical Guide for Parents
Martine Ives and Nell Munro
ISBN 1 85302 996 3

From Goals to Data and Back Again
Adding Backbone to Developmental Intervention for Children
with Autism
Jill Fain Lehman and Rebecca Klaw
ISBN 1 84310 753 8

The Development of autism
A Self-Regulatory Perspective

Thomas L. Whitman

Jessica Kingsley Publishers
London and New York

First published in the United Kingdom in 2004
by Jessica Kingsley Publishers Ltd
116 Pentonville Road
London N1 9JB, England
and
29 West 35th Street, 10th fl.
New York, NY 10001-2299, USA

www.jkp.com

Copyright © Thomas L. Whitman 2004

Library of Congress Cataloging in Publication Data
A CIP catalog record for this book is available from the Library of Congress

British Library Cataloguing in Publication Data
A CIP catalogue record for this book is available from the British Library

ISBN 1 84310 735 X
Printed and Bound in Great Britain by
Athenaeum Press, Gateshead, Tyne and Wear

Dedication

For Michael, Amy, Christopher, and Grandma Kathy.
Also for the many families who started me on the journey
to writing this book and helped me understand the real
meaning of autism.

Contents

Contents

Preface

Autism is a developmental disorder that has both fascinated and frustrated the scientific and clinical community. Although extensive research has attempted to isolate the neuropsychological basis of this complex disorder, its etiology remains elusive. Autism also presents major challenges to those providing services. Considerable controversy exists concerning how education and biomedical interventions should be structured and what constitutes best treatment practices. Further complicating this picture is the barrage of conflicting and incomplete information put forth in popular magazines, movies, television, and the Internet about autism. Not surprisingly, the formulation of useful public policy for dealing with autism awaits clarification from the scientific, medical, and educational communities. Despite the incomplete state of knowledge regarding the nature and treatment of autism, recent research and scholarly activity are beginning to yield a more precise picture of this disorder. In particular, there is intriguing new information about both the biological bases of this disorder and the role that the environment plays in its evolution. Moreover, new and more empirically based interventions are beginning to emerge.

This book was developed to address the needs of several different audiences, including parents, teachers, students taking a course in autism, therapists and health care professionals, and autism scholars/researchers. Because of the diversity of the intended readership, certain compromises have been made regarding the way materials are presented and developed. For parents, teachers, and beginning students of autism, the book serves as an introduction to autism, including its definition, assessment, basic characteristics, possible causes, and treatments. Family and social policy issues are also discussed at length. Teachers seeking a text on autism will find that this book not only covers the basics but also looks at autism from a broad theoretical and empirical perspective. For professionals who provide services to children with autism, this text can serve as a basic handbook on autism. It provides concise summaries and critical perspectives on assessment approaches, characteristics of autism, theories of autism, educational and treatment programs, and family stress and coping. For researchers, it is hoped this book will be theoretically provocative, stimulate a different way of thinking about autism, and suggest new research agendas.

This book differs from most previous works in a number of ways. It moves beyond current definitions of autism to discuss the complex and variable ways this disorder is manifested. In addition to summarizing popular theories of autism, it proposes a new comprehensive theoretical framework that is directed toward reconciling and integrating past theories. The broader social context in which autism occurs is examined, including its impact on the family. In addition to describing a wide range of educational and biomedical interventions, it takes a critical look at the present state of treatment for autism. More generally, the book looks at autism from a developmental perspective. It seeks to provide a dynamic picture of how it emerges and the role that emotional, sensory, motor, cognitive, and social processes play in its development. The book also provides the reader insights into the world of individuals with autism; more specifically why they isolate themselves from the social world and order their thoughts, emotions, behaviors, and environment through an unusual array of obsessions and compulsive behaviors.

The book consists of seven chapters. Chapter 1 discusses autism from a historical perspective; the definitions and criteria that are employed in the diagnosis of autism; distinctions between autism and related disorders; approaches to assessment; and finally, incidence and prevalence data, including recent information suggesting an increase in the incidence of autism. Chapter 2 describes in greater detail the key symptoms (i.e. its social, language, and stereotyped/ritualistic features) that define autism, as well as symptoms (sensory, motor, emotional, cognitive, and medical/physical) that are not included as part of its formal definition, but are important for understanding this disorder. Recent research examining this symptomatology is reviewed along with studies distinguishing autism from other developmental disorders.

In Chapter 3, historical and current theories of autism are summarized, including those emphasizing socioenvironmental, psychological, and biological factors. The psychological theories examine a number of processes that have been postulated to play a major role in autism, including cognitive (information processing, executive function, theory of mind, metacognition, and intersubjective), language, sensory integration, and arousal/activation. The biological theories reviewed examine the role of genetic, anatomical, and biochemical factors. Chapter 4 presents a new theory of autism that examines the diverse (emotional, motor, sensory, cognitive, language, and social) symptoms of autism within a developmental framework and seeks to explain individual differences in the ways this disorder is manifested in a way that makes sense from both a psychological and biological perspective. The unique self-regulatory system of individuals with autism is discussed, including reasons for its emergence and the functions this system serves in controlling emotions, cognitions, and behavior.

Chapter 5 describes a wide variety of educational and biomedical interventions that have been utilized to treat autism and examines their validity in the context of past theory and existing research. These intervention programs include behavior education (e.g., discrete trial learning), TEACCH, sensorimotor, speech and communication, play, behavioral deceleration, pharmacological, hormone, anti-yeast, homeopathic, immunologic, vitamin and dietary therapies, as well as other approaches. Chapter 6 describes the impact that children with autism have on their families and how these families influence the development of their children. More specifically, it examines the challenges that confront families of children with autism; the impact of autism, both positive and negative, on different family members; the characteristics of families that cope most successfully with these challenges (i.e. family resiliency); and family intervention and services. In Chapter 7, recommendations are made to parents, educators, and other health professionals regarding best treatment practices and enhancing family resiliency. Recommendations are made to researchers concerning areas in need of empirical investigation and specific suggestions about directions for applied and basic research. Finally, guidance is given to legislators and administrators to assist them in developing a coherent social policy that reflects current thinking on autism.

A number of people have been very helpful in preparing this book. Many students have provided me new insights about autism, through class discussion and their papers. Special thanks to Julie Van Weelden who assisted me immensely through her "library" research and editing comments; Jaelyn Farris, Leann Smith and Chelsea Weaver who helped me in making the book more reader-friendly; Amy Daynes for her many contributions and support; and Judy Stewart and Pauline Wright for their assistance in word processing and their patience. Finally, I would like to thank the many families who have allowed my students to come into their homes. It has been and remains my conviction that the real experts in the area of autism are the parents. They have taught me so much about autism and the meaning of family. In recognition of their contribution to this book, all royalties will be contributed to the Michiana Regional Autism Center.

CHAPTER 1

History, Definition, and Assessment

A young boy sits in the middle of a playroom floor rocking back and forth. After a while he ceases this activity and picks up a small toy truck. He tips the truck upside down and begins to spin its wheels around and around and around. As he spins the wheels, his eyes remain glued on the truck, his face expressionless. After ten minutes of this activity, his father comes over, calls the boy's name and asks him if he wants to go for a walk outside. The boy, seemingly oblivious to his father, continues to spin the truck's wheels and begins to rock gently. The father, disappointed, leaves the room and his son in his autistic world.

In recent years, public interest in autism has grown considerably. This interest has evolved in part because of the attention the mass media has given to this topic. For example, there have been a number of popular movies featuring persons with autism, such as *Rain Man*, *What's Eating Gilbert Grape*, and *Mercury Rising*. Discussions about autism are also commonplace on the radio and television and in newspapers and magazines. The public has been fascinated by the image of a beautiful child who has unusual abilities and lives in a secret world.

Media interest has been in turn catalyzed by the growing number of people speaking out on behalf of people with autism, including parents of children with autism, professionals involved in treatment and/or research, individuals with autism, and social policy-makers. Parents have advocated for specialized services for their children. Therapists, impressed by the achievements of children with autism when placed in educational programs, have argued for the development of intensive early intervention programs. Researchers, intrigued by the multifaceted nature of autism, have sought funding to understand the role that biological and environmental factors play in its emergence. Individuals with autism have described, sometimes with great eloquence, their struggles, desires, and needs. As a consequence of such advocacy for the development of quality services and research, community agencies and politicians have been compelled to address a public demand for action.

Autism is like a mystery novel in which it is not clear exactly what happened to one of the major characters, why it happened, and who or what is responsible. Autism has also been likened to a complex puzzle, with many parts that just do not seem to fit together. Sometimes it appears that the parts of the puzzle can be put together in various ways to create different pictures of autism. Questions then arise as to whether there is one or many correct solutions to this puzzle. In this book, the autism puzzle, and the possible ways this puzzle can be solved, will be examined within a developmental theoretical framework, drawing upon both traditional concepts of developmental psychology and more recently emerging perspectives espoused by scholars working in the areas of lifespan development and developmental psychopathology.

The examination of autism within a developmental context makes particular sense because it is a developmental disability. By definition, individuals diagnosed with autism display their symptoms before 36 months of age. Autism is a condition that emerges gradually, with its trajectory of development varying considerably from individual to individual. Children with autism vary not only in the severity and pattern of their symptoms, but also in their response to early intervention programs. Information gained from research in developmental psychology, which focuses on studying typical development, has helped to illuminate the nature of the deficiencies associated with autism. Conversely, the study of autism has provided researchers new insights into the diverse ways in which development can occur.

In this book we examine the multitude of ways in which autism manifests itself developmentally, including how it affects emotional, sensory, motor, cognitive, linguistic, and social functioning. Historically, theoreticians and researchers studying normal development have often focused on one of these processes to the exclusion of the others. In particular, developmental researchers, influenced by Piaget as well as more recent theoretical conceptualizations, have focused their attention on the study of cognitive development. Basic research in the area of autism has had a similar bias. As will be discussed in Chapter 3, many of the current psychological theories of autism have a distinctively cognitive flavor.

However, with the emergence of the areas of lifespan psychology and developmental psychopathology, there has been increasing emphasis on examining the interrelationships between different developmental domains, particularly the reciprocal influence of the emotional, cognitive, and social systems on each other. Moreover, interest in sensory, motor, and language development has increased. Considerable attention has also been placed on studying the evolution of these various developmental processes within the social context of the family and community.

In addition to examining the interrelationship of various psychological and social processes, developmental psychologists emphasize the study of individual differences; that is, how people differ from each other and why these differences occur. Two basic approaches have been employed in this regard. One approach examines the different ways that one group of persons vary from a second group, for example, how persons with autism differ socially or cognitively from persons without autism. A second approach examines differences within a particular group, for example, how individuals with autism differ from one another in characteristics such as social behavior and language. Although research on autism has been more of the first type, it will be argued in this book that the second approach is also very useful and can provide valuable insights into the development of autism and the possibility of different types of autism. Because autism is a spectrum disorder, in which individuals vary considerably from one another, theories and methodologies are needed that examine the reasons for these differences rather than using approaches that implicitly assume that all individuals with autism are alike.

The present book focuses on describing within a developmental framework the many ways in which autism is manifested, how these diverse manifestations can be explained, and what the implications of such diversity are for designing intervention programs. Chapter 2 will discuss in detail the common characteristics associated with autism, both those that are considered core for diagnostic purposes, as well as other non-core, but frequently occurring, features. Chapter 3 will examine the diverse conceptions, both psychological and biological, about the origins and development of autism. In Chapter 4, a new theory of autism will be proposed in an attempt to integrate existing theories into a broader conceptual framework. More specifically, a theoretical perspective will be presented that emphasizes the influence of the emotional, sensory, and motor systems on cognitive, linguistic, and social development in children with autism; and how these processes, in combination, influence the emergence of a unique self-regulatory system. Chapter 5 describes and evaluates educational and biomedical intervention approaches for "treating" autism, including nonvalidated and controversial treatments commonly employed by professionals and families. Chapter 6 examines the stressors confronted by families of children with autism and their effects, both positive and negative, on family functioning. In addition, the characteristics of resilient families who are able to cope successfully with these stressors, along with intervention strategies for promoting such resiliency, will be described. In the final chapter, specific recommendations are made to parents, therapists, researchers, and public officials regarding a variety of issues, including intervention programs, research, and social policy.

In this first chapter, a brief history of autism will be provided, followed by a discussion about the definition of autism, its diagnosis, and various types of assessment procedures. In addition, clarification of terms often encountered in the autism literature, such as "developmental disability", "pervasive developmental disorder", "autism spectrum disorder", "atypical autism", and "mental retardation", will be provided. Finally, there will be discussion about the demographics (distribution) of autism in the population, the reported increases in the incidence of autism, and prognosis.

A brief history of autism

Although in one sense the history of autism is a relatively short one, it is embedded in a longer history of mental illness and mental retardation. Since the nineteenth century, our knowledge about early childhood disorders, the role of biological and environmental factors in their development, and treatment approaches has grown exponentially. Although discussions about autism began over 60 years ago, full recognition of it as an entity separate from other disorders, such as childhood schizophrenia and mental retardation, only gradually evolved. Most histories of autism begin in the 1940s with the work of Leo Kanner, a child psychiatrist, who published a paper describing a new disorder, infantile autism, and the work of a pediatrician, Hans Asperger, who described a similar disorder that has become known as Asperger's Syndrome.

According to Kanner (1943), the major characteristics of autism included an inability to relate to people, a failure to use language for communication purposes in social situations, a resistance to change and an obsessive preoccupation with maintaining sameness, an orientation toward objects to the exclusion of people, and good cognitive/intellectual capabilities. He also noted a lack of response to their environment, strict adherence to routines, emotional turmoil when rituals were disrupted, and unusual language, which included tendencies to echo the speech of others, to respond literally to language, and to use pronouns inappropriately. Kanner believed that most children with autism had average to above average intelligence, a viewpoint not shared by most current scholars and researchers. In a later publication, Eisenberg and Kanner (1956) characterized autism in terms of three prime features: a sense of aloneness, a preoccupation with maintaining sameness, and an onset of the condition in the first two years of life.

Although Kanner is credited with the identification of and many insightful descriptions about infantile autism, he is frequently criticized for his ideas about its origins. He viewed autism, at least in part, as a response to a parenting style devoid of emotional warmth; a response in which the child withdraws from an unpleasant social reality into a private internal world. At one point, Kanner (1952) indicated that autism was difficult to treat because of lack of parental cooperation and suggested that children with autism might be better off if they were placed in a foster home. Whereas Kanner emphasized more the affective components of autism, others subsequently have focused on the cognitive deficits associated with this disorder, particularly problems in processing social and emotional information (Hobson, 1993; Rutter, 1983).

Shortly after Kanner's (1943) publication, Hans Asperger described a syndrome similar to that of Kanner's that was also characterized by social limitations and obsessive interests. In contrast to Kanner's description of autism, however, individuals with Asperger's Syndrome, as it has become called, were observed as being more typical in their language development. Asperger (1944) pointed out that the speech of this group of individuals, while not delayed, was nevertheless unusual and stereotyped. The nonverbal aspects of their communications were also odd, involving bland facial expressions and inappropriate gesturing. Wing (1981) brought Asperger's work (Asperger, 1944) to the attention of professional audiences, in an attempt to differentiate a form of autism that did not fit the Kanner stereotype of children who were uncommunicative. Currently, there is a debate about whether there is a real difference between children with autism who are high functioning and children with Asperger's Syndrome.

Although autism was not formally mentioned as a disorder prior to Kanner's 1943 publication, it almost certainly existed. Before Kanner, individuals with autism were likely included as part of other disorders, such as childhood psychosis or mental retardation, or were simply viewed as being odd and peculiar people. Some authors of books on autism suggest that Jean Itard's Wild Boy of Aveyron may have been autistic (Itard, 1962). Itard lived during a period, the later nineteenth century, when a more rational and scientific attitude about developmental disabilities was starting to emerge. According to Itard, a boy was found in 1879 wandering in a wood in France, where he apparently had lived for many years without human contact. When captured, the boy was animal-like in his behavior. After being examined by Pinel, commonly regarded as a father of modern psychiatry, the child was pronounced to be an incurable "idiot". However, Itard, a physician at a Paris institution for deaf mutes, suggested that the boy's condition resulted from his lack of social contact and was curable. Itard proceeded to treat the boy, who was named Viktor. Although Itard failed in his goal to normalize the boy, Viktor showed significant behavioral changes. As a consequence of his work, Itard instilled optimism in others concerning the treatability of children with significant developmental delays and influenced a student of his, Sequin, who later received acclaim for his influence on the development of special education programs in Europe and the United States.

Two other individuals of note in the early history of autism are Bruno Bettleheim and Bernard Rimland. Bettleheim, like Kanner, emphasized the importance of the social environment in the development of autism (Bettleheim, 1967). Perhaps influenced by his own personal history as a prisoner in a Nazi concentration camp, Bettleheim saw children with autism as victims of environmental trauma, and more specifically maternal neglect. From his perspective, autism, and in particular its symptoms of social withdrawal and apathy, evolved due to the emotional aloofness of "refriger-ator" mothers. Although Kanner and Bettleheim have been strongly criticized for their etiological perspective on autism, their viewpoint was not surprising given the Zeitgeist in which they lived: a time when psychoanalytic perspectives dominated thinking about mental illness and emphasized the influence of the early social environment on socioemotional development. Their theory of autism was subsequently disputed by most members of the medical and psychological communities, including Bernard Rimland, who put forth a bio-logically based theory of autism.

Rimland (1964) indicated that the evidence for a biological theory of autism was compelling. In support of this position, he cited research indicating that: 1) the personality patterns of most parents of autistic children did not fit Kanner's stereotyped characterization of them as cool and detached; 2) most siblings of children with autism were not autistic; 3) the ratio of autism in boys to girls was typically around three or four to one; 4) there was a high co-morbidity of autism in identical twins; and 5) autistic-like symptoms were associated with an organic brain dysfunction. In addition to his scholarly work, Rimland, a parent of a son with autism, was an active advocate for children with autism and played an instrumental role in forming the Autism Society of America, a national parents' organization with state and local chapters. Currently, his work and influence on the area of autism continues.

More generally, the area of autism was profoundly influenced by social movements, political activism, and research in the areas of mental retardation and developmental disabilities during the 1950s, 1960s and 1970s. At this point in history there was a growing concern in the United States that not enough was being done to help children with disabilities. Through the efforts of parents, the National Association for Retarded Children was formed, which helped catalyze the emergence of new services for children with developmental delays. The 1960s were a time of moral indignation in the United States when inhumane treatment practices in institutions were exposed in books such as *Christmas in Purgatory* (Blatt & Kaplan, 1966) and by visitors to the United States like Bengte Nirje, who characterized institutions for the mentally retarded as Nazi concentration camps (Nirje, 1969).

Nirje introduced the normalization principle into the American culture. Influenced by service models developed in the Scandinavian countries, the normalization principle guided program structure and delivery. Normalization, as defined by Nirje (1969), meant making available to persons with disabilities conditions of everyday life that were as close as possible to the norms and patterns of mainstream society. The normalization philosophy influenced what services were available, the quality of services, where services were delivered, and who delivered the services. At this same time, political activism in the United States during the Kennedy and Johnson presidencies led to the development of the President's Commission on Mental Retardation, the War on Poverty, early intervention programs, such as Head Start, and an array of other programs affecting the welfare of individuals with developmental disabilities. In the 1970s, rights to active treatment, education, due process, and freedom from harm were established through citizen and legal advocacy for individuals with disabilities.

In addition to these events, the emergence of behavior modification, a teaching and therapeutic approach based on learning theory, had a pronounced impact on the types of service delivered in residential institutions, schools, and home settings. Initially, behavior modification programs were utilized with difficult-to-treat populations, such as individuals with severe and profound levels of mental retardation. Eventually, because of the empirically documented success of this approach, behavioral techniques were employed in working with a variety of clinical populations as well as for teaching children in regular schools. It was within this context that another individual important in the history of autism emerged, Ivar Lovaas.

Lovaas developed a form of behavior modification, called discrete trial training, for use with children with autism. He found that they could be taught a wide variety of adaptive behaviors, including self-help, language, social, and academic skills. He offered evidence suggesting that some of these children, including individuals who originally had extensive developmental delays, were able to achieve a normal range of functioning. Important hallmarks of this behavioral approach include its emphasis on: 1) defining treatment goals; 2) the use of systematic prompts to assist children in learning; 3) the employment of individualized, motivational/reinforcement procedures; 4) starting early and intensive programming (20–40 hours per week); and 5) the ongoing evaluation of treatment effects. Perhaps the most important characteristic of this approach is its focus on training parents and teachers to deliver the intervention program in the children's everyday living environments.

Lovaas's influence has been extended through the work of second generation professionals, such as Robert Koegel and Laura Schreibman. For information on Lovaas and the behavioral approach, the reader is referred to Koegel and Koegel (1995), Lovaas (1977), Lovaas (1992), and Schreibman (1988). Further testimony to the influence and popularity of the behavioral approach is found in books by Catherine Maurice: *Let me hear your voice* (Maurice, 1993), and *Behavioral interventions for young children* (Maurice, Green & Luce, 1996). In these books, Maurice describes her search to help her children with autism. She provides extensive information about the process of establishing a behavior intervention program, along with anecdotal and clinical evidence concerning its effectiveness.

In addition to Lovaas, many other individuals have made significant contributions to the development of intervention programs as well as research on autism. For example, Eric Schopler and Gary Mesibov have contributed to the area of autism through their general scholarship, editorship of the *Journal of Autism and Developmental Disorders*, and particularly through their influence on the development of the TEACCH model of treatment. TEACCH, initially designed to serve children with autism and related communication handicaps in North Carolina, has been disseminated widely in the United States, as well as other countries of the world. It is a multidimensional program that addresses the needs of persons with autism throughout the lifespan. It integrates a variety of treatments in an effort to address the unique needs of each individual. Emphasis is placed on program evaluation. Because it is guided by research in other areas and best practices, the structure of TEACCH has evolved over time and continues to change.

The list of scholars and researchers who have made notable contributions to the field of autism is extensive and continues to expand. It includes many individuals cited in this volume, such as Marian Sigman, Eric Courchesne, Peter Hobson, Uta Frith, Helen Tager-Flusberg, Simon Baron-Cohen, Francesca Happé, James Russell, Michael Rutter, and many others too numerous to mention here. No history of autism would be complete without mentioning the considerable influence of the work of individuals with autism, such as Temple Grandin and Donna Williams, as well that of families who have children with autism. Their insider perspectives have provided considerable insights into the nature of autism as well as helping to catalyze the development of theory, research, and intervention programs.

Defining autism and its boundaries

Historically, there has been some confusion concerning exactly what autism is and how it differs from nonautistic disorders. This confusion is quite understandable, given that the definition of autism has changed somewhat over time as the boundaries between autism and other disorders have been gradually refined. Even currently, different professional organizations utilize slightly different definitions. The confusion concerning the meaning of autism is particularly apparent when autism is considered in the context of other terms, such as pervasive developmental disability, atypical autism, autism spectrum disorder, Asperger's Syndrome, mental retardation, developmental disability, and schizophrenia.

For a variety of reasons, it is important to clarify what is meant by the term "autism". A concrete definition allows for clear communication between professionals and parents concerning what autism is, helps researchers to study this disorder in an orderly fashion, and assists therapists in developing and evaluating intervention programs. In this section, autism will be first defined and then discussed in the context of other related terminology.

Autistic Disorder

It is beyond the scope of this chapter to review the wide variety of definitions of autism that have been put forth historically, as well as all those currently employed. For a discussion of some of these other definitions, the reader is referred to the *International classification of diseases* put out by the World Health Organization (1990) and Simpson and Myles (1998). Despite the multiplicity of definitions of autism, there has also been continuity in how they have been structured since Leo Kanner first described this syndrome. In general, most definitions have referred to the social, language, and unusual behavioral (e.g., stereotyped responses) characteristics of individuals with autism. Definitions of autism and discussions about the nature of this disorder have differed from each other in the specific subcharacteristics listed under the three aforementioned categories and in their degree of reference to other characteristics, such as atypical emotional, cognitive, motor, and sensory responses. In the next chapter, a comprehensive description and discussion of these characteristics will be presented.

The definition of autism used to guide discussion in this book is cited frequently in current texts on autism; specifically it is the definition put forth in the *Diagnostic and Statistical Manual of Mental Disorders, Fourth Edition* (DSM-IV) published by the American Psychiatric Association in 1994. This definition is commonly employed by professionals as a guide for classification and scientific study.

According to the DSM-IV, autism refers to a disorder in which persons manifest the following characteristics: social interaction impairments; communication problems; and repetitive, stereotypic, and restricted interests and activities. Autism is often referred to as a syndrome because it consists of a composite of different characteristics which occur in conjunction with each other. To be classified as autistic, individuals must manifest at least six of the symptoms described in the DSM-IV prior to three years of age. The DSM-IV diagnostic criteria for Autistic Disorder is summarized below:

SOCIAL INTERACTION IMPAIRMENTS (AT LEAST TWO OF THE FOLLOWING CHARACTERISTICS)

- Significant impairment in the use of nonverbal behaviors, such as eye-to-eye gaze, facial expression, body posture, and social interaction gestures
- Developmentally inappropriate peer relationships

- Failure to seek out others for the purpose of sharing enjoyment, interests, or achievements
- Poor social or emotional reciprocity

QUALITATIVE COMMUNICATION IMPAIRMENTS (AT LEAST ONE OF THE FOLLOWING CHARACTERISTICS)

- Delay in or absence of spoken language development as well as alternative modes of communication such as gestures
- Significant impairment initiating and/or maintaining a conversation with others (in persons with adequate speech)
- Idiosyncratic or stereotyped and repetitive language usage
- Lack of developmentally appropriate social-imitative or make-believe play

REPETITIVE, RESTRICTED, AND STEREOTYPED INTERESTS, ACTIVITIES, AND PATTERNS OF BEHAVIOR (AT LEAST ONE OF THE FOLLOWING CHARACTERISTICS)

- Preoccupation with one or several stereotyped and restricted interests which are abnormal either in their focus or intensity
- Inflexible adherence to nonfunctional routines or rituals
- Repetitive and stereotyped motor movements, such as hand flapping and rocking
- Persistent preoccupation with a specific part of an object

The reader is referred to DSM-IV for more specific information on this disorder (APA, 1994).

Autism and Pervasive Developmental Disorders

Within the DSM-IV classification system, Autistic Disorder is one of several disorders or subcategories within a larger category of Pervasive Developmental Disorders (PDDs). PDDs, including Autistic Disorder, are all "characterized by severe and pervasive impairment in several areas of development: reciprocal social interaction skills, communication skills, or the presence of stereotyped behaviors, interests and activities" (American Psychiatric Association, 1994, p. 69). Autism differs from the other Pervasive Developmental Disorders in the range and/or severity of its symptoms. The other disorders, besides Autistic Disorder, subclassified under PDD are: Rett's Disorder, Childhood Disintegrative Disorder, Asperger's Syndrome, and Pervasive

Developmental Disorder – Not Otherwise Specified (PDD-NOS). All of these disorders, which share many characteristics in common with autism, are sometimes referred to as nonautistic PDDs. Each of them will be briefly described and contrasted with the diagnostic criteria for Autistic Disorder.

RETT'S DISORDER

Individuals diagnosed with Rett's Disorder experience: "1) apparently normal prenatal and perinatal development, 2) apparently normal psychomotor development during the first five months after birth, and 3) normal head circumference at birth" (American Psychiatric Association, 1994, p. 77). The disorder manifests itself following a period of normal development, with its onset associated with the following features:

1. deceleration of head growth between ages 5 and 48 months

2. loss of previously acquired purposeful hand skills between ages 5 and 30 months with the subsequent development of stereotyped hand movements (e.g., hand wringing or handwashing)

3. loss of social engagement early in the course (although social interaction develops later)

4. appearance of poorly coordinated gait or trunk movements

5. severely impaired expressive and receptive language development with severe psychomotor retardation.

(American Psychiatric Association, 1994, p. 77)

Two other important features of Rett's Disorder are that it has only been reported in females and is typically associated with severe or profound mental retardation.

The features that most sharply distinguish Rett's Disorder from Autistic Disorder are its characteristic pattern of head growth deceleration, the loss of purposeful hand skills, the appearance of poorly coordinated gait or trunk movements, and the fact that Rett's Disorder occurs only in females, whereas Autistic Disorder occurs much more frequently in males.

CHILDHOOD DISINTEGRATIVE DISORDER

The critical feature of this disorder:

is a marked regression in multiple areas of functioning following a period of at least two years of apparently normal development in

age-appropriate verbal and nonverbal communication, social relationships, play, and adaptive behavior.

(American Psychiatric Association, 1994, p. 77)

After two years, but before ten years, the child loses previously acquired skills
in at least two of the following areas: expressive or receptive language, social
skills, or adaptive behavior, bowel or bladder control, play or motor skills.
Individuals with Childhood Disintegrative Disorder generally display all of
the characteristics cited for Autistic Disorder, including impairments in social
interaction, communication, and restrictive, repetitive, and stereotyped
features of behavior, interests, and activities. Thus, the main feature that distinguishes Childhood Disintegrative Disorder from Autistic Disorder is the
occurrence of developmental regression following at least two years of normal
development. If this regression cannot be documented, a diagnosis of Autistic
Disorder is recommended by DSM-IV (American Psychiatric Association,
1994).

ASPERGER'S SYNDROME

The diagnostic criteria for this disorder are like those of Autistic Disorder,
insofar as there are qualitative impairments in social interaction and the
presence of restricted, repetitive, and stereotyped patterns of behavior,
interests, and activities. However, it differs from Autistic Disorder in that there
is no significant general delay in early language development. There are also
no significant delays during the first three years of life in cognitive development or in the development of learning skills and other adaptive behaviors,
with the exception of those in the social interaction domain. Curiosity about
the environment is also displayed (American Psychiatric Association, 1994).
Asperger's Syndrome is nevertheless associated with clinically significant
impairments in social, occupational, and other important areas of functioning.
There is some disagreement in the research literature concerning whether
individuals with Asperger's Syndrome are really different from high functioning individuals with Autistic Disorder (Ghaziuddin, Leininger & Tsai,
1995).

PERVASIVE DEVELOPMENTAL DISORDER – NOT OTHERWISE SPECIFIED (PDD-NOS)

DSM-IV points out that:

This category should be used when there is a severe and pervasive
impairment in the development of reciprocal social interaction
associated with impairment in either verbal and nonverbal communica-

tion skills or with the presence of stereotyped behavior, interests, and activities, but the criteria are not met for a specific Pervasive Developmental Disorder, Schizophrenia, Schizotypal Personality Disorder, or Avoidant Personality Disorder.

(American Psychiatric Association, 1994, p. 84)

DSM-IV indicates that:

This category includes atypical autism – presentations that do not meet the criteria for autistic disorder because of the late age of onset, atypical symptomatology, or subthreshold symptomatology, or all of these.

(American Psychiatric Association, 1994, p. 84)

GENERAL COMMENTS

An attempt was made to capture here the essence of the criteria for diagnosing Autistic Disorder and its distinctions from other specific Pervasive Developmental Disorders (i.e. Rett's, Childhood Disintegrative, and Asperger's Syndrome as well as the less specific PDD-NOS). The reader is referred for additional information to the DSM-IV (American Psychiatric Association, 1994). Although significant progress has been made in defining the nature of Autistic Disorder, there remains, from this author's perspective, a diagnostic ambiguity that leads to a difficulty in distinguishing between high functioning individuals with Autistic Disorder and Asperger's Syndrome. Moreover, because of the broadness and somewhat amorphous nature of the PDD-NOS category (atypical autism), it seems likely that it will be overused and employed when it is not appropriate. Maes, Volkman, Hooks, and Cicchetti (1993) refer to PDD-NOS as a subthreshold category that is similar to atypical personality and defined negatively, in that the disorder is not autism. Research by these authors suggests children diagnosed with PDD-NOS show less severe disturbances in social relatedness than children with autism. (See also Buitelaar, VanderGaag, Klin & Volkman, 1999.)

Other terminological issues

In this section, autism will be discussed in relationship to other terms frequently encountered in the autism literature, including: autism spectrum disorder, schizophrenia, developmental disability, and mental retardation.

AUTISM SPECTRUM DISORDER

There are several ways that the term "autism spectrum disorder" has been employed. The term has been used to recognize the large individual differences that exist between persons diagnosed as autistic; persons with this diagnosis range from having all or most of the symptoms listed in the DSM-IV criteria for Autistic Disorder to those who have only the minimal requisite symptoms. This range includes individuals who are operating at a high developmental level as well as those who are much lower in their functioning level. A second way the term is employed suggests an even more extended continuum of symptomatology that includes individuals diagnosed with Autistic Disorders, Asperger's Syndrome and PDD-NOS. Sometimes, the spectrum appears to be defined even more broadly and is coequal with the entire range of Pervasive Developmental Disorders.

The argument for autism being on a spectrum or being a spectrum disorder is made based on the similarity of symptomatology of individuals on the spectrum. Ultimately, whether this continuum really makes sense awaits research into the causes and pathways of causality for the different types of individuals included in the spectrum. To the extent that individuals differing in symptom severity or symptom patterns have similar causes or underlying causal pathways, the notion of autism as a spectrum disorder makes theoretical sense. The possible causal pathways underlying the development of autism will be discussed in greater detail in Chapters 2, 3, and 4.

SCHIZOPHRENIA

Schizophrenia is part of a broader category of psychosis and shares some features in common with Autistic Disorder and the other Pervasive Developmental Disorders. According to the DSM-IV, the essential features of schizophrenia consist of a mixture of positive and negative signs that have been present for a significant portion of time (at least a month). Positive symptoms refer to an excess or distortion of normal functions, whereas negative symptoms refer to a loss or diminution of functioning. The symptoms of schizophrenia consist of a range of cognitive and emotional dysfunctions, including delusions, hallucinations, disorganized speech, and grossly disorganized or catatonic behavior (all positive signs) as well as affective flattening, alogia, and avolition (all negative signs).

More specifically, delusions consist of erroneous beliefs that typically involve a misrepresentation of perception or experiences. They may be quite bizarre in nature and include mistaken beliefs, for example of being spied on and/or persecuted. Hallucinations can occur in any sensory modality and involve a sensing of something that has no real external referent. Disorganized thinking is reflected in speech which ranges from incoherent to tangential, that is, involving loose associations. Grossly disorganized behavior manifests itself in a variety of ways, but typically includes a difficulty in performing goal-directed behaviors that are part of daily living and may be accompanied by silliness or unpredictable agitation. Catatonic behaviors have a motoric aspect in which the person has decreased reactivity to the environment and also may involve bizarre postures and/or excessive motor activity. Affective flattening is especially common, characterized for example by an immobile and unresponsive face, poor eye contact, and reduced body language. Alogia generally involves a poverty of speech, manifested by brief or empty replies. Avolition refers to an inability to initiate and persist in goal-directed activities. Finally, schizophrenia involves dysfunction in such areas as interpersonal relationships, work or education, or self-care. The reader is referred to the DSM-IV (American Psychological Association, 1994) for more complete information.

Although Autistic Disorder and schizophrenia were originally thought of as linked disorders, they are now viewed as separate entities. Comparison of the symptoms of Autistic Disorder and schizophrenia, however, suggests that the two disorders share several characteristics in common, particularly in the motor, language, affective, and social domains. A diagnosis of Autistic Disorder is warranted when it occurs early in life, is chronic in nature, and involves an interference in the development of language and social interaction; in contrast to the later emerging distortions in normal functioning that occur in schizophrenia. In individuals diagnosed with Autistic Disorder, an additional diagnosis of schizophrenia is made if prominent delusions or hallucinations are present. An additional diagnosis of schizophrenia is probably most appropriate when the person diagnosed with Autism Disorder has better developed language and thought processes.

Konstantareas and Hewitt (2001) point out that Asperger's Syndrome has been thought to be a more appropriate diagnosis than Autistic Disorder in individuals who show some of the signs of schizophrenia; specifically, because schizophrenia is at least in part a thought and perceptual disorder. This sort of dysfunction is difficult to detect in most individuals with Autistic Disorder. Research support for this hypothesis is mixed. Results of a study by Ghaziuddin, Leininger, and Tsai (1995) suggest greater levels of disorganized thinking in children with Asperger's Syndrome compared to children with autism who were higher functioning. In a study by Konstantareas and Hewitt (2001), the characteristics of a group of adults with chronic schizophrenia and men with Autistic Disorder, who were high functioning, were compared. Results indicated that none of the individuals in the schizophrenia group met the criteria for Autistic Disorder, whereas some of the individuals in the autistic group shared several symptoms in common with the schizophrenia group, including lack of interest in imitation and extremes of activity (negative signs of schizophrenia) and delusions or hallucinations (positive signs of schizophrenia). The authors interpret their results as supporting the position that Autistic Disorder and schizophrenia are two separate disorders which can exist together, that is, can be co-morbid.

DEVELOPMENTAL DISABILITY

Although developmental psychologists typically conceptualize development as a process that occurs across the lifespan, the term "developmental disability", as it is typically used, refers to a dysfunction that emerges during the earlier portion of the lifespan (0–22 years). Its definition originated as part of an effort by the federal government in the United States to identify and assist people in need of support services through federal legislation. The Developmental Disabilities Assistance and Bill of Rights Act of 1990 defines a developmental disability as a severe, chronic disability that:

- is attributable to a mental or physical impairment, or a combination of mental and physical impairments
- is manifest before 22 years of age
- is likely to continue indefinitely
- results in substantial functional limitations in three or more areas of major life activities, including self-care, receptive and expressive language, learning, mobility, self-direction, capacity for independent living, and economic self-sufficiency
- reflects the person's need for a combination of individualized and coordinated services that are of lifelong or extended duration.

The causes of developmental disabilities include factors that are genetic and environmental in origin. These factors, which manifest themselves prior to birth or after birth, during infancy, childhood or adolescence, adversely influence neurobiological and psychological functioning, resulting eventually in a disability. Table 1.1 outlines some of the major causes of developmental

Table 1.1 Causes, processes, and adaptive behavior deficiencies associated with developmental disabilities

Causes	Processes	Adaptive Behavior Deficiencies
Genetic/chromosomal deficiencies	Neurobiological (e.g., structural, neurochemical, and hormonal)	Self-care
Prenatal (e.g., teratogens such as alcohol, toxoplasmosis, rubella, and AIDS)	Sensory problems (e.g., blindness, deafness, and hypersensitivities)	Mobility
Perinatal (e.g., anoxia, prematurity, low birth weight)	Motor problems (e.g., in gross and fine motor skills)	Receptive and expressive language
Postnatal (e.g., diseases such as encephalitis, head injury, poverty, parental abuse/neglect, neighborhood violence)	Emotional problems (e.g., anxiety, and depression)	Learning
	Cognitive problems (e.g., in attention, perception, intelligence, and abstract thinking)	Academic Independent living Economic self-sufficiency

disabilities, the processes through which these causes operate, and the resulting deficiencies. The criteria as to what constitutes functional limitations in major life activities in the definition of developmental disabilities seems to have been left deliberately vague, referring to activities which can be typically performed by individuals in specific age groups, but for which a disabled person needs at least moderate assistance to perform.

Using this definition, most individuals with an autistic disorder would be defined as having a developmental disability, certainly early in their life, but typically also later. Because persons labeled as autistic have deficiencies in the areas of language and social interaction, they usually experience problems in other areas, such as academic and vocational functioning and independent living, all of which are central to the definition of developmental disabilities.

MENTAL RETARDATION

Questions concerning the relationship of Autistic Disorder and mental retardation are often posed. Although estimates vary, the percentage of persons with Autistic Disorder who meet the criteria of mental retardation may be around 75% (American Psychiatric Association, 1994). According to the American Association on Mental Retardation, mental retardation is defined as follows:

> Mental retardation refers to substantial limitations in present functioning. It is characterized by significantly subaverage intellectual functioning, existing concurrently with related limitations in two or more of the following applicable adaptive skill areas: communication, self-care, home living, social skills, community use, self-direction, health and safety, functional academics, leisure, and work. Mental retardation manifests before age 18.
>
> (AAMR, 1992, p. 1)

There are two critical components in this definition: subaverage intellectual functioning, and limitations in two or more adaptive skill areas. Depending on the IQ test, subaverage refers to IQ standard scores of approximately 70 to 75 or below. Similar to the definition of developmental disabilities, a second criterion of mental retardation refers to limitations in adaptive behavior. Most children with Autistic Disorder easily meet the adaptive behavior criteria for mental retardation; not all, however, manifest subaverage intellectual functioning as reflected by their score on an IQ test. The DSM-IV (APA, 1994) points out that it is sometimes difficult to determine if an additional diagnosis of Autistic Disorder is appropriate when the level of mental retardation is within the severe or profound range.

It can be argued that children with Autistic Disorder are put at a disadvantage when their intellectual functioning is evaluated through traditional IQ tests; specifically because most IQ tests place considerable weight on verbal ability as an index of intellectual ability, and furthermore because IQ tests are administered within a social context that may be confusing and fear-evoking to them. In an attempt to give a person diagnosed with autism a maximum opportunity to score well, many testers deviate from standard administration procedures through creating a more friendly and socially supportive testing environment. Even under these circumstances, the IQ scores of persons with a diagnosis of Autistic Disorder may represent an underestimation of their intellectual ability. Although traditional conceptions of intelligence view language proficiency as an important component, more recent conceptions of intelligence suggest that there are different types of intelligence, some of which do

not require high verbal ability and are not adequately assessed through traditional IQ tests.

Diagnosis and assessment of autism

In order for a treatment plan to be established, it is imperative that a thorough
evaluation occurs. The evaluation process typically begins with establishing
whether a child brought in for examination has autism or some other type of
developmental disorder. Once a diagnosis of autism is established, an array of
other assessment procedures are needed to establish a child's profile of
strengths and limitations. In this section the initial diagnostic process and
specific diagnostic procedures will be discussed, followed by a review of other
assessment procedures used for treatment planning and evaluation.

Obtaining a diagnosis

Many parents are reticent to bring their child in for diagnostic testing. Before
a diagnosis, parents live with the hope that their child is really okay. Although
they are often aware that their child does not seem to be developing normally,
they fear having to confront the unpleasant reality that their child may have a
serious problem, such as autism. This anxiety is certainly understandable.
Some parents also have concerns about the adverse effects of having their
child labeled autistic, such as being stigmatized by a public with prejudicial
attitudes.

Despite parental concerns associated with getting a diagnosis, this process
serves a variety of useful purposes. In some instances, a diagnosis enables a
clinician to isolate the cause of a disorder and provide treatment that leads to a
cure. However, this is not the case when a diagnosis of autism is made. Because
the biological causes of autism have not been determined, definitive or
curative treatments for this disorder are not yet possible. However, a
diagnostic evaluation in conjunction with other assessment procedures can
assist clinicians and educators in developing palliative treatments and
prevention programs for children with autism that can often reduce the
severity of this disorder. For example, programs can be put in place to reduce
sensory problems, enhance motor functioning, reduce eating problems,
address dietary deficiencies, develop language, and promote social behaviors.
If begun early, prevention efforts can sometimes significantly alter the developmental trajectory of a child.

Prevention programs are often subcategorized as primary, secondary, or tertiary. Primary prevention programs are designed to prevent the initial development of a disorder. For example, child inoculation programs were developed to prevent diseases such as polio, measles, mumps, tetanus, and diphtheria. Although there are currently no primary prevention programs for autism, secondary and tertiary prevention of autism is possible. Secondary prevention programs, although not curative, are designed to prevent the full development of the disorder. Some parents even report that secondary prevention programs have "normalized" their children's development, with the exception of a few residual "autistic" symptoms. An early diagnosis of autism allows secondary prevention programs to be put in place sooner, thus increasing the probability of their success. Tertiary prevention programs occur once a disorder is more fully manifested and are directed less at symptom prevention and more at symptom reduction and behavior management.

From a clinical and educational perspective, a diagnosis like autism also helps professionals communicate with one another as well as with parents. A diagnosis provides a precise description of a child's problem. Once received, a diagnosis allows for parents to search more strategically for services as well as information from other people, books, and the Internet. In addition, a diagnosis can establish a child's eligibility to receive free or partially compensated clinical and educational services.

From a scientific perspective, a diagnosis is critical for the scientific research enterprise. Before researchers can study autism and its causes, they have to first identify individuals with autism. Diagnostic and other assessment procedures help researchers to reliably identify people for inclusion in their study, as well as to describe the specific characteristics of their sample. Finally, a diagnosis can sometimes be useful in making prognostic statements about how a child will do in the future. More will be said about this issue later in the chapter.

Young children and early diagnosis

As scientific knowledge about the early development of autism increases, children with autism are being diagnosed at younger ages. Historically, a diagnosis of autism often did not occur until around age four or even later when children entered school. However, there is a current trend toward earlier diagnosis with many children now being diagnosed at age two or three. This trend has occurred because diagnostic procedures have improved, clinicians are more informed about autism, and children are being seen earlier by community agencies. Because of the importance of beginning interventions as soon as possible, it is critical to diagnose autism at the earliest possible stage. Although many diagnostic instruments have not been validated on children younger than three years of age, such instruments are starting to evolve.

Nevertheless, the task of diagnosing autism at an early age is challenging. Because autism is a developmental disorder, it manifests itself in various ways at different ages. Prior to age three, and particularly before age two, many of the core characteristics associated with autism are not fully manifested; in particular delays in social interaction and communication are difficult to detect. At earlier ages, the differences between children with developmental delays in these areas and typically developing children are considerably less pronounced than they will be at an older age. It is intrinsic to the nature of developmental delay that the disparity between children with delays and those without delays increases over time as development proceeds, especially during the period when behaviors such as language and social interaction begin to emerge in their more complex forms.

It is also difficult to obtain an early valid diagnosis of autism because infants and toddlers as a population show considerable variability in their developmental patterns. Before children are diagnosed as autistic, parents often report that they were told by their physicians about how children develop at quite different rates and that their child's development, while perhaps somewhat delayed, is not that unusual. Unless pediatricians or family practitioners refer a child for a formal developmental assessment, it is unlikely that a diagnosis of autism will be seriously considered at an early age. As a group, physicians have not been knowledgeable about autism and how it manifests itself over time; although this situation is slowly beginning to change.

Despite the difficulties associated with making an early diagnosis, researchers and therapists are gradually becoming aware of what many parents have known or suspected; that the early developmental history and behaviors of young children who are eventually diagnosed with autism are frequently quite different from typically developing children. Although children with autism are not born with all or perhaps any of the symptoms of this disorder, the symptoms often appear to emerge early. Parents who have no other children are less likely to perceive early differences in their child's development because they do not have a concrete reference point with which to compare their child's behavior. Typically, they become concerned when their child does not develop expressive language. However, before this point, most parents become uneasy when their child does not play normally, fails to respond to their social overtures, and/or when they fixate for long periods on objects in their environment rather than people.

Early social diagnostic features associated with autism include failures of the child to: make eye contact, look at faces, display imitative behavior, respond to their name, express interest in social games, and show enthusiasm as they interact with others. In addition, young children later diagnosed with autism often appear more flattened in their affect and show a preference for playing alone. Moreover, communication delays occur; not only is speech delayed, but also the use of social gestures (e.g., pointing) to solicit or to share attention. A variety of unusual, restricted and/or repetitive behaviors may also be present, including arranging objects in lines, attachment to unusual objects, object spinning, stereotyped play, and a failure to react to sensory stimuli, such as a loud sound (Lord & Risi, 2000; Ruble & Sears, 2001; Siegel, 1996; Stone & Ousley, 1996).

In an interesting study by Baranek (1999), a retrospective analysis of historical videotape was employed to study the sensorimotor and social behaviors of children with autism when they were 9–12 months of age; that is, at a point in their development that was well before they actually received their diagnosis. In contrast to both children with other developmental disabilities and children who were typically developing, children with autism showed poorer visual orientation/attention to nonsocial stimuli, greater mouthing of objects, more social touch aversion, and a more delayed response to their name. The authors suggest that infants with autism may have general problems with responsiveness (orientation/attention) to all sorts of sensory stimuli, social and nonsocial. Presently there is considerable optimism that new evaluation tools will be developed that will allow a preliminary diagnosis of autism to be made at 8–12 months, if not sooner (Bristol-Power & Spinella, 1999).

Diagnostic instruments

It is beyond the scope of this chapter to review in any comprehensive way the numerous instruments that have been employed for diagnosing autism. Rather the goal here will be to characterize them and provide general information about some of the more frequently employed types of instruments.

There are basically two ways of obtaining information to make a diagnosis of autism: direct observation of a child and questioning individuals who know the child well. Direct observational instruments are typically intended for use by a trained clinician. Such instruments can be employed during either structured or unstructured contacts with the child. In contrast to this observational approach, other instruments employ interviews or checklists to obtain information from parents, teachers, or others who frequently interact with the child being evaluated. Advantages associated with direct observation instruments are that they typically have high reliability and utilize observers who are quite familiar with and knowledgeable about autism. In contrast to trained observers, parents or teachers may not pay attention to critical child behaviors and/or appropriately interpret what they see. Conversely, a major advantage associated with using parent or teacher report data is that these individuals have greater general knowledge about their children, based on extensive contacts with them over long periods of time. Ideally, both types of assessments should be used in making a diagnosis.

Currently, a large number of diagnostic instruments are available. For example, observation instruments include the *Behavior Observation Scale for Autism, Behavior Rating Instrument for Autistic and Atypical Children* (BRIAAC), *Childhood Autism Rating Scale* (CARS), *Ritvo-Freeman Real Life Rating Scale* (RLRS), and the *Checklist for Autism in Toddlers* (CHAT). There are also several semi-structured interactive assessment instruments, such as the *Autism Diagnostic Observation Schedule* (ADOS-G) and the *Screening Tool for Autism in Two-Year-Olds* (STAT). A variety of parent–teacher questionnaires are available, including the *Diagnostic Checklist for Behavior Disturbed Children* (Form E-2) and the *Autism Behavior Checklist* (ABC). Finally, there are parent interview instruments, such as the *Autism Diagnostic Interview-Revised* (ADI-R) and the *Parent Interview for Autism* (PIA). For further information about these instruments, the reader is referred to Filipek, *et al.* (1999), Ruble and Sears (2001), and Scheuermann and Webber (2002).

Research by Sevin, Matson, Coe, Fee, and Sevin (1991) evaluated the psychometric characteristics of several instruments for assessing autism. In their study, the reliability and validity of three commonly employed scales, the *Autism Behavior Checklist* (ABC), the *Real Life Rating Scale* (RLRS), and the *Childhood Autism Rating Scale* (CARS), were examined. Although interrater reliability was for the most part within an acceptable range for all these instruments, the validity analyses yielded some intriguing results. In examining the correlation between the three scales, the RLRS and the CARS were significantly correlated ($r = 0.77$); but neither the CARS nor the RLRS were significantly correlated with the ABC. The authors suggested that the results may have been related to the way items were scored (binary versus Likert-type scales) or other method variance. Whereas the ABC data is based on parent report, the RLRS and the CARS data is derived from direct observation. Examination of items from the instruments suggested that the ABC may have been assessing different aspects of autism than the other two scales.

Evaluation of the relationship between these three autism scales and two measures of adaptive behavior (the *Vineland ABS-Survey Form* and the *ABS-School Edition* developed by the American Association on Mental Retardation) also indicated that the three autism scales were not related in the same way to the adaptive behavior assessments. Whereas no significant relationship was found between the adaptive behavior scores and the CARS, one set of dimensions of adaptive behavior (Social Adjustment, Personal Adjustment, and Personal-Social Responsibility) was associated with scores on the ABC, whereas another set of dimensions of adaptive behavior (Community Self-Sufficiency and Personal Self-Sufficiency) was associated with scores on the RLRS.

Finally, the diagnoses made using two of the autism scales (the ABC and the CARS) were checked against ones made based on the DSM-III-R and Autism Society of America (ASA) criteria for autism. These latter diagnoses were obtained by independent raters, using unstructured parent interviews and direct and/or videotaped observation of the participants. The participants were children and adolescents referred for testing because of marked autistic symptomatology. Results indicated that whereas only 50% of the sample diagnosed as autistic using the DSM-III-R criteria met the ABC cutoff criterion for autism, 92% of this same sample met the CARS criterion.

The results of this study by Sevin, Matson, Coe, Fee, and Sevin (1991) were not presented to suggest that one of these autism scales was necessarily better than the others, but rather to point out that different autism scales often have different items, as well as different approaches to gathering information, and as a result they may be measuring different dimensions of autism. Whereas one scale may provide more accurate information about the presence or absence of autism as defined by diagnostic criteria, such as those put forth in the DSM-III-R, another may provide better information about other types of impairment, adaptive behavior deficiencies, and/or behavior problems associated with the autism diagnosis.

Professionals involved in conducting diagnostic assessments need to be cognizant of the array of instruments available and their psychometric characteristics. Moreover, whichever diagnostic instrument is employed, it is important that a trained clinician interpret the results. When these instruments are used with very young children, definitive diagnoses are not always possible. In such instances, it is best to continue close monitoring of the child to observe how development proceeds. As a diagnosis of autism is being made, it is important to consider potential overlaps with other disorders, such as mental retardation, Developmental Language Disorder, and Attention Deficit Hyperactivity Disorder, as well as the various nonautistic Pervasive Developmental Disorders (i.e. Rett's, Childhood Disintegrative and Asperger's Disorders, and PDD-NOS).

Assessment and intervention

In addition to the diagnostic instruments just reviewed, there are a variety of other assessment procedures utilized in evaluating children with autism. The purpose of a comprehensive assessment program is to ensure that an appropriate intervention strategy is developed. Common types of assessments used with children with autism include: aptitude and achievement tests, adaptive behavior assessments, developmental evaluations, and an observational methodology that uses functional analysis. Each of these assessment strategies will be briefly described in this section.

APTITUDE, ACHIEVEMENT AND ADAPTIVE BEHAVIOR ASSESSMENTS

Aptitude tests have been most commonly employed with children to measure general intelligence. Examples of such tests include: the *Wechsler Intelligence Scale for Children*, the *Stanford-Binet Intelligence Scale*, the *Bayley Scales of Infant Development*, and the *McCarthy Scales of Children's Abilities*. Although in a sense all intelligence tests measure achievement, the distinction between intelligence and achievement tests is that intelligence tests are used to make inferences about a child's future ability to learn and his/her expected rate of learning, particularly in educational situations. In contrast, achievement tests are commonly used in schools to document the actual amount or level of learning obtained at a particular point in time.

Adaptive behavior assessments also evaluate achievement, but typically in nonacademic areas; for example, performance in motor, communication, self-help, daily living, recreational, social, and prevocational areas are commonly evaluated. Specific examples of this type of evaluation are the *Vineland Adaptive Behavior Scales* and the *American Association on Mental Deficiency (AAMD) Adaptive Behavior Scales*. Whereas ability and school achievement tests are completed by or with the active participation of the person being evaluated, adaptive behavior assessments are obtained either through direct observation or more typically through interviewing a child's primary care-taker and/or teacher. In an interesting study by Stone, Ousley, Hepburn, Hogan, and Brown (1999), the *Vineland Adaptive Behavior Scale* was used to investigate differences in adaptive behavior between children with autism and a comparison group of children who were developmentally delayed, but not autistic. Both groups were matched on chronological and mental age (CA and MA). Results indicated that relative to the comparison group, children with autism showed less developed socialization and communication skills even though the mental and chronological ages of the children were comparable.

Most ability, achievement, and adaptive behavior scales are normreferenced. A norm-reference test employs a norm or comparison group that is used in interpreting the test results. More specifically, when these types of evaluations are conducted, a student's performance is compared to the performance of a norm group and characterized as being within an average, below average, or above average range of functioning. For further information about the aforementioned assessments and other ability, achievement, and adaptive behavior evaluations, the reader is referred to Carlson, Hagiwara, and Quinn (1998).

DEVELOPMENTAL ASSESSMENTS

Although the aforementioned assessments are useful in comparing children with autism to children who are more typically developing, they provide only general information about areas in which intervention and education programs are needed, rather than specific information about program goals and how such programs should be structured. In contrast to ability, achievement, and adaptive behavior assessments (which evaluate a student's performance in comparison to a norm group), developmental assessments evaluate a student's performance along a continuum of skill acquisition seen in typically developing children. That is, this type of assessment reveals what a person can do currently in various developmental areas and what he/she needs to do next in order to increase in competency. For example, when examining expressive and receptive language, an evaluation may reveal that a child can label an object when presented alone, but not when it is placed with a group of other objects; or that a child may be able to respond to simple instructions involving a single motor response, but has difficulty with more complex instructions, requiring multiple responses. A good developmental assessment has direct implications for developing a curriculum. It specifies what particular skills, concepts, and behaviors need to be taught and the sequence in which they should be taught. Developmental assessments should be conducted through direct observation of a child's performance in specific task situations (Carlson, Hagiwara & Quinn, 1998).

FUNCTIONAL ANALYSIS

Functional analysis has its roots in the field of applied behavior analysis, which emerged in the 1960s. This approach to assessment is based on the premise that most behaviors are learned through a child's interaction with his/her environment. Behaviors that emerge serve a purpose; more specifically they allow a child to get what he/she wants or needs. Behaviors are initially learned and maintained by stimulus events which precede a response (often referred to as "antecedents", "setting events", or "discriminative stimuli"), as well as by stimulus events that follow a behavior (commonly referred to as "positive and negative reinforcers"). As learning proceeds, antecedent stimuli serve to signal to the child what behavior or response is likely to get the child what he/she wants. Stimuli that serve as reinforcers help ensure that the behavior will continue to occur in that circumstance.

For example, a child learns that when he/she sees a ball (an antecedent stimulus) and says "ball". his/her mother will smile and proceed to give him/her a hug and say "yes, that is a ball" (a positive reinforcer), thus motivating the child to repeat this response in the future. Alternatively, a child might learn when someone who the child "dislikes" approaches and talks to him/her that if he/she ignores them the person will go away (a negative reinforcer). Within a behavioral learning framework, it is postulated that although autism is rooted in biological causes, the specific symptoms or behaviors that children with autism display are often learned in the same fashion as more appropriate or adaptive behaviors. In behavioral educational programs, like discrete trial learning, maladaptive behaviors are reduced and adaptive behaviors are taught through arranging the physical and social environment in specific ways.

During a functional analytic assessment, information about the stimuli that influence a child's behavior and learning is obtained. When a behavior/response occurs, the characteristics of the general setting and specific events that precede (antecedents) and follow (consequents) are recorded. Through this process, hypotheses are formed about the environmental causes of maladaptive and adaptive behaviors and what types of stimulus events facilitate the development of these behaviors; these hypotheses are then used to guide the development of intervention programs. The reader is referred to Scheuermann and Webber (2002) for further information about how to conduct a functional analysis.

Functional analysis is similar to another type of evaluation, sometimes referred to as "ecobehavioral analysis", which evaluates how environmental features (such as room size, noise level, color, brightness, number of children, windows, task-irrelevant stimuli, and program structure) influence a child's behavior development and learning. Through ecobehavioral analysis, like in functional analysis, hypotheses are developed about the types of environmental stimuli that are associated with the development of maladaptive and adaptive behavior and then used to design interventions (Carlson, Hagiwara & Quinn, 1998).

OTHER ASSESSMENTS

In addition to the assessments already described in this section, there are a wide array of other important evaluations that are employed in helping children with autism. These assessments include: sensory evaluations, such as vision and hearing tests; speech evaluations, to examine receptive and expressive speech, as well as protocommunication (pre-speech) skills; motor evaluations, to assess gross and fine motor skills, as well as motor planning skills; play evaluations, to examine play complexity, appropriateness, and imagination; neurological examinations, to assess brain functioning and problems such as epilepsy; as well as a vast array of other biomedical evaluations, that assess, for example, dietary deficiencies, metabolic problems, immunological problems, and genetic anomalies.

Where to go for an evaluation?

Where and to whom should parents take their child for diagnostic and treatment planning evaluations? The answer to this question is not an easy one, in part because the answer varies from community to community. Ideally, professionals representing a variety of disciplines should be involved in a comprehensive and coordinated evaluation. It should be noted, however, that some professionals are not very knowledgeable about autism. Such ignorance may lead to the use of inappropriate evaluation instruments, clinical insensitivity in administering assessments, problems in interpreting the results of tests, and lack of awareness concerning when referrals to other professionals are appropriate.

Specific professionals that can be very helpful in the assessment process include: psychologists, educators, developmental therapists, speech pathologists, audiologists, physical therapists, occupational therapists, dieticians, and other medical personnel, particularly developmental pediatricians and pediatric neurologists. Clinical psychologists are often skilled psychometricians who are able to administer a variety of diagnostic instruments as well as tests that assess intellectual ability, adaptive behavior and developmental level, behavior problems, personality characteristics, and neuropsychological problems. They may also be skilled in conducting functional and ecobehavioral analyses. School psychologists can conduct some of these assessments, as well as evaluate, along with other educators, academic achievement.

Speech pathologists evaluate language and communication competencies as well as biological anomalies that might interfere with speech and communication. Audiologists assess children's hearing. Physical therapists and occupational therapists are skilled in the assessment of sensorimotor functioning. Whereas physical therapists emphasize the general evaluation of sensorimotor functioning, occupational therapists are more concerned with evaluating a child's use of sensorimotor skills in daily living situations. Dieticians can help in assessing a child's diet, dietary deficiencies, and the need for dietary interventions.

Some medical personnel, including family physicians, pediatricians, and psychiatrists, have not historically received much training in the area of autism and developmental disabilities. This trend is slowly changing with the emergence of new medical educational programs and through the growth of specialties in medicine, like developmental pediatrics, pediatric neurology, and child psychiatry. These specialties appropriately focus on the evaluation and treatment of medical problems but also often coordinate their efforts with other professions who conduct developmental and educational assessments.

Evaluations can occur in a variety of settings, including home, school, clinics, and hospitals. An optimal environment for evaluation occurs when assessment specialists are part of an interdisciplinary (transdisciplinary) team who possess the wide range of testing skills just discussed and have extensive experience in working with children with autism. These interdisciplinary teams are most likely to be found in autism centers, hospital settings, or clinics specializing in developmental disabilities. In an ideal situation, information from multiple assessments are collected before parents are given results concerning the status of their child. Sometimes, however, assessments occur in a sequential fashion and parents receive results in a piecemeal manner. Optimally, parents are emotionally supported when they receive news that their child is autistic, are actively assisted in developing a treatment plan, and are referred as appropriate to other agencies. Unfortunately, because professionals have not always received proper training in the area of autism, the overall needs of families may not be addressed. Parents need to be proactive in determining as best they can the expertise of the professionals with whom they consult. Parents should always feel free to seek out second and third opinions as necessary.

Incidence, demographic characteristics, and prognosis

Estimates of the incidence of autism vary widely, with recent estimates suggesting that autism may be on the increase. For example, early estimates suggested that autism occurred in about four to ten children per 10,000 births (APA, 1994; Jordan, 1999). In contrast, a variety of recent studies indicate a rising prevalence in autism. In a review of current studies, Charman and Baird (2002) suggest the rate may be as high as between 40 and 60 per 10,000 individuals. Estimates, such as that given by the Autism Society of America, similarly indicate that autism may occur as frequently as in two to six out of every thousand individuals (see ASA/www.autism-society.org).

Croen, Grether, Hoogstrate, and Selvin (2002), conducting a population-based study of eight successive birth cohorts of children born in California from 1987 to 1994, found an increase in prevalence from 5.8 to 14.9 cases of autism per 10,000 children. The authors indicated that during the same time period, the prevalence of mental retardation decreased from 28.8 to 19.5 per 10,000. This finding suggests that the increase in prevalence of autism may be due at least in part to the reclassification of children from the mental retardation to the autism category. The pattern of increase did not appear to be related to maternal age, race/ethnicity, education, child gender, or plurality. However, the authors did report that the age at which children entered into their service delivery system decreased across successive birth years from 1987 to 1994. Whereas in 1987 the mean age of entry was 6.9 years, it was 3.3 years in 1994. Not surprisingly, the total number of children enrolled in the California service delivery system increased across this same time period, almost tripling.

A similar but somewhat less dramatic increase in the prevalence of autism in Iceland was reported by Magnússon and Saemundsen (2001). Estimated prevalence rates for infantile autism/childhood autism were 3.8 per 10,000 for children born between 1974 and 1983 and 8.6 per 10,000 for children born between 1984 and 1993. The authors also reported that a higher proportion of the children in the younger compared to the older cohort fell into the retarded range, 95% versus 67%. They suggested, however, that research like their own may oversample lower functioning subjects who are more likely to enter the social service system.

These studies raise the question: Is autism really increasing in incidence or is it just being diagnosed more often? Arguments can be made on either side of this question. On one hand, it can be argued that a changing and more clearly articulated definition of autism, along with an increase in the types and quality of autism assessment instruments, have resulted in clinicians using this diagnostic category more often. Given that professional awareness about autism has risen, it may be that the incidence of autism has not changed, but rather the ability to diagnose it and distinguish it from other disabilities, such as mental retardation, has increased. Fombonne (1996) expresses skepticism about reports of increased incidence and suggests that they could be artifacts of the epidemiological methods employed, for example, the improved case-finding methods used in surveys. It may also be that the increase in autism, suggested by some estimates, are due to the inclusion of disorders similar to autism, such as nonautistic Pervasive Developmental Disorders. Moreover, it is also possible that as public recognition of autism has increased, parents are more actively seeking out diagnostic and treatment services for their children, thus increasing the opportunity for professionals to identify new cases of autism.

Arguments for a real increase in autism suggest that agents, such as environmental toxins or food additives, may be triggering additional cases of autism. Publicity about autism clusters in various geographic areas has led some individuals to wonder about the role that industrial pollutants in the air, water, and/or earth play in the development of autism. However, systematic studies of some of these reported clusters, such as in Brick Township, New Jersey, have not provided evidence for this hypothesis and instead suggested that the increases in autism were a function of other factors, such as data keeping and people moving into certain locales because of the availability of autism services (Wang, 2000).

Many parents of children with autism and some professionals have argued that changes in immunization procedures may be responsible for an increase in autism, providing a new trigger or pathway for the development of this disorder. In contrast to earlier decades, more immunizations are being given to children; moreover, more immunizations are being given at one time. Concern has also been expressed about the historical use of thimerosol, which contains mercury, as a vaccine preventative. Some people suggest that new immunization protocols may be overwhelming the developing immune systems of children, in particular those whose immune responses are for genetic and environmental reasons already compromised. Currently, empirical studies do not support the position that immunizations are a cause of autism. Nevertheless, as researchers examine more critically the interaction between immunization procedures and various specific characteristics of children with autism, it is possible that immunizations may be found to serve as a trigger for a select subpopulation of children who have certain types of immune system or metabolic problems. This issue will be further addressed in Chapter 3.

DEMOGRAPHIC AND OTHER CHARACTERISTICS

Although there are some uncertainties about whether the incidence of autism is changing, more is known about demographics of this disorder. By definition, for autism to be diagnosed it must occur within the first 36 months of life. Once diagnosed, most individuals retain this diagnosis over their lifetime; thus it is a chronic disorder. Symptomatically, individuals with autism experience a wide range of outcomes. For example, some individuals have good language skills, do well in school, and function without close supervision. At the other end of the autism continuum, individuals have pronounced developmental delays and mental retardation. Research suggests, however, that more individuals with autism operate developmentally at the lower range of functioning, with about 77% having mental retardation in addition to autism (Gillberg, 1984). With the implementation of earlier and more intensive interventions, this distribution of functioning level will likely change, at least to some extent, as individuals show greater developmental gains.

From a gender perspective, most studies indicate that autism is considerably more prevalent among males, with most studies indicating a male to female ratio somewhere between 3:1 and 4:1 (Volkman, Szatmari & Sparrow, 1993). However, females are more likely to have a severe form of autism that involves mental retardation. Socioeconomically, it was once thought that autism was a disorder that occurred more in higher socioeconomic status (SES) families. Recent research suggests, however, no differences in the incidence of autism between families of different social classes. In a summarization of research in this area, Mesibov, Adams, and Klinger (1997) noted that the apparent higher SES bias appears to be a function of social factors; more specifically that low income families are less likely to be aware of developmental problems in their children and are also less likely to find and use available autism services.

Although limited data is available concerning the life expectancy of persons with autism, both speculation and available data indicate that they have a higher mortality risk. Elevated early death rates are found in individuals diagnosed with autism and severe mental retardation and in females who, although less frequently diagnosed as autistic, are more likely than males to be severely retarded. In a study conducted in California, Shavelle, Strauss, and Pickett (2001) found elevated mortality rates in individuals with autism compared to general population mortality rates. Death rates related to seizure problems were particularly elevated. Increased mortality rates due to drowning, suffocation, and respiratory disorders were also noted.

Diagnoses are sometimes useful in making a prognosis, that is, in predicting what the course of development will be for a person with a particular disorder. Parents whose children have been diagnosed with autism want to know how much their children will benefit from treatment and education programs, and what their children's future will be like. In the case of autism, because relatively little is known about the disorder, definitive answers to questions about prognosis are difficult to give and even risky, particularly if they generate unwarranted or unrealistic expectations. At present, autism is considered a lifelong disability. Research is just beginning to provide useful information about how different children on the autism spectrum develop and respond to treatment. As new and more effective treatments evolve, the prognosis for children with autism is likely to change. Because pessimistic and overly optimistic predictions about the future can adversely influence the actions of both parents and professionals, it is better for diagnosticians and educators working in the area of autism to admit the limitations of their knowledge. They need to keep an open mind, to be optimistic, but also to be appropriately conservative in making predictions about future development.

Two general factors appear to influence how much children with autism will benefit from educational and medical treatments: the types and severity of their symptoms, and the quality and timing of the educational and medical programs to which they are exposed. Given our present state of knowledge and treatment capabilities, children with more severe forms of autism are not as likely to progress as quickly or as far as children whose autism is less severe. However, there is reason for optimism. Educational programs for children with autism are improving and being implemented at earlier ages. Moreover, as the biological causes of autism are better understood, it is quite possible that new effective medical treatments will be developed.

In the next chapter, the complex symptomatology associated with autism will be described in detail. In Chapters 3 and 4, theories regarding how the biological, psychological, and environmental factors influence the development of this symptomatology will be discussed, followed in Chapter 5 by a description of current treatment programs.

References

American Association on Mental Retardation (1992) *Mental retardation: Definition, classification, and systems of support* (Ninth edition). Washington, DC: American Associations on Mental Retardation.

American Psychiatric Association (1994) *Diagnostic and statistical manual of mental disorders* (Fourth edition). Washington, DC: American Psychiatric Association.

Asperger, H. (1944) "Die 'autistischen psychopathen' un kindersaltes." *Archiv. Fur Psychiatrie und Nervenkrankheiten 117*, 76–136.

Baranek, G. (1999) "Autism during infancy: A retrospective video analysis of sensory-motor and social behaviors at 9–12 months of age." *Journal of Autism and Developmental Disabilities 29*, 213–224.

Bettleheim, B. (1967) *The Empty Fortress.* New York: The Free Press.

Blatt, B. & Kaplan, F. (1966) *Christmas in Purgatory.* Boston: Allyn and Bacon, Inc.

Bristol-Power, M. & Spinella, G. (1999) "Research on screening and diagnosis in autism: A work in progress." *Journal of Autism and Developmental Disabilities 29*, 435–438.

Buitelaar, J., VanderGaag, R., Klin, A. & Volkman, F. (1999) "Exploring the boundaries of Pervasive Developmental Disorder Not Otherwise Specified: Analyses of data from the DSM-IV Autistic Disorder field trial." *Journal of Autism and Developmental Disorders 29*, 33–43.

Carlson, J. K., Hagiwara, T. & Quinn, C. (1998) "Assessment of students with autism." In R. L. Simpson & B. S. Myles (eds) *Educating Children and Youth with Autism* (pp. 25–53). Austin, TX: Pro-Ed.

Charman, T. & Baird, G. (2002) "Practitioner review: Diagnosis of autism spectrum disorders in 2- and 3-year old children." *Journal of Child Psychology 43*, 289–305.

Croen, K., Grether, J., Hoogstrate, J. & Selvin, S. (2002) "The changing prevalence of autism in California." *Journal of Autism and Developmental Disabilities 32*, 153–163.

Developmental Disabilities Assistance and Bill of Rights Act of 1990, Title 42, U.S.C. 6000–6083. *U.S. Statutes at Large*, 1191–1204.

Eisenberg, L. & Kanner, L. (1956) "Early infantile autism." *American Journal of Orthopsychiatry 26*, 556–566.

Filipek, P., Accardo, P. J., Baranek, G. T., Cook, E. H., Dawson, G., Gordon, B., Gravel, J. S., Johnson, C. P., Kallen, R. J., Levy, S. E., Minshew, N. J., Prizant, B. M., Rapin, I., Rogers,

S. J., Stone, W. L., Teplin, S., Tuchman, R. F. & Volkmar, F. (1999) "The screening and diagnosis of autistic spectrum disorders." *Journal of Autism and Developmental Disorders 29*, (6), 439–484.

Fombonne, E. (1996) "Is the prevalence of autism increasing?" *Journal of Autism and Developmental Disorders 26*, 673–676.

Ghaziuddin, M., Leininger, L. & Tsai, L. (1995) "Thought disorder in Asperger Syndrome: Comparison with high functioning autism." *Journal of Autism and Developmental Disorders 25*, 311–317.

Gillberg, C. (1984) "Infantile autism and other childhood psychoses in a Swedish urban region: Epidemiological aspects." *Journal of Child Psychology and Psychiatry 25*, 35–43.

Hobson, R. P. (1993) *Autism and the development of mind.* Hillsdale, NJ: Erlbaum.

Itard, J. (1962) *The Wild Boy of Aveyron.* New York: Appleton-Century Crofts.

Jordan, R. (1999) *Autistic spectrum disorders. An introductory handbook for practitioners.* London: David Fulton Publishers.

Kanner, L. (1943) "Autistic disturbances of affective contact." *Nervous Child 2*, 217–250.

Kanner, L. (1952) "Emotional interference with intellectual functioning." *American Journal of Mental Deficiency 56*, 701–707.

Koegel, R. & Koegel, L. (1995) *Teaching Children with Autism: Strategies for Initiating Positive Interactions and Improving Learning Opportunities.* Baltimore: Brookes.

Konstantareas, M. & Hewitt, T. (2001) "Autistic disorder and schizophrenia: Diagnostic overlaps." *Journal of Autism and Developmental Disorders 31*, 19–28.

Lord, C. & Risi, S. (2000) "Diagnosis of autism spectrum disorders in young children." In A. M. Wetherby & B. M. Prizant (eds) *Autism Spectrum Disorders* (pp. 11–30). Baltimore: Brookes.

Lovaas, O. I. (1977) *The Autistic Child: Language Development through Behavior Modification.* New York: Irvington.

Lovaas, O. I. (1992) *The Me Book.* Austin, TX: Pro-Ed.

Maes, L., Volkman, F., Hooks, M. & Cicchetti, D. (1993) "Differentiating pervasive developmental disorder not otherwise specified from autism and language disorders." *Journal of Autism Developmental Disorders 23*, 79–90.

Magnússon, P. & Saemundsen, E. (2001) "Prevalence of autism in Iceland." *Journal of Autism and Developmental Disorders 31*, 153–163.

Maurice, C. (1993) *Let me hear your voice.* New York: Knopf.

Maurice, C., Green, G. & Luce, S. (eds) (1996) *Behavioral intervention for young children with autism.* Austin, TX: Pro-Ed.

Mesibov, G., Adams, L. & Klinger, L. (1997) *Autism: Understanding the disorder.* New York: Plenum Press.

Nirje, B. (1969) "2The normalization principles and its human management implications." In R. Kugel & W. Wolfensberger (eds) *Changing patterns in residential services for the mentally retarded* (pp. 179–195), Washington, DC: President's Committee on Mental Retardation.

Rimland, B. (1964) *Infantile autism: The syndrome and its implication for a neural theory of behavior.* New York: Appleton-Century-Crofts.

Ruble, L. A. & Sears, L. L. (2001) "Diagnostic assessment of autistic disorder." In R. A. Huebener (ed) *Autism: A sensorimotor approach to management* (pp. 41–59). Gaithersburg, MD: Aspen.

Rutter, M. (1983) "Cognitive deficits in the pathogenesis of autism." *Journal of Child Psychology and Psychiatry 24*, 513–531.

Scheuermann, B. & Webber, J. (2002) *Autism: Teaching does make a difference.* Belmont, CA: Wadsworth.

Schreibman, L. (1988) *Autism.* Newbury Park, CA: Sage Publications.

Sevin, J., Matson, J., Coe, D., Fee, V. & Sevin, B. (1991) "A comparison and evaluation of three commonly used autism scales." *Journal of Autism and Developmental Disabilities 21*, 417–432.

Shavelle, R., Strauss, D. & Pickett, J. (2001) "Causes of death in autism." *Journal of Autism and Developmental Disorders 31*, 569–576.

Siegel, B. (1996) *The world of the autistic child: Understanding and treating autistic spectrum disorders.* New York: Oxford University Press.

Simpson, R. & Myles, B. (1998) "Understanding and responding to the needs of students with autism." In R. Simpson & B. Myles (eds) *Educating children and youth with autism: Strategies for effective practice* (pp. 1–24). Austin, TX: Pro-Ed.

Stone, W. L. & Ousley, O. X. (1996) "Pervasive developmental disorders: Autism." In M. L. Wolraich (ed) *Disorders of development and learning* (pp. 379–405). Boston: Mosley.

Stone, W., Ousley, O., Hepburn, S., Hogan, K. & Brown, C. (1999) "Patterns of adaptive behavior in very young children with autism." *American Journal on Mental Retardation 104*, 187–199.

Volkman, F., Szatmari, P. & Sparrow, S. (1993) "Sex differences in pervasive developmental disabilities." *Journal of Autism and Developmental Disabilities 23*, 579–591.

Wang, C. (2000) "High autism prevalence but no cluster found in Brick Township." *Advocate 33*, 11–12.

Wing, L. (1981) "Asperger's syndrome: A clinical account." *Psychological Medicine 11*, 115–129.

World Health Organization (1990) *International classification of diseases (10th rev.): Criteria for research.* Geneva, Switzerland: World Health Organization.

CHAPTER 2

Autism and Its Characteristics

What is it like to be a child with autism? How is the development of children with autism different from other children? Some insight into these questions is revealed by comparing their world with that of typical children. Prior to birth, infants are insulated by the protective cocoon of the womb. Their sensory environment is rich, but fairly orderly in its structure. It is noisy due to the beating of the mother's heart, her breathing, digestive sounds, movements, and voice. As the fetus explores the intrauterine environment, he/she receives diverse types of tactual, proprioceptive, and taste experiences (Maurer & Maurer, 1988). Compared to the world experienced after birth, this prebirth environment, although rich in sensory stimulation, is relatively muted, homogeneous, and predictable. After birth, the infant's world changes dramatically. I think it was William James who described the early postbirth world of the infant as a "blooming buzzing confusion". Although this world is chaotic and can be stressful, infants have protective mechanisms, including sucking reflexes, eye closure, and other primitive state-regulation behaviors, that help them to accommodate to their environment until their neurosensory and neuromotor systems mature. A sensitive care-taking environment also protects the infant from excessive stimulation and assists the infant in this adaptation process.

What happens, however, as appears to be the case with autism, if the environment continues to be experienced as chaotic? What happens if the biological system that assists the infant in adapting to the environment is different or compromised? What happens if the care-taking environment is not fully aware of the excessive demands being placed on the child who has biological and behavioral limitations? Based on the observations of parents and professionals who interact with children with autism, as well as the self-report of high functioning individuals with autism like Temple Grandin and Donna Williams, the world of persons with autism not only begins in chaos, but continues to be confusing, as well as frightening. It is sometimes too bright, too noisy, too abrasive, too pungent, and too bitter. The symptomatology associated with autism presents a picture of individuals with sensory, motor, and cognitive anomalies; who are severely challenged as they attempt to adapt to their environments; who are deficient in their coping resources; and who compensate for their limitations by developing unusual ways of regulating their emotions and controlling their physical and social surroundings. Although autism is a complex disorder with many faces, it ultimately represents a compromise that is reached by individuals who live in a world whose demands exceed their abilities to adapt in conventional ways.

In this chapter, the central characteristics contained in the definition of autism and other common characteristics associated with this disorder will be examined. Many misconceptions and myths exist regarding individuals with autism; for example, that they cannot make eye contact, smile, express affection, engage in reciprocal play, or think abstractly. These attitudes are derived from a time prior to the development of early intervention programs, an era when many of these children were institutionalized and/or given only basic physical care. More generally, these attitudes are based on a static view of autism, a snapshot of children with autism that misrepresents the essence of who they are and what they can become. These misconceptions are in contrast to a perspective in which children with autism demonstrate dynamic development over time and sometimes leave behind many of the "classic" signs of autism. Stereotypes of people with autism, like most stereotypes about people, ignore the fact that they are quite different from each other; not only in the way their autism is expressed, but also in their underlying temperaments, personalities, and competencies.

Although stereotypes of autism often present a false picture of this disorder, there are nevertheless core deficits that characterize individuals with autism. Some debate exists, however, about what these core deficits are and even about what constitutes a core deficit. Sigman (1994) describes three criteria that have been employed to define the meaning of a core deficit: specificity, universality, and primacy. Specificity refers to characteristics that are displayed only by individuals with autism, but not by children with other disorders. Although the majority of the symptoms associated with autism are not unique to this disorder, the overall configuration of symptoms is unique and is used to distinguish autism from other disorders. Universality means that a core deficit should be present in all individuals with autism. Employing this criterion, the general features (e.g., social and language deficiencies) used to describe Autistic Disorder in the DSM-IV definition (American Psychiatric Association, 1994) would be considered as core characteristics. Finally, primacy refers to the requirement that a core deficit should occur early in development. Relatedly, another aspect, not explicitly mentioned by Sigman (1994), is that a core deficit should help explain how other, later developing characteristics of autism emerge. As will be discussed in this chapter and Chapter 4, the literature on autism is replete with suggestions concerning what deficits are core in this latter sense; that is, which deficits precede other deficits and explain their emergence.

In this chapter, characteristics that are universal and used to diagnose autism, as well as other characteristics (e.g., sensory, motor, and emotional) which are commonly although not universally manifested, will be described. Research examining these characteristics will be presented, along with insider perspectives on these characteristics by people with autism. The general categories of characteristics to be described in order of their presentation include:

1. sensory processing problems

2. motor dysfunctions

3. arousal/activation problems

4. cognitive deficiencies

5. social interaction problems

6. language deficiencies

7. repetitive, restricted, and stereotyped interests, activities, and behaviors (self-regulation)

8. behavior problems

9. physical/medical features.

Table 2.1 presents an overview of the characteristics frequently associated with autism.

Table 2.1 Characteristics frequently associated with autism

Domain/Process	Characteristics
Sensory	Hypersensitive, hyposensitive, sensory avoidant, sensory seeking, vestibular, proprioception, and sensory integration problems
Motor	Motor development delays, fine and gross motor problems, low motor tone, motor planning problems, clumsiness, coordination difficulties
Arousal/activation/ emotion	Hyperarousal, hypoarousal, difficult or slow-to-warm-up temperament, high emotional reactivity, poor emotional regulation, fearfulness, anxiety, depression, motivational problems
Cognition	Attention difficulties, concrete thinking, good "visualization" skills, poor incidental and vicarious learning, lack of pretend play, metacognitive and executive functioning problems, problem- solving deficiencies, low self and social understanding (theory of mind deficiencies), low IQ and mental retardation, savant skills
Social interaction	Poor eye contact, imitation, joint attention and social referencing deficiencies, low social initiation, social withdrawal, aloneness, flat and inappropriate social affect, lack of empathy, low use of social gestures and lack of awareness of social protocol, superficial friendships
Language/ communication	Proto-communication problems (e.g., lack of social gestures), echolalia, expressive and receptive language deficiencies, idiosyncratic use of language, pronoun reversals, scripted language, pragmatic deficiencies, poor reading comprehension and conversational speech
Self-regulation	Lack of appropriate self-regulation skills, self-monitoring, self-instruction, and self-evaluation difficulties, problem-solving deficiencies, inability to solicit and use instrumental and emotional social supports, signs of poor self-regulation (impulsivity, distractibility, hyperactivity, ADHD, stereotyped and self-stimulatory behavior, obsessive and restricted interests, compulsive and ritualistic behaviors)
Behavioral problems	Noncompliance, aggression, self-injurious behavior, sleeping and eating problems
Physical characteristics/ medical problems	"Normal" looking, large head circumference, seizures

Sensory processing problems

Background and description

The senses alert us to events going on in our surroundings. They mobilize and guide behavior, influence emotions, and provide information that affects thinking at both a structural and content level. Through the senses, we learn about our environment as well as about ourselves, creating memories that contain records of our history of sensory experiences. Some philosophers, like John Locke, have even suggested that the mind is initially like a blank slate on which sensory experiences are written.

Although formal definitions of autism have not typically included sensory processing problems as a key defining characteristic of this disorder, the presence of sensory disturbances in children with autism is widely acknowledged. The range of such sensory dysfunctions is considerable and includes tactile, auditory, visual, olfactory (smell), and gustatory (taste) hypersensitivities and hyposensitivities. Problems of tactile defensiveness (hypersensitivity) are often noted in the autism literature. For example, tactile defensiveness may manifest itself through an aversion to being held, wearing certain items of clothing, walking on grass, and/or handling certain types of materials. Some individuals display very intense fear in social situations because of their tactual hypersensitivity. Temple Grandin (1995) describes the discomfort associated with being touched and hugged, as well as, paradoxically, her craving for physical affection. Similarly, auditory defensiveness involves oversensitivity to certain sounds, such as sirens, air conditioners, a hum from high voltage wires, or certain types of music. A visually defensive person may have a problem with bright lights or lights that flicker, such as fluorescent fixtures. Food aversions are also common among children with autism. It is not always clear whether the aversions are related to the taste, smell, or texture of the food or some combination of these features. As a consequence of such aversions, some children will eat only a small number of foods.

In addition to hypersensitivity, individuals with autism experience a variety of other sensory problems. Some individuals display reduced sensitivity (hyposensitivity) to pain, cold, and sound, as well as a wide variety of other sensory input. Conversely, other individuals with autism appear to be strongly drawn to certain types of stimuli, to the point of being fixated, and seek to perpetuate that stimulation through repetitive and compulsive behaviors. For example, some children crave deep pressure stimulation. Other individuals seem to be particularly attracted to odors and display a tendency to smell everything. For other individuals, a stimulus may not be fully perceived or may appear distorted. For example, there is speculation that some children's reading problems may be related to letters that appear wavy or even missing completely.

Some sensory problems may reflect an inability to coordinate or integrate sensory input from multiple sources and/or multiple sensory modalities. Children with this latter type of problem may have difficulty tracking a conversation when there are background noises or have problems attending to a visual stimulus when someone is talking. There is also speculation that sensory mixing (synesthesia) may occur in some individuals; for example, a person might see sounds or hear pictures. Finally, some sensory dysfunctions involve the vestibular system, which helps regulate balance and movement, and the proprioceptive system, which provides feedback from muscles, tendons, and ligaments about body position. Problems in both of these latter systems are likely responsible, at least in part, for the difficulties many children experience in gross and fine motor activities. The reader is referred to Huebner (2001) for a more complete description of sensory problems experienced by persons with autism.

O'Neill and Jones (1997), reviewing evidence from clinical and empirical studies, suggest that unusual sensory responses may be present in the majority of children with autism. They indicate that these responses are often present during early development and are linked to other aspects of autistic behavior. Similarly, Gillberg and Coleman (1992) suggest that abnormal sensory responses to stimuli may constitute the most characteristic symptom of autism not currently contained in the diagnostic criterion for this disorder. Summarizing research in this area, these authors further suggest that sensory abnormalities represent the most common type of symptom found in autism cases during infancy. They also point out that symptoms, like apparent deafness, strange reactions to sound, and empty gaze, distinguish autism from another developmental disorder, mental retardation.

Effects of sensory processing problems

Sensory processing involves the reception and organization of sensory experience, ideally in a way that leads to adaptive responses to the environment. To the extent that sensory processes are impaired, the sensory experience is incomplete or distorted. Children with autism, who sometimes appear to be living in a different world, may indeed be; specifically if their sensory experience of the world is quite different from that of other people. Temple Grandin (1988) reports:

> Noise was a major problem for me. When I was confronted with loud or
> confusing noises, I could not modulate it. I either had to shut it all out
> and withdraw, or let it all in like a freight train. To avoid its onslaught, I
> would often withdraw and shut the world out. As an adult, I still have
> problems modulating auditory input. (p. 3)

Similarly, Ornitz (1983) suggests that the behavior of children with autism
becomes disorganized because of their inability to modulate sensory input.
Disorganization can occur for a variety of reasons, including an inability to
focus on incoming stimuli, a failure to filter out irrelevant aspects of the
stimuli, and/or a failure to process completely information contained in the
stimuli. These problems then may produce disruptions at an autonomic
(emotion) level that further inhibit effective sensory processing and elicit a
fight or flight response; both of these responses prevent coordinated and
strategic action. Behaviorally, such an individual can appear at one extreme
hypoactive and withdrawn or at the other extreme hyperactive and disorganized.

Although sensory problems are often reported in terms of a specific
modality, such as touch, problems in one sensory modality often influence
functioning in other sensory modalities, thus creating sensory integration
problems (see review by Anzolone & Williamson, 2000). In turn, sensory
integration difficulties can lead to problems in other areas, such as in motor
functioning. The influence of sensory problems on the motor system can be
far-reaching and profound. For example, Paris (2000a) suggests that problems
in discriminating tactile information can result in impairments in: gross motor
control (decreased body scheme, impaired balance reactions, postural
insecurity, and motor clumsiness), hand control (impairments in grasp,
isolated finger control, manipulation skills, and tool usage), oral motor control
(decreased isolated tongue movements, poor lip closure, instability of the jaw,
and articulation problems), and physical problems, such as shortening of the
hand. More generally, Paris (2000a) points out that tactile discrimination
problems can affect standing, walking, speech, feeding, and many other
activities of daily living.

As mentioned previously, the sensory disturbances observed in individuals with autism vary widely across sensory modalities and include problems
of hyposensitivity and hypersensitivity. Dunn (1997) points out that some
children who are hypersensitive may display a high level of arousal and
activity. However, for other children hypersensitivity may result in sensory
overload and an ensuing behavioral lethargy and flatness of affect, which in
turn may be associated with either an underlying high physiological arousal

or physiological shutdown (perhaps due to exhaustion). Cognitively, hyper-sensitive children may appear distractible, narrowly focused on one aspect of their environment, or inwardly focused. They may also adapt by attempting to tightly control their environment through ritualistic, compulsive, and stereo-typed behavioral patterns.

In contrast to hypersensitive children, hyposensitive children appear to have a high sensory threshold, and thus require more stimulation to evoke a response. Dunn (1997) indicated that hyposensitive children often appear to be unemotional. Behaviorally, they may appear to be either nonresponsive or disorganized in their responses. Cognitively, hyposensitivity is associated with lower levels of attention to incoming stimuli. Hyposensitivity can be viewed as an attempt on the part of children to deal with the problem of overstimulation by shutting out a world that is too intense or chaotic. Such children may show a mixed pattern of reactivity to stimulation, sometimes appearing hypersensitive and other times seeming to be hyposensitive. Other children with hyposensitivity may appear stimulus-deprived and seem to engage in activities for the purpose of gaining sensory input, for example, through rocking, spinning, or tapping. Sometimes selected hyposensitivity can be viewed as developmentally normal, in that repeated presentation of a stimulus typically leads an individual to habituate, that is, to be less attentive to a stimulus as it loses its novelty.

Dunn (1997) suggests that children can be classified from a sensory processing perspective along two continua: a neurological threshold continuum, which relates to whether a stimulus is registered, and a behavioral response continuum, which describes how actively an individual responds to a given level of stimulation. Individuals who are operating at the extremes of these two continua fall into one of four categories:

1. low registration, passive behavioral response

2. low registration, high behavioral response (sensory seeking)

3. high registration, low behavioral response

4. high registration, high behavioral response (sensory avoiding).

This classification scheme emphasizes the importance of the distinction between what is sensed and the reaction to what is sensed, and more generally the complex relationship that exists between the sensory system and the motor system.

Motor dysfunction

According to Paris (2000b), the motor control system consists of a set of processes that help organize and coordinate functional movements. Motor control evolves over time as a consequence of feedback both from the environment and from the body. Motor behaviors, particularly intentional acts, involve motor planning, a process which requires conscious attention and effort. Similarly, motor learning involves a cognitive phase in which information is obtained from the senses and a practice phase in which feedback is used to direct performance.

Motor problems are often observed in children with autism. Although fine motor abilities are affected more than gross motor abilities, problems in both areas are often observed. To what extent these problems are a function of defects in the motor regions of the brain, sensory system, or a combination of these and other defects is unclear. Parents, clinicians, and researchers have noted that infants and toddlers later diagnosed with autism often display early problems in self-feeding, dressing, and general manual dexterity, as well as delays in meeting the major milestones of early motor development (e.g., sitting, crawling, and walking) (Teitelbaum, Teitelbaum, Nye, Fryman & Mauer, 1998). Other problems noted in this population include: postural control problems, unusual postures, clumsiness, impairment in complex motor skills (e.g., bike riding), general motor slowness, repetitive motor behaviors, low motor tone, eye-gaze and visual tracking abnormalities, low movement, lack of endurance, balance disturbances, sucking and swallowing difficulties, speech difficulties, choreiform movements, and dyspraxia.

Dyspraxia, or a dysfunction in praxis, refers to problems in formulating a goal, figuring out how to accomplish a goal (motor planning), and the actual execution of the action: steps which obviously have a strong cognitive as well as a motor component. Children with dyspraxia find it difficult to learn new tasks. Considerable effort and repetition is required on their part to achieve a specific level of competency. Children with Asperger's Syndrome or a high functioning form of autism often have dyspraxia, even if their general level of motor competence is good. Murray-Slutsky (2000) summarizes four different types of dyspraxias that have been identified:

1. visuodyspraxia

2. problems with praxias on verbal command

3. problems withbilateral integration and sequencing

4. somatodyspraxia.

Children with visuodyspraxia have poor form and space perception and problems in visual–motor coordination. Children with praxis-on-demand problems are unable to assume physical postures on verbal command and have difficulty with motor sequencing. Children with bilateral integration and sequencing problems have difficulty coordinating the two sides of their body. They fail to develop hand dominance and avoid crossing the midline of their body. Finally, children with somatopraxia manifest tactile discrimination, fine and gross motor coordination, hand control, oral–motor, and body scheme problems. More generally they appear clumsy. Children with autism and Asperger's Syndrome frequently display somatodyspraxia.

Motor control can be adversely affected by impairments within the central nervous, musculoskeletal, and peripheral nervous systems, as well as by systems controlling motor planning and sensory processing. Because each of these components plays a critical role in motor control, an impairment in any one of them can adversely influence the other components and ultimately motor learning and performance. The sensory systems, particularly the visual, tactual, vestibular, and proprioceptive systems, play a central role in motor performance by providing information that guides motor activity.

In a review of research, Paris (2000b) suggests that motor control problems in individuals with autism may be related to a loss of Purkinje cells in the vermis portion of the cerebellum. The cerebellum plays a key role in coordination of complex movements, balance coordination, and fine motor control. Interestingly, the vermis has connections to regions that control attention, arousal level, and assimilation of sensory information. (See also review by Murray-Slutsky, 2000.) Thus, it is perhaps not surprising that motor problems in children with autism can contribute to deficiencies in other areas such as behavioral regulation, play, communication, and social interaction. Moreover, motor deficits can affect a child's general ability to explore his/her environment, thereby potentially impacting their overall cognitive development (see reviews by Anzalone & Williamson, 2000; Huebner & Kraemer, 2001).

Motor control problems have been mentioned as one of the key characteristics of individuals with Asperger's Syndrome. In a group study, Gillberg (1989) found that 83% of the individuals with this disorder had relatively poor motor skills; in particular he noted that they were generally clumsy and had an awkward way of walking. A variety of other research suggests that between 50% and 90% of individuals with Asperger's Syndrome display motor coordination problems (Attwood, 1998). Specific motor problems that have been observed include: difficulties in throwing and catching a ball, problems with balance (e.g., standing on one leg with eye closed), and lack of manual dexterity (e.g., difficulties in tying shoelaces, handwriting). The movements of individuals with Asperger's Syndrome have also been described as rapid and arrhythmic. It has been suggested that the motor problems of children and adults with Asperger's Syndrome are similar to motor symptoms displayed in other syndromes that feature a movement disorder, such as Tourette's Syndrome, catatonia, and Parkinson's disease (see review by Attwood, 1998).

Whereas motor control problems are viewed as an important feature of Asperger's Syndrome, children with autism have been portrayed historically as displaying normal motor development and sometimes even possessing special competencies in this domain. However, a variety of recent research challenges this perspective and suggests that many children with autism may have a similar or greater incidence of motor problems than children with Asperger's Syndrome (Manjiviona & Prior, 1995; Rinehardt, Bradshaw, Brereton & Tonge, 2001). For example, Manjiviona and Prior (1995) reported similar levels of motor impairment in groups of children with Asperger's Syndrome and children with autism who were high functioning. Rinehardt et al. (2001) also found similar performances on a simple motor reprogramming task in individuals with autism as compared to individuals with Asperger's Syndrome. Although both groups had difficulty in movement preparation, the authors suggested that the nature of the two groups' motor planning problems may have been somewhat different. Results of a study by Baranek (1999) are intriguing in that they suggest that motor and sensory problems are present early in children with autism, when they are 9–12 months old, and that these symptoms can be used, in conjunction with social deficiencies, to distinguish children with autism from typically developing children.

If the position is accepted that most if not all children with autism have motor problems and that these problems manifest themselves during the early stages of development, two critical questions arise: What impact do these motor problems have on the development of the child? And what produces these motor problems in the first place? One answer to these questions is that the early sensory problems associated with autism create great stress in the infant, which in turn leads to disorganized motor behavior. In turn, the motor problems restrict the availability of motor coping resources available to the infant for dealing with their stress, which then further exacerbates the infant's sensory and motor problems. It is also possible that a more basic dysfunction in the arousal/activation system of the infant is responsible for these sensory and motor problems in the first place. In the next section the arousal/activation system of individuals with autism will be described.

Arousal/activation problems

Descriptions of persons with autism by those around them, as well as by themselves, suggest that they are easily stressed, anxious, and fearful. Not only do they often show strong reactions to the environment, but they may have difficulty regulating their emotions when they become upset. Temple Grandin described herself as living in a constant state of fear, with seemingly minor events at times causing an intense reaction. She stated that as she got older her anxiety attacks got worse, escalating into a constant state of physiological alertness, panic attacks, and ultimately depression. She further indicated that about half of high functioning individuals with autism have similar problems (Grandin, 1995). Clinical observation of children with autism also suggests that they display high autonomic reactivity, particularly in new situations, as well as a difficulty in self-regulating this reactivity. Waterhouse (2000), drawing from clinical descriptions, self-descriptions of persons with autism, research, and theory, points out the primacy of anxiety in the lives of both autistic children and adults; lives that are ruled by fear and terror. She speculates that the root of such anxiety may be biologically based and perhaps even genetically rooted as part of the individual's basic temperament (see Table 2.1, p. 53).

Thomas and Chess (1977) suggest that most children can be placed into one of three temperament categories: easy, difficult, or slow to warm up. Based on their research, the authors indicate that about 40% of infants show an easy temperament, about 10% display a difficult temperament, and about 15% are slow to warm up. The remainder of the children, about 35%, display a mixture of traits that do not fit readily into any of these three categories. Easy infants display rhythmicity (e.g., regular eating, sleeping, and toileting habits); approach new situations and people with ease and are adaptable, that is, they tolerate changes in routine; are positive in mood; and demonstrate a low to moderate intensity of affect when happy or sad. In contrast, difficult infants are arrhythmic, have a high activity level, are avoidant of new situations and people, display low adaptability, are more negative in mood, and show a high intensity in their affect when sad or upset. Finally, slow-to-warm-up infants are low in activity level, avoidant in new situations, low in adaptability, and low in the intensity of their affect when happy or sad. Although children with autism differ in their temperaments, the majority of them seem to display traits associated with difficult and/or slow-to-warm-up (shy) categories (Chess & Thomas, 1989). Both of these temperament types share a common component, an arousal problem. Whereas children with a difficult temperament overtly manifest their overarousal, children in the slow-to-warm-up category seem to control their overarousal through avoidance and withdrawal.

A number of individuals have speculated about the role that arousal plays in autism. For example, Tinbergen and Tinbergen (1972) indicate that overarousal might be responsible for the social deficiencies observed in individuals with autism. Ornitz (1983) postulated that at least some of the symptoms associated with autism may result from an inability to modulate sensory input, which is reflected in problems of underreactivity and overreactivity. Paris (2000a) suggests that because their level of arousal is less than optimal, learning and performance in individuals with autism are adversely affected. This impact on learning and performance could be mediated through the attentional problems that result from overarousal and/or underarousal, with inattention or selective attention leading to problems of encoding, processing, and recalling the information necessary for learning to occur.

In summary, in order to function effectively, a calm–alert state is necessary. Paris (2000a) suggests that individuals with autism demonstrate levels of arousal that are either lower than desirable or so high that decompensation results. If understimulated, for either biological and/or environmental reasons, hyporesponsivity (an inability to respond quickly or even at all) results. If overstimulated, again for similar reasons, responding becomes disorganized, impulsive, or even inhibited as a consequence of avoidance or withdrawal. A critical question that needs investigation is whether the anxiety and fears of persons with autism are related to arousal and state-regulation problems, poor social and cognitive coping skills, or a combination of these. From a neurological perspective, problems like those just described may result from a defect in the reticular activating system. This part of the brain, which influences alertness, has ties to many types of sensory information and plays a role in controlling sensory input (see review by Paris & Murray-Slutsky, 2000). In Chapter 4, a theory of autism will be put forth that emphasizes the critical roles that the arousal-activation system and emotions play in the development of autism through their influence on sensory, motor, cognitive, social, and linguistic processes.

Cognitive deficiencies

There is more discussion, research, and theorization about the cognitive characteristics of persons with autism than any other feature of this disorder. There is also fairly uniform agreement that this population displays deficits in: complex memory, metacognitive abilities, knowledge of other people, recognition of emotions, knowledge of self, problem-solving skills, and abstract thinking. These deficits in turn have often been used to explain their social interaction and language difficulties. Many of the social and language deficiencies associated with autism have cognitive components, including those related to pragmatic communication, question-asking, joint attention, imitation, and pretend play. In contrast, there is also recognition of "islands" of cognitive abilities in this population and evidence that cognitive processes, such as attention, discrimination, rote memory, visual–spatial perception, and certain types of object knowledge, are unimpaired or less impaired. Indeed, sometimes there are even areas of special cognitive abilities, such as those displayed by autistic savants. In this section, several cognitive characteristics associated with autism will be discussed including: attention and memory difficulties; concrete thinking; metacognitive, executive process, and theory of mind deficiencies; deficits in emotional and cognitive intelligence; and savantism (see Table 2.1, p. 53).

Attention difficulties

The most rudimentary of the cognitive processes, attention, is a prerequisite for the development of more complex cognitive processes. It is quite common for persons with autism to have attention difficulties, with estimates of this type of problem being as high as 64%. A companion problem, hyperactivity, also occurs with great frequency (36–48%) in this population (Tsai, 1998). Thus, it is not surprising that many children with autism are initially diagnosed as having Attention Deficit Hyperactivity Disorder (ADHD).

Parents and teachers commonly report that children with autism have difficulties with attention in learning situations. Although they can be easily distracted and their focus may often wander, paradoxically, their attention is sometimes captured by task-irrelevant cues upon which they fixate for long periods of time. This problem, which is also sometimes referred to as "stimulus overselectivity" because it involves a limited consideration of environmental cues, is often observed in children who appear poorly motivated to learn (Simpson & Myles, 1998). This "selective inattention" may, however, have little to do with the motivational level of children with autism but rather may occur because they are unable to discover/discriminate cues in the environment that are considered important or relevant by others.

Hypotheses regarding the precise nature of the attention problems of children with autism suggest a range of potential deficits, including an inability:

- to orient to a stimulus
- to sustain attention to a stimulus for long periods
- to shift attention from one stimulus to another, that is, to disengage attention from one object in order to re-engage another
- to broaden their attention focus.

Children with autism at times seem to engage in paradoxical behaviors, sometimes seeming to ignore completely their environment and at other times continually changing the focus of their attention. In general, research suggests that many of the aforementioned attention characteristics may not be reflective of a basic underlying deficiency or defect. That is, children with autism can and do orient to a stimulus; can sustain attention to a stimulus for long periods of time; can disengage and shift attention from one stimulus to another; and are not always overselective in the attention focus (see review by Mesibov, Adams & Klinger, 1997).

If the attention problems of individuals with autism do not represent in and of themselves basic defects, a question is raised as to why they occur. In this regard, there are many potential answers. They may attend to one stimulus to the exclusion of others because it is intrinsically reinforcing; that is, because of its appealing sensory qualities. For example, some children with autism are drawn to objects that have a certain sound quality or cadence. Alternatively, selective inattention may represent a way of dealing with situations that produce a state of overarousal. The developmental theory described in Chapter 4 suggests that the unique attentional style of individuals with autism may evolve, at least in part, as a way of regulating unpleasant emotions. From this perspective, inattention and selective attention represent general coping mechanisms through which children with autism deal with situations that are overdemanding. Attention characteristics such as eye-gaze avoidance, a tendency to look at objects using peripheral perception, and "unwillingness" to share attention with other people are specific examples of these coping mechanisms.

A final explanation for the attentional problems of children with autism is that they focus on narrow aspects of the environments because they have difficulty perceptually integrating or deriving meaning from "complicated" stimulus patterns; so instead they attend to stimuli that are simpler in nature (see Mesibov *et al.*, 1997). Relatedly, some researchers suggest that children with autism have a problem using cues to direct their actions if the cues contain information, particularly information that is social in nature, that must be interpreted (Leekam & Moore, 2001). This theory may also explain why children have difficulty sharing attention with others and following the gaze of others. That is, children with autism may not share attention or follow the gaze of others because such acts require an understanding of complex social cues which they do not process. This type of deficiency could also explain why children with autism have difficulties in educational situations which emphasize social communication.

Research by Pierce, Glad, and Schreibman (1997) provides some support for this perspective. In their study, children were shown videotaped vignettes of children interacting, in which the number of cues required for correct inter-pretation of the interaction varied from one to four; the cues that varied included verbal content, tone of voice, and nonverbal cues, such as smiling (either accompanied by or not accompanied by an object, such as giving a present). In general, children with autism were able to reply to specific attention (information) and social perception questions relating to the stories as accurately as typically developing children and children with mental handicaps when the stories contained only one cue. However, when the stories contained multiple cues, the children with autism had greater difficulty responding to the questions than the other groups of children. This research leaves open the question of whether the inferior performance of the children with autism was related to their difficulty in attending to multiple cues and integrating and interpreting these cues and/or was due to the fact that these cues were social in nature.

One of the explanations offered by the authors concerning why children with autism did not perform as well in the multiple-cue situation is particu-larly intriguing. They suggested that the multiple-cue situation placed more attention strain on the children because it required more attention-shifting and integration of information; in turn this strain caused the participants to be overaroused, thus interfering with their capacity to attend to the information.

If children with autism are indeed, as suggested earlier, more easily subject to overarousal and have problems self-regulating their arousal level, this explanation makes particularly good sense.

Results of other research also support the view that children with autism do not have a general problem orienting to tasks, sustaining attention, or encoding information; their task performance deteriorates, however, when a task requires assimilation of complex information, rapid shifting of attention, strategic planning, or conceptual responses (Goldstein, Johnson & Minshew, 2001). It is possible that the difficulties that children display in interpreting social cues and behaving appropriately in social interaction situations may be a function of the fact that the cues in these social situations are intrinsically more complex and dynamic (changing) than those contained in most of the nonsocial tasks they confront in everyday life. This interpretation may also explain why higher functioning children with autism and Asperger's Syndrome often perform well in their academic work, but not in their social interactions.

Memory

Early perspectives on memory functioning in children with autism suggest that they have good rote memories (Kanner, 1943). Case studies have indicated that some individuals with autism, including some autistic savants, display better than average and even exceptional memories for certain kinds of material. Research has provided a more refined view of memory processes in this population. For example, research has established that like typical children, memory improves with age in children with autism. Individuals with autism often do as well as nonautistic persons when material to be remembered is visual in nature, but have more problems recalling material when it is presented auditorially, particularly if the material is verbal in nature. Moreover, they appear to have more difficulty in remembering information that is complex and meaningful. There is also evidence that autistic individuals who are mentally retarded have more severe memory impairments (see review by Renner, Klinger & Klinger, 2000). Although research on memory in children with autism is increasing, less work has been done in this area relative to other cognitive processes, such as attention and social perception. Many findings have not been replicated, possibly because of the differences in the characteristics of the sample studied, tasks utilized, and other variations in experimental procedures.

Nevertheless, some of the results of more recent research are fascinating. For example, Millward, Powell, Messer, and Jordan (2000) found that children with autism were less likely to recall events performed by themselves than those performed by a peer. In contrast, nonautistic children were more likely to remember events performed by themselves. The authors point out that these results are consistent with theories that suggest children with autism are less aware of themselves, less self-conscious, and less likely to self-monitor, and as a consequence do not develop a well-defined sense of self. Moreover, the results are consistent with theory of mind and metacognitive perspectives which contend that children with autism do not understand their own minds.

Concrete thinking

People with autism tend to understand the world in more concrete terms (Waterhouse, 2000). They have difficulty comprehending abstract ideas; instead they react in a literal fashion to the words of others, thus making it difficult for them to understand humor, deceitful behavior, metaphorical expressions, and idiomatic speech. This autistic style of thinking may be a function of the way language is learned and the tendency to connect words to specific visual images. Temple Grandin discusses how she had to convert abstract ideas into pictures to understand them. For example, she points out that words like church conjure up for her specific images of all the churches she has ever seen, rather than a general image of a church (Grandin, 1995). One consequence or correlate of concrete visually oriented thinking is that it leads to an interesting pattern of strengths within a context of many limitations. For example, on IQ tests, like the *Wechsler Intelligence Scales for Children*, individuals with autism often do better on subtests requiring visualization skills, like the block design, but have difficulty with subtests that require interpretation of word meanings, concepts, and social situations like the similarities and information subtests (see review by Lerea, 1987).

Metacognition, executive processes, and self-regulation

Both research and clinical literatures are full of examples indicating that persons with autism can learn simple as well as complex behavioral and cognitive skills needed in specific situations, for example like those taught in academic programs, but that they have difficulty transferring or generalizing these skills to other situations in which they would be appropriate. This type of difficulty could be explained in terms of their concrete and visual thinking characteristics. Another possible explanation for this inability to transfer what they have learned to other contexts is that they have a self-regulatory disorder.

In most formal educational programs, children are first taught how to respond in one situation and then are taught about other situations in which the response is applicable. Cognitive and educational psychologists have suggested that in order to transfer learning from one situation to another, a person must have a metacognitive understanding of their capabilities as well as knowledge about the environments with which they interact. More specifically, a person has to know what skills they possess, what skills are required in new situations they encounter, and whether they possess the skills necessary to perform in the new situations. Individuals with a metacognitive understanding of themselves and their environment not only understand their abilities and what they can do, but also comprehend what their limitations are and what they cannot do.

In order to cope with new situations requiring action a person must also be able to utilize or execute what he/she knows. Thus, in addition to metacognitive knowledge, the concept of an executor is important. For example, in a specific problem-solving situation a person not only needs to examine the problem at hand and characterize what is required to solve a problem, but also implement the solution. Individuals with these *metacognitive* and *executive skills* are often characterized as self-regulating their behavior. Within this framework, successful problem-solvers attend to their behavior (self-monitor), make judgments about the acceptability of that behavior through comparing what one is doing with what needs to be done (self-evaluation), and feel a sense of accomplishment when they succeed (self-reinforcement). Depending upon the outcome of their self-evaluation, individuals decide whether or not to change their behavior. If a problem is not solved, they need to reevaluate what they are doing and search for a new solution. Individuals with good self-regulation skills recognize that they are capable of controlling their environment through their actions and as a consequence gain confidence and a sense of self-efficacy (Whitman, 1990).

Persons with autism are often characterized as having metacognitive and executive process deficiencies, in part because they have great difficulty in transferring what they have learned to new situations. They are viewed as having little insight into their own minds and what they know and do not know. When they are put in new learning situations, they may:

- appear confused, helpless, and distractible
- act in an impulsive and seemingly mindless fashion
- perseverate, repeatedly using ineffective strategies.

(Adrien, Martineau, Barthélémy, Bruneau, Garreau & Sauvage, 1995)

Individuals with autism do not appear to self-monitor or self-evaluate their actions; and even when they are successful, they do not seem to understand the reasons for their success or experience a sense of self-accomplishment (see for example, Millward *et al.*, 2000). Although they may have scripts, social or otherwise, for dealing with specific situations, they often have difficulty modifying these scripts in order to adapt to new situations (Volden & Johnston, 1999). To the extent that this characterization is correct, it is not surprising that children with autism appear unmotivated in new learning situations and uninterested in expanding their range of interests.

Theory of mind and emotional intelligence

Individuals with autism are not only characterized as lacking insights into their own minds, but also the minds of other people. Hobson (1993) suggests that the emergence of self-reflective thought is dependent on advances in social understanding, which in turn is dependent on the development of inter-personal relationships. Many of the social impairments that persons with autism display have been attributed to their inability to understand what other people are thinking and that the perspectives of other people may be different from their own. Because they have problems comprehending the thoughts, beliefs, and attitudes of other people, they also have difficulty understanding their own and other people's feelings. A lack of understanding of the feelings of others makes it difficult for them to understand their own emotions and vice versa. It also appears that they do not experience certain emotions (e.g., embarrassment, pride, and guilt), or at least do not experience these emotions in the same way as other people (Grandin, 1995). In describing their own emotions, individuals with autism tend to give scripted, less personally relevant, and tangential responses (Kasari, Chamberlain & Bauminger, 2001). In turn, this type of problem likely makes it difficult for them to empathize with other people. As a consequence of the aforementioned difficulties, autistic persons are often viewed as being low in emotional intelligence or emotional competence.

In discussing emotional competence, Sarni (1999) suggests that a variety of skills are necessary in order to develop a sense of psychological well-being in social situations. These skills include the capacities:

- to be aware of one's emotional state, and that one might be experiencing multiple, and sometimes contradictory emotions simultaneously

- to discern the emotions of others, using physical and social cues

- to use emotion vocabulary and emotional expressions in conventional ways

- to empathize with others

- to recognize that inner emotional states and outer behavioral expressions of emotions need not necessarily correspond, either in oneself or others

- to cope with aversive or distressing emotions

- more generally, to recognize that the nature of social relationships is defined in a large part by the quality of the emotional communication that occurs within those relationships.

Through these skills, people not only manage their own emotions but also gain an overall sense of self-esteem and emotional self-efficacy in social situations.

Sarni (1999) views emotional competence as developing within the context of social relationships and a person's emotional experiences. She suggests that children with autism, because of a major cognitive deficit in the way they interpret their emotional experiences and those of others, are unable to convey emotions in conventional ways. Celani, Battacchi, and Arcidiacono (1999) point out that emotion recognition is a complex skill that requires the interpretation of facial expressions within a specific social and physical context. To the extent that children with autism have difficulty attending to and integrating cues from different sources, they would be expected to have problems interpreting the meaning of particular emotional expressions and "emotional" circumstances as well as reacting appropriately to such circumstances.

Research examining emotions in children with autism suggests that they, like typical children, experience the world at an emotional level, but that they convey their emotions in unconventional ways; for example, by showing happy expressions more often in solitary situations than social situations or by displaying emotions such as joy in situations that appear to an observer to be unpleasant. Reddy, Williams, and Vaughan (2002) found, after analyzing videotapes and comparing the responses of children with Down's Syndrome and children with autism in free play and toy play situations, that children with autism displayed lower frequencies of attention and smiles in response to the laughter of others. Such observations suggest that children with autism do not learn the cultural scripts of emotion or know the steps of the social inter-action "dance", thus seemingly marching to the beat of a different drummer (Sarni, 1999).

IQ and mental retardation

It has been frequently stated that the majority of children with autism are also mentally retarded (Sigman & Capps, 1997). From a formal perspective, this is probably an accurate assessment. According to the definition put forth by the American Association on Mental Retardation (AAMR):

> Mental retardation refers to substantial limitations in present func-
> tioning. It is characterized by significantly subaverage intellectual func-
> tioning, existing concurrently with related limitations in two or more of
> the following skill areas: communication, self-care, home living, social
> skills, community use, self-direction, health and safety, functional
> academics, leisure, and work. Mental retardation manifests before age
> 18.

> (AAMR, 1992, p. 5)

Thus, to receive a diagnosis of mental retardation, an individual must display both intellectual and adaptive behavior deficiencies before age 18.

Using these criteria, it should not be surprising that children with autism are often diagnosed as having mental retardation. They typically display a variety of skill or behavioral limitations, most frequently in the communica-tion, social interaction, leisure, academic, and vocational areas. Children with autism, who are considered functioning at a lower developmental level, often display deficiencies in all of the skill areas listed in the AAMR definition. In addition, many children with autism score in the "significantly subaverage" range of intellectual functioning on intelligence tests, defined as an IQ score of approximately 70–75 or below.

Intelligence, as evaluated by IQ tests, is a measure of rate of development; that is, it describes how much development has occurred in a particular period of time and is also an index that projects how much development is likely to occur in the future. Individuals with lower IQs are described as developing more slowly than persons with higher IQs; over time the disparity in develop-ment level and achievement between these two groups increases. It is often difficult to detect differences early on in development, for example at age two or three, between individuals in an IQ range of 65–75 compared to individ-uals with IQs around 100; however, with increasing age, the disparity becomes increasingly obvious. When children's assessed IQs fall below 50, it becomes much easier to detect developmental problems at an early age.

Estimates of the incidence of IQ scores in the range of mental retardation in persons with autism vary considerably, from around 25% to 80% (see Zahner & Pauls, 1987). Most commonly, estimates are in the 50% to 80% range. When examining intellectual ability, the IQ scores of persons with autism are less revealing than the variation in their performance on specific subtests of an IQ assessment (Lerea, 1987). Persons with autism display an uneven pattern of strengths and weaknesses. Typically, they score higher on subtests that measure nonverbal abilities than on those that assess verbal abilities. They do better on subtests that assess short-term memory than on subtests that assess social knowledge and comprehension. They also do better on subtests evaluating perceptual organization abilities, but are more likely to have problems with subtests that require sequencing skills. If one subscribes to the notion that intelligence is composed of not one general ability but multiple abilities, persons with autism would be characterized, relative to their overall IQ, as having a profile of contrasting abilities and disabilities.

A distinction is sometimes made between the basic process or processes underlying intelligence and the developmental achievements in various domains assessed by intelligence tests. At its most basic process level, researchers often view intelligence as an index of the speed with which infor-mation is processed. One provocative hypothesis put forth suggests that even though persons with autism are impaired in certain areas like social compre-hension, most are unimpaired in their speed of processing, that is, in the basic underlying foundation of intelligence. In a study by Scheuffgen, Happé, Anderson, and Frith (2000) this hypothesis was examined. The speed of processing of children with autism on an inspection time task was compared with that of age-matched, normally developing children, who had IQs one standard deviation above average. The results suggested that children with autism have preserved this basic processing capacity, despite the fact that they had lower IQ scores than the comparison group. More generally, the results imply, at least for some children with autism, that their low scores on intelli-gence tests are not a function of a deficit in speed of processing, but rather are due to defects in other areas, for example in attentional, regulatory, or social-cognitive processes that also influence performance on IQ tests.

There is also considerable discussion in the IQ testing literature about whether autism and Asperger's Syndrome are really separate disorders or if they are one disorder on a continuum. Based on results of an analysis of the performance of children and youth with Asperger's Syndrome on various subtests of the Wechsler IQ test, Barnhill, Hagiwara, Myles, and Simpson (2000) concluded that children with Asperger's Syndrome are more like typically developing children in their performance profile than children with other autism-related disorders. Because their conclusions were based on comparisons of their results (which provided information only about individuals with Asperger's Syndrome) with the results from other studies, caution must be taken in accepting their interpretation. In an interesting study by Miller and Ozonoff (2000), the authors found participants with Asperger's Syndrome to have higher verbal and full-scale IQ scores, significantly larger verbal-performance IQ discrepancies, and better visual-perceptual skills than children with high functioning autism. However, and most interestingly, when the IQ differences between the two groups were statistically controlled, the performance profiles of the two groups were quite similar. The authors suggest that their results provide support for the hypothesis that Asperger's Syndrome may be simply "high IQ autism".

Some people question whether the IQ tests that are given to children with autism are fair, because these children frequently have language deficiencies and IQ tests have a strong verbal component. Even when their language skills are well developed, children with autism appear to have difficulty tracking the directions of the test administrator, perhaps because of the unconventional ways children with autism use and understand language. They also have difficulty attending in the structured social situations in which the test is given. Thus, estimates of the IQs of children with autism may be low because of the social nature of testing situations and the verbal format of the IQ test. Such estimates may also disguise the children's competencies in nonverbal areas. In this regard, Temple Grandin has expressed her frustration with a society that evaluates thinking and intelligence in only one way and points out that many successful thinkers are visual, not verbal, in their thinking style (Grandin, 1995). Nevertheless, it should be noted that IQ tests that assess verbal skills and verbal learning are good predictors of academic achievement in schools; however, most of these schools have a conventional language-based curriculum. Such a test may not be a good predictor of the performance of children with autism who are placed in a curriculum that is more visually oriented and takes into consideration their social limitations; that is, a curriculum that is more individualized and utilizes the special competencies of the student.

Savant characteristics

Savant characteristics, or the savant syndrome, refers to the presence of remarkable and sometimes amazing abilities that exist within a context of mental deficits. These characteristics are most common in individuals with autism, but are also found in individuals with mental retardation and various types of brain damage. Rimland (1978) reports that savant abilities may occur in about 10% of people with autism. Estimates of the frequency of savantism rely, however, on how this syndrome is specifically defined. Examples of savantism, which are more common than clear definitions of this syndrome, include people whose gifts involve special sensory (particularly visual and auditory), motor, memory, or nonsymbolic abilities, and accomplishments in areas like art and music (Treffert & Wallace, 2002). More specifically, savants may have a prodigious memory, an ability to produce a musical piece after hearing it only once, special drawing abilities, or may display amazing feats of calculation. The special abilities that autistic savants demonstrate are, however, not typically useful from a social or vocational standpoint.

Theories abound concerning why such abilities exist and how they develop. Perhaps the most prominent theory is that a defect or injury in the left hemisphere results in a reorganization of the brain and the enhancement of functions associated with the right hemisphere. Mottron and Burack (2001) emphasize that both autistic savants, as well many nonsavant individuals with autism, display patterns of relative strengths in the context of limitations. They suggest that a vertical imbalance exists in autism; specifically that the relationship between lower and higher psychological (and brain) processes is disrupted and that overdeveloped lower processes, such as sensory recognition and reproduction, interfere with the development of higher processes, such as abstract thinking and social reflection. Conversely, it could be argued that the lack of development of higher processes could catalyze the development of special abilities that emerge to compensate for abilities that are lost or diminished. Because of the striking and often similar patterns of abilities and disabilities in autistic savants, some researchers suggest that this unusual syndrome may provide unique windows into the functioning of the brain.

Social interaction deficiencies

Persons with autism display a broad pattern of deficiencies in social interaction situations. From a diagnostic perspective, these social deficits are considered a core characteristic of autism. During the early stages of development, deficiencies in the social development of children with autism are not always apparent, either because their early social development is on track or more likely because differences in this area are more subtle and less easy to detect. As they enter into the second year of life, their social difficulties become increasingly apparent. By the time they are three years of age, their overall development in the social realm is often markedly delayed.

Although children with autism become attached to their parents; sometimes use nonverbal skills, such as gestures to make requests; and may show turn-taking skills during play, they usually show marked limitations in these and other areas of social interaction, particularly in situations requiring joint attention, social initiation, and dynamic social reciprocity. They are less able to benefit from experiences in social environments that are less structured, and which require that they learn vicariously through observation. Children with autism also manifest specific difficulties in maintaining appropriate eye contact, using adults as a social reference to interpret ambiguous social situations, expressing empathy, engaging in social play with peers, following social protocols, and developing friendships. Their facial expressions, which are sometimes bland or inappropriate, seem to reflect a lack of understanding of social cues (see Table 2.1, p. 53).

In a study of 50 individuals, ranging in age from 28 months to 33 years and having a history of infantile autism, Volkmar, Cohen, and Paul (1986) examined parental responses to a series of questions concerning their children's early social development. The authors found that the majority of these individuals were described by their parents as appearing emotionally distant, ignoring people, avoiding eye contact, displaying little affection or social interest, ignoring displays of affection or withdrawing from such displays, appearing to look through people, and seeming to be unaware of their mothers.

Although the social deficiencies of children with autism become more apparent as they grow older, there are considerable individual differences in their general pattern of development. Some children are almost totally nonresponsive to the social environment. Others react to social overtures and even initiate social interaction, but do so in less mature and more unusual ways (Waterhouse & Fein, 1998; Wing & Gould, 1979). Wing and Gould (1979) suggest that the social interaction styles of individuals with autism spectrum disorders can be grouped into three types: aloof; passive; and active, but odd. Children who are aloof are cut off from social contact, become upset when close to others, and typically reject social overtures. In contrast, children in the passive group, while not making social overtures, accept such overtures from others without becoming upset and may even enjoy such social contact. The last group consists of individuals who spontaneously approach people, but do so in unusual, one-sided, and inappropriate ways. This group often has a higher level of overall competency than the other two groups.

Like individuals with Autistic Disorder, children with Asperger's Syndrome show impaired social behavior, despite their more normal language and intellectual development. Gillberg and Gillberg (1989) suggested that to be labeled as having Asperger's Syndrome a child should have at least two of the following social impairments: an inability to interact with peers, a lack of desire to interact with peers, a lack of appreciation of social cues, and/or socially and emotionally inappropriate behavior. Gillberg and Gillberg (1989) also indicated that nonverbal communication impairments should be present for a diagnosis to be made. Specifically, the child should have at least one of the following characteristics: a limited use of gestures, clumsy/gauche body language, limited facial expressions, inappropriate expressions, and/or a peculiar stiff gaze.

Several factors are associated with the social development of children with autism, including age, IQ, and social supports. Growth in social competencies typically occurs with increasing age. Moreover, IQ correlates positively with the degree of social development, with higher IQ individuals with autism acquiring more extensive social skills. Finally, with proper support structures and interventions, social behavior improves. In fact, since the inception of early intervention programs, the historical stereotype of children with autism being withdrawn, nonaffectionate, and noninteractive has changed. For reviews describing the social behavior of individuals with autism, the reader is referred to Paris (2000a), Sigman and Capps (1997), and Waterhouse (2000).

In the remainder of this section, some of the more salient social characteristics of children with autism will be examined in greater detail. More specifically, their attachment behaviors will be examined along with deficiencies they display in joint attention, social referencing, imitation, play, and friendship formation.

Attachment

From an evolutionary perspective, attachment behaviors serve to keep children close to their parents, thus ensuring their physical safety and the preservation of the species. Secure attachment relationships are also considered necessary because they provide emotional security to children, which in turn allows them to actively explore their environment. In addition, attachment relationships are important because they influence the perceptions children have of people other than their parents. As a consequence of a child's early attachment experiences, a "working model" is formed concerning what people are like and how they are likely to treat the child, particularly in close relationships. Theoretically, a variety of child factors have been hypothesized to inhibit the development of attachment behaviors in children with autism including: anxiety, problems in interpreting nonverbal expressions of emotion, an inability to make inferences about other people's mental states, and neurotransmitter and hormonal disturbances (e.g., abnormal levels of oxytocin, vasopressin, cortisol, and norepinephrine) (see reviews by Gillberg & Coleman, 1992; Huebner & Kraemer, 2001). Clinical reports of children with autism treating parents as objects, for example, like pieces of furniture, has led to the suggestion that they have an attachment deficit. Although autistic children have often been characterized as being unable to develop close emotional bonds with people, a variety of research suggests that they do become attached to their parents/care-takers (see Sigman & Mundy, 1989).

Studies that employ the "strange situation" paradigm for assessing attachment indicate that children with autism miss their parents when they are left alone in a room, that they are relieved when they are reunited with their parents, and that they prefer the company of their parents to a stranger: all signs that a specific attachment has been formed. Research by Sigman and her colleagues suggests that while children with autism display a variety of attachment behaviors, their specific attachment style is difficult to categorize. For example, Sigman and Mundy (1989) found that of the 15 children they could categorize, all were classified initially as disorganized/disoriented. However, a subsequent and more detailed analysis of their attachment style suggested that six of the children were securely attached, two were inse-cure-ambivalent, two were avoidant, three were disorganized, and three could not be subclassified. Although these results suggest that children often do form attachments, they also indicate that such attachments are not always of a secure type. It should be pointed out that this type of study is typically conducted later in the children's lives due to the fact that the diagnosis of autism is not usually made until a child reaches two or three years of age. For this reason, such studies are not able to provide information on when such attachments develop or whether attachment formation is delayed.

A number of critical questions concerning the attachment relationships of children with autism are in need of answers. For example, are attachment relationships more impaired in certain subgroups of children with autism, like Wing and Gould's (1979) aloof group? What is the relationship between child IQ and attachment style? How do the attachment styles of children with autism differ from children without a developmental disability? It seems likely that a number of the characteristics commonly associated with autism, including hyposensitivity, hypersensitivity, inattention, hyperactivity, language difficulties, self-regulation deficiencies, social-cognitive problems, and behavioral problems (e.g., irregular sleep habits) could exert considerable influence on the formation, nature, and complexity of the attachment relationship. In addition to the characteristics of children with autism, it is quite possible that the social context surrounding these children influences attachment formation, including social factors such as parental grief, depression, stress, and difficulty in interpreting their children's signals. Even if children with autism form secure emotional attachments with their care takers, as some research suggests, it does not follow that these children form articulated conceptualizations about who their parents are, what other people are like, and human relationships in general. The development of such a conceptual model assumes an ability on the part of the child to understand their own minds and those of other people, to empathize with others, and to generalize attributions formed in one interpersonal situation to other people: cognitive abilities that are often deficient in children as well as adults with autism (see review by Sigman & Capps, 1997).

Joint attention

What distinguishes children with autism from typically developing children is not so much the fact that they do not interact with others or form relationships, but rather the ways in which they interact. For example, although they show some attachment behaviors, approach care-takers to make requests, make occasional eye contact, and even take part in games requiring turn taking, they are not inclined to actively share their interests and achievements with others or share in the interests of others; that is, they do not share attention jointly with others. Early in development they are unlikely to point to objects in order to engage the attention of others, look where others are looking, or shift their gaze back and forth from an object to an adult. Because joint attention appears to be critical for acquiring oral language, deciphering other people's oral communications and the nonverbal facial expressions that accompany such communications, learning vicariously through observation, developing empathy, and understanding the minds of others, some researchers feel that it may be a key to understanding the development of autism. Joint attention is also thought to be a critical prerequisite for improving the social behavior of children with autism. (See reviews by Carpenter & Tomasello, 2000; Mundy & Stella, 2000.)

In a typically developing child, attention is directed more to social than nonsocial stimuli, often toward a person's eyes (see review by Klin, Jones, Schultz, Volkmar & Cohen, 2002). Klin *et al.* (2002) found reduced fixation time on the eye region to be a good predictor of autism. Interestingly, however, greater fixation on the mouth predicted better social adjustment and less impairment in individuals with autism. In contrast, greater fixation on objects was associated with more extensive autistic symptomatology. As the authors point out, the results raise a variety of intriguing hypotheses about the pattern of relationships between mouth and eye fixation times and the development of language and social competence. For example, it may be that both mouth and eye fixation are important for language acquisition because the mouth provides information about the formation and structure of sounds and words and the eyes provide nuanced information about the referents and meanings of words. More generally, attention to facial cues would seem to be a critical prerequisite for joint attention.

Joint attention has been defined as involving "behaviors used to follow or direct the attention of another person to an event or object and to share an interest in that event or object" (Siller & Sigman, 2002, p. 77). In a review of research, Mundy and Crowson (1997) point out that joint attention deficiencies alone have been able to reliably discriminate samples of young children with autism from children with other developmental delays and suggest that this deficiency, along with play and imitation, is one of the best early predictors of autism. Moreover, these authors speculate that because joint attention is linked to later social and cognitive development, it may be a pivotal skill that should be targeted at the onset of early intervention programs. It seems likely that joint attention influences later social and cognitive development through its impact on the development of imitation and play, skills in which children with autism are also deficient. In an interesting study, Leekam and Moore (2001) examined but did not find support for the theory that these children's difficulty in imitating and responding to the attention of others is related to a more general problem of attentional dis-engagement (disengaging their attention from one object and shifting it to another). This intriguing theory needs to be further investigated, along with another theory proposed by the authors: that children with autism have difficulty interpreting and using the information obtained through the attentional processes.

Social referencing

Another characteristic closely related to joint attention is social referencing. As infants grow and become interested in their care-takers and other people, they tend to spend more time looking at them. This interest likely springs from the fact that adults provide infants stimulation, objects of value (e.g., food), and emotional support. Along with this general social interest comes a specific tendency for infants to focus visually on adults in situations that are unusual, ambiguous, or confusing, a phenomenon known as social refer-encing. Adults become sources of information for infants in such situations, as a consequence influencing the infants' behavior and feelings. During social referencing infants shift attention from a new or strange object (or person) to a parent in a back and forth manner, apparently for the purpose of gaining information about how to interpret the meaning of the object and whether it constitutes a threat.

Deviating from this normative pattern, autistic children spend less time looking at their care-givers, even in situations that are unusual or ambiguous. When they do look at their care-taker's face, they do not appear to use the information contained in nonverbal facial cues to guide their behavior. For example, if children with autism encounter a strange object, their reaction to the object does not seem to be greatly influenced by whether their care-takers are smiling or showing fear. Perhaps this social referencing deficit occurs because children with autism are overwhelmed by the sensory complexity of their physical and social environment and become distracted, consequently obtaining little information or assistance from others to resolve their confusion. Moreover, if they find their environment chaotic and fear-evoking, they may attempt to control it through withdrawal, rigid routines, and attentional fixations, further restricting the ways in which they engage their social environment (see review by Sigman & Capps, 1997).

Imitation

Imitation is a skill that is manifested early in the human life cycle. Infants may show imitative behavior a few weeks after birth. During normal development, infants are drawn to the faces of their care-taker and imitate or attempt to imitate with increasing frequency their facial expressions. These imitations are part of a larger social interactional dance that begins shortly after birth between infants and parents. In contrast, children with autism often show deficiencies in spontaneous as well as elicited (requested) imitation. These imitation deficiencies are thought to be so important that they have been given the status of a core or basic deficit. Through imitation, children acquire new skills, including language, motor behaviors, emotional expressions, and social protocols. Some researchers theorize that imitation helps a child to understand the minds of other people and social conventions as well as to self-regulate during social interactions (Smith & Bryson, 1994).

Along with joint attention and play, imitation is an early reliable discriminator of autism (Mundy & Crowson, 1997). Because social imitation requires attending to other people, imitative deficiencies may occur because of an attentional and/or social interpretational deficiency (Leekam & Moore, 2001). Although children with autism often improve their imitative skills over time, their disability in this area often differentiates them from both typically developing children and children with other handicaps, including mental retardation. As a consequence, intervention programs for children with autism typically focus early on developing imitative behavior as a prelude to teaching other specific nonverbal and verbal behaviors (see Cox, 1993; Rogers & Bennetto, 2000). It is also hoped that once children with autism become imitators, they will be able to learn more informally through observing others in social situations like play.

Play

Play is a process that evolves from infancy into adulthood. Play can be distinguished in a variety of ways, including by its diversity, complexity, functionality, its social versus asocial orientation, and its symbolic versus concrete nature. Typically, children show a progression from object exploration to using toys in specific and conventional ways; from solitary play to parallel play, and eventually to cooperative play with other children; and from concrete to symbolic and imaginary (pretend) play. Play is a vehicle through which children learn about their environment and how to interact with it, thereby influencing their sensorimotor, cognitive, and socioemotional

development. As Murray and Paris (2000) point out, "by touching, manipulating, exploring and testing", children find out about the world, themselves,
and their relationships with others (p. 370). Play helps children try out new
roles, solve problems, work cooperatively with others, and formulate and
execute plans.

An inability to engage in appropriate play in nonsocial, and particularly
social, contexts is considered to be one of the early distinguishing characteristics of children with autism. Although they do play, research indicates that the
play of children with autism is characterized by its:

1. stereotyped nature, with objects often serving as sources of repetitive
    self-stimulation

2. preoccupation with specific toys, as well as specific aspects of a toy

3. absence of functional and normative interactions with toys

4. lack of imagination and a pretend orientation

5. concrete and nonsymbolic nature

6. solitariness and nonsocial quality

7. simplistic and scripted structure.

Parents notice early on that their children with autism: do not play with toys
in usual ways, are interested in developmentally simpler toys, are quite limited
in what toys they play with, and may develop obsessive attachment to toys,
often keeping them close but not playing with them. Children with autism
who are operating at a higher intellectual level may show more functional
play, more diverse and complex interactions with toys, more social play, and a
greater tendency to engage in imaginary or pretend play. Nevertheless, their
approach to play still has a certain fixed and nonspontaneous quality (Siegel,
1996; Sigman & Capps, 1997). Researchers have variously suggested that
children with autism have play difficulties because of the problems they
display in sensory processing, arousal modulation, selective attention, and
shifting attentional focus. Others have suggested that their play deficiencies
may be related to their dyspraxia and executive control problems (integrating
sensory information, forming representations, and transferring this representation into action) (see review of theory and research in this area by Baranek,
Reinhartsen & Wannamaker, 2001). Because play provides a major context
for the development of friendships, it is not surprising that children with
autism have difficulty forming meaningful social relationships with others.

Friendship

Friendships and other peer relationships provide a context in which children develop social skills, an understanding of social rules, a sense of personal identity, and an appreciation of individual differences. They also are a source of emotional satisfaction. Although children with autism have peer acquaintances, their contacts with them are often casual in nature. Although they can be taught a range of social skills, such as appropriate eye contact, greeting responses, initiating, and responding to social contacts, they find it difficult to use these skills in a spontaneous fashion in social situations. Higher functioning children with autism who develop more complex linguistic competencies and social skills have a better chance of developing and sustaining a relationship with others than autistic children who are functioning at a lower level. Despite their superior social skills, their relationships are nevertheless typically superficial in nature. It is frequently assumed that children with autism cannot develop deep friendships because of their inability to understand the minds and emotions of others.

In a review of theory and research on friendship, Bauminger and Kasari (2001) point out that even though children with autism can explain what a friend is, they appear to view friendship in more instrumental terms; for example, it allows them to say that they have a friend. Their descriptions of pictures of friends and friendships tend to emphasize physical details like color of clothing or frequency of contact, rather than the social, cognitive, or affective aspects of the individual or relationship. Although children with autism seem to understand what loneliness means, they do not seem to associate loneliness or lack of friends with feelings of sadness. Bauminger and Kasari (2001) suggest that interventions directed at friendship development should be individualized, according to the developmental level of the person, and optimally contain components that not only target the acquisition of specific behavioral skills, but also focus on developing the social and emotional meaning of friendship. They further recommend that peers, parents, and teachers should be recruited to develop, support, and sustain friendships.

Language deficiencies

There is a dynamic relationship between children's language and their social and cognitive functioning. Through language children express their needs, make demands, regulate their own and other people's behavior, communicate their feelings, explore and respond to their social environment, come to better understand themselves, and imagine worlds different than the one in which they live. Language helps children escape reality and become in their minds whoever and whatever they wish to be. It also allows them to more readily understand the minds of other people. During typical development, preverbal gestures and joint attention acts help to pave the way for language. Intentional communication develops early (9–13 months) followed by first words (13–18 months), word combinations (18–30 months), sentences (30 months–5 years), and discourse grammar (5–8 years) (see Prizant & Wetherby, 1993).

Language deficiencies are a core diagnostic characteristic of autism. Estimates suggest that around 50% of children with autism do not acquire speech as a primary mode of communication (Prizant, 1996). It is common for children with autism who have great difficulty with expressive language to echo words spoken to them. This echolalia is also found more generally in children who are just beginning to acquire language. Based on parental report, it appears some children with autism lose their language abilities after a period of normal development (see Table 2.1, p. 53).

Although children with autism vary considerably in their language development, all have difficulty in communicating. Some children have minimal receptive and expressive speech while others develop more elaborate language skills; however, even this latter group has difficulty engaging in dynamic discourse with others and comprehending the intricacies of social communications. The fact that children with autism have language deficiencies is not surprising given their problems in preverbal communication (e.g., limited use of social gestures) and deficiencies in maintaining eye contact, joint attention, social referencing, and imitation.

In a review by Sigman and Capps (1997), the language deficiencies of children with autism are summarized as including problems in: words and grammar, pragmatics (which includes the prosodic features of language), conversational conventions, taking the listener's perspective into consideration, and the use of narrative. In their review, the authors cite research suggesting that phonological (sound) development in children with autism, while slower, resembles that of other children, but that the meanings children with autism attach to words are idiosyncratic as well as highly tied to specific concrete objects.

Among children with autism who develop more complex language, their grammar and syntax, while similar to typical children, show a variety of anomalies, such as unusual word strings, less sophisticated grammar rules, past-tense difficulties, pronoun reversals (e.g., I for you), use of passive sentences, and problems in production and comprehension of questions. Although some children with autism develop fairly normal grammar, their use of language nevertheless remains problematic. Sigman and Capps (1997) suggest these children have less experience with dynamic reciprocal social interactions that would help them understand the nuances of words and more generally the pragmatics of language.

Children with autism who are higher functioning use language, at least early on, more to satisfy their needs than to share attention with others or to understand another's point of view. Their conversations are often characterized by perseveration on specific topics, irrelevant detail, and tangential shifts in topic. They tend not to initiate a conversation. They frequently show idiosyncratic interpretations of others' speech, as well as problems in modulation, loudness, pitch, stress (prosody), and rhythm. They are less likely to use intonation stress to convey meaning or interpret utterances. Conversations with children with autism typically break down when they are questioned. They also have a tendency to interrupt others, as well as difficulties in elaborating on others' comments and maintaining a logical dialogue flow. These latter problems probably relate to a broader difficulty that children with autism have with being able to understand the perspective of others (see Sigman & Capps, 1997).

Many of the aforementioned characteristics are also displayed by children with Asperger's Syndrome. Gillberg and Gillberg (1989) include among the diagnostic criteria for this disorder the following speech and language characteristics: delayed development, superficially perfect expressive language, formal pedantic language, odd prosody, peculiar voice characteristics, and impairments in comprehension, including a tendency to misinterpret both the literal and implied meanings of words (see Attwood, 1998 for a further discussion of these characteristics).

Tager-Flusberg (1996) points out that children with autism seldom use language to share or seek information from others. As a consequence, their conversations are restricted. Even though they may have a good vocabulary and syntax and may be generally responsive to others' verbalizations, they do not frequently initiate, expand, or elaborate as they converse. Tager-Flusberg (1996) suggests that children with autism, even if they are high functioning, do not understand that other people often have viewpoints that are not the same as theirs; that is, they do not have a theory of mind.

In contrast to this perspective, Prizant (1996) suggests that there is increasing evidence that speech problems in individuals with autism may be caused by factors other than or in addition to their social-cognitive impairments. More specifically, he suggests that general motor difficulties, including motor speech impairments and motor planning problems, may be responsible for their speech and communication delays. Similarly, Murray-Slutsky (2000) points out that effective speech and language require that a child register sensory information, formulate an idea, plan and sequence thoughts, and then speak. She points out that this is the same process that occurs in motor planning and executing total body activities, and hypothesizes that motor planning (praxis) and language share overlapping neural structures.

Travis and Sigman (2001) suggest that two developmental reorganizations, hypothesized to be critical for language development, do not occur in the same way in children with autism as in other children. These two landmarks relate to the emergence of communicative intentions and symbolic ability. Communicative intentions occur typically around nine months when infants begin to show awareness that their behaviors/signals have an effect on others. As a result, they reproduce these behaviors in order to reelicit the consequences. Symbolic ability begins typically around 11–13 months when infants become aware that signs are substitutable for the objects to which they refer. This recognition leads to "symbolic" gestures and words to communicate their needs and interests. Despite the fact that children with autism manifest marked and characteristic limitations in these areas, Travis and Sigman (2001) suggest, based on their review of research, that these intentional and symbolic acts can be acquired; for example, most children with autism can and do learn how to make requests and reject the requests of others.

In contrast to expressive language, less is known about language comprehension in children with autism. Nevertheless, research suggests children with autism do not attend to speech in the same way as other children and are better at visual than auditory/verbal processing. Because of their attentional problems and the fact that the meaning of speech is acquired within a social context, it is not surprising that they have problems understanding the meanings of speech, particularly those aspects of speech that are more symbolic in nature (see review by Watson, 2001).

Repetitive, restricted, and stereotyped activities, interests, and patterns and self-regulation

Perhaps the most intriguing of the core characteristics used to define autism are those that describe repetitive and restricted activities, interests, and patterns of behavior. In contrast to social and language/communication deficiencies, this third set of core characteristics consists of behaviors that are unusual and even bizarre in nature, perhaps because their origin and function are not well understood. Specific examples of such behaviors include: body rocking, body twirling, head weaving, object spinning, finger twisting, toilet flushing, feet touching, lining up objects, intense attachment to specific objects, rigid adherence to fixed routines, and excessive talking about a particular topic, such as dinosaurs. In a review of research, Tsai (1998) presents data indicating that the occurrence of these characteristics in persons with autism is quite high; for instance, morbid or unusual preoccupations (43–88%), obsessive phenomena (37%), compulsive rituals (16–86%), stereotyped utterances (50–89%), and stereotyped mannerisms (68–74%). Table 2.1 (p. 53) suggests that these responses are reflections of a poorly developed self-regulatory system that evolves because more sophisticated cognitive and social forms of self-regulation are not learned. In this section, stereotypy and obsessive–compulsive behavior will be discussed in greater detail.

Stereotypy

Considerable attention has been given to the study of stereotyped behavior or stereotypy, sometimes also referred to as "self-stimulatory behavior". Although definitions of stereotypy vary, they usually include reference to behaviors that are: repetitive, often occurring with high frequency; invariant in topography or pattern; and nonfunctional, in the sense that they do not seem to have an obvious or conventional explanation for their occurrence. Although there are considerable differences in the structure of specific stereotyped behaviors across individuals with autism, there is considerable intraindividual consistency; that is, the particular stereotyped responses engaged in by a given individual are relatively invariant.

Another response, sometimes classified under stereotypy, is self-injurious behavior, for example, head banging. Although historically head banging frequently occurred in individuals with autism in institutional settings, it is only occasionally observed in home environments. Self-injurious behaviors are like other stereotyped responses in that they are often invariant in form, repetitive, and can occur with a high frequency. Self-injurious behaviors differ from other stereotyped responses, however, in that they can result in physical harm. In Chapter 4, it will be argued that stereotyped and self-injurious behaviors serve an important regulatory function for children with autism.

In addition to occurring in persons with autism, stereotypy occurs in individuals with mental retardation, particularly in those who are in the lower IQ range (IQ 55). It also is frequently displayed by children and adults who live in nonstimulating institutional environments; individuals who have a genetic and/or organic disorder (e.g., Lesh-Nyan, schizophrenia, and blindness); and persons who are on certain drugs, such as amphetamines. Moreover, simple, repetitive motor responses, such as head rolling and kicking, routinely occur as part of human development during infancy. Normal adults also engage in similar responses, such as leg swinging, rocking, or finger tapping. In normal populations, however, these behaviors do not typically occur with as high a rate as in individuals with autism. Finally, stereotypy is observed in animals reared in isolation or kept in confined spaces.

Theories abound as to what causes stereotypy. In young infants, it appears that repetitive responses are part of normal motor development and indeed are probably essential to the development of the motor system and later adaptive behavior. Another explanation for stereotypy suggests that there is an optimal level of stimulation necessary for adaptive human functioning. In order to maintain homeostasis, individuals self-activate or seek stimulation when their level of arousal is low, or conversely decrease stimulation when their overall level of arousal is high. From this perspective, stereotyped behavior serves either a self-stimulatory function directed at increasing stimulation, or as a filtering mechanism, directed at reducing external stimulation.

A second major, albeit related, explanation for the occurrence of stereotyped behavior is that it is utilized to reduce tension or anxiety. Stereotyped responses are activated when an individual becomes stressed or experiences a high level of arousal. Repetitive behavior, such as rocking, serves to reduce tension. Both the homeostatic and the tension/arousal hypothesis suggest that although the external environment plays a role in stereotypy, the critical factor is not what is happening in the environment per se, but what impact the environment has on the state of arousal/activation within the individual; that is, high or low internal states of arousal/activation mediate the effects that the external environment has on the occurrence of stereotyped behavior.

A third explanation for stereotypy is based on learning theory and the concepts of positive and negative reinforcement. By definition a reinforcer is any event (stimulus) that follows after a behavior and increases the future probability of behavior. Positive reinforcement is said to occur when a stimulus, for example social attention, follows a response and leads to an increase in that response. In contrast, negative reinforcement involves the termination of a stimulus, typically thought of as unpleasant, such as social or physical coercion, after a response occurs. It also by definition results in an increase in responding. Stimuli that serve as positive or negative reinforcers may vary widely across individuals. From a learning perspective, stereotypy in individuals with autism can be increased either through negative reinforcement, for example, if teachers cease to make demands of them after they engage in stereotyped behavior; or through positive reinforcement, for example, if parents give attention to a child after the onset of stereotyped behavior. Even if learning theory can explain and be used to control the rate with which stereotyped behavior occurs in individuals with autism, it does not fully account for why these behaviors develop in the first place.

A number of biological explanations for stereotypy have also been proposed. For example, it has been observed that amphetamine users often manifest stereotyped behavior patterns. Other evidence suggests involvement of the dopamine and opiate systems. It has been suggested that stereotyped behaviors produce a biochemical state that reinforces the individual for engaging in such behavior (see Chapter 3). For further information on theories about the origins of stereotypy, the reader is referred to Baumeister and Forehand (1973), Berkson (1983), Charman and Swettenham (2001), Lewis and Baumeister (1982), O'Brien (1981), and Whitman, Scibak, and Reid (1983).

Obsessive–compulsive behavior

In addition to stereotypy, individuals with autism frequently engage in a number of other unusual behaviors that can be categorized as obsessive and/or compulsive in nature. Obsessions usually relate to behaviors that are more cognitive in nature, whereas compulsions typically are nonverbal or motoric in nature. Tsai (1996) reports a variety of research suggesting a very high incidence of obsessive/compulsive behaviors in individuals with autism. These behaviors appear to be used by the individual to create or maintain a specific type of order in the environment. Examples of these behaviors include: playing continually with a specific toy, repetitively writing words or numbers, lining up objects, adhering rigidly to a routine, talking incessantly about a certain topic, and asking repeatedly to engage in a particular activity.

Estimates of obsessive/compulsive behaviors in children with autism who have normal intelligence are high, typically well above 50% (Tsai, 1998). These behaviors tend to increase in frequency when an individual is having difficulty adapting to a new environment and/or is under stress. In contrast to people with Obsessive–Compulsive Disorder (OCD), autistic children who display obsessive or compulsive symptoms seem less concerned about their symptoms and do not resist them (Tsai, 1992). Nevertheless, it seems that people with autism, like individuals with OCD, use their symptoms as a way to reduce anxiety. In Chapter 4, reasons for the emergence of obsessive/compulsive behaviors will be discussed at greater length as part of a developmental theory of autism.

Behavior problems and co-morbid conditions

A variety of other characteristics of individuals with autism have been examined by researchers, including behavioral/socioemotional problems and co-morbid psychiatric disorders. Bryson (1996) suggests that over 50% of persons with autism have some type of significant behavioral or medical problem. A few of the more prominently mentioned of these problems will be briefly discussed in this section, including noncompliance, aggression, sleep disorders, eating problems, and co-morbid psychiatric disorders.

Noncompliance and aggression

Like typically developing children, children with autism are noncompliant. Some researchers and clinicians suggest that noncompliance occurs in children with autism because of their limited communication skills and thus represents an alternative way of communicating. Some interventions use the occurrence of noncompliant responses as occasions to teach speech. When successful, such interventions have been associated with not only a reduction in noncompliance but also improved expressive language as well as other types of adaptive behavior (Paul, 1987). If untreated, simple noncompliance sometimes escalates into aggression.

Aggressive behavior represents one of the more debilitating responses displayed by children with developmental disabilities. Aggressive responses not only make intervention programs more difficult, but can lead to children being excluded from mainstreamed educational settings. Perhaps the most devastating effect of aggressive behavior is the impact it has on other people's perception of the individual who displays such behavior. As young children with autism become adolescents and adults, their aggressive behavior elicits not only concern but also fear in others, which in turn can result in the further isolation of persons who are already isolated because of their social deficiencies. Such aggressive behavior can also present a major obstacle to inclusive education, community involvement, and the development of friendships (Fox, Dunlap & Buschbacher, 2000).

Sleep disorders

Sleep disorders are often categorized as falling into two categories: dyssomnias and parasomnias (American Sleep Disorders Association, 1990). Dyssomnias include difficulties in initiating sleep, maintaining sleep, and/or excessive sleepiness. Parasomnias involve disruptions in transitions between sleep stages and partial arousals that disrupt quality of sleep. Research employing both objective and self-report methodologies suggest that sleep problems among children with developmental disorders, including children with autism, are higher than in groups without such disabilities. However, research in this area is sparse.

Estimates of sleep problems in individuals with autism range from 36% to 83% (see review by Schreck, 2001). There is disagreement in the literature, however, as to whether the sleep patterns of children with autism are really that different from other children (Hering, Epstein, Elroy, Iancu & Zelnek, 1999). Sleep problems noted in populations with autism include: problems in getting to sleep, poor quality of sleep, night waking, sleepwalking, early waking, and irregular sleep patterns (Arbelle & Ben-Zion, 2001). Sleep researchers have documented links between sleep problems and poor behavior regulation, behavior problems, and psychopathology in both clinical and nonclinical populations (see review by Sadeh, Gruber & Raviv, 2002). The list of causes and correlates of sleep problems are many, including age, IQ level, irregular day and bedtime routines, parental limit-setting practices, environmental disturbances, frightening dreams, and fear upon awakening, as well as a host of biological problems related to diet, eating patterns, allergies, drugs, and melatonin production.

Eating/feeding problems

Although aberrant eating habits and eating-related problems are widely reported in children with autism, these reports are based mostly on anecdotal evidence. For example, Schopler (1995) notes reports of problems such as eating inedibles, picky eating, overeating, eating too fast, limited self-feeding, and allergic responses to food. Ahearn, Castine, Nault, and Green (2001) review evidence suggesting that individuals with developmental delays, particularly persons with severe and profound mental retardation, frequently have eating problems. Results of their own research, based on an examination of the feeding patterns of 30 children diagnosed with autism or PDD-NOS, indicated that over half of the participants exhibited one or more of the following: low levels of food acceptance, individual patterns of food refusal, food-type selectivity, and food-texture selectivity. The authors suggest that although their results are consistent with other reports of feeding problems in children with autism spectrum disorders, they may not be unique to children with this type of developmental problem. They also point out that eating problems are commonly noted by parents of typically developing children.

Co-morbid disorders

A variety of symptoms reported in individuals with autism, some of which have already been mentioned, suggest the presence of other disorders. For example, persons with autism frequently display symptoms such as inattention, anxiety, depression, inappropriate affect, bizarre behaviors, hallucinations, delusions, obsessive–compulsive behaviors, hyperactivity, and aggression. These symptoms can be diagnostically indicative of other psychiatric conditions, such as schizophrenia, depressive disorder, anxiety disorder, Obsessive–Compulsive Disorder, Attention Deficit Hyperactivity Disorder, and Conduct Disorder. Conversely, children with these latter disorders sometimes also manifest autistic symptoms (see Tsai, 1996). Clinically, dual diagnoses are useful if they lead to additional appropriate treatments. From a research perspective, the more frequent use of dual diagnoses, where appropriate, could also assist researchers in examining the conditions under which such co-morbid disorders develop.

Physical characteristics and medical conditions

Children with autism are often described as looking physically like any other child. Sometimes they have also been characterized as being beautiful children. One distinguishing physical feature frequently mentioned in the autism literature is head size. Although head size at birth appears to be normal, head growth reportedly accelerates after birth. During early childhood the head circumference of children with autism is somewhat larger than other children, on average around 10% (see review by Tager-Flusberg, Joseph & Folstein, 2001). This larger head size is thought to be related to a larger brain size. In combination, the larger head size and brain size of these children may be related to a gene defect. Brain growth acceleration in autism is discussed further in Chapter 3.

Barton and Volkmar (1998) indicate that there is considerable evidence that neurobiological causes play a critical role in the development of autism. They point out it is less clear what role medical conditions that are commonly associated with autism play in the etiology of this disorder. They review evidence indicating that 10–30% of persons with autism have a known associated medical condition. Genetic conditions, such as Fragile X, Tourette's Syndrome, and Down's Syndrome; neurological conditions, including seizure disorders; environmental and infectiously produced diseases, like lead poisoning and encephalitis; and prenatal risk factors, like maternal rubella, have been implicated in the development of autism. Although Barton and Volkmar (1998) present general evidence for such relationships, they point out that the fundamental relationships may not be between these medical conditions and autism, but between these conditions and low IQ, specifically severe mental retardation.

Among the many medical conditions associated with autism, epilepsy is probably the most frequent. Epilepsy is a neurologically based disorder which is typically diagnosed through the observation of clinical seizures. Children who have observable seizures also show abnormal brain electrical activity on an electroencephalogram (EEG). There is a group of individuals, however, who have abnormal EEGs but who do not manifest observable clinical seizures. Estimates of the incidence of seizures in children with autism vary widely, ranging from around 11% to 42%. The types of seizures vary, but generalized motor seizures appear to be particularly common.

There are varying perspectives regarding the relationship between autism and epilepsy. One view is that both are manifestations of a common underlying neurological cause. Another perspective is that seizure activity influences the course of autism and its associated symptoms. In this regard, there is speculation that epilepsy may play a role in the emergence of autism in children who initially develop normally but later show regression in areas such as language and social interaction. Research support for this position, and more generally for a causal relationship between epilepsy and autism, is minimal at best. There is evidence, however, that seizure activity is more common in individuals with autism who have severe mental deficiency and motor deficits, as well as in girls with autism; perhaps because girls are more likely than boys to manifest severe mental deficiency (Tuchman, Rapin & Shinnar, 1991).

The resolution of the question of whether epilepsy plays a causal role in the development of autism is important from a treatment perspective. If such a relationship exists, it suggests that a more aggressive approach toward the treatment of both clinical and subclinical seizure activity would be appropriate, using therapeutic approaches like anticonvulsant drugs, corticosteroid therapy, or surgical treatment. At present, however, research is needed to examine whether any actual therapeutic benefits occur through the use of such therapies. Particular caution is suggested about the use of surgery, except for intractable epilepsy (Kanner, 2000). For further information on autism and epilepsy, the reader is referred also to Ballaban-Gil and Tuchman (2000), Kanner (2000), and Tuchman (2000). In the next chapter, medical conditions associated with autism and possible biological causes of this disorder will be discussed in greater detail.

General summary

Several points have been emphasized in this chapter. First, individuals with autism display a number of common characteristics/symptoms, including sensory, motor, and emotional deficiencies, that are not part of the diagnostic criteria for this disorder. Second, there are considerable individual differences in the characteristics/symptoms displayed by persons with this disorder even though they share general core diagnostic features. Third, it appears that there is a dynamic relationship between the various types of symptoms, with symptoms in the different domains likely exerting considerable influences on each other. As will be pointed out in Chapter 4, most existing theories of autism do not systematically address the reasons for the broad individual differences that exist in the way this disorder is manifested, nor do they examine the implications of such differences for development.

References

Adrien, J., Martineau, J., Barthélémy, C., Bruneau, N., Garreau, B. & Sauvage, D. (1995) "Disorders of regulation of cognitive activity in autistic children." *Journal of Autism and Developmental Disorders 25*, 249–263.

Ahearn, W., Castine, T., Nault, K. & Green, G. (2001) "An assessment of food acceptance in children with Autism or Pervasive Developmental Disorder – Not Otherwise Specified." *Journal of Autism and Developmental Disorders 31*, 505–511.

American Association on Mental Retardation (1992) *Mental Retardation: Definition, classification, and systems of support* (Ninth edition). Washington, DC: American Association on Mental Retardation.

American Psychiatric Association (1994) *Diagnostic and statistical manual of mental disorders* (Fourth edition). Washington, DC: American Psychiatric Association.

American Sleep Disorders Association (1990) *The international classification of sleep disorders: Diagnostic and Coding Manual.* Rochester, MN: American Sleep Disorders Association.

Anzalone, M. E. & Williamson, G. G. (2000) "Sensory processing and motor performance in autism spectrum disorders." In A. M. Wetherby & B. M. Prizant (eds) *Autism spectrum disorders* (pp. 143–166). Baltimore: Brooks Publishing Co.

Arbelle, S. & Ben-Zion, I. (2001) "Sleep problems in autism." In E. Schopler, N. Yirmuja, C. Shulman & L. Marcus (eds) *The research basis for autism intervention* (pp. 219–228). New York: Kluwer Academic Plenum.

Attwood, T. (1998) *Asperger's Syndrome: A guide for parents and professionals.* London: Jessica Kingsley Publishers.

Ballaban-Gil, K. & Tuchman, R. (2000) "Epilepsy and epileptiform EEG: Association with autism and language disorder." *Mental Retardation and Developmental Disabilities Research Reviews 6*, 300–308.

Baranek, G. (1999) "Autism during infancy: A retrospective analysis of sensory-motor and social behaviors at 9–12 months of age." *Journal of Autism and Developmental Disorders 29*, 213–224.

Baranek, G., Reinhartsen, D. & Wannamaker, S. (2001) "Play: Engaging young children with autism." In R. Huebner (ed) *Autism: A sensorimotor approach to management* (pp. 313–351). Gaithersburg, MD: Aspen.

Barnhill, G., Hagiwara, T., Myles, B. & Simpson, R. (2000) "Asperger's Syndrome: A study of the cognitive profiles of 37 children and adolescents." *Focus on Autism and Other Developmental Disabilities 15*, 146–153.

Barton, M. & Volkmar, F. (1998) "How commonly are known medical conditions associated with Autism?" *Journal of Autism and Developmental Disorders 28*, 273–278.

Baumeister, A. & Forehand, R. (1973) "Stereotyped acts." In N. Ellis (ed) *International review of research in mental retardation* (Vol. 6) (pp. 55–96). New York: Academic Press.

Bauminger, N. & Kasari, C. (2001) "The experience of loneliness and friendship." In E. Schopler, N. Yirmiya, C. Shulman & L. Marcus (eds) *The research basis for autism intervention* (pp. 151–170). New York: Kluwer Academic/Plenum Publishers.

Berkson, G. (1983) "Repetitive stereotyped behaviors." *American Journal of Mental Deficiency 88*, 239–246.

Bryson, S. (1996) "Brief report: Epidemiology of Autism." *Journal of Autism and Developmental Disorders 26*, 165–167.

Carpenter, M. & Tomasello, M. (2000) "Joint attention, cultural learning and language acquisition: Implications for children with autism." In A. Wetherby & B. Prizant (eds) *Autism spectrum disorders: A transactional developmental perspective* (pp. 31–54). Baltimore: Brookes Publishing Co.

Celani, G., Battacchi, M. & Arcidiacono, L. (1999) "The understanding of emotional meaning of facial expressions in people with autism." *Journal of Autism and Developmental Disorders 29*, 57–66.

Charman, T. & Swettenham, J. (2001) "Repetitive behaviors and social-communicative impairments in autism: Implication for developmental theory and diagnosis." In J. Burack, T. Charman, N. Yirmiya & P. Zelazo (eds) *The development of autism: Perspectives from theory and research* (pp. 325–345). Mawah, NJ: Erlbaum.

Chess, S. & Thomas, A. (1989) "Temperament and its functional significance." In S. Greenspan & G. Pollock (eds) *The course of life: Early childhood* (pp. 163–225). Madison, CT: International Universities Press.

Cox, R. (1993) "Normal development from birth to five years." In E. Schopler, M. Van Bourgondrein & M. Bristol (eds) *Preschool issues in autism* (pp. 39–57). New York: Plenum Press.

Dunn, W. (1997) "The impact of sensory processing on the daily lives of young children and their families: A conceptual model." *Infants and Young Children 1*, 23–35.

Fox, L., Dunlap, G. & Buschbacher, P. (2000) "Understanding and intervening with children's challenging behavior." In A. Wetherby (ed) *Autism spectrum disorders: A transactional developmental perspective* (pp. 307–332). Baltimore: Brooks.

Gillberg, C. (1989) "Asperger syndrome in 23 Swedish children." *Developmental Medicine and Child Neurology 31*, 520–531.

Gillberg, C. & Coleman, M. (1992) *The biology of autistic syndromes* (Second edition). London: McKeith Press.

Gillberg, C. & Gillberg, I. C. (1989) "Asperger's Syndrome. Some epidemiological considerations: A research note." *Journal of Child Psychology and Psychiatry 30*, 631–638.

Goldstein, G., Johnson, C. & Minshew, N. (2001) "Attentional processes in autism." *Journal of Autism and Developmental Disabilities 31*, 433–440.

Grandin, T. (1988) "Teaching tips from a recovered autistic." *Focus on autistic behavior 3*, 1–8.

Grandin, T. (1995) *Thinking in pictures.* New York: Vintage Books.

Hering, E., Epstein, R., Elroy, S., Iancu, D. & Zelnek, N. (1999) "Sleep patterns in autistic children." *Journal of Autism and Developmental Disorders 29*, 143–147.

Hobson, R. P. (1993) *Autism and the development of mind.* Hillsdale, NJ: Erlbaum.

Huebner, R. A. (2001) *Autism: A sensorimotor approach to management.* Gaithersburg, MD: Aspen.

Huebner, R. A. & Kraemer, G. (2001) "Sensorimotor aspects of attachment and social relatedness in autism." In R. A. Huebner (ed) *Autism: A sensorimotor approach to management* (pp. 209–244). Gaithersburg, MD: Aspen.

Kanner, A. (2000) "Commentary: The treatment of seizure disorder and EEG abnormalities in children with autism spectrum disorders: Are we getting ahead of ourselves?" *Journal of Autism and Developmental Disorders 30*, 491–495.

Kanner, L. (1943) "Autistic disturbances of affective contact." *Nervous Child 2*, 217–250.

Kasari, C., Chamberlain, B. & Bauminger, N. (2001) In J. Burack, T. Charman, N. Yirmiya & P. Zelazo (eds) *The development of autism: Perspectives from theory and research* (pp. 309–325). Mawah, NJ: Erlbaum.

Klin, A., Jones, W., Schultz, R., Volkmar, F. & Cohen, D. (2002) "Visual fixation patterns during viewing naturalistic social situations as predictors of social competence in individuals with autism." *Archives of General Psychiatry 59*, 809–816.

Leekam, S. & Moore, C. (2001) "The development of attention and joint attention in children with autism." In J. Burack, T. Charman, N. Yirmiya & P. Zelezo (eds) *The development of autism: Perspectives from theory and research* (pp. 105–130). Mawah, NJ: Erlbaum.

Lerea, L. E. (1987) "The behavioral assessment of autistic children." In D. Cohen, A. Donnellan & R. Paul (eds) *Handbook of autism and pervasive developmental disorders* (pp. 273–288). Silver Springs, MD: Winston & Sons.

Lewis, M. & Baumeister, A. (1982) "Stereotyped mannerisms in mentally retarded persons: Animal models and theoretical analysis." In N. Ellis (ed) *International review of research in mental retardation* (Vol. 11) (pp. 123–161). New York: Academic Press.

Manjiviona, J. & Prior, M. (1995) "Comparison of Asperger Syndrome and high functioning autistic children on a test of motor impairment." *Journal of Autism and Developmental Disorders 25*, 23–39.

Maurer D. & Maurer C. (1988) *The World of the Newborn.* New York: Basic Books, Inc.

Mesibov, G., Adams, L. & Klinger, L. (1997) *Autism: Understanding the disorder.* New York: Plenum.

Miller, J. & Ozonoff, S. (2000) "The external validity of Asperger's Disorders: Lack of evidence from the domain of neuropsychology." *Journal of Abnormal Psychology 109*, 227–238.

Millward, C., Powell, S., Messer, D. & Jordan, R. (2000) "Recall for self and other in autism: Children's memory for events experienced by themselves and their peers." *Journal of Autism and Developmental Disorders 30*, 15–28.

Mottron, L. & Burack, J. (2001) "Enhanced perceptual functioning in the development of autism." In J. Burack, T. Charman, N. Yirmiya & P. Zelazo (eds) *The development of autism: Perspectives from theory and research* (pp. 131–148). Mawah, NJ: Erlbaum.

Mundy, P. & Crowson, M. (1997) "Joint attention and early social communication: Implications for research on intervention with autism." *Journal of Autism and Developmental Disorders 27*, 653–676.

Mundy, P. & Stella, J. (2000) "Joint attention, social orienting and nonverbal communication in autism." In A. Wetherby & B. Prizant (eds) *Autism spectrum disorders: A transactional developmental perspective* (pp. 55–77). Baltimore: Brookes Publishing Co.

Murray, M. & Paris, B. (2000) "The importance of play in learning and development." In C. Murray-Slutsky & B. Paris (eds) *Exploring the spectrum of autism and pervasive developmental disorders* (pp. 370–384). Therapy Skill Builder (Harcourt Health Sciences Co.).

Murray-Slutsky, C. (2000) "Somatopraxia and intervention strategies." In C. Murray-Slutsky & B. Paris (eds) *Exploring the spectrum of autism and pervasive developmental disabilities* (pp. 237–277). Therapy Skill Builder (Harcourt Health Science Co.).

O'Brien, F. (1981) "Treating self-stimulatory behavior." In J. Matson & J. McCartney (eds) *Handbook of behavior modification with the mentally retarded.* New York: Plenum Press.

O'Neill, M. & Jones, R. (1997) "Sensory-perceptual abnormalities in autism: A case for more research." *Journal of Autism and Developmental Disorders 27*, 283–293.

Ornitz, E. (1983) "The functional neuroanatomy of infantile autism." *International Journal of Neuroscience 19*, 85–124.

Paris, B. (2000a) "Characteristics of autism." In C. Murray-Slutsky & B. Paris (eds) *Exploring the spectrum of autism and pervasive developmental disorders* (pp. 7–23). Therapy Skill Builder (Harcourt Health Sciences Co.).

Paris, B. (2000b) "Motor control and coordination difficulties." In C. Murray-Slutsky & B. Paris (eds) *Exploring the spectrum of autism and pervasive developmental disorders* (pp. 278–332). Therapy Skill Builder (Harcourt Health Sciences Co.).

Paris, B. & Murray-Slutsky, C. (2000) "Sensory integration and treatment." In C. Murray-Slutsky & B. Paris (eds) *Exploring the spectrum of autism and pervasive developmental disorders* (pp. 80–98). Therapy Skill Builder (Harcourt Health Sciences Co.).

Paul, R. (1987) "Communication." In D. Cohen, A. Donnellan & R. Paul (eds) *Handbook of autism and pervasive developmental disorders* (pp. 61–87). Silver Springs, MD: V. H. Winston & Sons.

Pierce, K., Glad, K. & Schreibman, L. (1997) "Social perception in children with autism: An attention deficit." *Journal of Autism and Developmental Disorders 27*, 265–282.

Prizant, B. (1996) "Brief report: Communication, language, social and emotional development." *Journal of Autism and Developmental Disorders 26*, 173–178.

Prizant, B. & Wetherby, A. (1993) "Communication in preschool. Autistic children." In E. Schopler & M. Bourgondien (eds) *Preschool issues in autism* (pp. 95–128). New York: Plenum.

Reddy, V., Williams, E. & Vaughan, A. (2002) "Sharing humor and laughter in autism and Down's syndrome." *British Journal of Psychology 93*, 219–242.

Renner, P., Klinger, L. & Klinger, M. (2000) "Implicit and explicit memory in autism: Is autism an amnesic disorder?" *Journal of Autism and Developmental Disorders 30*, 3–14.

Rinehardt, N., Bradshaw, J., Brereton, A. & Tonge, B. (2001) "Movement preparation in high-functioning autism and Asperger Disorder: A serial choice reaction time task involving motor reprogramming." *Journal of Autism and Developmental Disorders 31*, 79–88.

Rimland, B. (1978) "Savant capabilities of autistic children and their cognitive implications." In G. Serban (ed) *Cognitive defects in the development of mental illness* (pp. 43–65). New York: Brunner/Mazel.

Rogers, S. & Bennetto, L. (2000) "Intersubjectivity in autism: The roles of imitation and executive function." In A. Wetherby & B. Prizant (eds) *Autism spectrum disorders: A transactional developmental perspective* (pp. 79–107). Baltimore: Brookes.

Sadeh, A., Gruber, R. & Raviv, A. (2002) "Sleep, neurobehavioral functioning and behavior problems in school-age children." *Child Development 73*, 405–417.

Sarni, C. (1999) *The development of emotional competence.* New York: Guilford Press.

Scheuffgen, K., Happé, F., Anderson, M. & Frith, U. (2000) "High 'intelligence', low 'IQ'? Speed of processing and measured IQ in children with autism." *Development and Psychopathology 12*, 83–90.

Schopler, E. (1995) *Parent survival manual: A guide to crisis resolution in autism and related developmental disorders.* New York: Plenum.

Schreck, K. (2001) "Behavioral treatments for sleep problems in autism: Empirically supported or just universally accepted." *Behavioral Interventions 16*, 265–278.

Siegel, B. (1996) *The world of the autistic child: Understanding and treating autism spectrum disorders.* New York: Oxford University Press.

Sigman, M. (1994) "What are the core deficits in autism?" In S. Broman & J. Grafman (eds) *Atypical cognitive deficits in developmental disorders* (pp. 139–158). Hillsdale, NJ: Erlbaum.

Sigman, M. & Capps, L. (1997) *Children with autism: A developmental perspective.* Cambridge: Harvard University Press.

Sigman, M. & Mundy, P. (1989) "Social attachments in autistic children." *Journal of American Academy of Child and Adolescent Psychiatry 28*, 74–81.

Siller, M. & Sigman, M. (2002) "The behaviors of parents of children with autism predict the subsequent development of their children's communication." *Journal of Autism and Developmental Disorders 32*, 77–89.

Simpson, R. & Myles, B. (1998) "Management of students with autism." In R. Simpson & B. Myles (eds) *Educating children and youth with autism* (pp. 55–172). Austin: Pro-Ed.

Smith, I. & Bryson, S. (1994) "Imitation and action in autism: A critical review." *Psychological Bulletin 116*, 259–273.

Tager-Flusberg, H. (1996) "Brief report: Current theory and research on language and communication in autism." *Journal of Autism and Developmental Disorders 26*, 169–172.

Tager-Flusberg, H., Joseph, R. & Folstein, S. (2001) "Current directions in research in autism." *Mental Retardation and Developmental Disabilities Research Reviews 7*, 21–29.

Teitelbaum, P., Teitelbaum, O., Nye, J., Fryman, J. & Mauer, P. (1998) "Movement analysis in infancy may be useful for early diagnosis of autism." *Proceedings of the National Academy of Sciences 95*, 13982–13987.

Thomas, A. & Chess, S. (1977) *Temperament and development.* New York: Brunner/Mazel.

Tinbergen, E. & Tinbergen, N. (1972) *Early childhood autism: An ethological approach. Advances in ethology, Journal of Comparative Ethology,* Supplement No. 10. Berlin: Paul Berry.

Travis, L. & Sigman, M. (2001) "Communicative intentions and symbols in autism. Examining a case of altered development." In J. Burack, T. Charman, N. Yirmiya & P. Zelazo (eds) *The development of autism: Perspectives from theory and research* (pp. 279–308). Mawah, NJ: Erlbaum.

Treffert, D. & Wallace, G. (2002) "Islands of genius." *Scientific American, June,* 76–85.

Tsai, L. (1992) "Medical treatment in autism." In D. Berkell (ed) *Autism: identification, education, and treatment* (pp. 151–184). Hillsdale, NJ: Erlbaum.

Tsai, L. (1996) "Brief report: Co-morbid psychiatric disorders." *Journal of Autism and Developmental Disorders 26*, 159–163.

Tsai, L. (1998) "Medical interventions in students with autism." In R. Simpson & B. Myles (eds) *Educating children and youth with autism* (pp. 277–314). Austin: Pro-Ed.

Tuchman, R. (2000) "Treatment of seizure disorders and EEG abnormalities in children with autism spectrum disorders." *Journal of Autism and Developmental Disorders 30*, 485–489.

Tuchman, R., Rapin, I. & Shinnar, S. (1991) "Autistic and dysphasic children II: Epilepsy." *Pediatrics 88*, 1219–1225.

Volden, J. & Johnston, J. (1999) "Cognitive scripts in autistic children and adolescents." *Journal of Autism and Developmental Disorders 29*, 203–211.

Volkmar, F., Cohen, D. & Paul, R. (1986) "An evaluation of DSM-III criteria for infantile autism." *Journal of American Academy of Child Psychiatry 25*, 190–197.

Waterhouse, S. (2000) *A positive approach to autism.* London: Jessica Kingsley Publishers.

Waterhouse, L. & Fein, D. (1998) "Autism and the evolution of human social skills." In F. R. Volkmar (ed) *Autism and pervasive developmental disorders* (pp. 242–267). New York: Cambridge University Press.

Watson, L. (2001) "Issues in early comprehension development of children with autism." In E. Schopler, N. Yirmiya, C. Shulman & L. Marcus (eds) *The research basis for autism intervention* (pp. 135–150). New York: Kluwer Academic Plenum Publishers.

Whitman, T. L. (1990) "Self-regulation and mental retardation." *American Journal on Mental Retardation 94*, 347–362.

Whitman, T. L., Scibak, J. & Reid, D. (1983) *Behavior modification with the severely and profoundly retarded.* New York: Academic Press.

Wing, L. & Gould, J. (1979) "Severe impairments of social interaction and associated abnormalities in children: Epidemiology and classification." *Journal of Autism and Developmental Disorders 9*, 11–29.

CHAPTER 3

Theories of Autism

with Kathleen J. Kolberg

Within the scientific enterprise, theories about disorders such as autism serve a variety of functions. Some theories are more descriptive, acting as conceptual organizers about what is known. For example, they describe the nature of a disorder, how it develops, and how it differs from other disorders. A more sophisticated theory also allows predictions to be made; for example, about how people with a particular disorder will behave in the future given their present symptoms. In addition to these descriptive and predictive functions, a comprehensive theory formulates hypotheses regarding the critical processes underlying the development of a disorder and speculates about how interventions might be best structured. Theories are not either wrong or right, but rather are more or less useful. Theories that allow more precise and accurate predictions to be made and/or lead to the design of effective interventions are more useful and for that reason are characterized as having greater validity.

Theories of autism can be typically subdivided into those that are psychological or biological. Psychological theories specify the role that different processes, such as those involving the attention or the sensory system, play in symptom development. In contrast, biological theories emphasize how various factors such as genes, neurochemical processes, neurological structures, and environmental toxins influence symptom formation. Ideally, psychological theories should be consistent with what is known biologically about autism. Conversely, biological theories should be consistent with what is known psychologically.

A variety of theories of autism have been proposed. Many of these theories are quite descriptive and not very formalized in their presentation. Most theories of autism are quite speculative and in need of empirical verification. Moreover, most theories are narrow in scope, focusing on only a few of the symptoms associated with autism. Theory formulation in the area of autism is particularly difficult because of the number and heterogeneous nature of the symptoms. At present, it is not clear which symptoms of autism are primary, that is, are a critical part of an early process leading to other symptoms. Ideally a comprehensive theory of autism should emphasize how biological, psychological, and environmental factors can work in conjunction to explain the development of autism. Moreover, to be really useful, a theory of autism should specify how biological and/or psychobehavioral interventions can be structured to address the underlying causes of autism so as to prevent or ameliorate the symptoms associated with this disorder. Although there is empirical support for some theories of autism, no one theory has emerged that has gained broad acceptance. Because of the rapidly increasing scientific interest in autism, it is likely that the theoretical landscape will change dramatically in the next decade.

In this chapter current theories of autism are briefly reviewed. Special attention is given to social–environmental, psychological, and biological theories. The social–environmental theories focus on how the family and other social factors influence the development of autism. The psychological theories emphasize the importance of cognitive, language, sensory integration, or arousal/activation processes. The biological theories discuss the role of genetic, neurostructural, neurochemical, and environmental factors. Our discussion begins with an examination of theories that emphasize the influence of the social environment on the development of autism.

Social–environmental theories

Parenting influences

Historically, as discussed in Chapter 1, there was considerable speculation about whether autism was caused by poor parenting. Kanner (1943) observed that many of the parents of children with autism appeared to be cold and aloof, more preoccupied with their occupational and personal pursuits than their children. As a consequence of this type of thinking, some professionals thought it might be in the children's best interest for them to be separated from their parents (Bettleheim, 1967). Currently, there is no support for the theory that parents or a certain type of parenting style causes autism. It is now generally acknowledged that the parents of children with autism are quite variable in their parenting characteristics and that whatever their characteristics, parents are not responsible for their children's autism.

There is some evidence, however, that the characteristics of parents and their autistic children may be at least somewhat correlated. For example, some parents of children with autism manifest themselves autistic-like characteristics and/or socioemotional problems. One proposed explanation for this similarity between parents and children emphasizes the importance of genetic factors. Children are thought to inherit not autism per se, but a predisposition to develop autism; a predisposition that is perhaps triggered by certain prenatal and/or postnatal environmental factors. This theory and other biological theories will be described in greater detail later in this chapter.

Although not typically discussed in the autism literature, another possible reason for the correlation between the characteristics of parents, such as those cited by Kanner (1943), and those of their autistic children could be that the children influence the behavior of their parents. For example, children who do not make eye contact with or respond to the overtures of their parents may produce anxiety and a sense of helplessness in the parents, who in turn distance themselves from their children, thus making it appear that both children and parents are emotionally detached.

Even though there is no empirical evidence to suggest that parents are responsible for their children's autism, and considerable evidence to the contrary, it is not unreasonable to assume that parents of children with autism, like parents of any child, exert considerable influence on the general development of their children. Parents who become knowledgeable about autism and how to treat it, aggressively seek out services for their children, and become active teachers of their children, are likely to have a different impact on their children than if they are less knowledgeable, proactive, and involved. Although intervention programs vary in terms of how actively they incorporate parents into the program, most recognize that parents should be part of the treatment process. Some approaches to teaching children with autism, such as applied behavior analysis and TEACCH, require extensive involvement of parents in the administration of the program (see Chapter 5 for a discussion of these programs). Research suggests that therapeutic structures developed by professionals and implemented by parents and volunteers can have a pronounced effect on how children with autism develop. More generally, social scientists have long acknowledged the critical role that the social and physical environment plays in the development of disorders such as autism. One such environment is a residential setting.

Institutionalization effects

Currently children with autism are seldom placed in institutions or residential programs. Historically, institutionalization of these children was common. It has been suggested, and partially documented, that residential settings that provide only custodial care and no active treatment/education programs have serious adverse effects on the children's development. Early research in the areas of learning and developmental psychology indicates that behavioral delays and deviant behaviors can be produced by restrictive, depriving, and punitive environments.

For example, in an early seminal book, Hunt (1961) summarizes evidence that depicts human intelligence, with its genetic foundation, as very plastic and capable of being greatly enhanced or suppressed by the social experiences and environments in which a person is placed. He describes a wide variety of animal and human research indicating that not only cognitive but also sensory and motor development can be inhibited when environmental stimulation is restricted. Hunt (1961) also cites research suggesting that institutional environments such as those that existed in the middle of the last century were responsible for developmental delays in children, including mental and physical growth retardation. After the publication of Hunt's (1961) book, research describing the adverse impact of environmental deprivation and poverty, and the positive effects of different types of environmental interventions on development, proliferated.

One line of research, particularly relevant to the area of autism, investigated the effects of restricted environmental arrangements on the development of stereotyped behaviors. In a review of this research, Lewis and Baumeister (1982) report findings suggesting that stereotyped behaviors, such as rocking and pacing back and forth, develop when children and animals are reared in isolation situations. Another intriguing set of studies they reviewed describe the disabling effects that separation from mother can have on early behavioral, cognitive, and autonomic functioning of offspring, as well as potential links between social isolation and symptoms, such as anxiety, hyperactivity, and other behavioral problems. It is interesting to note that, even though children with autism are not typically physically separated from their mothers or currently institutionalized, the nature of autism results in a psychological isolation of these children from their mothers and other care-takers, as well as symptoms not unlike those described in the review by Lewis and Baumeister (1982). Research by Lovaas (1977) also points to the profound effects social environments can have on children with autism. The children in their study showed a marked reduction in autistic symptoms and improvements in adaptive behavior while in a community-delivered, behavior education program; however, the children later regressed when returned to a residential institutional setting that did not have the resources to implement intensive educational programs.

In summary, a variety of research has suggested that numerous developmental problems, including sensory, motor, language, and cognitive delays, and maladaptive or peculiar responses, such as self-injurious and stereotyped behaviors, may be produced, at least in part, by institutional and other environments that are nonstimulating, atypical, and/or insensitive in their care-taking arrangements. Although there is no evidence that autism is actually caused by such environmental factors, there is growing clinical and research evidence indicating that the environment can have a marked influence on the development of autistic symptoms and that carefully structured interventions can lead to reduction in autistic symptomatology.

Psychological theories

In contrast to social–environmental theories of autism that emphasize the influence of the social context on autism, other theories suggest that autism may develop as a consequence of a psychological defect or deficiency which has environmental and biological origins. In this section, major psychological theories of autism will be briefly summarized that point to the importance of cognitive, language, sensory, and emotion arousal processes. Beginning students of autism, who do not have a background in psychology, may find the description of a few of these theories, particularly the cognitive theories, as too technical. If this is the case, the reader is advised to skim these sections to get a general overview.

Cognitive theories

Early in the history of autism, claims of a general intellectual deficit underlying this disorder were common. This view seemed to be based on the fact that persons with autism were frequently assessed as having IQs that fell into the range of mental retardation. As the area of cognitive psychology evolved and as data from intelligence testing was more closely analyzed, another perspective emerged: that the cognitive deficits associated with autism are of a more specialized nature. For example, some investigators pointed out that the verbal IQ of individuals with autism is lower than their performance IQ. They further pointed out that individuals with autism are fairly proficient on certain subtests from IQ scales, such as those that assess rote memory and visual/motor skills, but less proficient on other subtests, for example those that evaluate social comprehension and vocabulary (see review by Tager-Flusberg, Joseph & Folstein, 2001). Moreover, it was acknowledged that intelligence tests provide only limited information about many of the cognitive abilities and disabilities reportedly associated with autism and that more attention needs to be given to examining specific cognitive processes and possible deficits in areas such as information processing, executive functioning, social cognition, and metacognitive knowledge. Theories suggesting the importance of these processes are briefly summarized in this section.

CENTRAL COHERENCE

Frith and Happé (1994) suggest that persons with autism display an abnormality in information processing, more specifically a failure of holistic processing or what they refer to as "weak central coherence". Individuals with weak central coherence prefer to attend to specific aspects of a task or an environment rather than examining the task as a whole. Although such a processing style can be a disadvantage in tasks that require global consideration of an overall task, it can be useful when the solution requires attention to specific parts of a task. For example, in completing the block design task from the Wechsler IQ test, the authors suggest that individuals with autism have an advantage because they look at the component parts of the designs which they are asked to reproduce rather than the overall configuration of the design. This part-oriented processing can also be of advantage in other situations when tasks involve the identification of "hidden" parts, such as in an embedded figures task, but a disadvantage when tasks require that a person look at the interrelationships of different parts of a figure (see review by Happé, 2000).

Jordan (1999), in a review of research of the central coherence hypothesis, suggests that research support for this theoretical position is mixed. Nevertheless, the work of Frith and Happé (1994) and others points out that individuals with autism have difficulty in processing complex material, particularly when that material has semantic meaning. Confronted with a complex task, they appear to be as likely to attend to irrelevant as relevant features. The question is why. Some researchers suggest that their performance problems on complex tasks are related to an executive function deficiency.

EXECUTIVE FUNCTION DEFICIENCY

Whereas some theorists have suggested the cognitive deficiencies associated with autism lie in the information processing domain and are related to problems such as weak central coherence, other theorists have asserted the deficits relate more to the executive control of the information that is processed and the behaviors flowing from that information (see review by Tager-Flusberg *et al.*, 2001). Executive functioning involves processes such as planning, searching, strategy selection, impulse control (including inhibiting prepotent responses that are not useful), shifting attention, and monitoring: all processes that facilitate flexibility of thought and action. These processes are more intentional and conscious in nature rather than automatic and reflexive.

Executive control involves active self-control rather than control from the external environment. Control is mental, guided by knowledge, goals, ideas, plans, and scripts (see Jordan, 1999). Russell (1997) refers to executive functioning as "a set of mental processes necessary for the control of action" (p. 258). Action can be behavioral or mental. Executive functioning is commonly thought to be mediated neurologically through the frontal lobes of the brain, although other parts of the brain are also mentioned as playing a role in this complex set of processes (Robbins, 1997).

It has been hypothesized that children with autism have a variety of problems because of a deficit in their executive control system (Turner, 1997). For example, they have trouble on tasks that require switching responses, such as a discrimination task that initially involves reinforcing a child for selecting squares rather than circles, and then subsequently reinforcing the child for selecting circles, not squares. Children with autism tend to perseverate on such a task, continuing to select squares even though reinforcement is only given for selecting circles. This perseverative tendency is consistent with the characterization of individuals with autism as being obsessive and compulsive.

Turner (1997) suggests that the repetitive behavior observed in children with autism is related to executive process problems. He hypothesizes that they engage in repetitive behaviors because they are unable to generate alternative ways of acting. He points out that if children have an executive dysfunction, they might be expected to act in one of several ways in new situations; specifically they might be less flexible, less spontaneous, slow to act, or unresponsive in their behavior, or conversely they might be impulsive, acting in either a random, mindless fashion or a repetitive manner. Moreover, they might also be expected to be more distractible in new situations and less likely to monitor their actions and make adjustments based on the feedback they receive.

Jarrold (1997) points out that children with autism may also have problems with pretend play because of an executive dysfunction, including a difficulty inhibiting a dominant response. During pretend play children have to inhibit actions normally elicited by an object; for example, in pretending a pencil is a telescope, a make-believe response, looking, has to be imposed in place of an established response, drawing. Based on his empirical research, he suggests that other executive control problems, relating to goal selection and representation, may also account for their pretend-play deficit.

Russell (1997) outlines the developmental features of the executive system and how an early dysfunction in this system might impact self-awareness. He suggests that during early normal development, a primitive action-monitoring system emerges that allows the nervous system to record perceptual inputs and code actions that originate in the world as well as those initiated by the child. Awareness or knowledge of action develops as a result of the feedback received from these actions and their consequences, along with a primitive self-awareness of how specific actions and their consequences are related. Subsequently, in an automatic rather than intentional way, the child is able to instigate movements in order to control and achieve certain types of perceptual inputs. Through this process a sense of agency or intentionality develops; that is, an expectation by the child that he/she can change their perceptual input through action.

Russell (1997) speculates that in autism the development of this primitive awareness may be disrupted because of action-monitoring and memory problems; and that as a consequence children with autism have problems developing knowledge regarding their own actions and imitating the actions of others, as well as regulating their actions through inner speech. Moreover, he raises the possibility that this dysfunction could also impair their understanding of others' intentions because of their own impoverished self-awareness; that is, they have difficulty understanding other people because they do not understand themselves. Thus, from this perspective, executive processing dysfunctions lead to theory of mind problems, more specifically, problems in comprehending what is going on in the minds of other people.

In discussing other factors that might adversely influence executive functioning, Russell (1997) points to research suggesting that children with autism have executive control problems because they have trouble with working memory, particularly when the amount of information to be processed is great or semantically meaningful. Relatedly, Russell (1997) suggests that children with autism are impaired in their ability to use inner speech to help them retain important information and use it to guide behavior. This position will be described in greater detail later in this chapter and Chapter 4. Although Russell (1997) favors the position that executive control problems lead to theory of mind deficiencies, he allows that it is possible, although less likely, that theory of mind problems are responsible for executive processing dysfunctions. In the next section, theory of mind deficiencies are discussed.

SOCIAL COGNITION, THEORY OF MIND, AND METACOGNITION

The area of social cognition involves the study of how a person's thought processes are related to their social context. Research in this area focuses on how a person comes to understand both their own thought processes as well as the thought processes of other people. Hypotheses concerning the latter topic are part of a prominent literature that has been referred to as theory of mind. Theory of mind researchers study how the mental states of others (their desires, beliefs, intentions, and knowledge) come to be understood by those around them (see review by Tager-Flusberg *et al.*, 2001).

Within the experimental literature, children's "theory of mind" has been studied in structured situations, including one that utilizes a false belief paradigm. In this type of research, a child is asked a question about a situation in which he/she holds knowledge in common with another child as well as possesses unique knowledge. For example, two children are shown crayons placed in a blue box. Subsequently, one (informed) child becomes privy to additional information (he/she knows the crayons have been subsequently taken out of the blue box and put in a red box) that the other (uninformed) child does not have. Informed children, who have developed an understanding of the minds of others, will report that the uninformed children, who have not seen the crayons taken out of the blue box and put in the red box, will think the crayons are still in the original blue box. Children less advanced in their understanding of the minds of others will indicate that uninformed children will think as they do: that the crayons are in the red box.

Theories about how children in general and children with autism understand the world around them are embedded in a more general developmental and cognitive psychology literature. These theories raise questions about the ability of children with autism to think abstractly; to distinguish between mental and physical reality; to differentiate between imaginary, fictional, and real events; and to understand their own selves. Some researchers suggest that autistic children have a primary deficit in understanding the minds of other people and how people's mental states (desires, beliefs, and knowledge) influence their behavior in social interaction situations (Baron-Cohen, Tager-Flusberg & Cohen, 2000). Other researchers disagree and suggest that children with autism do not understand others' minds because they do not develop a sense that they themselves have a mind, or if they do possess this general knowledge, do not understand or appreciate the contents of their own mind. One literature suggests that although children in general vary in their ability to know their own minds and to understand what they know and do not know, children with autism have particular difficulty thinking about their own thinking patterns; that is, they have a metacognitive deficit. Metacognition refers to the self-knowledge that individuals have about their cognitive states and mental processes (Flavell, 1978). The reader is referred to books by Baron-Cohen, Tager-Flusberg, and Cohen (1993), and Russell (1997) for further discussions of theory of mind theories.

Theories about why children with autism have difficulty understanding their own and other minds vary in their conceptions about the processes underlying the origins of this high-level cognitive dysfunction. Some theories focus on possible neurological reasons for the deficiency, such as a deficit in the prefrontal area of the brain. Other theories describe an impairment in a basic cognitive mechanism, such as the ability to form metarepresentations, and still others focus on social processes to explain theory of mind problems. This latter type of theory emphasizes that cognitive development occurs in an interpersonal context and that to understand the mind as a social entity, the social context in which it arises must be considered. One influential theory of this type has been proposed by R. Peter Hobson.

Hobson (1993) points out that what children typically learn in social transactions is not a theory of other people's minds, but a knowledge about people. Children "come to know about people's subjective states through having subjective experiences" with people (p. 5). According to Hobson (1993), an understanding of other people and the nature of their minds is acquired through "an individual's experience of affectively patterned, intersubjectively coordinated relations with other people" (p. 5). Through social encounters with people, children gain a sense of self, a capacity for symbolization, and a sense of others' attitudes and feelings.

Hobson (1993) views autism as a condition where individuals have limited understanding that people have subjective and psychological experiences. In contrast to Leslie's (1987) view that autistic individuals have an innate problem with metarepresentation, that is, in developing mental representations of what is going on in other people's minds, Hobson (1993) sees the development of this metarepresentational deficiency as having social roots in autistic children's problems with engaging others at an intersubjective level. Hobson (1993) emphasizes that autistic individuals manifest a "relative incapacity for intersubjective contact" (p. 3) and a problem emotionally connecting with others, a connection he refers to as one of "hearts and minds" (p. 3). As a consequence of this impairment in intersubjective engagement, other problems evolve in the cognitive, linguistic, and social areas.

Hobson (1993) views the difficulties that children with autism have in peer and adult interactions—including those relating to social gesturing, sharing experiences, joint attention, affect coordination, emotion perception and expression, imitation, attachment behavior, and self-development—as evidence of their broader difficulty in intersubjective engagement. As a consequence of this intersubjective difficulty, children with autism are constrained in their ability to acquire knowledge about other people's mental and emotional states, their own selves, language and communication, and more generally in their ability to symbolize and form mental representations about others and themselves. Hobson (1993) emphasizes that the emotional origins of psychological understanding involve cognitive processes, including the ability to make inferences about others' emotional states based on knowledge of one's own internal states, a process typically referred to as empathy. Language is a critical component involved in the development of empathy. It both influences and is influenced by the way social interactions and intersubjective engagements occur.

Language theories

As mentioned earlier, there is evidence that children with autism score lower on the verbal section of IQ tests than the performance section. Findings from multiple studies suggest, however, that the verbal-performance IQ discrepancy is most evident in autistic children who have lower IQs and that the discrepancy is negligible among higher (IQ) functioning children with autism. It appears that among higher functioning autistic children, who typically develop language later, that the verbal-performance IQ discrepancy reduces over time as their language development accelerates (see review by Tager-Flusberg *et al.*, 2001).

Nevertheless, even among those autistic children who have well-developed receptive and expressive language skills, a good vocabulary, and grammatical skills, there are language features that distinguish them from children without autism. Specifically, children with autism have what are called pragmatic deficits that become apparent in their social interchanges. For example, they often have difficulty interpreting and responding to the conversations of others, particularly if unfamiliar, nonliteral, figurative, and abstract terms are employed. They also have difficulty responding to the questions of others as well as in asking questions. In contrast, they are more proficient when the conversational topic is concrete and familiar.

As indicated earlier in the section on executive control theory, Russell (1997) suggests that autistic children may have difficulty both retaining and using information to guide their behavior because of an inability to use inner speech, a process that has been conceptualized as having social roots. Some theorists emphasize that inner speech or self-verbalization is part of a developmental process in which the interpersonal nature of thought is transferred or internalized into an intrapersonal process; one in which children's actions become controlled less by external verbal directives and more by their own verbal responses. This theoretical perspective has been influenced by the conceptualizations of Luria (1961) and Vygotsky (1978).

The general premise of Vygotsky's developmental theory, elaborated upon by Wertsch (1979), is that development occurs in the context of social interaction. According to these theorists, children's verbal control over motoric behavior increases with age. During the early stages of human development, adults verbally guide and direct children's behavior. Later, adults gradually relinquish verbal control to the child as the child acquires the capacity for independent action. Whereas adults initially provide considerable and specific assistance to guide children's behavior, children eventually verbally regulate their own behavior with assistance from the adults given only as needed. Finally, children assume complete verbal regulatory control over their behavior, a process that eventually becomes increasingly covert and "cognitive" in nature. Because of the problems autistic children have in their interpersonal relationships, many of which were just outlined in the discussion of Hobson's (1993) intersubjective theory, it seems likely that this internalization process will not proceed in a typical fashion and that language and the cognitive processes that assist children in self-regulating their behavior will not develop normally. More will be said about this in Chapter 4.

In theories of language acquisition, explanations of language development emphasize both the aforementioned processes that are social in nature, involving people in the child's context who support language learning, as well as linguistic mechanisms that are part of the neurological architecture of the brain. In contrast, a more recent theory of language acquisition, espoused by Bloom and Tinker (2001), views the child less as an object or passive recipient of social or physical cues, but rather as an active agent in her/his language development. From their perspective, language is acquired and emerges out of and in conjunction with the child's social, cognitive, and emotional development during the first three years of life. Within this developmental context, children acquire knowledge and develop perceptions that influence their representation of the world, including their beliefs, desires, and feelings about their world. The emphasis in this model is less on the brain and/or the environment for explaining language acquisition and more on the child's cognitions and actions. Although Bloom and Tinker's theory of language acquisition was not developed to explain language development in children with autism, their theory implies that to understand the language acquisition process in children with autism, the unusual cognitive, emotional, and social characteristics of this population must all be considered, a position that will be further developed in Chapter 4.

In contrast to the many theories that emphasize the primacy of cognitive and language processes in the development of autism, other theories point out the importance of more basic and earlier emerging processes, specifically those involving the sensory and arousal/activation systems.

Sensory integration theory

Sensory integration involves a series of processes that include the receipt of sensory input, the assimilation (processing) of that input in the brain, and the subsequent organization of behavior (action) in response to that input. Although the different sensory modalities are specialized for detecting different attributes of a sensory stimulus, the sensory systems have a similar underlying organization. Sensory integration theory attempts to explain both typical and atypical functioning through an understanding of stimulus–brain–behavior relationships.

During human development, sensory experiences with the environment influence the emerging structure of brain and the processes that flow from it.

Developmental problems are especially likely to occur if this sequence is disrupted during the early stages of development, either prenatally, perinatally, or postnatally during infancy and toddlerhood. Sensory integration theory in conjunction with genetic research suggests autism may result from a disruption of brain development during the gestational period. Within a developmental framework, the impact of small, early occurring changes in the environment and/or brain structure can result in large changes in functioning over time. Biological or environmental stressors may change the microstructure of the brain, resulting in impaired sensitivity and a cascade of events that leads to a cycle of increasing impairments at both a biological and behavioral level.

In general, there are considerable individual differences in the ways that children and adults process and respond to sensory experiences. Some individuals respond slowly to sensory stimuli in their environment, others quickly. They may also respond emotionally in various ways to a particular stimulus: with pleasure, neutrality, or pain. Some people seem to seek sensory stimulation, others seem to be sensory avoidant. There are also variations in the specific modality that people experience oversensitivity and undersensitivity. One person may show special sensitivity to certain auditory stimuli, another to touch. Many children with autism appear to experience the sensory world at the extreme, either showing hypersensitivity or hyposensitivity. The impact that dysfunction in the sensory system has on development is potentially considerable, and includes emotional problems and delays in the motor, language, cognitive, and social domain. The impact of this system on the development of autism will be described further in Chapter 4. For additional information regarding sensory integration theory and autism, the reader is referred to Chapter 2 and also a review by Huebner and Dunn (2001). In addition, the close connection between the sensory and the arousal/activation system is discussed in the next section.

Arousal and self-regulation

Individuals with autism are frequently characterized as experiencing the world at one or both ends of the arousal continuum. Arousal-activation problems in this population have been variously connected to neurological problems, sensory problems, and the social context. As Huebner and Dunn (2001) point out, arousal has been variously defined as a physiological state of readiness and a general state of nervous excitation. Arousal has a neurological substrate that can be influenced by the environment and a person's perception of the environment. Arousal as a state lies along a continuum from low to high. Cognitively, it is associated at one extreme with inattention and sleepiness; in the middle, with focused attention and alertness; and at the other extreme with distractibility and flight of ideas. Affectively the continuum is associated variously with apathy, boredom, calmness, excitement, anxiety, fear, and terror. Optimal arousal, which lies in the middle of the continuum, is associated with effective performance and learning. In contrast, hypoarousal is frequently connected with lethargy, indifference, and sleep, whereas hyperarousal is associated with intense, often uncomfortable feelings, avoidance, or immobility (Huebner and Dunn, 2001).

Some theorists and researchers suggest that the primary problem of children with autism does not lie in a dysfunctional arousal system per se, but rather in their inability to modulate or regulate that arousal. From this perspective, what differentiates them from children who develop more typically is their failure, when they become upset or conversely bored, to be able to regain a sense of calmness, alertness, and focused attention. This failure could be attributed to their inability to develop and/or employ effective motor (e.g., self-soothing), cognitive (e.g., problem-solving), or social (e.g., comfort-seeking) self-regulation strategies. Observation of individuals with autism suggests, however, that they do use self-regulation strategies, and that these strategies are in a sense effective, at least in the short run; however, these strategies involve unconventional behaviors that create secondary problems. More specifically, many of the unusual behaviors that individuals with autism display (e.g., failure to make eye contact, inattention, extreme withdrawal, social aloofness, rocking, self-injurious behaviors, ritualistic behaviors and insistence on sameness, hyperactivity, and active avoidance through flight) can be viewed as functional in the sense that they serve to reduce states of high arousal that are unpleasant. Moreover, some theorists have suggested that a number of the aforementioned strategies, as well as behaviors like body twirling and spinning objects, can also serve to provide sensory stimulation, to individuals who have low arousal and are understimulated (see Lewis & Baumeister, 1982). Both of these perspectives are consistent with a model of sensory processing proposed by Dunn (1997).

In his model, Dunn (1997) proposes that people vary both in the threshold at which they experience stimulation as well as in the way they handle that stimulation. More specifically, some individuals who have a high threshold of stimulation react only to higher intensities of stimulation, and often appear passive in their response to the environment, seemingly not registering or acknowledging that stimulation has occurred and thus appearing apathetic or self-absorbed. At the other end of the activity continuum, some individuals with this same high threshold of stimulation actively seek out stimulation, as if stimulus-deprived, and often appear excitable. Conversely, some individuals with a low threshold of stimulation, that is, who are very quick to sense even very low intensity levels of stimulation, may at the low end of the activity continuum appear to react normally or perhaps appear to experience mild discomfort and distractibility. In contrast, individuals with a similar low threshold of stimulation, but who operate at the high end of the activity continuum, may quickly acknowledge receipt of a stimulus, become emotionally upset, and attempt to terminate stimulation through active avoidance or controlling the stimulation in some other manner.

Extrapolating from Dunn's (1997) model, a number of intriguing questions are suggested about the nature of autism. For example, do individuals with autism show greater variation in the thresholds at which a specific stimulus is experienced and in how this stimulus is responded to than individuals without autism? That is, do individuals with autism have a different and more extreme threshold of stimulation than individuals without autism? Relatedly, do children with autism show greater extremes of response (from very passive to very active) to specific levels of stimulation? Anecdotal data suggest that individuals with autism, as a population, do operate at the extreme in terms of their sensory threshold compared to individuals without autism. Moreover, it also appears that persons with autism may also respond behaviorally, whatever their sensory threshold, at the extreme: either by ignoring the stimulation, through active avoidance of it, or conversely by actively and compulsively seeking it out. Thus, it is possible that people with autism differ from people without autism in the way they experience a stimulus (i.e. the threshold at which they sense the stimulus), in the way they react and cope with a stimulus that is sensed (i.e. how they regulate their affective response to a stimulus), or in both their sensitivity and coping style. It is also possible that children with autism vary considerably from each other in their sensitivity and coping style. For example, it may be that some children with autism not only are more sensitive (reactive) to a given level of stimulation, but also lack the capacity to cope with and modulate their affective responses. In contrast, other children with autism may be hyposensitive to environmental stimulation and actively mobilize themselves to seek out stimulation. Another intriguing possibility is that all children are hypersensitive, but that some develop self-regulatory mechanisms, such as cognitive withdrawal, that makes them appear hyposensitive. In Chapter 4, a theory that describes autism as a self-regulation disorder will be developed at greater length.

Biological theories of autism

In addition to socioenvironmental and psychological theories of autism, there has been a proliferation of biological theories of autism. In this section an overview of these theories is presented, which emphasize variously genetic, environmental, genetic and environmental, biochemical, neurostructural, and immunological factors. All of these theories, either directly or indirectly, suggest that autism is a neurological disorder affecting the brain. Before discussing these theories, an overview of brain development and methods for studying its development and activity is presented.

Brain development and dysfunction

The brain is the first organ to develop, with development beginning at 18 days after conception, and extending after birth into early adulthood. In general, the structures regulating basic physiologic organization (e.g., control of heart rate and breathing) mature first, then the structures responsible for sensory and motor, state regulation (sleep/wake), cognitive, and movement coordination functions. Early prenatal processes lead to the formation of three major areas of the brain, the forebrain, midbrain, and hindbrain, which eventually differentiate into the specific structures described in Table 3.1 (p. 128). The cells within these areas divide rapidly during the later stages of fetal development—with 250,000 new neurons formed every minute. During pregnancy and postnatal life, cells migrate to the proper layer, mature, and form connections with other nerve cells. These cells are also involved in a process of programmed cell death, in which excess nerve cells are "pruned". During this process, fully functioning nerve tracts are preserved and excess or inactive neurons are killed. Pruning takes place at a rapid rate in late pregnancy and early childhood. During late pregnancy and childhood, the neural pathways are gradually surrounded by a myelin sheath that increases the speed of transmission and prevents cross-signaling with other nerve paths (Michel & Moore, 1995).

Both genes and environment affect the development of the nervous system. Genes play a particularly critical role in the early prenatal period, when the basic structures are set up and basic cell layers are formed. Even during these early phases of neurological development, environmental forces can alter development in critical or disruptive ways. During the later prenatal and postnatal stages, the environment plays an increasingly active role in development, especially in the formation of connections between neural cells, as well as in the pruning process.

Throughout nervous system development, the brain is especially vulnerable to environmental insult. This vulnerable period extends from a few days after conception through early childhood, a longer period of vulnerability than any other organ system. The environment can damage the nervous system in a variety of ways through toxins, infections, or trauma. Agents that interfere with developmental processes are called "teratogens". Early insults to brain tissue often have more severe effects. In contrast, later insults may be less severe because the brain has built in redundancy of later processes so that if some cells are disrupted, other cells can take over. Although this protective design reduces, it does not completely eliminate developmental problems in the nervous system.

The environment also plays a positive role in nervous system development. Even before birth, sensory pathways that transmit touch, vestibular (position in gravity), smell, taste, and auditory stimuli begin to function and fire as they are stimulated by the environment. This nerve activity facilitates synapse formation. Absence of environmental stimulation can lead to pruning of critical neural pathways (LeDoux, 2002). Sometimes, environmental experience can adversely affect brain maturation and sensory integration. For example, the senses are normally stimulated in a set order before birth, with touch and movement earliest, then smell, taste, hearing, and finally sight. If this order is changed, sensory function may be altered. Quail chicks that have premature visual stimulation do not learn to distinguish their mothers by sound, and quail chicks that experience augmented auditory stimulation do not develop normal visual recognition (Sleigh & Lickliter, 1997). Early environmental trauma can also produce tragic developmental consequences. For example, research indicates that when young children are abused, long lasting changes in prefrontal cortex functioning occur, which are associated with threat assessment and self-regulation problems (Teicher, Andersen, Polcari, Anderson & Navalta, 2002).

Developmental disabilities, particularly those in which marked adaptive behavior impairments occur, have been frequently associated with different types of neurological dysfunction. Researchers working in the area of autism believe that most of the symptoms associated with this disorder have a neurological basis. Although the exact genetic and environmental causes have not been yet identified, researchers are making progress in identifying specific parts of the brain that are associated with autistic symptomatology. This identification process is likely to accelerate, given the amount of research being conducted and the increasing sophistication of the methods for studying neurological functioning. These methods include: clinical assessment; monitoring techniques, such as the electrocardiogram (ECG), electroencephalogram (EEG), magnetoencephalography (MEG), and evoked potential records (EPS); neurochemical analysis; autopsy examinations; and neuroimaging techniques, such as computerized transaxial tomography (CT scan), magnetic resonance imaging (MRI), and position emission tomography (PET).

Genetic theories

OVERVIEW

Evidence for a genetic basis for autism comes from various types of research, including twin, family, and genetic linkage studies. Increasingly, it has been recognized that autism is highly heritable. However, the pattern of inheritance and expression of autism are complicated. If genetics were the complete story, then the percentage of identical twins who are both affected would approach 100%. Simple patterns of inheritance are detectable in approximately 10% of cases of autism, often co-morbid with other syndromes, such as Fragile X and tuberous sclerosis. Genetic linkage studies suggest that a number of genes (perhaps 15–20) are needed to produce the characteristics associated with the phenotype of autism. These studies also provide preliminary evidence of the location of these genes on specific chromosomes (see review by Jones & Szatmari, 2002; Risch *et al.* 1999; Tager-Flusberg *et al.* 2001). Some research suggests that what is typically inherited is a genetic susceptibility for autism, at least for some, if not most, cases of autism (Andres, 2002); that is, a vulnerability to a secondary insult, such as an environmental toxin or infection, is inherited. A susceptible person responds to the insult by developing autistic symptoms, while a nonsusceptible person does not.

TWIN, SIBLING, AND FAMILY STUDIES

In twin studies, concordance rates of autism in monozygotic (identical) twins vary considerably, but typically are higher than 60%; that is, if one of the twins has autism the probability that a second member of a twin set will have autism is higher than 60% (Bailey, Le Couteur, Gottesman, Bolton, Simonoff,

Yuzda & Rutter, 1995; Smalley, 1997). Concordance rates vary across studies in part as a function of whether the formal definition of Autistic Disorder is used or a broader definition is used that includes other disorders on the autism spectrum, such as PDD-NOS and Asperger's. When a broader definition of autism is employed concordance rates are higher.

Studies examining different-aged (non-twin) siblings in families, in which one of the children is autistic, also indicate a higher than expected incidence of autism in the other siblings: about a hundred times more likely than in the general population. Concordance rates among dizygotic twins, who are genetically as dissimilar as siblings of different ages, are similar to general sibling rates in most, but not all, studies (Hallmayer, Glasson, Bower, Petterson, Croen, Grether & Risch, 2002) (for an exception, see Greenberg, Hodge, Sowinski & Nicoll, 2001). Family studies also find higher rates of occurrence of autistic characteristics (e.g., social interaction problems and communication deficiencies), as well as characteristics of other psychiatric disorders (e.g., depression and Obsessive–Compulsive Disorder) in the parents and other relatives of children with autism. What these concordance rates tell us in general is that the more genetic information people have in common, the more likely they will share the traits of autism.

GENETIC ANALYSIS

Genetic analysis is employed to locate genes involved with autism. Analytical methods include chromosomal analysis which looks at larger changes on the chromosome; linkage analysis which is employed to search for small common DNA sequences in affected individuals which are absent in nonaffected individuals; and trait analysis which looks at genes associated with specific traits (e.g., speech delay).

Methodologically, a genetic analysis usually begins with looking for chromosomal anomalies, such as extra (duplications) or missing (deletions) chromosomal segments. Approximately 5% of individuals with autism have an identified chromosomal abnormality. The most commonly reported anomaly in research studies is the duplication of a section of the long arm of chromosome 15, an area also associated with Angelman and Prader-Willi Syndromes, which share some symptoms in common with autism (Andres, 2002; Folstein & Rosen-Sheidley, 2001). For example, Buxbaum et al. (2002), examining 80 families with multiple cases of autism, found that autistic traits were associated with the gene for the GABA (gamma aminobutyrate, an inhibitory neurotransmitter) receptor on the long arm of chromosome 15.

Linkage analysis, one of the most common methods in genetic analysis, looks at small changes in DNA (as detected by DNA restriction enzyme cuts) that occur in affected individuals in a family but not in nonaffected individuals. The changes detected may be in or adjacent to the gene that causes the problem, but it serves to narrow the area of the genome of interest. Although linkage studies of autism have been inconsistent in their findings, several linkage areas have been found on the long arm (q) of chromosomes 3, 7, 2, 13, 15, and 6 and the short arm (p) of chromosomes 16, 19, 11, 13, and 1 (Andres, 2002; Auranen et al., 2002; Folstein & Rosen-Sheidley, 2001; Sultana et al. 2002).

When specific traits of autism are used to sort linkages, additional location information is obtained. For example, Alarcon, Cantor, Liu, Gilliam and Geschwind (2002) found, in a study of 152 families, that age at first word was strongly linked to area 7q. Repetitive behaviors were also localized to 7q in an overlapping region. The 7q region is expressed in the development of the fetal brain in the frontal, parietal, and temporal areas, making it an even more interesting genetic region (Sultana et al., 2002). Several other specific gene sites have been implicated by linkage studies and are being explored further (McKusick et al., 2002).

Some studies, focusing on the genetic markers of autism, use trait analysis. This technique assists in the search for patterns of genes associated with specific autistic characteristics, which occur across family members who may or may not be autistic. For example, trait analysis for an autistic-like behavior, "insistence on sameness", led researchers to a set of three GABA receptor genes on chromosome 15 (Shao et al., 2003). Speech delay has been linked to an area on chromosome 2 (Shao et al., 2002). Trait analysis is a particularly important technique for multigene disorders like autism.

Current genetic research on autism is accelerating, partially due to the availability of large cooperative genetic databases. For example, Cure Autism Now (CAN) and the UCLA Neuropsychiatric Institute have formed the AGRE (Autism Genetic Resource Exchange) gene bank. The goal of the AGRE is to collect and store the genetic information of large numbers of people with autism and their family members and then make it available to researchers who study autism. Findings using AGRE data are already expanding our understanding of the genetics of autism (Alarcon et al., 2002). For the most up-to-date summary of genetics and autism, see Online Mendelian Inheritance in Man (OMIM) (McKusick *et al.*, 2003).

Early environmental theories

Although autism is a genetically determined disorder, the environment likely plays a role in how this disorder is explicitly genetically expressed (manifested). Evidence for a variability of expression comes from identical twin studies. In studies by Bailey *et al.* (1995) and Smalley (1997), concordance rates of 40% and 60% were found when a narrow definition of autism was used. When a broader definition was employed that included Asperger's Syndrome and other autistic spectrum disorders, the concordance or co-occurrence rate rose to above 90%. These data strongly suggest that in persons with identical "autism genes", the expression of these genes may lead to autism or some other disorder on the autism spectrum. Some studies also show that nonidentical twins have a higher rate of autism than siblings from different pregnancies (Betancur, Leboyer & Gillberg, 2002; Greenberg *et al.*, 2001). If, indeed, this is the case, the pattern of results suggests that prenatal environmental factors may play an important role in the development of autism. Not all studies, however, have found a difference between nonidentical twins and other siblings (Hallmeyer *et al.*, 2002; Hultman, Sparen & Cnattingius, 2002).

Recent interest in the role environmental factors play in the development of autism has also been evoked by the reportedly high incidence of autism in places like the Brick Township in New Jersey (Centers for Disease Control, 2000). It has been suggested that environmental factors, such as a toxin in the air, water, or earth, influence the expression of genes or even cause autism directly. Although specific environmental triggers for autism have not yet been isolated, it is known more generally that specific environmental factors can cause and/or place a person at increased risk for developmental disorders. For example, maternal alcohol consumption during pregnancy can lead to fetal alcohol syndrome and associated symptoms (e.g., mental retardation, social deficiencies, and physical defects). An example of a genetic disorder that requires an environmental input is phenylketonuria. Persons with this gene disorder are unable to metabolize phenylalanine, an amino acid. When exposed to phenylalanine in their diet (an environmental factor), children with this disorder typically experience severe mental and growth retardation, but if they are placed on a special diet without phenylalanine, they develop normally.

The search for environmental triggers of autism has in part been guided by a supposition that this trigger likely occurs early in development, specifically because of the pattern of brain anomalies associated with autism. Support for this supposition is provided by the studies that show differences in the placement and number of Purkinje cells in the cerebellum of persons with autism, anomalies that are initiated during early stages of cell migration (Rodier, Ingram, Tisdale, Nelson & Romano, 1996). Thalidomide is an example of a possible trigger for autism. Stromland, Nordin, Miller, Akerstrom and Gillberg (1994) evaluated 86 persons who had been exposed to thalidomide in utero. They found four individuals with autism within this population. These four were members of a larger group of 15, all of whom were exposed to this drug between days 20 and 24 of pregnancy. Although thalidomide is not likely a source of autism today, specifically because its use during pregnancy has been discontinued, research like this helps make the general case for early environmental triggers of autism.

More recent studies have found a variety of other environmental factors linked to autism. For example, Juul-Dam, Townsend, and Courchesne (2001), examining data from several studies including their own, found that low contraceptive use, second and third trimester uterine bleeding, Rh incompatibility, induced labor, prolonged labor, oxygen supplementation at birth, and high bilirubin levels were all associated with autism. Hultman *et al.* (2002) also found an association between autism and prenatal/perinatal factors such as intrauterine growth retardation, daily smoking during pregnancy, and Caesarian birth. In nonhuman research, the offspring of pregnant mice, injected with human influenza, were found to have changes in the size and number of their pyramidal cells and abnormal cortex development, as well as behavioral characteristics similar to those found in autism (Fatemi, Halt, Stary, Kanodia, Schulz & Realmuto, 2002). Viral infections in humans have also been associated with schizophrenia in offspring, a disorder that shares symptoms in common with autism (see Brown & Susser, 2002). Although factors like the ones listed above are not sufficient to explain autism, since they commonly occur in pregnancies that do not result in autism, they may be part of a larger environmental and genetic process that leads to autism.

An intriguing factor that affects the prenatal environment is the genetic makeup of the mother, particularly genes that influence metabolism, blood chemistry, and other processes that support pregnancy. Results of a study by

Robinson, Schutz, Macciardi, White, and Holden (2001) suggest that a maternal deficiency in a gene that codes for an enzyme that controls the conversion of dopamine to norepinephrine is a moderate, but significant, risk factor for having a child with autism. This study provides another example of how genes and environment may act in combination to produce autism.

At present, environmental agents that occur later in development are also under consideration as risk factors, especially in autism that appears to have its onset in the second year of life, after a period of seemingly normal development. Such agents include: anticonvulsant medications (e.g., valproic acid); lymphocytic choriomeningitis virus; and the measles, mumps, and rubella (MMR) vaccine. Although specific teratogens, toxins, proteins, and viruses have not yet been shown to be associated with autism, considerable interest and speculation exists concerning the potential role of such agents in producing brain damage and autistic symptomatology (see discussion of vaccines later in this chapter).

Neurochemical theories

Brain function is derived from a seemingly impenetrable tangle of nerves and their extensions, axons and dendrites. Neurons speak to one another through axons which release chemical signals that cross a small gap and bind to the dendrites or cell body of the next nerve cell. When these chemicals, called "neurotransmitters", or their receptors are present at abnormal levels (high or low), they affect how the brain functions. Neurotransmitters vary in their channel of influence. They may stimulate some functions and suppress others. For example, serotonin and dopamine are neurotransmitters that occur at lower levels in depressed patients. Raising these levels often leads to a reduction in depressive symptoms. Other neurotransmitters like norepinephrine are important in attention, alertness, and the stress response. GABA, another neurochemical, is important in inhibiting neural activity which in turn is associated with a feeling of relaxation. Neurotransmitters, including monoamines (which consist of serotonin, dopamine, epinephrine, and norepinephrine), have captured the interest of autism researchers because they are commonly found in areas of the brain that control emotions and goal-directed behavior. In this section we will examine various neurochemicals being investigated for their role in autism, specifically serotonin, dopamine, GABA, opioids, and oxytocin.

Research has consistently found that autistic individuals have high serotonin levels in their blood (Anderson, Horne, Chatterjee & Cohen, 1990; Cook, 1996; Cook, Arora *et al.*, 1993). Whereas low serotonin levels are associated with psychological disorders, such as depression, high serotonin levels have been associated with schizophrenia and autism (Jakovljevic, Muck-Seler, Pivac & Crncevic, 1998). Chugani *et al.* (1999) examined 30 autistic children and found that the levels of serotonin in autism increased with age, whereas control children showed declining serotonin levels. Serotonin is of particular interest to autism researchers because of the critical role it plays in brain development. For example, it influences neuron removal, dendrite development, synapse formation and maintenance, cell migration, and cellular organization within areas such as the hippocampus and sensory cortex. If research finds that levels of serotonin are altered during fetal and early postnatal development, this could explain some of the structural and functional problems found in autism.

Dopamine (DA) is another neurotransmitter implicated in autism. Dopamine and norepinephrine play an important role in the development of the prefrontal cortex, which is associated with functions such as complex thought, threat appraisal, problem solving, and emotions, all of which are affected by autism. In therapeutic studies it has been found that drugs that increase DA and other monoamines (norepinephrine) also reduce some of the symptoms of autism, such as inattention, self-stimulation, and self-injury (Volkmar, 2001). In a study by Ernst, Zametkin, Matochik, Pascualvaca & Cohen (1997), accumulation of 18-F-DOPA (a tracer chemical for dopamine) in the anterior medial prefrontal cortex was reduced in autistic patients as compared to nonautistic subjects. The enzyme that converts dopamine to norepinephrine was also found to be significantly lower in autistic family members, including in one-third of mothers of autistic patients; however, 20% of women without autistic children also showed this characteristic (Robinson *et al.*, 2001).

GABA, an inhibitory neurotransmitter that serves to modulate reactivity in the brain, may also play a role in autism. Several tranquilizers produce relaxation by magnifying GABA action. Elevated GABA levels have been found in the blood and urine of autistic children (Dhossche, Applegate, Abraham, Maertens, Bland, Bencsath & Martinez, 2002). Moreover, in a small autopsy study, the number of receptors for GABA in the hippocampus was found to be lower in four male subjects with autism than age-matched controls (Blatt, Fitzgerald, Guptill, Booker, Kemper & Bauman, 2001). Genes related to the receptors for GABA on chromosomes 7 and 15 have also been linked to autism (Menold *et al.,* 2001; Serajee, Zhong, Nabi & Huq, 2003). In addition, enzymes that are involved in the conversion of glutamate to GABA have been observed to be at lower levels in the parietal lobe and the cerebellum of autistic subjects compared to controls (Fatemi *et al.,* 2002).

Oxytocin is an interesting neurohormone that is being increasingly examined because of its relationship to autism and stress modulation. Oxytocin is normally released during labor and breastfeeding as well as through ventral vagal stimulation which occurs during cuddling. Oxytocin has been associated with social behaviors in animals. For example, a strain of mice with an oxytocin knockout gene (ensuring oxytocin is not made) have been found to display abnormal social behaviors (e.g., they did not recognize familiars). In contrast, knockout mice with oxytocin injections did not show these deficiencies (Winslow & Insel, 2002). Human data also suggest a relationship between oxytocin and autistic symptoms. In a comparison of autistic and nonautistic children, Modahl *et al.,* (1998) found lower average levels of oxytocin in a group of autistic children compared to a group of age-matched controls. Whereas the nonautistic group showed increased levels of oxytocin with age, autistic children did not show this increase. Moreover, nonautistic children had wider variability in their oxytocin levels; interestingly, those with higher levels of oxytocin were found to have better social skills. Autistic children with higher oxytocin levels were more likely to have a preferred friend. The relationship between oxytocin level and social behavior in autistic children was, however, more complex than these findings suggest. Children in the autism group also showed a negative correlation between oxytocin levels and some socialization skills such as verbal and nonverbal imitation. A study by Green, Fein, Modahl, Feinstein, Waterhouse and Morris (2001), showed that autistic children with low oxytocin levels had elevated levels of Oxytocin-X, a precursor of active oxytocin, denoting a possible error in the synthetic pathway for oxytocin.

Other biochemical explanations of autism have also been proposed. For example, some theorists have suggested that the brains of individuals with autism produce too many opioids, a form of opiates, and that such productions might be associated with autistic symptoms, particularly self-stimulation and social withdrawal. The production of opioids is thought to be triggered in normally developing children through social behaviors, such as seeking out mother. If, as some researchers suggest, opiates are produced through other mechanisms in children with autism, such as rocking or twirling, this could explain their low motivation to seek out other people, and their appearance of being socially withdrawn. For this reason medications designed to reduce the levels of opioids have been suggested as a treatment to reduce self-stimulatory and social withdrawal behaviors (see review by Tsai, 1998).

Structural theories

A number of neurological structures have been proposed as playing a critical role in the development of autism. These sites include the brain stem, cerebellum, reticular formation, and the cerebrum, particularly the frontal and temporal lobes. Table 3.1 describes these and other structures and the functions commonly associated with them. Neuroanatomical studies of autism examine these structures and the underlying cellular anatomy, including cell size, axons, dendrites, and the synapse between cells. These studies use a number of the methodologies including those described previously (e.g., autopsy, CT scans, PET scans, and functional MRI).

One of the more intriguing sites that has been examined for its association with autism is the brain stem. This structure begins at the top of the spinal cord and is composed of the medulla oblongata and the pons, which is in the midbrain (see Table 3.1). Another structure, the reticular activating center, runs through the brain stem and serves a sensory gating function. As part of the state regulation system, this center helps to regulate arousal, control sleep/alert cycles, and maintain homeostasis. Defects in the brain stem may account for some of the arousal defects, attentional difficulties, and sensory problems (e.g., hypersensitivity and hyposensitivity) displayed by individuals with autism (Huebner & Lane, 2001).

Another structure that has received close attention from researchers is the cerebellum, which is a large area on the dorsal surface of the brain, consisting of two hemispheres connected by the vermis (Table 3.1). The cerebellum helps coordinate movement in the absence of conscious control, modulates sensory input, and integrates sensory responsiveness throughout the brain. Defects in the cerebellum are associated with sensorimotor problems, low muscle tone, motor coordination difficulties, and sensory modulation impairments: all characteristics commonly associated with autism. Moreover, the cerebellum may play special roles in: associating affect with nonverbal communication movements, regulating the speed of cognitive processes and the timing of social interactions, supporting nonmotor aspects of language, and

Table 3.1 Brain areas and functions

Primary Brain Area	Specific Brain Structures	Functions
Forebrain	Cerebral hemispheres (includes prefrontal, frontal, temporal, parietal, and occipital lobes)	Higher order processing of information, sensory processing, voluntary motor control
		Prefrontal—assessment of threat, problem-solving
		Frontal—speech, behavior, sensory, movement
		Temporal—sensory integration, comprehension of language
		Parietal—receiving sensory information
		Occipital—visual input
	Limbic system	Mood, emotional response, and memory
	Thalamus	Pain, sensory transfer to the cerebral hemispheres, and attention
	Hypothalamus	Control of breathing, heart rate, water balance, temperature, hormone levels
Midbrain	Pons	Large bundle of nerve fibers, serves as a bridge between the cerebrum, the lower brainstem, and the cerebellum
Hindbrain	Cerebellum	Receives sensory input from the ears used to maintain balance, receives feedback from muscles and other body parts about their current movement and position, regulates muscle tone, coordinates muscle movement, and coordinates movement ordered by the cerebrum
	Lower brainstem (medulla oblongata)	Regulates heart rate, breathing, blood pressure, vomiting reflex, relay center for most of the sensory and motor nerves, arousal, and attention

the learning of movement patterns— all processes that appear disrupted in individuals with autism (Huebner & Lane, 2001).

The temporal lobe is an associative area highly connected with the frontal cortex, parietal lobe, limbic system, auditory cortex, and visual cortex. Many autistic individuals have seizure disorders which involve this area of the brain. Children with infantile seizures who show early bilateral hypoperfusion (lower blood flow) of the temporal lobe are more likely to later be diagnosed with Autistic Disorders (Chugani, DaSilva & Chugani, 1996). In children with tuberous sclerosis, tuberous growth in the temporal lobe has been strongly correlated with autism (Bolton & Griffiths, 1997). Moreoever, primate experiments show behavioral changes similar to autism when the temporal lobe is damaged (Bauman & Kemper, 1997). Waterhouse, Fein, and Modahl (1996) present a model that attributes many of the symptoms of autism to a dysfunction in the medial-temporal lobe. This area includes structures of the temporal lobe and the parietal association areas, and more specifically, the amygdala, limbic, and hippocampal systems, as well as neurochemistry circuits for serotonin, oxytocin, vasopressin, and beta endorphins. A dysfunction of portions of the temporal lobe could explain the difficulties that individuals with autism have in processing auditory and visual stimulation as well as associating meaning and emotions with such stimuli.

A final area of the brain often associated with autism is the frontal lobe. Problems in the prefrontal portion of this structure have been associated with executive function and information processing defects, and could account for the problems individuals with autism have in strategy formation, planning, cognitive flexibility, response inhibition, judgment, metacognition, parallel processing, social cognition, and performance monitoring (Happé et al., 1996; Luna et al., 2002). There has been a debate, however, whether the frontal lobe plays a primary role in the development of autism or whether problems in this area result from dysfunctions in lower neurological structures.

Research on brain anatomy, histology, and activity patterns in autism

The behavioral symptoms of autism are striking, yet evidence for their neurological basis is elusive. Although enlargement of several brain structures and unusual activity patterns have been consistently reported, a cohesive picture of structural changes associated with autism has not yet emerged. Because of new tools for examining brain activity, chemistry, and microanatomy, there is optimism that research will provide information that will help improve diagnosis and target treatments. Analyzing the results of research utilizing these tools is complicated because autism manifests itself in different ways. In this section, examples of typical findings will be presented on brain enlargement, cellular level changes in the brain, and unusual activity patterns in the brain.

Several studies have found an enlarged brain in persons on the autism spectrum (Lainhart, Piven, Wzorek, Landa, Santangelo, Coon & Folstein, 1997; Piven, 1997; Woodhouse, Bailey, Rutter, Bolten, Baird & Le Conteur, 1996). For example, Gillberg and deSouza (2002) found macrocephaly during the first year of life in children later diagnosed with Asperger's Syndrome. These enlargements, present at birth, sometimes become more distinct later in childhood (Lainhart et al., 1997). Enlargements have been found in the cerebellum, amygdala, hippocampus, and the parietal, temporal, and occipital lobes of the cerebrum (Piven, Arndt, Bailey & Andreason, 1996; Sparks et al., 2002). Enlargement of the amygdala is more common among children with autism than in children with Asperger's Syndrome or other Pervasive Developmental Disorders, an effect that disappears during adolescence (Sparks et al., 2002). In a study of brain growth, Courchesne et al. (2001) evaluated 30 two-to four-year-old boys with autism, born with normal head circumference. They found that 90% of the boys had larger than average brain volume and 37% met the criteria for developmental macrocephaly. They also had more cerebral and cerebellar white and cerebral gray matter. With age the picture changed; a sample of adolescent boys with autism were not found to have above average gray matter or white matter volumes. The authors concluded that autism is associated with an alteration in the timing and control of brain growth (Courchesne et al., 2001).

The cerebellum, which plays a role in attention, sensory function, linguistic function, and motor coordination, was examined in several other studies. The neocerebellum, which comprises the VI and VII lobules of the vermis and the posterior lobe of the lateral hemispheres, is particularly interesting because of the role it plays in attention (shifting of attention), cognitive, and linguistic functions. Deficits in vermis lobules VI and VII have been linked to reduced exploratory behavior in GS guinea pigs and L1CAM knockout mice. The vermis of the cerebellum has been analyzed using MRI with human subjects. A number of these studies found abnormalities in the cerebellum to be correlated with autism generally, as well as specific autistic traits such as low exploration and verbal expression. For example, Courchesne et al. found less cerebellar gray matter and smaller vermis lobules VI and VII in autistic boys than in nonautistic boys (Courchesne *et al.*, 2001). Measures of reduced toy exploration negatively correlated with vermis lobule VI–VII volume and positively correlated with frontal lobe volume (Pierce & Courchesne, 2001). Lower verbal IQ scores have also been associated with abnormal vermis measures (Courchesne, Saitoh *et al.*, 1994). It appears, however, that hypoplasia of the neocerebellum may be more linked to mental retardation (which is found in at least 60–70% of individuals with autism) or other nonspecific neurodeficits than to autism per se (Schaefer *et al.*, 1996).

In addition to studies of brain anatomy, studies of brain activity have been helpful in examining brain–autism symptom relationships. For example, functional imaging has been employed to examine living brain tissue and the brain at work. Functional imaging looks mainly at glucose utilization or blood flow changes as an index of brain activity. These studies are either done with subjects at rest or while performing specific tasks.

Several studies of subjects at rest show a decrease in left side blood flow in the frontal and temporal lobes and increased flow in the right side frontal, temporal, and parietal areas of the brain, most significantly in the sensorimotor, auditory cortex, and in Broca's area (Chiron, Leboyer, Leon, Jambaque, Nuttin & Syrota, 1995; Hashimoto, Sasaki, Fukumizu, Hanaoka, Sugai & Matsuda, 2000; Zilbovicius *et al.*, 2000). These studies also show some age-related effects. For example, Zilbovicius *et al.*, (1995) examined autistic children at age three to four and found lower regional cerebral blood flow (rCBF) in the frontal lobe, but by age six to seven the rCBF was closer to that of nonautistic children.

Brain activity studies performed on subjects while they perform tasks of interest in autism have produced a variety of results. Their performance on visual and auditory language processing tasks is associated with unusual patterns in the cingulate gyrus and activity differences between the right and left cerebral hemispheres (Haznedar *et al.*, 2000; Muller *et al.*, 1999; and review by Boddaert & Zilbovicius, 2002). Auditory language processing task studies showed a predominant pattern of right side temporal lobe activity, as opposed to the left side predominance for language in nonautistic subjects (Muller *et al.*, 1999). These studies demonstrate reversal of hemispheric dominance when processing auditory stimuli, with auditory language processing occurring in an area more commonly connected to logic and spatial relationships (Boddaert & Zilbovicius, 2002; Muller *et al.*, 1999). Autistic and nonautistic individuals also show a different pattern of brain activity during theory of mind tasks. In general, subjects with an autistic spectrum disorder have less activity in the frontal lobe and amygdala and greater activity in the superior temporal gyri (Baron-Cohen *et al.*, 1999; Critchley *et al.*, 2000; Schultz *et al.*, 2000). Thus, in general, these studies indicate that individuals with autism show unusual patterns of brain activation compared to nonautistic individuals on a variety of different tasks.

Immune theories of autism

The immune system, even under normal circumstances, has a marked impact on behavior. Chemicals secreted by the immune system, called cytokines, are known to bind to sites in the brain and cause changes in areas such as sleep, attention, and mood. Recently there has been speculation that immune system problems may trigger the development of autistic symptoms. This system has drawn attention because of:

1. the unusual patterns of production of immune chemical signals and antibodies observed in individuals with autism

2. the recent reported rise in the rates of autism

3. the suggestion that autism could be related to inoculation procedures and/or inflammatory disease of the intestine

4. the use of diet therapies to reduce possible food allergies in autistic children.

Research in this area has thus far not produced any major revelations. There is, however, some evidence of reduced immune function as well as overactive immune system function in children with autism (for a detailed review, see Krause, He, Gershwin & Shoenfeld, 2002). For example, Croonenberghs, Bosmans, Deboutte, Kenis, and Maes (2002), analyzing whole blood from autistic children, found a significantly higher production of two inflammatory response signaling chemicals—signs of an overactive immune system. It is possible that some symptoms of autism, such as sleep, mood, and attention problems, are reduced after treatment of an infection or removal of allergens from the child's diet because the activity of the immune system is reduced.

AUTOIMMUNE DISEASE

A serious problem arises when the immune system attacks tissues within the body instead of outside foreign agents; such a response can lead to autoimmune disease. The term "auto" in front of immune system refers to a response against "self". For example, in myasthenia gravis, the tissue attacked is in the nervous system. Research indicates an increased rate of autoimmune diseases in families of children with autism, the most common being Type 1 Diabetes, rheumatoid arthritis (adult form), systemic lupus, and hypothyroidism (Comi, Zimmerman, Frye, Law & Peeden, 1999).

Although very early autoimmune diseases could conceivably alter the developmental trajectory of the nervous system, there is no direct evidence that this occurs in children with autism. There is speculation, however, that children with autism may have an abnormal immune system response to common proteins. Antibodies to measles and to human herpesvirus-6 have been shown to cross-react to nervous system proteins, such as myelin basic protein and neuronal-axon filament protein in some subjects with autism (Cook, Perry, Dawson, Wainwright & Leventhal, 1993; Singh, Fudenberg, Emerson & Coleman, 1988; Singh, Warren, Odell, Warren & Cole, 1993; Singh, Lin & Yang, 1998). Such a reaction could lead to an autoimmune disease. More research is needed before any definitive statements about the role of autoimmune system disease in autism can be made.

"LEAKY GUT SYNDROME"

Researchers have also shown some interest in the relationship between autism and antibodies associated with specific allergies to foods, such as those containing casein, glutein, and lactalbumin (Lucarelli et al., 1995). There is speculation that these antibodies might, in conjunction with an inflammatory disease of the intestine, lead to "leaky gut syndrome" and that in turn this disorder might lead to the emergence of autistic symptoms. In leaky gut syndrome, an inflamed intestinal lining allows increased passage of incompletely digested proteins and other antigens across the gut lining into the blood and lymph circulation, thereby eliciting an immune response to these chemicals which can be severe depending on the level of antigen exposure. At present, there is no definitive research supporting a causal link between leaky gut syndrome and autism; however, some, but not all, studies point to gastrointestinal inflammatory symptoms in at least a significant subset of children with autism (D'Eufemia et al., 1996; Horvath & Perman, 2002). Because inflammatory disease of the gut is quite common, occurring in 10–18% of the general population, research needs to explain why autism would occur in only a small subset of those with this disease (Barbezat, Poulton, Milne, Howell, Fawcett & Talley, 2002; Soderholm et al., 2002) (see discussion of treatments based on gut theories of autism in Chapter 5).

VACCINES

An antigen that has received considerable attention in the past few years has been the measles-mumps-rubella (MMR) vaccine. This vaccine can elicit antibodies that cross-react with nervous system proteins. Because of anecdotal reports of autistic symptoms appearing after immunizations, there has been an increase in research investigating a potential vaccine–autism relationship. In response to public and scientific interest in vaccines and autism, and the public health impact that would result if people avoid vaccination, the World Health Organization requested that studies with larger sample sizes be conducted. Although earlier studies suggested a possible link between the MMR vaccine and autism, later, better-controlled studies, using larger samples, have failed to find evidence of such a relationship (Peltola, Patja, Leinikki, Valle, Davidkin & Paunio, 1998; Taylor, Miller, Lingam, Andrews, Simmons & Stowe, 2002). In one such study, Madsen et al (2002) examined the medical records of children born in Denmark from 1991 to 1998, which consisted of 537,303 children, 82% of whom were vaccinated. In this cohort 316 children were diagnosed with Autistic Disorder and 422 with Autistic Spectrum Disorder. Based on their analyses, these researchers found no evidence of increased risk of autism related to use or timing of vaccination. There is, however, significant risk of death and disease in avoiding immunizations.

CONCLUSIONS

In summary, the role that the immune system plays in the development of autism is under active investigation. At present, there does not seem to be a link between vaccines, inoculation protocols, and autism. In general, research has been difficult to conduct in this area for a number of reasons including: the relatively small numbers of subjects available for study; the diversity of symptoms associated with the autism spectrum (and the possible subtypes of autism); measurement problems and the overall expense associated with the use of sophisticated techniques; insufficient animal models for immune system diseases; and finally the problems evaluating cause–effect relationships due to the delays that occur between exposure to a potential insult, such as dietary proteins or inoculation, and development of symptoms.

General perspectives

There is a growing consensus that the answer to what biologically causes autism is not a simple one. Evidence indicates that there are multiple neurological sites involved in autism, suggesting that the etiological process leading to autism is complex, and that this process is genetically based, involving perhaps 15–20 different genes. The consensus of opinion is that autism is most likely not caused by postnatal injury or defective sensory receptors. The environment may, however, play a role in the development of autistic symptoms, most likely during early fetal development. This complexity regarding etiology is reflected in the changing and diverse theoretical perspectives on autism.

Huebner and Lane (2001) reviewed three of the prominent theoretical perspectives on autism: neurological immaturity, heterogeneous etiology, and other etiology. The first perspective, neurological immaturity, proposes that autism results from a failure of brain development. It is based on evidence that multiple structures of the brain (e.g., the cerebellum, amygdala, limbic system, and hippocampus) show a reduced number of neurons, increased cell density, a reduction in dendritic growth, and an enlargement of the brain. In combination these types of problems suggest early disruption in brain formation during fetal development. This disruption could be produced genetically or in combination with some environmental agent. From this theoretical perspective, later developing structures, such as the cortex, are affected in a secondary, but important, way as the cascade of effects from lower to upper brain structures unfolds.

A second perspective reviewed by Huebner and Lane (2001) suggests that autism, as a spectrum disorder, is associated with different symptom patterns, which result from different etiologies. That is, different subcategories or subtypes of autism have different biological causes. A variant of this theory, not mentioned by Huebner and Lane, is that each of the specific symptoms associated with autism is influenced through separate causal pathways, that is, different symptoms have different causes. Another variant suggests that there may be a final common pathway through which all pathways converge.

The final perspective mentioned by Huebner and Lane (2001) does not have the coherency or simplicity of the first two. It suggests a wide variety of explanations for autism that involve diverse genetic and environmental factors. For example, there is speculation that autism occurs in conjunction with other genetic disorders, such as Fragile-X and tuberous sclerosis, although only 10–30% of the individuals with these disorders develop autism; and that the genes responsible for these disorders are involved in the production of some types of autism or autistic symptoms. The findings that a number of environmental factors (e.g., second semester bleeding in mothers) appear to be associated with autism have led other researchers to suggest that various environmental factors may cause autism or trigger an underlying genetic predisposition. Some attention has also been given to the roles that subclinical seizures may play in autism, particularly their roles in inhibiting the functioning of structures, such as the amygdyla and hippocampus, and in producing later clinical seizures. This process, if clarified, could explain why some children with autism develop their symptoms after an apparent period of normal development. For further information on the neurobiological causes of autism the reader is referred to Akshoomoff (2000), Courchesne and Pierce (2000), Huebner and Lane (2001), Simpson and Zionts (2000), and Tager-Flusberg *et al.* (2001).

In the next chapter, a developmental theory of autism will be presented that attempts to incorporate current psychological and biological theory and research into a broader conceptual framework.

References

Akshoomoff, N. (2000) "Neurological underpinnings of autism." In A. M. Wetherby & B. M. Prizant (eds) *Autism spectrum disorders: A transactional developmental perspective.* (Vol. 9) (pp. 109–142). Baltimore: Brookes Publishing Co.

Alarcon, M., Cantor, R., Liu, J., Gilliam, T. & Geschwind, D. (2002) "Autism Genetic Research Exchange Consortium. Evidence for a language quantitative trait locus on chromosome 7q in multiplex autism families." *American Journal of Human Genetics 70* (1), 60–71.

Anderson, G., Horne, W., Chatterjee, D. & Cohen, D. (1990) "The hyperserotonemia of autism." *Annals of the New York Academy of Science 600*, 331–340.

Andres, C. (2002) "Molecular genetics and animal models in autistic disorder." *Brain Research Bulletin 57*(1), 109–119.

Auranen, M., Vanhala, R., Varilo, T., Ayers, K., Kempas, E., Ylisaukko-oja, T., Sinsheimer, J. S., Peltonen, L. & Jarvela, I. (2002) "A genomewide screen for autism-spectrum disorders: evidence for a major susceptibility locus on chromosome 3q25–27." *American Journal of Human Genetics 71*, 777–790.

Bailey, A., Le Couteur, A., Gottesman, I., Bolton, P., Simonoff, E., Yuzda, E. & Rutter, M. (1995) "Autism as a strongly genetic disorder, evidence from a British twin study." *Psychological Medicine 25*(1), 63–77.

Barbezat, G., Poulton, R., Milne, B., Howell, S., Fawcett, J. P. & Talley, N. (2002) "Prevalence and correlates of irritable bowel symptoms in a New Zealand birth cohort." *New Zealand Medical Journal 115(1164), U220.*

Baron-Cohen, S., Ring, H. A., Wheelwright, S., Bullmore, E. T., Brammer, M. J., Simmons, A. & Williams, S. C. (1999) "Social intelligence in the normal and autistic brain: an fMRI study." *European Journal of Neuroscience 11*(6), 1891–1898.

Baron-Cohen, S., Tager-Flusberg, H. & Cohen, D. (1993) *Understanding other minds.* Oxford: Oxford University Press.

Baron-Cohen, S., Tager-Flusberg, H. & Cohen, D. J. (eds) (2000) *Understanding other minds: Perspectives from autism and developmental neuroscience* (Second edition). Oxford: Oxford University Press.

Bauman, M. & Kemper, T. (1997) (eds) *The neurobiology of autism.* Baltimore: The Johns Hopkins University Press.

Betancur, C., Leboyer, M. & Gillberg, C. (2002) "Increased rate of twins among affected sibling pairs with autism." *American Journal of Human Genetics 70*(5), 1381–1383.

Bettleheim, B. (1967) *The empty fortress: Infantile autism and the birth of self.* New York: The Free Press.

Blatt, G., Fitzgerald, C., Guptill, J., Booker, A., Kemper, T. & Bauman, M. (2001) "Density and distribution of hippocampal neurotransmitter receptors in autism, an autoradiographic study." *Journal of Autism and Developmental Disorders 31*(6), 537–543.

Bloom, L. & Tinker, E. (2001) "The intentionality model and language acquisition: Engagement, effort and the essential tension in development." *Monographs of the Society for Research in Child Development 66,* 1–104.

Boddaert, N. & Zilbovicius, M. (2002) "Functional neuroimaging and childhood autism." *Pediatric Radiology 32*(1), 1–7.

Bolton, P. & Griffiths, P. (1997) "Association of tuberous sclerosis of temporal lobes with autism and atypical autism." *Lancet 349*(9049), 392–395.

Brown, A. & Susser, E. (2002) "In utero infection and adult schizophrenia." *Mental Retardation and Developmental Disabilities Research Reviews 8*(1), 51–57.

Buxbaum, J. D., Silverman, J. M., Smith, C. J., Greenberg, D. A., Kilifarski, M., Reichert, J., Cook, E. H., Jr., Fang, Y., Song, C.Y. & Vitale, R. (2002) "Association between a GABRB3 polymorphism and autism." *Molecular Psychiatry 7,* 311–316.

Centers for Disease Control (CDC) (2000) *Prevalence of autism in Brick Township, New Jersey, 1998: Community Report.* www.cdc.gov/ncbddd/pub/BrickReport.pdf.

Chiron, C., Leboyer, M., Leon, F., Jambaque, I., Nuttin, C. & Syrota, A. (1995) "SPECT of the brain in childhood autism, evidence for a lack of normal hemispheric asymmetry." *Developmental Medicine and Child Neurology 37*(10), 849–860.

Chugani, H., DaSilva, E. & Chugani, D. (1996) "Infantile spasms: III. Prognostic implications of bitemporal hypometabolism on positron emission tomography." *Annals of Neurology 39*(5), 643–649.

Chugani, D. C., Muzik, O., Behen, M., Rothermel, R., Janisse, J. J., Lee, J. & Chugani, H. T. (1999) "Developmental changes in brain serotonin synthesis capacity in autistic and nonautistic children." *Annals of Neurology 45*(3), 287–295.

Comi, A., Zimmerman, A., Frye, V., Law, P. & Peeden, J. (1999) "Familial clustering of autoimmune disorders and evaluation of medical risk factors in autism." *Journal of Child Neurology 14*(6), 388–394.

Cook, E. H. (1996) "Brief report: pathophysiology of autism: neurochemistry." *Journal of Autism and Developmental Disorders 26*(2), 221–225.

Cook, E. H., Arora, R., Anderson, G., Berry-Kravis, E., Yan, S., Yeoh, H., Sklena, P., Charak, D. & Leventhal, B. L. (1993) "Platelet serotonin studies in hyperserotonemic relatives of children with autistic disorder." *Life Sciences 52*(25), 2005–2015.

Cook, E. H., Courchesne, R., Lord, C., Cox, N. J., Yan, S., Lincoln, A., Haas, R., Courchesne, E. & Leventhal, B. L. (1997) "Evidence of linkage between the serotonin transporter and autistic disorder." *Molecular Psychiatry 2*(3), 247–250.

Cook, E., Perry, B., Dawson, G., Wainwright, M. & Leventhal, B. (1993) "Receptor inhibition by immunoglobulins: specific inhibition by autistic children, their relatives, and control subjects." *Journal of Autism and Developmental Disorders 23*(1), 67–78.

Courchesne, E., Karns, C., Davis, H., Ziccardi, R., Carper, R. A., Tigue, Z. D., Chisum, H. J., Moses, P., Pierce, K., Lord, C., Lincoln, A. J., Pizzo, S., Schreibman, L., Haas, R., Akshoomoff, N. & Courchesne, R. (2001) "Unusual brain growth patterns in early life in patients with autistic disorder, an MRI study." *Neurology 24*, 57(2), 245–254.

Courchesne, E. & Pierce, K. (2000) "An inside look at neurobiology, etiology, and future research of autism." *Advocate* (July-August), 18–22.

Courchesne, E., Saitoh, O., Yeung-Courchesne, R., Press, G.A., Lincoln, A. J., Haas, R. H. & Schreibman, L. (1994) "Abnormality of cerebellar vermian lobules VI and VII in patients with infantile autism: identification of hypoplastic and hyperplastic subgroups with MR imaging." *American Journal of Roentgenology 162*(1), 123–130.

Courchesne, E., Townsend, J. & Saitoh, O. (1994) "The brain in infantile autism: posterior fossa structures are abnormal." *Neurology 44*(2), 214–223.

Critchley, H. D., Daly, E. M., Bullmore, E.T., Williams, S. C., Van Amelsvoort, T., Robertson, D. M., Rowe, A., Phillips, M., McAlonan, G., Howlin, P. & Murphy, D. G. (2000) "The functional neuroanatomy of social behaviour: changes in cerebral blood flow when people with autistic disorder process facial expressions." *Brain 123* (Pt. 11), 2203–2212.

Croonenberghs, J., Bosmans, E., Deboutte, D., Kenis, G. & Maes, M. (2002) "Activation of the inflammatory response system in autism." *Neuropsychobiology 45*(1), 1–6.

D'Eufemia, P., Celli, M., Finocchiaro, R., Pacifico, L., Viozzi, L., Zaccagnini, M., Cardi, E. & Giardini, O. (1996) "Abnormal intestinal permeability in children with autism." *Acta Paediatrica 85*(9), 1076–1079.

Dhossche, D., Applegate, H., Abraham, A., Maertens, P., Bland, L., Bencsath, A. & Martinez, J. (2002) "Elevated plasma gamma-aminobutyric acid (GABA) levels in autistic youngsters: stimulus for a GABA hypothesis of autism." *Medical Science Monitor 8*(8), PR1–6.

Dunn, W. (1997) "The impact of sensory processing abilities on the daily lives of young children and their families: A conceptual model.2 *Infants and Young Children 9*, 23–35.

Ernst, M., Zametkin, A., Matochik, J., Pascualvaca, D. & Cohen, R. (1997) "Low medial prefrontal dopaminergic activity in autistic children." *Lancet 350*(9078), 638.

Fatemi, S., Halt, A., Stary, A., Kanodia, J., Schulz, R. & Realmuto, G. (2002) "Glutamic acid decarboxylase 65 and 67 kDa proteins are reduced in autistic parietal and cerebellar cortices." *Biological Psychiatry 52*, 805–810.

Flavell, J. (1978) "Metacognitive development." In J. Scandura & C. Brainerd (eds) *Structural process theories of complex human behavior.* Leyden, The Netherlands: Sijthoff.

Folstein, S. & Rosen-Sheidley, B. (2001) "Genetics of autism: complex aetiology for a heterogeneous disorder." *Nature Reviews Genetics 2*(12), 943–955.

Frith, U. & Happé, F. (1994) "Autism: 'Beyond theory of mind'." *Cognition 50*, 115–132.

Gillberg, C. & deSouza, L. (2002) "Head circumference in autism, Asperger syndrome, and ADHD: a comparative study." *Developmental Medicine Child Neurology 44*(5), 296–300.

Grandin, T. (1996) *Thinking in pictures: And other reports from my life with autism.* New York: Random House.

Green, L., Fein, D., Modahl, C., Feinstein, C., Waterhouse, L. & Morris, M. (2001) "Oxytocin and autistic disorder: alterations in peptide forms." *Biological Psychiatry 50*(8), 609–613.

Greenberg, D. A., Hodge, S. E., Sowinski, J. & Nicoll, D. (2001) "Excess of twins among affected sibling pairs with autism: implications for the etiology of autism." *American Journal of Human Genetics 69*(5), 1062–1067.

Hallmayer, J., Glasson, E. J., Bower, C., Petterson, B., Croen, L., Grether, J. & Risch, N. (2002) "On the twin risk in autism." *American Journal of Human Genetics 71*(4), 941–946.

Happé, F. (2000) "Parts and wholes, meanings and minds: Central coherence and its relation to theory of mind." In Baron-Cohen, S., Tager-Flusberg, H. & Cohen, D. (eds) *Understanding other minds, perspectives from autism and developmental neuroscience* (Second edition) (pp. 203–221). Oxford: Oxford University Press.

Happé, F., Ehlers, S., Fletcher, P., Frith, U., Johansson, M., Gillberg, C., Dolan, R., Frackowiak, R. & Frith, C. (1996) "'Theory of mind' in the brain. Evidence from a PET scan study of Asperger syndrome." *Neuroreport 8*(1), 197–201.

Hashimoto, T., Sasaki, M., Fukumizu, M., Hanaoka, S., Sugai, K. & Matsuda H. (2000) "Single-photon emission computed tomography of the brain in autism: effect of the developmental level." *Pediatric Neurology 23*(5), 416–420.

Haznedar, M. M., Buchsbaum, M. S., Wei, T. C., Hof, P. R., Cartwright, C., Bienstock, C. & Hollander, E. (2000) "Limbic circuitry in patients with autism spectrum disorders studied with positron emission tomography and magnetic resonance imaging." *American Journal of Psychiatry 157*(12), 1994–2001.

Hobson, R. P. (1993) *Autism and the development of the mind.* Hillsdale, NJ: Erlbaum.

Horvath, K. & Perman, J. (2002) "Autism and gastrointestinal symptoms." *Current Gastroenterology Report 4*(3), 251–258.

Huebner, R. A. & Dunn, W. (2001) "Introduction and basic concepts." In R. Huebner (ed) *Autism: A sensorimotor approach to management* (pp. 1–40). Gaithersburg, MD: Aspen.

Huebner, R. A. & Lane, S. J. (2001) "Neuropsychological findings, etiology and implications for autism." In R. A. Huebner (ed) *Autism: A sensorimotor approach to management* (pp. 61–99). Gaithersburg, MD: Aspen.

Hultman, C. M., Sparen, P. & Cnattingius, S. (2002) "Perinatal risk factors for infantile autism." *Epidemiology 13*(4), 417–423.

Hunt, J. McV. (1961) *Intelligence and experience.* New York: Ronald Press.

Jakovljevic, M., Muck-Seler, D., Pivac, N. & Crncevic, Z. (1998) "Platelet 5-HT and plasma cortisol concentrations after dexamethasone suppression test in patients with different time course of schizophrenia." *Neuropsychobiology 37*(3), 142–145.

Jarrold, C. (1997) "Pretend play in autism: Executive explanations." In J. Russell (ed) *Autism as an executive disorder* (pp. 101–140). Oxford: Oxford University Press.

Jones, M. & Szatmari, P. (2002) "A risk-factor model of epistatic interaction, focusing on autism." *American Journal of Medical Genetics 114*, 558–565.

Jordan, R. (1999) *Autism spectrum disorders: An introductory handbook for practitioners.* London: David Fulton.

Juul-Dam, N., Townsend, J. & Courchesne, E. (2001) "Prenatal, perinatal, and neonatal factors in autism, pervasive developmental disorder–not otherwise specified, and the general population." *Pediatrics 107*(4), E63.

Kanner, L. (1943) "Autistic disturbances of affective content." *The Nervous Child 2*, 217–250.

Krause, I., He, X. S., Gershwin, M. E. & Shoenfeld, Y. (2002) "Brief report: immune factors in autism: a critical review." *Journal of Autism and Developmental Disorders 32*(4), 337–345.

Lainhart, J. E., Piven, J., Wzorek, M., Landa, R., Santangelo, S. L., Coon, H. & Folstein, S. E. (1997) "Macrocephaly in children and adults with autism." *Journal of the American Academy of Child and Adolescent Psychiatry 36*(2), 282–290.

LeDoux, J. (2002) *Synaptic self: How our brains become who we are.* New York: Viking Press.

Leslie, A. M. (1987) "Pretense and representation: The origins of 'theory of mind'." *Psychological Review 94*, 412–426.

Lewis, M. & Baumeister, A. (1982) "Stereotyped mannerisms in mentally retarded persons: Animal models and theoretical analyses." In N. Ellis (ed) *International review of mental retardation* (Vol. 7) (pp. 123–161). New York: Academic Press.

Lovaas, O. I. (1977) *The autistic child: Language development through behavior modification.* New York: Irvington.

Lucarelli, S., Frediani, T., Zingoni, A. M., Ferruzzi, F., Giardini, O., Quintieri, F., Barbato, M., D'Eufemia, P. & Cardi, E. (1995) "Food allergy and infantile autism." *Panminerva Medicine 37*(3), 137–141.

Luna, B., Minshew, N. J., Garver, K. E., Lazar, N. A., Thulborn, K. R., Eddy, W. F. & Sweeney, J. (2002) "Neocortical system abnormalities in autism: an fMRI study of spatial working memory." *Neurology 59*(6), 834–840.

Luria, A. R. (1961) *The role of speech in the regulation of normal and abnormal behaviors.* New York: Liverright.

Madsen, K. M., Hviid, A., Vestergaard, M., Schendel, D., Wohlfahrt, J., Thorsen, P., Olsen, J. & Melbye, M. (2002) "A population-based study of measles, mumps, and rubella vaccination and autism." *New England Journal of Medicine 347*(19), 1477–1482.

McKusick, V. *et al.* (not listed) (eds) (2003) *Online Mendelian Inheritance in Man (OMIM).* National Center for Biotechnology Information, US National Institutes of Health. www.ncbi.nlm.nih.gov/entrez/query.fcgidb=OMIM.

Menold, M., Shao, Y., Wolpert, C., Donnelly, L., Raiford, K., Martin, E., Ravan, S., Abramson, R., Wright, H., Delong, G., Cuccaro, M., Pericak-Vance, M. & Gilbert, J. (2001) "Association analysis of chromosome 15 gabaa receptor subunit genes in autistic disorder." *Journal of Neurogenetics 15*, 245–259.

Michel, G. & Moore, C. (1995) *Developmental psychobiology: An interdisciplinary approach.* Cambridge, MA: MIT Press.

Modahl, C., Green, L., Fein, D., Morris, M., Waterhouse, L., Feinstein, C. & Levin, H. (1998) "Plasma oxytocin levels in autistic children." *Biological Psychiatry 43*, 270–277.

Muller, R. A., Behen, M. E., Rothermel, R. D., Chugani, D. C., Muzik, O., Mangner, T. J. & Chugani, H. T. (1999) "Brain mapping of language and auditory perception in high-functioning autistic adults: a PET study." *Journal of Autism and Developmental Disorders 29*(1), 19–31.

Peltola, H., Patja, A., Leinikki, P., Valle, M., Davidkin, I. & Paunio, M. (1998) "No evidence for measles, mumps, and rubella vaccine-associated inflammatory bowel disease or autism in a 14-year prospective study." *Lancet 351*(9112), 1327–1328.

Pierce, K. & Courchesne, E. (2001) "Evidence for a cerebellar role in reduced exploration and stereotyped behavior in autism." *Biological Psychiatry 49*(8), 655–664.

Piven, J. (1997) "The biological basis of autism." *Current Opinions Neurobiology 7*(5), 708–712.

Piven, J., Arndt, S., Bailey, J. & Andreason, N. (1996) "Regional brain enlargement in autism: a magnetic resonance imaging study." *Journal of the American Academy of Child Adolescent Psychiatry 35*(4), 530–536.

Risch, N., Spiker, D., Lotspeich, L., Nouri, N., Hinds, D., Hallmayer, J., Kalaydjieva, L., McCague, P., Dimiceli, S., Pitts, T., Nguyen, L., Yang, J., Harper, C., Thorpe, D., Vermeer, S., Young, C., Wiese-Slater, S., Rogers, T., Salmon, B., Nicholas, P., Petersen, P. B., Pingree, C., McMahon, W., Wong, D., Cavalli-Sforza, J. J., Kraemer, H. C. & Myers, R. M. (1999) "A genomic screen of autism: evidence for a multilocus etiology." *American Journal of Human Genetics 65*, 493–507.

Robbins, T. (1997) "Integrating the neurobiological and neuropsychological dimensions of autism." In J. Russell (ed) *Autism as an executive disorder* (pp. 21–53). Oxford: Oxford University Press.

Robinson, P., Schutz, C., Macciardi, F., White, B. & Holden, J. (2001) "Genetically determined low maternal serum dopamine beta-hydroxylase levels and the etiology of autism spectrum disorders." *American Journal Medical Genetics 100*, 30–36.

Rodier, P. M., Ingram, J. L., Tisdale, B., Nelson, S. & Romano, J. (1996) "Embryological origin for autism: developmental anomalies of the cranial nerve motor nuclei." *Journal of Comparative Neurology 370*(2), 247–261.

Russell, J. (1997) "How executive disorders can bring about an inadequate 'theory of mind'." In J. Russell (ed) *Autism as an executive disorder* (pp. 256–304). Oxford: Oxford University Press.

Schaefer, G. B., Thompson, J. N., Bodensteiner, J. B., McConnell, J. M., Kimberling, W. J., Gay, C. T., Dutton, W. D., Hutchings, D. C. & Gray, S. B. (1996) "Hypoplasia of the cerebellar vermis in neurogenetic syndromes." *Annals of Neurology 39*(3), 382–385.

Schultz, R. T., Gauthier, I., Klin, A., Fulbright, R. K., Anderson, A. W., Volkmar, F., Skudlarski, P., Lacadie, C., Cohen, D. J. & Gore, J. C. (2000) "Abnormal ventral temporal cortical activity during face discrimination among individuals with autism and Asperger syndrome." *Archives General Psychiatry 57*(4), 331–340.

Serajee, S., Zhong, H., Nabi, R. & Huq, A. (2003) "The metabotropic glutamate receptor 8 gene at 7q31: partial duplication and possible association with autism." *Journal of Medical Genetics 40*, e42.

Shao, Y., Cuccaro, M. L., Hauser, E. R., Raiford, K. L., Menold, M. M., Wolpert, C. M., Ravan, S. A., Elston, L., Decena, K., Donnelly, S. L., Abramson, R. K., Wright, H. H., DeLong, G. R., Gilbert, J. R. & Pericak-Vance, M. A. (2003) "Fine mapping of autistic disorder to chromosome 15q11–q13 by use of phenotypic subtypes." *American Journal of Human Genetics 72*(3), 539–548.

Shao, Y., Raiford, K. L., Wolpert, C. M., Cope, H. A., Ravan, S. A., Ashley-Koch, A. A., Abramson, R. K., Wright, H. H., DeLong, R. G., Gilbert, J. R., Cuccaro, M. L. & Pericak-Vance, M. A. (2002) "Phenotypic homogeneity provides increased support for linkage on chromosome 2 in autistic disorder." *American Journal of Human Genetics 70*(4), 1058–1061.

Simpson, R. L. & Zionts, P. (2000) *Autism: Information for professionals and parents.* Austin, TX: Pro-Ed.

Singh, V. K., Fudenberg, H., Emerson, D. & Coleman, M. (1988) "Immunodiagnosis and immunotherapy in autistic children." *Annals of the New York Academy of Sciences 540*, 602–604.

Singh, V. K., Lin, S. X. & Yang, V. C. (1998) "Serological association of measles virus and human herpesvirus-6 with brain autoantibodies in autism." *Clinical Immunology Immunopathology 89*(1), 105–108.

Singh, V. K., Warren, R. P., Odell, J. D., Warren, W. L. & Cole, P. (1993) "Antibodies to myelin basic protein in children with autistic behavior." *Brain Behavior and Immunity 7*(1), 97–103.

Sleigh, M. & Lickliter, R. (1997) "Augmented prenatal auditory stimulation alters postnatal perception, arousal, and survival in bobwhite quail chicks." *Developmental Psychobiology 30*(3), 201–212.

Smalley, S. L. (1997) "Genetic influences in childhood-onset psychiatric disorders: autism and attention-deficit/hyperactivity disorder." *American Journal of Human Genetics 60*(6), 1276–1282.

Soderholm, J. D., Yang, P. C., Ceponis, P., Vohra, A., Riddell, R., Sherman, P. M. & Perdue, M. H. (2002) "Chronic stress induces mast cell-dependent bacterial adherence and initiates mucosal inflammation in rat intestine." *Gastroenterology 123*(4), 1099–1108.

Sparks, B. F., Friedman, S. D., Shaw, D. W., Aylward, E. H., Echelard, D., Artru, A. A., Maravilla, K. R., Giedd, J. N., Munson, J., Dawson, G. & Dager, S. R. (2002) "Brain structural abnormalities in young children with autism spectrum disorder." *Neurology 59*(2), 184–192.

Stromland, K., Nordin, V., Miller, M., Akerstrom, B. & Gillberg, C. (1994) "Autism in thalidomide embryopathy: a population study." *Developmental Medicine and Child Neurology 36*(4), 351–356.

Sultana, R., Yu, C.-E., Yu, J., Munson, J., Chen, D., Hua, W., Estes, A., Cortes, F., de la Barra, F., Yu, D., Haider, S. T., Trask, B. J., Green, E. D., Raskind, W. H., Disteche, C. M., Wijsman, E., Dawson, G., Storm, D. R., Schellenberg, G. D. & Villacres, E. C. (2002) "Identification of a novel gene on chromosome 7q11.2 interrupted by a translocation breakpoint in a pair of autistic twins." *Genomics 80*, 129–134.

Tager-Flusberg, H., Joseph, R. & Folstein, S. (2001) "Current directions in research on autism." *Mental Retardation and Developmental Disabilities Research Reviews 7*, 21–29.

Taylor, B., Miller, E., Lingam, R., Andrews, N., Simmons, A. & Stowe, J. (2002) "Measles, mumps, and rubella vaccination and bowel problems or developmental regression in children with autism: population study." *British Medical Journal 324*(7334), 393–396.

Teicher, M. H., Andersen, S. L., Polcari, A., Anderson, C. M. & Navalta, C. P. (2002) "Developmental neurobiology of childhood stress and trauma." *Psychiatric Clinics of North America 25*(2), 397–426, vii–viii.

Tsai, L. (1998) "Medical interventions for students with autism." In R. Simpson & B. Myles (eds) *Educating children and youth with autism* (pp. 151–184). Austin, TX: Pro-Ed.

Turner, M. (1997) "Toward an executive dysfunction account of repetitive behavior." In J. Russell (ed) *Autism as an executive disorder* (pp. 57–100). Oxford: Oxford University Press.

Volkmar, F. R. (2001) "Pharmacological interventions in autism: theoretical and practical issues." *Journal of Clinical Child Psychology 30*(1), 80–87.

Vygotsky, L. S. (1978) *Mind in society: The development of higher psychologiscal processes.* (Edited by M. Cole, V. John-Steiner, S. Scribner & E. Souberman) Cambridge, MA: Harvard University Press.

Waterhouse, L., Fein, D. & Modahl, C. (1996) "Neurofunctional mechanisms in autism." *Psychological Review 103*(3), 457–489.

Wertsch, J. V. (1979) "From social interaction to higher social processes: A clarification and application of Vygotsky's theory." *Human Development 22*, 1–22.

Winslow, J. T. & Insel, T. R. (2002) "The social deficits of the oxytocin knockout mouse." *Neuropeptides 36*, 221–229.

Woodhouse, W., Bailey, A., Rutter, M., Bolten, P., Baird, G. & Le Conteur, A. (1996) "Head circumference in autism and other pervasive developmental disorders." *Journal of Child Psychology and Psychiatry 37*(6), 665–671.

Zilbovicius, M., Boddaert, N., Belin, P., Poline, J. B., Remy, P., Mangin, J. F., Thivard, L., Barthelemy, C. & Samson, Y. (2000) "Temporal lobe dysfunction in childhood autism: a PET study. Positron emission tomography." *American Journal of Psychiatry 157*(12), 1988–1993.

Zilbovicius, M., Garreau, B., Samson, Y., Remy, P., Barthelemy, C., Syrota, A. & Lelord, G. (1995) "Delayed maturation of the frontal cortex in childhood autism." *American Journal of Psychiatry 152*(2), 248–252.

CHAPTER 4

Toward a Developmental Theory of Autism

In the last chapter a variety of theories of autism were summarized. What should strike any student of autism is that there is a considerable difference of opinion about the origins of this disorder. Existing theories vary considerably in the specific biological and psychological factors focused upon to explain its emergence. This theoretical diversity is a reflection of the status of empirical research. Although intriguing insights into the development of autism have been revealed through research, no definitive cause or set of causes has been found. Both theory and research have typically focused on only one or two pieces of the autism puzzle, such as a particular cognitive, sensory, motor, affective, social, or biological process. In this chapter, an attempt will be made to put together theoretically the different pieces of the autism puzzle in order to develop a broader and more dynamic perspective regarding its origins. A theory of autism is presented that, although not novel in the explanatory constructs it includes, strives to integrate these constructs into a single, comprehensive, developmental framework. Before describing this theory, several assumptions that guided its development will be discussed.

Assumptions about a developmental theory of autism

Theories of autism are constructions; that is, best guesses about what it is and how it evolves. The scientific process of theory formation is not really that different from the speculative enterprise engaged in by anyone who attempts to understand the unfamiliar and mysterious happenings in the world around them. In the area of autism, parents, clinicians, and researchers all develop their own unique theories about the origins of this disorder. Theories are formed from one or more of the following sources:

1. facts established through empirical research and/or clinical observation

2. basic assumptions about the nature of the phenomenon studied

3. other theories

4. through logic, in which inferences are made from what is known and assumed to that which is not yet known.

The theory of autism to be presented in this chapter was influenced in part by the factual information presented in Chapter 2 and the theories described in Chapter 3. It was also influenced by a set of general assumptions about autism, how a theory of autism should be structured, and what this theory should try to achieve. These assumptions are described in this section. Because of the academic nature of this discussion, some readers, after examining the overview section, may want to skip to the next section which describes a developmental theory of autism.

Overview

The first assumption that guided theory development is that a comprehensive theory of autism should acknowledge that autism is a developmental disorder that emerges during the first two years of life; a disorder that is not easily identifiable in its initial stages and that substantially changes in its characteristics over time. A comprehensive theory of autism should attempt to describe the processes underlying its initial emergence and later development.

Second, a comprehensive theory should recognize that autism is a complex disorder that involves a variety of symptoms, deficiencies, and atypical behaviors which fall into the domains (arousal/affective, sensory, motor, cognitive, language, social, and self-regulation) described in Chapter 2. The task of a comprehensive theory is to describe how these various symptoms and the processes underlying them are interrelated.

Third, a comprehensive theory should account for the considerable individual differences in the characteristics and development of persons labeled autistic. For example, it should attempt to explain why some children with autism have motor and/or sensory problems and others do not, and what the developmental implications are of having problems in these various areas. Ideally, a comprehensive theory should provide insights not only into the reasons for differences in individuals diagnosed with Autistic Disorder, but also differences between individuals with this diagnosis and other individuals on the autism spectrum with other diagnoses, particularly those with Asperger's Syndrome and PDD-NOS. Such a theory should allow for the possibility that different causal pathways will be needed to explain individual differences in outcomes.

Finally, a comprehensive theory of autism should make sense at both a biological and psychobehavioral level. In the theory of autism described in this chapter, it is assumed that at one level autism is a biologically based disorder, at least in part genetically based, which affects brain development and functioning at an anatomical and neurophysiological level. At another level, autism is a dynamic composite of psychological/behavioral processes that are affected by both biological and environmental factors. A comprehensive theory should describe the interface of these biological and psychological/behavioral processes; that is, make sense of the diverse symptomatology associated with autism and integrate what is known biologically and psychologically about them into a coherent conceptual framework.

The development of a theory that incorporates these assumptions/characteristics is a demanding task. The theory presented in this chapter represents a first approximation of how it might be best constructed. In the remainder of this section, these assumptions/characteristics of a developmental theory of autism will be discussed in greater detail.

Developmental features

The theory of autism presented in this chapter is influenced by lifespan conceptualizations of human development. The lifespan perspective has been heavily influenced by the work of Paul Baltes and his colleagues (Baltes, 1987; Baltes, Reese & Lipsitt, 1980). Within a lifespan conceptual framework, development is viewed as a process that is *lifelong*, continuing from conception to death and involving both change and continuity. Development occurs in *multiple domains*, somewhat arbitrarily referred to as: *physical*, which includes sensory and motor processes; *cognitive*, which includes language, learning, perceptual, and thought processes; *emotional*, which includes activation-arousal processes, as well as primary and secondary emotional states such as anxiety, fear, pleasure, joy, and guilt; and *social*, which includes a variety of behavioral skills and processes that are necessary for effective social interaction. Development in all of these domains is influenced by biological factors, operating in conjunction with social-learning processes.

The lifespan perspective emphasizes not only that development is lifelong, but also that it is *multidirectional*, with some processes experiencing growth, and others showing decline or not changing. In this regard, it is inter-esting to note that autism represents a fascinating pattern of uneven develop-ment, involving both strengths and limitations. Development is also viewed as having *plasticity*; that is, it can be significantly altered in either positive or negative directions depending on the experiences of the individual. Although genes set limits and genetic deficiencies can restrict the boundaries in which development occurs, the environment, including programs of prevention and intervention, also has a powerful influence on how development occurs. Moreover, development is significantly influenced by the *historical and cultural context* in which it takes place. In the area of autism, significant changes have occurred in the last 50 years in our knowledge about this disorder and the types of intervention approaches that are available, including our realization about how critical it is for interventions to begin as early as possible and to be multidimensional in nature. As a consequence of these changes, the ways autism manifests itself has been altered, sometimes in very significant ways.

Development is also viewed as being *multiply influenced*, not only at a general level by biological, maturational, and environmental factors, but also at a more specific level by interactions between the various developmental processes (e.g., sensory, motor, and cognitive). This multivariate and interactional perspective is a prominent feature of the theory of autism discussed later in this chapter.

A final feature of the lifespan approach to the study of development is that it utilizes the perspectives and knowledge of *different disciplines*. In the area of autism a multidisciplinary perspective has been invaluable. Research and treatment on autism has come from fields such as neurobiology, neurophysiology, immunology, developmental biology, dietary science, psychopharmacology, physical and occupational therapy, audiology, optomalogy, speech and communication, education, developmental psychology, clinical psychology, and public policy. For a more complete discussion of Baltes' and other conceptions about the nature of development, the reader is referred to Sigelman and Shaffer (1995).

Individual differences

As a subdiscipline within psychology, developmental psychology has emphasized the importance of studying individual differences. Historically, two general approaches have been utilized by researchers studying human behavior. One approach attempts to understand the differences between char-acteristics of two or more groups of individuals by looking at their average or typical behavior; for example, individuals with autism, and how they are different from other groups without developmental delays or with delays not related to autism. The other approach emphasizes looking at differences between individuals within a group and what produces this variation; for example, differences within a group of individuals with a label of Autistic Disorder or differences between individuals who lie on the broader autism spectrum. Both of these approaches have merit.

Developmental psychologists argue that in order to understand the dynamics of development it is at least as important to focus on the reasons why variation occurs within a specific group of persons as between different groups of people. Developmentalists note that the differences within a specific group, such as people of a certain gender, race, or disability, are often as large, if not larger, than differences between groups. This focus on individuals has particular merit when the differences that exist within a group are marked, such as is the case in persons with autism. For example, the range of IQs of people with autism is greater than that of people who display typical development. This variability should raise questions about whether the biological and psychological factors that influence development in autistic individuals at the low end of the IQ continuum are the same as those that influence development in autistic individuals at the high end of the IQ continuum. Similarly, other questions that are in need of answers include whether autistic individuals with sensory and/or motor problems develop differently from autistic individuals without these problems.

The theory to be presented in this chapter is directed at understanding the differences within groups of people on the autism spectrum, as well as differences between groups of people with and without autism; that is, the theory has broad implications for understanding not only autism, but also other types of developmental disorders as well as normal development. Examination of variation within autistic groups and between autistic and nonautistic groups should assist researchers in their search for the specific etiologies of autism and clinicians in their decision-making concerning how best to structure prevention and intervention programs.

Biology, behavior, and the environment

Although historically there has been a tendency for theories of autism to emphasize explanatory constructs that are either biological, environmental, or psychological in nature, the contention here is that a comprehensive theory should attend to all of these processes. Figures 4.1 and 4.2 (p. 151) present a way of thinking about the relationships between these processes.

Figure 4.1 describes the emergence of the phenotype and the influence of the genotype and environment on the phenotype, as well as other relationships between these constructs. The genotype consists of those genes that an individual inherits from their parents. Some, but not all, of the genes an individual inherits influence the development of the phenotype. As genes are expressed, the phenotype is formed. The phenotype consists of the biological and behavioral expressions of the gene, including brain anatomy, brain neurochemistry, and observable psychobehavioral processes (e.g., motor, sensory, emotion, cognitive, and language). The formation of the phenotype is influenced by the genotype working in close conjunction with the environment. The genotype also influences the environment in the sense that it places restrictions on the range of ways an environment can influence the phenotype. For example, light from the environment would not be able to influence the development of the retina in the eye if genes did not first influence the production of retinal cells. The environment, however, is critical to the devel-

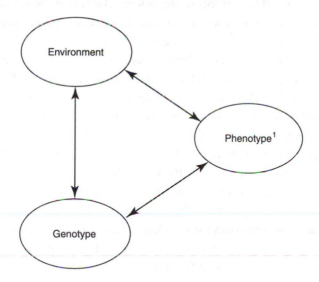

Figure 4.1 A bioenvironmental model of development

---

1   Includes both biological and behavioral systems (e.g., brain anatomy and neurochemical processes as well as motor, sensory, cognitive, affective, and linguistic processes).

opment of vision. Without appropriate light stimulation from outside of the retinal cells, vision—along with supportive brain structures—would not develop appropriately.

The environment consists of both genetically and nongenetically produced biological agents within the individual, such as proteins and toxins, and also external physical and social factors outside of the individual, such as factories that produce toxins, and home intervention programs. Although the environment is not typically thought of as being able to influence the genotype, it can do so, for example, through radiation that leads to gene mutation or through its influence on mating patterns (who marries whom). Some researchers have speculated that the pattern of mating in Silicon Valley (between partners who both have high "technological" abilities) in California has resulted in an increase in autism in this geographic area. The biochemical environment within an individual also influences which genes within the genotype are expressed, as well as how genetically based structures evolve. The environment which is operative from conception influences the development of the phenotype throughout the life span. Some researchers suggest that environmental factors, operating during the first trimester of pregnancy, trigger autism in individuals who are already genetically predisposed to this disorder (see Chapter 3). The phenotype not only is influenced by the environment but also influences both the social and nonsocial aspects of the environment through the biological and behavioral characteristics and actions of the individual. The phenotype also influences the genotype in the sense that it affects what genes are expressed as well as the assortative mating process. In summary, the model presented in Figure 4.1 describes development as a very dynamic process, a product of continuous reciprocal interactions between the genotype, the environment, and the phenotype.

Figure 4.2 depicts further the process through which the environment influences the development of the phenotype. The physical and social environment directly influences the development of biological structures, such as the brain, as well as the biochemical functions associated with these structures, and indirectly influences the development of an array of psychobehavioral processes. Biological processes mediate the relationships between the environment and psychobehavioral development. As development proceeds, the behavioral characteristics of an individual in turn influence his/her environment.

For example, the environment can facilitate development through the provision of appropriate forms and amounts of sensory (sound, light, touch, etc.) and dietary inputs, as well as inhibit, arrest, or distort development through sensory deprivations and harmful biochemical (bacterial, viral, and toxic) agents. The environment influences both typical and atypical development by affecting how the brain is wired, how neurochemical and hormonal processes occur, the size of different neurological structures, and more generally through its impact on the maturation of the brain. Through its influence on biological structures such as the brain, the physical and social environment indirectly affects the development of arousal/activation, sensory, motor, cognitive, language, and socioemotional processes. In turn, as these processes emerge they exert a reciprocal influence on development at the biological level as well as on the environment.

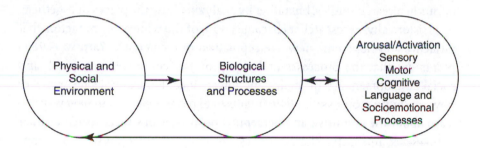

Figure 4.2 Environmental and biological influences on development

A question that is sometimes raised is, If autism is biologically caused through genetic pathways, why should research be concerned with examining the environmental context in which autism emerges? One reason, suggested earlier, is that the environment may provide essential triggers that combine with genetic mechanisms to produce the disorder. A second reason is that the environment also influences the specific ways autism is manifested at a symptomalogical level, including its severity. Thus, although genes provide a broad blueprint for the development of autism, the environment plays a vital role in determining how that blueprint is enacted. Research suggests that through early prevention and intervention programs, the trajectory of this disorder may be significantly altered from a behavioral perspective, as well as at a neurobiological level. The reader is referred to Chapters 3 and 5 for further discussion of the environment's role in biological and psycho-behavioral development.

Systemic development and analysis

In the social and biological sciences, the importance of maintaining a systemic perspective has often been advocated (Smith & Thelen, 1993). This perspective emphasizes that in studying a phenomenon like human development it is often misleading to concentrate on one domain of development in isolation from other domains, that is, without considering the interrelationships between different domains of development. If this perspective is adopted, a phenomenon such as autism cannot be adequately studied by studying only one of its characteristics, but rather the various characteristics of this disorder must be examined in terms of their relationships with each other. Metaphorically, adoption of this perspective means that the puzzle of autism cannot be solved by looking only at separate pieces of the puzzle, as often occurs in research studies, but rather by analyzing how the pieces fit together.

Historically, as researchers became aware of the wide array of factors that influence development, new conceptualizations emerged. Yarrow (1981) points out that the processes underlying motor, cognitive, emotional, and social development are all "delicately" intertwined. For example, he describes how emerging motor skills allow infants to explore the world in new ways, to learn about the cognitive and perceptual properties of objects (such as their permanence and spatial characteristics), to cope with their physical surroundings, and to develop a sense of independence. Through various motor behaviors (e.g., sucking, crawling, and walking) and early protocommunications (crying, gestures, sounds), infants also learn to regulate emotions, elicit social interactions, and satisfy their needs. Yarrow further points out that emotions of the infant, when controlled, enhance alertness and cognitive functioning but, if uncontrolled, interfere with attention, learning, and motor coordination. Moreover, as infants learn to make finer discriminations, adult facial features become familiar and evoke pleasure, or if unfamiliar elicit fear. Infant emotional states become associated with people and lead to social approach or avoidance behaviors. Infants and parents engage in a complex dance that progresses with development. Thus, in attempting to understand both typical and atypical child development, there has been increasing recognition that the relationships between the component processes within the child, as well as the relationships between these processes and the social/physical environment, must be examined.

From a systems theory perspective, different levels of development, including the biological, psychological, and behavioral, are dynamically interconnected (Thelen, 1995). In place of simple models emphasizing unidirectional relationships between a specific psychological function or environmental event and a developmental outcome, development is viewed as emerging through interaction of individual and environmental processes, with the pattern of relationships between these processes changing across time. Behavior and the context in which it occurs give meaning to each other; the child cannot be understood without examining the present and historical context in which development occurs, and the environment, including socialization and parenting practices, cannot be understood without examining the characteristics of the child. From a goodness of fit perspective, child development is viewed in terms of how well the social environment interfaces with the characteristics of the child (Thomas & Chess, 1977).

With the advent of increasingly complex conceptualizations about infant development, investigators have been challenged to formulate new and more appropriate research strategies. Because of a gap between these complex conceptual models and existing empirical methodologies, theories often served more as a general guide for research rather than as specific templates to be tested. However, as new designs, creative measurement schemes, and multivariate statistical methods (e.g., structural modeling) evolved for examining the multiple and changing characteristics of children and their environments, such multidimensional theories were able to be evaluated. This paradigmatic and methodological shift has revolutionized the way development is studied.

In autism research, however, studies still focus on specific pieces of the infant puzzle, typically in a cross-sectional fashion. At present, new dynamic theoretical conceptualizations are needed to study this disorder and how it develops over time. It is contended here that in order to understand autism, the collective activity of all its component processes must be examined, along with the changes resulting from their dynamic interplay. As Smith and Thelen (1993) have pointed out, emergent behaviors show patterns over time that are not contained in any of their components when evaluated in a cross-sectional fashion. In the next section, a theory for studying autism is presented that incorporates the aforementioned systemic and developmental characteristics. This theory is presented in Figure 4.3 (p. 156).

A developmental theory of autism

Before discussing this theory in detail, several of its general characteristics will be noted.

1. It is a multivariate theory that postulates that a number of factors have to be considered in order to understand the development of autism in its diverse manifestations. Three of the constructs in the theory relate to symptoms/processes referred to in the DSM-IV definition of autism (social interaction, communication/language, and stereotypical responses) and four other constructs consist of symptoms/processes (arousal/activation/emotion, sensory, motor, and cognitive) that are not a formal part of this definition.

2. The self-regulatory construct in Figure 4.3 (p. 156) refers to both adaptive and maladaptive coping processes that can be motoric, cognitive, linguistic, or social in nature. Stereotyped patterns of interests, activities, and behaviors are viewed as maladaptive coping mechanisms that serve to reduce anxiety in the short term, but create long-term problems for the individual.

3. All of the theoretical constructs can be considered either directly or indirectly as "causes" that exert influence on the other constructs, thus constituting a complex chain of "causality" that results in the emergence of the symptoms of autism.

4. The theory postulates that the characteristics referred to in the seven constructs change over time, that is, with development; thus the system as a whole is in a constant state of reorganization.

5. All of the constructs in the theory can be considered at either a psychobehavioral or a neurobiological level; thus the theory can be considered as psychobiological in nature.

6. Although all of the processes exert influence, either directly or indirectly on the other processes, the three processes on the left of Figure 4.3 (arousal/activation/emotion, sensory, and motor processes) emerge developmentally earlier than the other processes (cognition, language/communication, and social interaction characteristics) and for that reason may play a primary role in the emergence of autism.

7. The theory allows, however, for the possibility that a specific process may play either a primary, secondary, or minimal role in the development of different symptom patterns on the autism spectrum. For example, individuals who have motor problems are hypothesized to have a different trajectory of development than individuals without motor problems. Thus, the theory is directed at explaining individual differences in people with autism.

8. The six processes to the left of the self-regulatory construct in Figure 4.3 (arousal/emotion, sensory, motor, cognition, communication, and social interaction) all influence the development of the self-regulatory system, which in turn reciprocally influences these six processes.[1]

In summary, the developmental theory outlined in Figure 4.3 emphasizes the important role that early emerging processes, specifically the sensory, motor, and the arousal/activation/emotion processes, play in the development of the cognitive, language/communication, and social interaction processes. All of these processes in turn play a critical role in the development of the self-regulatory system. The self-regulatory system, which has motor, cognitive, linguistic, and social response components, influences the manner in which individuals control their emotions, cognitions, and behaviors. Thus, self-regulation plays an essential role in the completion of physical, academic, and social interaction tasks. Self-regulatory skills assist individuals not only in learning but also in maintaining and transferring what they have learned to new situations without external assistance. Although individuals with autism differ in their specific pattern of symptoms, they share in common an inability to self-regulate.

In the remainder of this section each of the constructs in the theory, outlined in Figure 4.3, will be described along with their interrelationship to the other constructs.

Arousal/activation and emotion processes

As discussed in Chapters 2 and 3, research and clinical observations of individuals with autism suggest that considerable variability exists within as well as across individuals in their level of arousal/activation and the types of emotions they display. Children with autism appear to operate at the extremes. For example, they may react to the environment with high emotional intensity, show little emotional response, and/or fluctuate

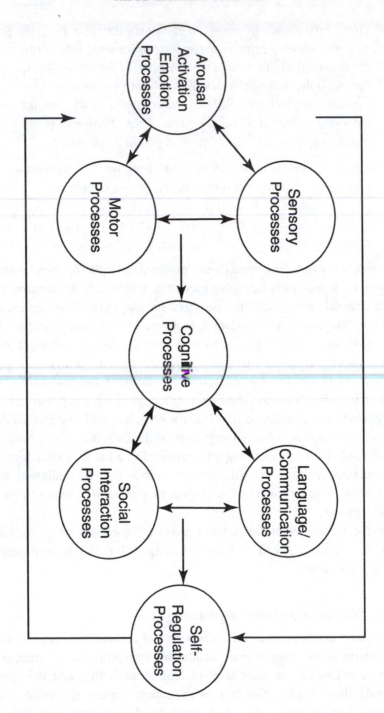

Figure 4.3 A developmental theory of autism

emotionally between these extremes; sometimes displaying great anxiety, fear, or panic and at other times displaying little or no overt response, thus appearing affectively flat. Not only do specific individuals show variability in their emotional behavior over time, they also frequently differ from one another in their specific response style or temperament. For example, they may be either highly arrhythmic in their eating, sleeping, and elimination habits or highly routinized in these behaviors. They may be extremely upset when confronted with new or novel situations or they may be indifferent to such situations. Biologically, the existence of an arousal/activation problem in children with autism is suggested by research indicating structural anomalies in the development of brain stem, the limbic system, and the reticular activation system as well as biochemical anomalies (see Chapter 3).

The theory outlined in Figure 4.3 postulates that problems in the arousal/activation and emotion system may have a major influence on the development and functioning of the sensory, motor, cognitive, language, social, and self-regulatory systems. At a sensory level, autistic children who are experiencing a high state of arousal would be expected to show a pattern of hypersensitivity, particularly in environments that are changing, novel, and/or more intense. In contrast to more typically developing children, they would also be expected to show slower habituation responses to sensory input; that is, it would take them longer to adapt to new patterns of stimulation. Conversely, problems of hyposensitivity and the absence of an orienting response toward stimulus inputs, such as pain, hot, and/or cold, could be explained by a state of low arousal. As suggested in Chapter 2, hyposensitivity could also be reflective of the operation of a primitive self-regulatory mechanism for dealing with a sensory environment that is overwhelming, specifically withdrawal. In summary, the theory described in Figure 4.3 suggests that hypersensitivity and hyposensitivity to auditory, visual, tactual, gustatory, and/or olfactory stimuli could be explained via a temporary fluctuation in and/or a more permanent defect in the arousal/activation system.

A state of hyperarousal could also explain at least some of the motor symptoms associated with autism, including problems related to the development of gross and fine motor skills, as well as problems of muscular tension, coordination, balance, and motor planning. Hyperarousal would also be expected to be associated with a state of hyperactivity. In contrast, low arousal would be compatible with a state of low muscle tone, lethargy, and inactivity.

Cognitively, individuals in a state of hyperarousal would likely be distractible and experience problems in attentional focusing, attention span, scanning, and processing information as well as in short-term and long-term memory (Dawson & Levy, 1989). As a consequence, learning would be slower, and more complex cognitive processes, such as abstract thinking, problem-solving, social comprehension, and self-understanding, would show particularly adverse effects. Although the process would be somewhat different, low arousal would likely lead to a similar pattern of problems due to inattention rather than distractibility.[2]

In the theory of autism outlined in Figure 4.3, arousal/activation and emotion processes are also hypothesized to play a critical role in the development of the language/communication system. Not only is language development affected directly, but also indirectly through the impact that hyperarousal and hypoarousal have on other processes, such as those which are a part of the cognitive (e.g., attention and monitoring) and motor (speech) systems. For example, Bloom (1993) links affective expression, a motor response, with the development of language. She points out that emotional expression competes with language learning for an infant's attention, and suggests that neutral expression of emotion allows infants to use their limited cognitive resources for early language learning. Her research indicates that one-year-old infants who spend more time in neutral emotional states achieve language milestones, such as first words and multiword speech, earlier than infants who are more emotionally expressive (Bloom & Capatides, 1987).

Social development is also directly affected by states of hyperarousal and hypoarousal, in part because of how individuals in such states are perceived by others. For example, individuals with arousal/activation problems appear more anxious and agitated, if hyperaroused; or socially indifferent, withdrawn, and emotionally bland, if hypoaroused. In addition, social functioning is likely affected in an indirect fashion through the effects the arousal/activation/emotion system has on sensory, motor, and cognitive functioning. For example, children who are extremely anxious are less likely to be aware of their social environment, less strategic in their social decision-making, and less able to carry through a plan of action. As a consequence, they will be less able to use the social skills they possess and to acquire new social skills in social interaction situations.

Finally, the theory described in Figure 4.3 suggests that the emotions of children with autism indirectly influence the development of self-regulation through their impact on sensory, motor, social, cognitive, and language/communication processes. These latter processes directly affect the development of self-regulatory behavior through the tools they provide for self-regulation and for recruiting supports from others when self-regulation is not possible. In turn, the theory points out that self-regulation processes provide individuals the capacity to control their emotions.

Insight into the critical role emotions play during early development, including the development of self-regulation, is provided by Als (1982). Emotions develop from an innately determined biological response system, involving the autonomic nervous system, into a more complex system, characterized by increasing cognitive input. More specifically, Als conceptualizes development as a process involving multiple systems that emerge in a dynamic fashion. In the order of their development, these systems include: the autonomic, motor, state-organization, attentional/interactive, and self-regulatory. Each of the later emerging systems is influenced by the earlier developing systems. If one of the earlier emerging systems is immature or damaged, the development of later emerging systems is delayed or inhibited. Even after the various systems develop, they can become disorganized as a consequence of emotional stress. Early stress, before adequate coping techniques develop for dealing with it, is particularly disorganizing and can have potentially devastating, long-term effects.

According to Als (1982), during normal development, when a child becomes autonomically disorganized or overaroused, the motor, state-regulation, attention, and social interactive systems also become disorganized. When disorganization occurs, children eventually reorganize themselves unless repeatedly stressed. This reorganization process can be greatly assisted by a sensitive social environment that provides emotional supports. With development, the capacity of the child to cope with stressful environments gradually increases; unless the stressors are too great and prolonged, proper social supports are not provided, and/or biological defects are present. Social supports from parents and care-takers serve not only to reduce stress and soothe the child, but also to teach the child how to cope and self-regulate his/her emotions.

The critical point to be emphasized here is that both "simpler" motor and cognitive responses, such as cuddling and attention, as well as more complex motor, cognitive, and social responses, can become operational only when the child is emotionally organized. Gardner and Karmel (1983) suggest that during early infancy, maladaptive arousal patterns, such as hyperarousal, may alter central nervous system (CNS) organization in permanent ways. Citing research that shows that highly aroused infants prefer less complex and informative stimuli, they point out that under conditions of prolonged stress such preferences may be permanently established as functional and structural connections in the brain, thus having a detrimental effect on cognitive development. The preference for noncomplexity displayed by distressed infants bears close similarity to the attention fixations and stereotyped routines engaged in by children with autism who are under stress. For a review of research on the role of emotion in cognitive development, the reader is referred to Whitman, O'Callaghan, and Sommer (1997).

Children with autism may be especially vulnerable to stress if their arousal and state-regulation systems are dysfunctional, environment stressors are too intense and prolonged, and/or their self-regulatory system is poorly developed. If early stress is not managed, the development of their motor, cognitive, language, and social interaction systems may be placed at risk for delays. Moreover, if the social signaling system of children with autism is compromised, they may not receive the emotional supports from care-takers necessary to control their arousal levels. As will be discussed later, social supports may play a critical role in the development of self-regulation in children with autism.

A number of studies indicate that when emotionality and self-regulation are considered in conjunction, they can serve as either risk or protective factors in children's social adjustment. In a study by Lengua (2002) self-regulation was defined as including processes that modulate emotional responses, such as attention shifting and focusing. Lengua (2002) found that negative emotionality predicted adjustment problems, and positive emotionality predicted positive adjustment in third-to fifth-grade children, whereas self-regulation predicted both types of adjustment. Although not directly reported, the data from this study seem to indicate that children with better self-regulatory skills were not only less negative in their emotionality, but also that their ability to control emotions led to better social adjustment.

Consistent with this pattern of results, Belsky, Friedman, and Hsieh (2001) found nonhandicapped children who reacted negatively and intensely to their environment were more limited in their social skills. This relationship occurred, however, only when children also had poor self-regulatory control; that is, when they were unable to control their emotions through manipulating their attention focus (Belsky *et al.*, 2001). Similar results were obtained by Eisenberg, Pidada, and Liew (2001) with a sample of children who were third graders and from another culture, Indonesia. Children who displayed higher negative emotionality and a lower ability to self-regulate were viewed as less appropriate in their social behavior, more likely to display problematic behavior, and more likely to be rejected by their peers. Finally, results of a study by Denham, Blair, DeMulder, Levitas, Sawyer, Auerbach-Major, and Queenan (2003) also indicate the important contribution of emotional regulation, as well as emotional expressiveness and emotion knowledge, to social competence. In combination the results of these studies are generally consistent with the linkages proposed in Figure 4.3 between emotionality, social adaptation, and self-regulation.

Sensory processes

As already described, children with autism often display problems of hyper-sensitivity and/or hyposensitivity. Available information seems to suggest that their sensory problems appear to be secondary to problems in other areas, such as the arousal/activation system, rather than due to basic defects in the sensory system. In particular, there is no compelling evidence that these children's sensory problems are related to problems in the peripheral sensory structures, although there are some reports in the literature of children with autism having different types of visual and hearing difficulties (Carmody, Kaplan & Gaydos, 2001; Klin, 1993; Rosenhall, Nordin, Sandstrom, Ahlsen & Gillberg, 1999). Whatever the case, it is clear that children with autism often have problems processing certain types of stimulation as well as inte-grating sensory inputs from multiple modalities. From a sensory standpoint, persons with autism, particularly children, seem to often experience the world as chaotic, unpleasant, and sometimes painful (see Chapter 2). In turn their sensory problems affect functioning in other areas.

Problems in the sensory system, whether primary or secondary, are likely to influence level of arousal, with hypersensitivity further increasing arousal and hyposensitivity either reinforcing an existing state of low arousal or serving to decrease a state of hyperarousal. As mentioned, hyposensitivity, or sensory inattention to the environment, may be functional if it allows a person to disconnect from a situation that is confusing and/or painful. Sensory problems can also deter the development of the motor system; for example, coordination of the sensory and motor systems is critical to development of both gross and fine motor skills. Research by Gepner and Mestre (2002) suggests that children with autism are less reactive posturally to visually perceived environmental motion than a comparison group of typically developing children, and that hyporeactivity to such visual input is associated with motor impairments. Such a disassociation between the motor system and visual input may account for the delays children with autism experience in achieving motor milestones, as well as the motor problems observed in this population, such as rigid gait and awkward posturing. Finally, sensory problems are likely to adversely, albeit indirectly, affect social and language development through their impact on attention and cognitive learning processes (Huebner, 2001).

Motor processes

Motor problems are common in children with a Pervasive Developmental Disorder. They are mentioned explicitly as part of the diagnostic criteria for Rett's and Childhood Disintegrative Disorder. Although motor problems are not formally a part of the diagnosis for the other pervasive developmental disabilities, the literature makes frequent reference to such problems among children with Asperger's Syndrome and children with Autistic Disorder, particularly those who are lower functioning (see Chapter 2).

The importance of the motor system for a child's overall development is only beginning to be understood. It is known, however, that this system plays a particularly important role in the regulation of emotional arousal. For example, during infancy sucking helps pacify the child, as does drawing the limbs into the trunk of the body (Als, 1982). Therapeutically, routines involving exercise and deep muscle massage are frequently part of programs for managing stress in children and adults, including individuals with autism (Escalona, Field, Singer-Strunck, Cullen & Hartshorn, 2001). Motor overactivity is also symptomatic of disorders, like Attention Deficit Hyperactivity Disorder (ADHD), that affect learning and social functioning. In the occupational therapy literature, motor sequencing problems, such as walking without first crawling, have been hypothesized to have adverse effects on general development. Many of the occupational therapy regimens for children with developmental abilities, including autism, integrate motor and exercise routines into the overall therapeutic program (Huebner, 2001). From a sensory perspective, children who are more motorically competent experience their environment in a different way than those who are less motorically competent. A more motorically advanced child not only comes into contact with more of the environment, but is also able to explore more fully and competently that environment through active manipulation.

Motor development has also been proposed as playing a critical early role in the development of the cognitive system as outlined in theories like that of Jean Piaget (1970). Children's perception of the world changes dramatically as locomotion increases. In addition, the relationship between sensorimotor functioning and speech acquisition and communication skills has been of interest to researchers, although the importance of these relationships is only beginning to be appreciated in the area of autism (Abrahamsen & Mitchell, 1990). The motor system also plays a critical role in social development, through its influence on the acquisition of motorically based speech and communication skills as well as social behaviors. Delays in the motor arena not only hamper social interaction, but also mark children as different, sometimes stigmatizing them.

Cognitive, language/communication, and social processes

The cognitive, language/communication, and social characteristics of children with autism have already been discussed at length in Chapters 2 and 3. The presence of deficiencies in the latter two domains is central to the diagnosis of autism. The symptoms in these three areas range from marked problems in joint attention, expressive language, and imitation to deficiencies in abstract thinking, interactive play, and social comprehension. As shown in the theory described in Figure 4.3, these types of deficiencies, while prominently featured in any discussion of autism, enter developmentally later into the causal chain; that is, cognitive, social, and language symptoms are hypothesized as developing, at least in part, as a function of defects in the arousal/activation, sensory, and motor systems. The theory leaves open the question of whether the deficiencies in the cognitive, social, and language areas are primary defects, exacerbated by preexisting problems in the arousal/activation, sensory, and/or motor systems; or secondary defects, a consequence of more fundamental defects in these earlier emerging systems.

What is clear, however, is that the cognitive, social, and language systems have reciprocal influences on each other and more generally have a profound effect on the development of children with autism (see Chapters 2 and 3). For example, deficiencies in joint attention have been linked to later language problems and difficulties in understanding the state of mind of other people (Phillips, Baron-Cohen & Rutter, 1992; Uvlund & Smith, 1996). Moreover, cognitive deficiencies, including difficulties in interpreting the perspectives, emotions, and behaviors of others, influence individuals with autism as they attempt to initiate, respond to, and sustain social interactions. Just as the cognitive system influences language and social development, social interactions provide the context for cognitive and language development. Finally, the language/communication system has a profound influence on the child's ability to socially interact, as well as providing critical tools that influence the child's cognitive understanding of the world.

In addition to outlining the critical role that the cognitive, language, and social systems play in each other's development, the theory presented in Figure 4.3 also points out the impact that these three processes have on the development of the self-regulatory system. For example, the theory suggests that the self-regulatory problems associated with autism develop in part because of their cognitive deficiencies, including the problems they have attending to the environment, processing information, and using such information in strategic ways. These deficiencies make it difficult for individuals to engage in independent, intentional, goal-directed action. In a study by Ruble (2001), children with autism were found to engage less frequently in goal-directed behaviors in social situations; moreover, such behaviors were less complex and less often self-initiated. The author suggests that parents need training in ways to encourage and sustain their children's independence that take into consideration their children's cognitive limitations; that is, parents have to learn how to provide social supports for their children until they learn to self-regulate. In the next section, the emergence of the self-regulation system will be described along with its impact on the development of autism.

Self-regulation

As previously discussed, the theory presented in Figure 4.3 points out that self-regulation is influenced by emotional, sensory, motor, cognitive, language, and social factors. Effective self-regulation requires an optimal level of arousal, with both hyperarousal and hypoarousal associated with diminished functioning. The sensory system is critical for self-regulation because it provides information to the individuals about the environment and their behavior. The motor system enables individuals to engage in rudimentary self-regulation acts, such as cuddling when distressed, as well as more complex linguistic and social forms of self-regulation, such as self-instruction and the solicitation of social supports. The cognitive, language, and social interaction systems provide individuals the tools they need to strategically guide their behavior. Moreover, the social environment surrounding the child provides instrumental and emotional supports that gradually allow children to assume control of their thoughts, emotions, and behavior. The importance of the social environment will be discussed further in the last section of this chapter.

THE NATURE OF SELF-REGULATION

Because of the critical role that self-regulation plays in the theory of autism proposed in this chapter, this process will be described in some detail. Self-regulation creates both short-term and long-term benefits for the individual, especially in societies that emphasize the importance of independent and autonomous functioning. Although theoretical perspectives on self-regulation vary, there is general agreement that it involves an action on the part of an individual that results in the self-control of their behavior, emotions, and/or cognitions. Self-regulation has been described by Kopp (1982) as the:

> ability to comply with a request, to initiate and cease activities according to environmental demands, to modulate intensity, frequency, and duration of verbal and motor acts in social and in educational settings, to postpone acting upon a desired object or goal and to generate socially approved behavior in the absence of external monitors. (p. 149)

From a developmental perspective, although self-regulation is initially grounded in more primitive motor (e.g., sucking and cuddling) and attentional responses (e.g., eye closing and gaze aversion) that are initially reflexive in nature, this system undergoes change with development and becomes increasingly intentional and tied to cognitive development (Kopp, 1989). This more mature form of self-regulation is similar to the concept of effortful control described by Kochanska, Murray, and Harlan (2000). As the process of self-regulation emerges over time, the target of self-regulation changes from a focus on controlling emotions to also controlling overt behaviors and thoughts. As a consequence, children are able to delay gratification, resolve conflict, and adapt to new situations.

Within a social-learning framework, more complex forms of self-regulation include self-monitoring, self-evaluation, and self-reinforcement responses. To self-regulate, persons must first observe their social and physical environment, as well as their own behavior. Through information gained from self-observation, cognitive strategies are designed and selected to guide behaviors that will help the individual obtain a desired goal. Performance standards are established that allow an individual to evaluate whether they have achieved a desired goal. Through the evaluative process, the individual either experiences satisfaction or dissatisfaction. If dissatisfied, the individual reexamines the situation, formulates a new strategy, and exercises a new response (see Bandura, 1986; Kanfer & Gaelick, 1986; Karoly, 1982; Whitman, 1990).

In contrast to a social-learning conceptualization of self-regulation, other cognitive perspectives not only discuss the importance of basic cognitive strategies for behavior regulation, but also emphasize the interrelationship between metacognitive and higher control processes and lower-order cognitive processes (Flavell, 1979). For example, in order to self-regulate, the person must examine what he/she knows about a challenging situation that is being confronted, what resources he/she has to meet this challenge, and how these resources can be best utilized. Such an act requires the individual to understand what is in his/her own mind and sometimes to make guesses about what is in the minds of other people—processes in which individuals with autism are thought to be deficient (see Chapter 3).

Thus, self-regulation involves the capacity to change behavior based on past experience, inhibiting responses that are not useful, selecting behaviors that have proved useful, anticipating the effects of selected responses, and more generally initiating and maintaining behavior in a planful and organized manner. These capabilities are commonly regarded as functions associated with the prefrontal cortex, an area in which structural anomalies have been reported in individuals with autism (see Chapter 3). This ability to be planful and use memories of past experiences to guide new behavior and discard ineffective response patterns has been found in animal research to be disrupted by lesions in the frontal part of the cortex and replaced by ineffective preservative behaviors (see Diamond & Goldman-Rakic, 1989). This research lends support to the perspective that the ritualistic, compulsive, stereotyped behaviors found in an autistic population are symptoms of a poorly developed and defective self-regulatory system.

SELF-REGULATION IN CHILDREN WITH AUTISM

Definitions and descriptions of autism typically make reference to the social, language, and cognitive deficiencies of this population as well as emphasize the obsessive and compulsive aspects of their interests, activities, and behaviors. From an educational perspective, there is considerable evidence that individuals with autism can with proper instruction improve their social, language, and cognitive functioning. The instructional programs are, however, seldom viewed as unqualified successes. Although children with autism can learn behavioral and cognitive scripts and even maintain what they have learned over time, they often fail without external support structures to generalize what they have learned to new contexts. That is, their responses are tied to the environment in which instruction occurs and are not spontaneously utilized in other situations.

Because of this type of generalization problem, autism could be described as a self-regulatory disorder. Due to their inability to self-regulate their behavior, individuals with autism depend on others for guidance or utilize a variety of self-regulatory behaviors that are not adaptive, behaviors that are symptomatic of their disorder. The repetitive, restricted, and stereotyped patterns of interests, activities, and behaviors of children and adults with autism can be construed as their attempts to cope with environments and situations that are too complex and stressful. Their unique approaches to dealing with such challenges include: withdrawing into their private world, physically escaping a situation, restricting their interactions with the environment, engaging in stereotyped motor behaviors, narrowing their attentional focus to small parts of a task, persevering in their response patterns, and developing rigid routines and ritualistic behaviors.

If autism is viewed as a self-regulatory disorder, an interesting question arises as to whether children with autism are more undercontrolling or more overcontrolling in their self-regulatory style. The argument can be made that they are undercontrolled because they do not develop more complex forms of self-regulation, such as executive control processes (e.g., planning and monitoring), or sometimes even simpler forms of self-regulation, such as soliciting social support. Moreover, children with autism share other characteristics in common with undercontrolled children. They often appear impulsive and distractible, seek immediate gratification, and are easily influenced by shifting environmental contingencies (Kremen & Block, 1998). Conversely, they appear overcontrolled in that they use the primitive self-regulatory techniques that they do possess to compulsively order their environment. Children who are overcontrolled share many features in common with children with autism. Overcontrolled children have been variously described as: obsessive, preservative, uncomfortable with ambiguities, demonstrating a particular preference for structuring their environment, reactive to novel situations, temperamentally wary, difficult to soothe, and socially withdrawn (Kremen & Block 1998, Rubin, Coplan, Fox & Calkins, 1995). The answer to the question just posed seems to be that children with autism are both undercontrolled and overcontrolled, with perhaps overcontrol developing because of the stress that occurs when they cannot gain control in more conventional and acceptable ways.

In summary, it can be argued that individuals with autism learn to self-regulate their emotions and behaviors through their obsessions and compulsive routines. These coping techniques, however, are problematic in that self-regulation is achieved at a great social cost; they are unable to enter fully into interactions with others. Their primitive self-regulatory mechanisms, while not ultimately useful, may be inadvertently reinforced by their social milieu, and sometimes even deliberately allowed to occur because more mature techniques of self-regulation have not been able to be taught. Thus far, attempts to help children with autism to generalize what they have learned and to self-regulate have not been successful. There are reasons to be optimistic, however, that they can be taught to self-regulate. The process through which self-regulation develops is being actively studied by researchers (e.g., Kochanska *et al.*, 2000). Much has already been learned about this process.[3] Moreover, it is interesting to note that self-regulatory training programs have been designed and successfully employed with children with other developmental problems, including mental retardation (see Whitman, 1987, 1990). In Chapters 5 and 7, it will be argued that more attention needs to be given to the development of self-regulation skills in children with autism.

The social environment and the development of autism

As indicated in Chapter 3, there is considerable evidence that autism is a genetically based disorder. Although the specific defects that produce autism have yet to be identified, research within the last decade has provided initial insights into their general neurobiological foundation. In contrast, less is known about how the social and physical environment influences the emergence of autism and its underlying biological substrate (see Figure 4.2, p. 151). It is likely that research examining the impact of the social environment and parenting on autism has been inhibited, both because of the vigorous rejection by the professional community of early theories suggesting that autism was caused by aloof and affectively disengaged parenting styles, as well as by the growing realization that autism is a genetically based disorder. However, as discussed earlier, even though autism has genetic origins, perhaps with some early biological triggers, it does not follow that the social environment has no influence on the trajectory of this disorder. Research suggests otherwise.

For example, Stiller and Sigman (2002) found that parents of children with autism vary in the degree to which they are able to synchronize their

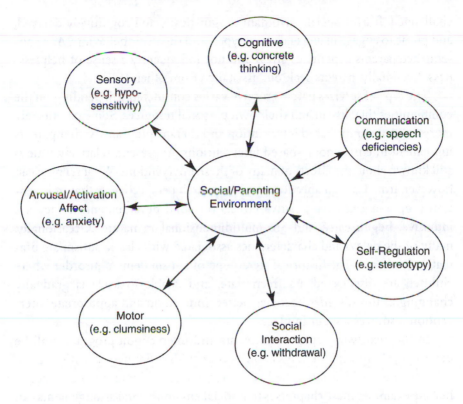

Figure 4.4 The reciprocal influences between the social/parenting environment and the characteristics of children with autism

behaviors with their children and that their level of synchronization is related to the children's joint attention and language skills. Parents who synchronize are able to respond to the needs of their children in a sensitive and contingent fashion, thereby promoting social development. Overall, the results of this type of research, as well as early intervention research, suggests that parents and primary care-takers of children with autism, like parents of typically developing children, can have a substantial impact on their children's behavior. This observation should not be interpreted, however, as meaning that parents are responsible for their children's autism.

Figure 4.4 describes some of the reciprocal influences that likely occur as autism is manifested in a social context. As autism emerges, parents are confronted with children whose characteristics are peculiar and confusing. At least initially, they have little insight into why their children act as they do and what they as parents should do to help their children. For example, they may be bewildered by their children who are hypersensitive, motorically challenged, fearful, socially avoidant, linguistically and cognitively delayed, and prone to engage in unusual stereotyped and ritualistic behaviors. As a consequence parents experience stress and not infrequently a sense of helplessness. Eventually, parents seek out assistance from others.

The type of services parents receive varies considerably depending on the communities they live in and their own personal resources. Some parents rely more on community-based intervention and therapy programs. Other parents implement intensive home-based interventions. At present, relatively little is still known about the effects of many of these interventions. What seems clear, however, from both an anecdotal and a research perspective, is that intervention programs can have positive effects on child development, if they are intensive, begun early, and are multidimensional in nature. Occasionally, many of the delays and characteristics associated with classic autism are dramatically altered. The historical stereotype of autism being a disorder where children are disengaged, unaffectionate, and unable to learn is gradually changing as this disorder becomes better understood and appropriate intervention resources are put in place.

In the next two chapters, treatments and intervention programs will be described, along with the ways families cope with children with autism. Even though autism still awaits a medical cure, what should impress the reader as he/she examines these chapters is that social environmental arrangements can positively alter the development of children with autism and the characteristics described in Figure 4.4.

Notes

1   An important part of a systems perspective is its recognition that the pattern of influence on the development of autism can be complex. Rather than single influences or causes, autism is viewed as having multiple influences. From a theoretical perspective, researchers studying autism need to consider not only the number of factors that may explain autism and its development, but also to reflect on the different ways these variables may act in conjunction with each other to influence development.

One way that the variables in Figure 4.3 might influence autism is through their *reciprocal interaction* with one another; that is, both variables act on the other: Variable A influences Variable B, which in turn influences Variable A, and so on. For example, the arousal level of infants with autism may affect their cognitive functioning, producing either inattention or attention refocusing, which in turn may result in a reduction in arousal level.

A second way these variables may influence one another is through a different type of interaction, what mathematicians refer to as a *statistical interaction*. The way that Variable A acts on Variable B depends on the characteristics or level of a third variable, Variable C. For example, some parents and professionals have argued that immunizations (Variable A) may produce autistic symptoms (Variable B), but only when a child's immune system is extremely compromised (Variable C).

A third way that the development of autism might occur is through a *mediational relationship* between variables. Variable A influences Variable B, which in turn influences Variable C. The effect of Variable A on Variable C operates indirectly through Variable B. Thus, Variable B helps explain more precisely how A influences C. For example, as a result of a sensory problem, such as hypersensitivity to certain sound frequencies (Variable A), a child becomes stressed (Variable B), which in turn results in a child engaging in a stereotyped response (Variable C), such as body rocking. Thus, the effect of hypersensitivity on self-stimulatory behavior is explained in terms of the stress it produces in the child.

A final way that influence might occur is through the *arithmetic summing* of effects of two or more variables on a third variable: Variable A plus Variable B influence Variable C. For example, two sources of stress, such as the presence of an unfamiliar person in a room and an unfamiliar task, each of which separately produces anxiety in a child, sum to produce greater anxiety than either one of them in isolation.

2 Within the past two decades developmental models have increasingly emphasized the influence of emotions on cognitive functioning; historically, however, this was not the case. In the adult literature, when emotional responses were examined, cognitive activities were typically viewed as a necessary and sufficient condition for emotional activity (Lazarus, 1982); that is, cognition and emotion were fused together in such a way that cognitive evaluation was considered crucial to the emotional response. Thus, feeling and cognitive states were not viewed as different domains of development, but rather as aspects of a unified developmental process (Lewis & Michalson, 1983). Increasingly, however, researchers have acknowledged the existence of a dynamic interrelationship between affective and cognitive processes during infancy (Cicchetti & Schneider-Rosen, 1984). Although a new zeitgeist has been evolving, Barrett and Campos (1987) stressed that theories of emotional development are prisoners of old paradigms. They asserted that most theories neither adequately addressed how emotions evolve nor explained why rudimentary emotions like fear are less driven by an emerging cognitive system than previously thought.

3 During infancy and early childhood, when a child becomes distressed and behaviorally disorganized, he/she is typically assisted in reorganizing and gaining control of themselves by care-takers who provide emotional supports and help the child reengage their social environment. The amount and types of support provided vary depending on the child and their developmental maturity as well as the sophistication of the care-takers. Through sensitive care-taking, a child gradually acquires the ability to self-regulate in stressful circumstances, thereby also gaining a sense of self-efficacy. As children develop, the signs of their emotional disorganization change, as does the complexity of a child's self-regulatory strategies for controlling emotions, but the objectives of effective self-regulation remain the same: to reduce unpleasant emotions, and to gain cognitive and behavioral control of a situation. With development, language becomes a critical tool for directing their behavior and influencing thinking.

From a social cognitive perspective, self-verbalization is part of a developmental process in which thinking becomes internalized and the interpersonal nature of thought, as reflected in social conversation, is transferred into an intrapersonal process, that is, within the person. Behaviorally what occurs during this process is that a child's actions become progressively less controlled by external verbal directives from others. As self-regulation evolves, the child's behavior is controlled initially by the child's own overt verbalizations but eventually by his/her covert verbal/thinking responses. Thus, children learn to respond in the absence of external social cues from adults by "cognitively" directing their own behavior. Language provides one vehicle for becoming aware of one's actions and allows the individual to extrapolate from their thoughts about such actions to understanding the thoughts/minds and actions of other people (see Whitman, 1990).

Parents, care-takers, and teachers help infants and children to regulate their behavior through a process sometimes referred to as scaffolding (Day, Cordon & Kerwin, 1989; Vygotsky, 1978). Although scaffolding is often discussed in the context of teaching cognitive self-regulation, this approach can also be used to teach younger children emotional self-regulation. Both simple and complex cognitive tasks, such as an infant attending to a parent or a child completing a math problem, cannot be completed unless a child is emotionally organized. Scaffolding consists of socialization agents providing structure and assistance to children as they engage in a task or a challenging environment. Through procedures like physical guidance, verbal prompting, and modeling, socialization agents transfer knowledge, cognitive strategies, and behaviors to children. Parents/teachers help children reduce their cognitive workload by assuming responsibility for parts of the task while the child concentrates on other parts. The ultimate goal of the scaffolding process is to introduce, as necessary, social supports to assist the child and then to remove in a gradual fashion these supports as the child acquires the cognitive and behavioral competence to self-regulate (Whitman, O'Callaghan & Sommer, 1997). In order to facilitate development, parents/teachers typically become proficient at providing appropriate emotional and cognitive scaffolding supports. When a child is incapable of self-regulation for whatever reason, such as severe environmental stress, biological problems, and/or language deficiencies, the provision of appropriate supports becomes even more critical for promoting optimal functioning and self-regulatory competencies. In such situations children can be explicitly taught to verbally control their behavior through a variety of procedures, including self-instruction and correspondence training (Whitman, 1987; Whitman et al., 1997).

References

Abrahamsen, E. & Mitchell, J. (1990) "Communication and sensorimotor functioning in children with autism." *Journal of Autism and Developmental Disorders 20*, 75–85.

Als, H. (1982) "Toward a syntactic theory of development: Promise for the assessment and support of infant individuality." *Infant Mental Health 3*, 229–243.

Baltes, P. B. (1987) "Theoretical propositions of life-span developmental psychology. On the dynamics between growth and decline." *Developmental Psychology 23*, 611–626.

Baltes, P. B., Reese, H. W. & Lipsitt, L. P. (1980) "Life-span developmental psychology." *Annual Review of Psychology 31*, 65–110.

Bandura, A. (1986) *Social foundations of thought and action: A social cognitive theory.* Englewood Cliffs, NJ: Prentice-Hall.

Barrett, K. & Campos, J. J. (1987) "Perspectives on emotional development: II. A functional approach to emotions." In J. D. Osofsky (ed) *Handbook of infant development* (Second edition) (pp. 555–578). New York: Wiley.

Belsky, J., Friedman, S. & Hsieh, K. (2001) "Testing a core emotion-regulation prediction: Does early attentional persistence moderate the effect of infant negative emotionality on later development?" *Child Development 72*, 123–133.

Bloom, L. (1993) *The transition from infancy to language: Acquiring the power of expression.* New York: Cambridge University Press.

Bloom, L. & Capatides, J. B. (1987) "Expression of affect and the emergence of language." *Child Development 58*, 1513–1522.

Carmody, D., Kaplan, M. & Gaydos, A. (2001) "Spatial orientation adjustments in child with autism in Hong Kong." *Child Psychiatry and Human Development 31*, 233–247.

Cicchetti, D. & Schneider-Rosen, K. (1984) "Theoretical and empirical considerations in the investigation of the relationship between affect and cognition in atypical populations of infants: Contributions to the formulation of an integrative theory of development." In C. Izard, J. Kagan & R. Zajonc (eds) *Emotions, cognition and behavior* (pp. 366–408). Cambridge: Cambridge University Press.

Dawson, G. & Levy, A. (1989) "Arousal, attention and the socioemotional adjustment of individuals with autism." In G. Dawson (ed) *Autism: Nature, diagnosis and treatment.* New York: Guilford.

Day, J. D., Cordon, L. A. & Kerwin, M. L. (1989) "Informal instruction and development of cognitive skills: A review and critique of research." In C. B. McCormick, G. Miller & M. Pressley (eds) *Cognitive strategy research: From basic research to educational applications.* New York: Springer-Verlag.

Denham, S., Blair, K., DeMulder, E., Levitas, J., Sawyer, K., Auerbach-Major, S. & Queenan, P. (2003) "Preschool emotional competence: Pathway to social competence." *Child Development 74*, 238–256.

Diamond, A. & Goldman-Rakic, P. (1989) "Comparison of human infants and rhesus monkeys on Piaget's task: Evidence for dependence on the dorsolateral prefrontal cortex." *Experimental Brain Research 24*, 24–40.

Eisenberg, N., Pidada, S. & Liew, J. (2001) "The relationship of regulation and negative emotionality to Indonesian children's social functioning." *Child Development 72*, 1747–1763.

Escalona, A., Field, T., Singer-Strunck, R., Cullen, C. & Hartshorn, K. (2001) "Improvements in the behavior of children with autism following massage therapy." *Journal of Autism and Developmental Disorders 31*, 90–95.

Flavell, J. H. (1979) "Metacognition and cognitive monitoring: A new era of cognitive-developmental inquiry." *American Psychologist 34*, 906–911.

Gardner, J. M. & Karmel, B. Z. (1983) "Attention and arousal in preterm and full-term neonates." In T. Field & A. Sostek (eds) *Infants born at risk* (pp. 69–98). New York: Grune & Stratton.

Gepner, B. & Mestre, D. (2002) "Brief report: Postural reactivity to fast visual motion differentiates autistic from children with Asperger Syndrome." *Journal of Autism and Developmental Disorders 12*, 231–238.

Huebner, R. (2001) *Autism: A sensorimotor approach to management.* Gaithersburg, MD: Aspen.

Kanfer, F. H. & Gaelick, L. (1986) "Self-management methods." In F. H. Kanfer & A. P. Goldstein (eds) *Helping people change* (pp. 283–345). New York: Pergamon.

Karoly, P. (1982) "erspectives on self-management and behavior change." In P. Karoly & F. H. Kanfer (eds) *Self-management and behavior changes: From theory to practice* (pp. 3–31). New York: Pergamon.

Klin, A. (1993) "Auditory brainstem responses in autism: Brainstem dysfunction or peripheral hearing loss." *Journal of Autism and Developmental Disorders 23,* 15–35.

Kochanska, G., Murray, K. & Harlan, E. T. (2000) "Effortful control in early childhood: Continuity and change, antecedents, and implications for social development." *Developmental Psychology 36,* 220–232.

Kopp, C. B. (1982) "Antecedents of self-regulation: A developmental perspective." *Developmental Psychology 18,* 199–214.

Kopp, C. B. (1989) "Regulation of distress and negative emotions: A developmental view." *Developmental Psychology 25,* 343–354.

Kremen, A. M. & Block, J. (1998) "The roots of ego-control in young adulthood: Links with parenting in early childhood." *Journal of Personality and Social Psychology 75,* 1062–1075.

Lazarus, R. S. (1982) "Thoughts on the relations between emotion and cognition." *American Psychologist 37,* 1019–1024.

Lengua, L. (2002) "The contribution of emotionality and self-regulation to the understanding of children's response to multiple risk." *Child Development 73,* 144–161.

Lewis, M. & Michalson, L. (1983) *Children's emotions and moods.* New York: Plenum Press.

Phillips, W., Baron-Cohen, S. & Rutter, M. (1992) "The role of eye contact in goal detection: Evidence from normal infants and children with autism or mental handicap." *Development and Psychopathology 4*(3), 375–383.

Piaget, J. (1970) "Piaget's theory." In P. H. Mussen (ed) *Carmichael's manual of child psychology* (Vol. 1, Third edition) (pp. 703–732). New York: Wiley.

Rosenhall, U., Nordin, V., Sandstrom, M., Ahlsen, G. & Gillberg, C. (1999) "Autism and hearing loss." *Journal of Autism and Developmental Disorder 29,* 349–357.

Rubin, K. H., Coplan, R. J., Fox, N. A. & Calkins, S. D. (1995) "Emotionality, emotion regulation, and preschoolers' social adaptation." *Development and Psychopathology 7,* 49–62.

Ruble, L. (2001) "Analysis of social interactions as goal-directed behaviors in children with autism." *Journal of Autism and Developmental Disabilities 31,* 471–482.

Sigelman, C. K. & Shaffer, D. R. (1995) *Life-span human development* (Second edition). Pacific Grove, CA: Brooks/Cole.

Smith, L. B. & Thelen, E. (1993) *A Dynamic Systems Approach to Development: Applications.* Cambridge, MA: MIT Press.

Stiller, M. & Sigman, M. (2002) "The behaviors of parents of children with autism predict the subsequent development of their children's communication." *Journal of Autism and Developmental Disorders 32,* 77–89.

Thelen, E. (1995) "Time-scale dynamics and the development of an embodied cognition." In R. F. Port & T. van Gelder (eds) *Mind as motion: Explorations in the dynamics of cognition.* Cambridge, MA: MIT Press.

Thomas, A. & Chess, S. (1977) *Temperament and development.* New York: Brunner/Mazel.

Uvland, S. & Smith, L. (1996) "The predictive validity of nonverbal communicative skills in infants with perinatal hazards." *Infant Behavior and Development 19*, 441–449.

Vygotsky, L. S. (1978) *Mind in society: The development of higher psychological processes* (edited by M. Cole, V. John-Steiner, S. Scribner & E. Souberman). Cambridge, MA: Harvard University Press.

Whitman, T. L. (1987) "Self-instruction, individual differences, and mental retardation." *American Journal of Mental Deficiency 92*, 213–223.

Whitman, T. L. (1990) "Self-regulation and mental retardation." *American Journal on Mental Retardation 94*, 347–362.

Whitman, T. L., O'Callaghan, M. & Sommer, K. (1997) "Emotion and mental retardation." In W. McLean (ed) *Handbook of mental deficiency: psychological theory and research* (Third edition) (pp. 77–98). Mawah, NJ: Erlbaum.

Yarrow, L. J. (1981) "Perspectives on Interactional Research." In E. Shapiro & E. Weber (eds) *Cognitive and affective growth* (pp. 97–108). Hillsdale, NJ: Erlbaum.

CHAPTER 5

Educational and Biomedical Interventions

with Kathleen J. Kolberg

No topic has generated more controversy within the area of autism than that concerning how it should be treated. Although this controversy has become more public due to mass media attention, it has arisen basically because of the lack of consensus concerning the causes and exact nature of autism. At present, it can only be said with any certainty that autism is a genetically based disorder. Considerably less is known about the specific genetic, biochemical, and anatomical bases of autism and the role that the environment, particularly the prenatal and early postnatal environment, plays in its emergence. For this reason and because of the complexity of the symptomatology associated with autism (as well as the considerable individual differences in the way this disorder is manifested), it has been difficult to establish what the focus of treatment should be. Controversy has also been generated because many of the treatments for autism have been developed outside of a scientific framework. They have been designed by clinicians and educators who have not known how, or thought it necessary, to evaluate treatment effectiveness through controlled scientific research.

Because of a lack of consensus about the appropriate treatments for autism, parents have been confused concerning how to best help their children. They have often been forced into a choice of either doing nothing or adopting untested treatment approaches. In their search for assistance, parents have frequently selected treatments based on the testimonies of other parents and well-meaning professionals. From a scientific perspective, such testimonies do not constitute a compelling source of evidence regarding a treatment's efficacy. Nevertheless, parents have proceeded the best they could in helping their children, given that most popular treatments have not yet been scientifically shown to be effective.

In this chapter, educational and biomedical programs that have been employed with children with autism will be described. These programs are quite diverse and include the following interventions: behavior education, TEACCH, sensorimotor, speech and communication, alternative communication, play, humanistic/spiritual, behavior reduction, and biomedical. The biomedical treatments reviewed include: pharmacologic, hormone, anti-yeast, homeopathic, immunologic, vitamin and diet, and craniosacral manipulation. Special attention will be given to programs that have been more visible and widely employed. As will be discussed later in the chapter, surprisingly little attention has been given by educators to the development of interventions that address the emotional and cognitive needs of children with autism, characteristics postulated in Chapters 3 and 4 to be critical in the development of autism.[1] Finally, brief mention of some of the more controversial treatments will be made. For each intervention, the rationale for its employment, its basic structure and procedures, and available evidence for its efficacy will be summarized where possible.

Behavior education programs

In comparison to other intervention programs described in this chapter, behavior education programs have been the focus of considerable research. In fact, general research on these programs has been so extensive that numerous journals have evolved, devoted solely to the publication of work in this area, such as the *Journal of Applied Behavior Analysis, Behavior Therapy*, and *Behavior Modification*. Behavior education interventions have developed from basic research conducted over the past 80 years with humans and animals. In conjunction with this basic research, major theories have emerged describing how children and adults learn. Principles derived from classical conditioning, operant conditioning, and cognitive-behavioral theories of learning have provided the foundation for the development of an array of therapeutic and educational techniques. These techniques have been used for over 30 years in home, school, and community settings to teach children and adults a wide variety of behaviors, including motor, self-help, language, social, academic, and vocational skills, as well as to treat numerous clinical and developmental problems, including anxiety disorders, depression, attention-deficit/

hyperactivity problems, mental retardation, and autism (Bandura, 1969; Kazdin, 2001; Plaud & Eifert, 1998; Sulzer-Azaroff & Mayer, 1991).

Although each of the aforementioned learning theories and the interventions associated with them have general relevance for understanding autism and the design of educational programs for this population, only one of these theories, operant conditioning, has thus far had significant impact on the area of autism. Basic research in the area of operant learning has led to the emergence of intervention programs, variously described as behavior modification, applied behavior analysis (ABA), and discrete trial learning. These interventions are quite similar to one another and will be referred to in this chapter as behavior education.

Behavioral modification, based on well-established principles of learning, employs procedures, such as positive and negative reinforcement, extinction, stimulus control, prompting, shaping, and chaining, to increase adaptive behavior and decrease maladaptive behavior. The field of applied behavior analysis emphasizes that these and other techniques used in behavior education programs should be evaluated through reliable measurement procedures and single-subject research designs. Discrete trial learning interventions, which have come to be widely employed in the area of autism as a result of Ivar Lovaas' research and training programs, utilize the aforementioned behavior modification techniques as well as many of the evaluation methodologies developed within the area of applied behavioral analysis.

When the area of behavior education first evolved, one of the major targets of this intervention was individuals thought to be incapable of learning, particularly children with "severe and profound" mental retardation (Whitman, Scibak & Reid, 1983). After demonstrating the utility of this approach for teaching children with marked behavioral deficiencies, the procedures were quickly extended to assist children and adults with a variety of difficult-to-treat problems, as well as to teach typically developing children in regular education classrooms and home situations (Bandura, 1969).

Numerous myths have developed surrounding the field of behavior education, often perpetuated by individuals who have not been very familiar with learning theory and applied research in this area. For example, many people view behavior education as an intervention or set of interventions basically designed to reduce inappropriate or maladaptive behavior. Although this emphasis was present in some early behavior education programs, the basic target of behavior interventions has been teaching new behaviors, such as self-help, language, social, and academic skills. Relatedly, many people perceive that the behavior education approach actively relies on the use of punishment techniques. In point of fact, however, most current behavioral programs emphasize the use of positive reinforcement techniques and seldom, if ever, use punishment procedures. Later in this chapter, techniques for reducing inappropriate behaviors will be discussed; those that are recommended do not involve the use of punishment.

Basic characteristics of behavior education programs

Although it is beyond the scope of this chapter to discuss in detail the behavior education approach and its specific offshoots, like discrete trial learning, some of the basic assumptions and characteristics of this approach will be discussed. One important assumption is that most behaviors are learned, both behaviors that society considers adaptive as well as maladaptive. A second assumption is that the environment (social and nonsocial) plays a critical role in the learning process. Behavior is controlled by antecedent events or stimuli that precede behavior (e.g., verbal commands, visual stimuli, and general features of the physical environment) and also, and most importantly, by stimulus events that follow a response, including events that involve the administration and withdrawal of stimuli. These latter stimulus events, when they result in an increase in behavior, are referred to respectively as "positive reinforcers" and "negative reinforcers".

Critical features of behavior training programs include:

1. selecting and carefully defining the target behavior(s) to be changed/developed

2. deciding on the training technique, which typically includes some type of prompting and reinforcement procedure

3. programming the target behavior to occur with sufficient frequency so that it can be reinforced

4. implementing the intervention in a way so as to ensure that the target behaviors are maintained over time and generalized to appropriate social settings.

The process of selecting target behaviors to be taught in an intervention program is guided by a number of considerations, including whether they are developmentally appropriate, useful, and meet a general criteria for social acceptability. Thus, emphasis is placed not only on the selection of target behaviors that are practical, in that they help the individual cope with the demands of daily living, but also on goals that make developmental sense and systematically build on the child's existing patterns of skills and capacities. Before beginning a behavior education program, it is necessary to define precisely the target behaviors so that the intervention program can be consistently applied and changes in the target behaviors can be reliably evaluated. Precise definitions specify the observable characteristics of the behaviors to be taught and provide concrete examples of behaviors that meet the definition's requirements. In behavior education programs for children with autism, a myriad of target behaviors are taught as part of programs for developing self-help, social, communication, and academic skills. The target behaviors to be taught are part of what is typically referred to as their "individualized education program".

The identification of reinforcers is a critical step in any behavior education program. A reinforcer is any stimulus or activity that follows a response and serves to increase the occurrence of that response. The process of selecting stimuli that will serve as reinforcers is guided by theory, observation of the student, information from persons significant in the student's life, and student self-report. In order to ensure that the target behaviors occur and can be reinforced, a variety of response-induction techniques are employed, including modeling, physical guidance, shaping, and verbal instruction. In the final step, maintenance and generalization of the target behavior is programmed through a variety of procedures including: discrimination training, variable intermittent reinforcement schedules, use of naturally occurring reinforcers, gradual withdrawal of social supports, and teaching self-regulatory skills. Wherever possible, educational programs take place in the child's everyday living environment, and "natural" reinforcers like praise and affection are employed.

In contrast to many interventions, which are administered by professionals, behavior education programs are designed so that they can be transferred to parents, teachers, and other important people in the child's life. Behavior education programs should begin as early as possible in the child's life and be applied consistently in both structured and unstructured situations. Certified professionals and/or paraprofessional consultants are required to establish a formal behavior education program and to train critical teaching personnel. Because the program needs to be applied around 20–40 hours per week, parents of children with autism typically seek outside help from volunteers and paid teachers to assist them in the implementation of the home program.

As mentioned previously, extensive research evaluating the validity of behavior education programs for children with autism and other developmental problems has been conducted. This research is published in numerous journals in the areas of autism and behavior education. In addition to applied research, a clinical evaluation component is incorporated into all behavior intervention programs. Research indicates that children with autism benefit most when a behavior education program is applied at least 20–40 hours a week. Although this approach has been found to be particularly efficacious with higher functioning autistic children, it has also been effectively employed with lower functioning children with autism and mental retardation. For a review of the behavioral approach, the reader is referred to Lovaas (2003), Scheuermann and Webber (2002), and Whitman et al. (1983).

In summary, the behavior education approach has been more extensively evaluated than other interventions described in this chapter. The use of behavior techniques continues to expand as they are incorporated into approaches used by other disciplines, such as education, speech therapy, and occupational therapy. The behavior education approach has emphasized what is one of the most important goals in regular and special education programs, that is, ensuring that behaviors taught are maintained and generalized to new situations (Stokes & Baer, 1977). Unlike many treatment approaches, behavior education approaches place almost as much emphasis on the maintenance and generalization of behavior skills as on initial response acquisition. Behavioral and cognitive-behavioral researchers have been actively involved in evaluating new approaches, such as self-regulation training for use with populations with developmental disabilities to promote changes that are lasting and dynamic (Whitman, 1990).

The TEACCH approach

In contrast to other approaches described in this chapter, TEACCH is broader in its educational focus, and eclectic in that it integrates a wide variety of different methods, including behavior education techniques, into its total program. TEACCH stands for the Treatment and Education of Autistic and related Communication-Handicapped Children. It was developed under the direction of Eric Schopler at the University of Carolina and is now utilized throughout the state of North Carolina. The TEACCH approach views autism as a permanent condition. It was designed to help autistic individuals (and their families) throughout their life. Since its inception, the TEACCH program has been widely disseminated and is now part of autism education programs in many places in the United States as well as in other countries.

A number of principles have guided the development of the TEACCH program. For example, assessment is a critical component that allows the program to be tailored to the needs of each individual. Programs begin with a detailed evaluation of the individual's psychological, physical, and developmental needs. Evaluation is also employed to assess program success and the changing needs of the individual. The general focus of treatment is upon improving adaptation by building on an individual's strengths and addressing limitations through the utilization of those strengths. In implementing the program, a structured teaching environment is employed to help students anticipate what they will be doing, and to minimize their frustration and anxiety. This structured teaching component stipulates where teaching occurs, what is taught, and the procedures and materials to be used in teaching. The physical aspects of the teaching environment are systematically arranged to provide stability and to reduce student distraction. Structure is also controlled through ensuring uniform implementation of specific programs across therapists. As curriculum changes, new activities are gradually integrated to reduce their disruptive influence.

Parents are a critical part of the TEACCH treatment team. Parents are considered to be the child's first and most important teachers. Parents are respected because of the knowledge they possess about their children, the amount of time they spend with them, and the considerable influence they exert on their children's lives. Parents act as teachers and also assist in program decision-making. Through parent involvement, programs are extended from the school and workplace to home. As a consequence of their active involvement, parents are thought to become more motivated participants in their children's program and to have a greater sense of program ownership.

The TEACCH program adheres to a generalist training model. It emphasizes not only that professionals and paraprofessionals should implement their programs, but also that they should become knowledgeable of and acquire expertise in the implementation of all the child's programs. It is argued that this breadth helps ensure consistency of program implementation and increases the probability of a program's success through generalizing its employment across environments. Moreover, by involving all teaching personnel in the total program, it is felt that they will make better educational decisions because of their awareness of the overall nature of the child's program.

The TEACCH model is implemented in home, preschool, primary and secondary schools, and job settings. Although this approach emphasizes the use of validated techniques and the evaluation of student progress, systematic research on the overall program is difficult to find. The task of conducting such research is made more difficult because TEACCH is evolutionary, with changes in the program occurring as new treatments emerge and also as the child develops. Individuals interested in learning more about this approach are encouraged to explore the extensive program literature on TEACCH (e.g., Schopler, Mesibov & Hearsey, 1995) as well as to visit the TEACCH website (www.teacch.com).

Sensorimotor therapies

As pointed out in Chapter 2, sensory and motor impairments are common among individuals with autism. Autistic children as a population have difficulties in registering sensory inputs—seemingly ignoring incoming stimulation—as well as in modulating sensory inputs, with the consequence that they appear oversensitive and anxious in certain situations. They also have difficulty integrating sensory data from their environment. In addition, they commonly display problems in orienting responses, filtering incoming stimulation, habituating to stimulation, processing and interpreting sensory information (particularly information that is complex and requires integration from multiple modalities), and using sensory information to guide motor action. Motor deficits observed in children with autism include: low muscle tone, eye gaze and tracking problems, dyspraxia, and problems in imitation. They also show hyporeactivity and hyperreactivity. Many children with autism spectrum disorders, particularly those with Asperger's Syndrome, have problems in motor planning and initiation, as well as in the regulation of movement.

Different general approaches to sensorimotor training have been identified by Schneck (2001). One approach involves the systematic arrangement of sensory stimulation to elicit appropriate motor responses. Treatment can include more passive procedures, which involve the therapist guiding an individual's movement, or more active procedures, which integrate the child into activities that provide specific sensory inputs and require certain movements. In contrast, a second approach gradually introduces challenging sensory input for the purpose of helping individuals to adapt or habituate to that input. Unlike the first approach, it is not typically applied in the context of a goal-directed activity. Finally, a third approach is directed toward organizing sensory input for the individual when sensory processing deficits lead to problems in adaptive responding, the goal being to improve the way the sensory system integrates and uses sensory input. It contrasts with the other approaches in that it is more individualized, often involves active participation of the child, and typically uses a variety of equipment.

Sensorimotor approaches are most commonly employed by occupational and physical therapists. Occupational therapy focuses on the development of fine and gross motor skills and the reduction of sensory processing problems. Occupational therapists are found in a variety of settings including hospitals, schools, and private clinics. Occupational therapy bears many similarities to physical therapy, but differs in its emphasis on specific skill development. In contrast, physical therapy is often directed at developing or retraining general mobility and is more likely to focus on gross motor problems, low muscle tone, gait problems, and strength deficits. For more specific information on sensorimotor programs and occupational therapy, the reader is referred to Schneck (2001) and Rydeen (2001).

In addition to the therapies mentioned, there are a variety of programs developed for autistic children that emphasize physical activity, physical exercise, movement, and sports activities such as Daily Life Therapy (Kitahara, 1983/1984). Some programs also use physical activities to help modulate arousal and increase attention in children with autism. In the remainder of this section, the sensory system and several specific sensory integration therapies will be described.

Sensory integration therapies

The senses provide humans information about the world that surrounds them. During sensory integration, stimuli are received, organized, interpreted, and used to guide behavior. From a theoretical perspective, sensory integration is viewed as a response that is not only neurologically based, but also influences the developing neurological structure of the brain. The senses help individuals become aware of their environment and prepare them for action. In order for information to be received, the brain must be aroused into an alert state and the body prepared for action. Although the senses are often discussed in isolation, information from the various senses needs to be integrated in order for an adaptive response to occur. As novel stimuli impinge upon the senses, the body becomes mobilized for action. As specific stimuli are repeatedly encountered, the brain habituates or accommodates to these stimuli, thus freeing up its attentional processes for new stimuli.

Problems occur if the sensory system is not able to register input from the environment and mobilize action or conversely registers input in a way that produces overarousal; that is, the individual displays oversensitivity to incoming stimuli. Children who do not register incoming stimulation may either not react at all and/or engage in actions designed to increase the intensity of stimulation. Children who are overly sensitive to certain types of stimulation may become disorganized and show disruptions in their behavior, sometimes initiating responses designed to directly reduce that stimulation or to avoid the context in which the stimulation occurs.

Sensory integration therapies have been developed to assist individuals who have problems of either poor registration and/or oversensitivity— problems that in turn can lead to other problems related to the processing, analysis, and organization of sensory input as well as the retention (short-term and long-term memory) of information. The sensory integration therapies, while often focusing on one specific modality (auditory, visual, touch, taste, smell, vestibular, or proprioception), involve of necessity other modalities; thus it is holistic and involves the entire body, including all the senses and the motor system. For individuals who have poor registration of stimuli, thera-peutic procedures typically involve the introduction of stimuli that vary in level of intensity, rate of presentation, duration, contrast, points of contact, and/or predictability to enhance functioning. The ultimate goal is to develop in the individual an increasing level of alertness and activation as they confront specific stimulus inputs. For individuals who are overly sensitive to specific stimulus inputs, therapy generally focuses on gradually introducing these stimuli in a way so as to facilitate habituation.

Although sensory integration therapy is typically viewed as being a subspecialty of occupational therapy, which focuses on helping individuals perform purposeful activities, in reality this therapy often involves a variety of disciplines, including physical therapy, as well as specialties that focus on hearing and vision. For further information on the sensory integration approach the reader is referred to Cook and Dunn (1998) and Schneck (2001). In the remainder of this section, examples of therapies that have been classified under the rubric of sensory integration will be discussed.

SENSORY INTEGRATION THROUGH EQUIPMENT-BASED EXERCISES

Although disturbances can occur in any of the senses, sensory integration programs often emphasize exercises that promote motor development through affecting three systems: the tactile (a system based on the skin surface and the nerves that serve it), the proprioceptive (a system based in the muscle joints and ligaments that provides information about where the body is in space), and the vestibular (a system, based mostly in the inner ear, that influences body movement and balance). Ayres (1979), in what has become a classic work, *Sensory integration and the child*, outlines a variety of therapeutic activities that were designed to promote overall sensory integration. One such activity involves the use of the scooter board, which consists of a board mounted on four wheels that allows movement in any direction. Typically, the child lies in a prone position on the scooter. A variety of activities designed to provide a complex array of sensory inputs are engaged in, such as spinning and riding down a ramp.

A second piece of equipment frequently utilized in sensory integration therapy is a bolster swing. The swing consists of a core, with padding and a cover, that is around six feet in length and three feet in circumference. Ropes attach the swing to an overhead hook. The child sits or lies on the core and swings back and forth. Various activities, such as picking up objects from the floor while the bolster is moving, provide the child with a variety of vestibular, proprioceptive, and tactual inputs, as well as other types of stimulation. Ayres (1979) points out one of the prime purposes of these activities is to develop an inner sense of direction and locus of control during interactions with the physical and social environment, which in turn leads to a general sense of self-confidence and mastery.

A variety of other techniques have also been used by sensory integration therapists. For example, to address problems of tactile oversensitivity, techniques that involve the handling of different textured materials, deep pressure (e.g., hugs and massage), and habituation (gradual introduction of materials that produce unpleasant sensations) have been employed. For proprioceptive problems, jumping on a trampoline and joint-compression have been used. For vestibular problems, techniques such as walking on a balance beam, balancing on a large moving ball, and engaging in exercises that involve crossing the midline of the body (e.g., right hand on left part of torso and stair climbing) have been employed.

AUDITORY INTEGRATION

Hearing is essential for perception, speech, and learning. In typically developing children, auditory input influences arousal levels and attentional responses. Disruptions in auditory processing can lead to a variety of problems of a cognitive, linguistic, and socioemotional nature. Children with autism have considerable difficulty in sound and speech processing. They also sometimes engage in what appear to be socially unusual behaviors in order to avoid or to produce certain sound stimuli: behaviors that some clinicians theorize originate from an auditory integration deficiency. In order to assist children with such problems, several approaches have evolved to facilitate auditory integration.

One such approach is the Berard Method, which was developed by Guy Berard, a French otolaryngologist (Berard, 1993). This method assumes that people vary in their level of sensitivity to sounds and that for some individuals hypersensitive hearing can result in pain and consequently attentional and learning problems. As part of the Berard Method, an audiogram is obtained to evaluate auditory abnormalities in order to establish the thresholds at which a person hears a sound at different frequency levels, and to establish a baseline against which to evaluate treatment effectiveness. Treatment is directed at reducing hypersensitivity problems and more generally at flattening out the audiogram.

Berard believes that the hearing system can be retrained, just as muscles can be retrained through physical exercises. In order to retrain the auditory system, a broad range of low and high frequency sound stimuli are presented randomly through headphones to a listener. Frequencies at which hearing is painful are attenuated through a filtering system. Treatment typically consists of 20 half-hour sessions over a 10–20-day period. Although Berard does not maintain that the auditory problems of children with autism cause their disorder, he believes that treatments directed at improving auditory functioning can reduce problems that are associated with hearing difficulties, such as attentional problems.

Theoretically, it is not clear how the Berard Method produces its effects. Because sound frequencies associated with hypersensitivity are attenuated, a simple habituation explanation does not seem feasible. In order to habituate to a sound frequency, it needs by definition to be repeatedly presented. Another related explanation, based on counter-conditioning theory, is possible. If the process of hearing can be made not only less painful through the filtering of sounds, but actually pleasurable because of the many secondary gains associated with hearing, then the positive experience associated with hearing may serve to inhibit the adverse effects related to specific auditory stimuli.

Support for the efficacy of this method is mixed. Anecdotal reports suggest improvements in language, tactile, and social functioning, as well as a reduction in sound hypersensitivities. Although such reports of successes abound, including those described in Stehli (1990, 1995), empirical research yields at best a mixed picture regarding the method's efficacy (Goldstein, 2000; Mudford, Cross, Breen, Cullen, Reeves, Gould & Douglas, 2000). At present, more research is needed to evaluate the general utility of this approach, to assess what types of individuals benefit most from the procedure, and to provide insights into why this procedure is effective, if indeed it is.

A second, less frequently utilized method of auditory integration training was developed by Tomatis in the middle of the last century (Thompson & Andrews, 2000). Tomatis emphasized that sounds that travel through bones go straight to the middle ear, bypassing the inner ear, and that these sounds tend to be loud and distracting. His method focused on reducing sound hypersensitivity by directing sound first to a vibrator and then to the middle ear. A variety of sound patterns, including music, the child's own speech, and the child's mother's speech are used in this program. The mother's voice is filtered during therapy in an attempt to recreate how her voice would have been heard during fetal development, at birth, and during infancy. The rationale for this procedure is to reproduce how listening should have occurred developmentally. That is, the procedure attempts to redevelop listening under "normal" developmental conditions in order to change the child's response to sound and language. Autistic children often receive 150–200 hours of therapy over a 6–12-month period. As with the Berard Method, research support for its efficacy is lacking.

THE WILBARGER PROTOCOL

Developed by Wilbarger and Wilbarger (1991), the Wilbarger Protocol is used as a treatment for sensory defensiveness. The method involves brushing, using a nonabrasive brush, in conjunction with proprioceptive input to all joints. The treatment is repeated multiple times (8–12 times) throughout the day over several weeks. Theoretically, the technique would appear to exert its effects through habituation as the tactual system is challenged through repeated brushing. Empirical data supporting the efficacy of this approach were not found.

IRLEN LENSES

At present there is reason to believe that at least some people with autism experience the visual world in unusual ways. Such visual anomalies have been described by Williams (1992, 1996). One specific disorder that has attracted attention has been referred to variously as the Irlen Syndrome, scoptic sensitivity, visual perceptional discomfort, and visual dyslexia. Waterhouse (2000) points out that people with this disorder have a family history of dyslexia and hyperactivity and a variety of more specific symptoms, such as sensitivity to bright lights, problems in focusing, poor depth perception, and an inability to see print without distortions. If 15% of the population suffers from this visual disorder, as Waterhouse (2000) suggests, it is likely that at least a similar percentage of children with autism also have this problem. To the extent that they do have visual problems, it could explain a variety of their other problems, such as inattention, hyperactivity, lack of coordination, information processing problems, and situation-specific anxiety responses. Work at the Irlen Institute suggests that tinted lenses may relieve many of these symptoms (see Waterhouse, 2000, for a more complete review of this problem and the Irlen Institute solution).

SENSORY DIET

Sensory diet, as it is described here, is not so much a treatment as a strategy for developing a specific treatment. As originally discussed by Wilbarger and Wilbarger (1991), it refers to the type and amount of sensory input received by an individual. To evaluate a person's sensory diet, careful observation is necessary to assess the patterns and types of sensory input toward which an individual migrates, as well as avoids. Observation focuses not only on the behavior, but also on the emotional response of the individual to the sensory input.

An ideal sensory diet is one that helps an individual maintain a level of alertness that is accompanied by emotional calmness and effective performance. Using this ideal sensory diet, sensory interventions are developed that integrate preferred activities and sensory inputs, and avoid activities and inputs that produce overarousal. In order to expand a person's sensory diet, while maintaining effective functioning, challenging tasks are interwoven with activities that are satisfying; that is, challenging activities are gradually introduced in a way that allows the child to maintain an optimal level of arousal. Thus, sequencing of activities is important. Activities that precede challenging events, as well as activities that occur during and after such events, are critical to the design of an effective sensory intervention program.

In addition to these external supports, children can be taught, when challenged, to monitor and self-regulate their arousal level (Williams & Shellenberger, 1996). A prime example of this type of self-regulation is the use of the squeeze machine employed by Temple Grandin to decrease her anxiety level (Grandin, 1995). The use of deep pressure, as well as the Wilbarger Protocol (Wilbarger & Wilbarger, 1991), can be self-introduced either before, during, and/or after challenging activities. Some behavioral programs use an individual's stereotypies as an allowed activity after engaging in challenging tasks. This type of access to stereotypies may serve not only as a reward for good performance, but also as a response that reduces tension and anxiety.

Speech and communication training

Language and communication deficiencies are one of the core characteristics used to diagnose autism. Individuals with autism vary considerably in their language proficiency. Whereas some individuals have minimal or no expressive and receptive language, others have well-developed language, but have difficulties using this language in social interaction situations. Probably the most frequent intervention employed with young children with autism is speech therapy.

The goals of speech therapy vary considerably, depending on the developmental level and capabilities of the recipient. For example, some programs focus on speech articulation and on the paralinguistic or prosodic features of speech, including pitch, timing, volume, and stress. Other programs emphasize speech morphology, syntax, and content, or its pragmatic components; that is, how speech is used in maintaining a conversation, taking turns, responding in a relevant fashion, staying on topic, being clear, and recognizing the speaker's intent. Still other programs work on developing basic expressive skills and language comprehension. Not all programs focus on speech and language usage; some emphasize preverbal or nonverbal communication, that is, communications that convey messages without words. For example, nonverbal communication programs might concentrate on developing appropriate eye contact, use of gestures, appropriate facial expressions, joint attention, and alternative communication systems, such as signing.

Specific programs for achieving these goals vary considerably, for example, in where they take place (the clinic, school, and/or home), and in the degree to which they focus on the practical and/or the developmental needs of the child. Home-and clinic-based speech programs are more likely to be used with younger children, whereas school-based programs are more often employed with older children. Ideally, parents and other significant care-takers should be involved to ensure that the program is as intensive as possible and arranged so as to extend speech achievements to different environments and people. Although historically, behaviorally oriented speech programs were often directed at meeting the immediate functional needs of the child and family, they are now more frequently utilized as part of a broader developmentally oriented language program. Developmental programs are directed at systematically building language from its simple to more complex forms. This type of program is particularly appropriate for children whose language is developing more rapidly. In contrast, children whose language development is significantly delayed are more likely to receive a program directed at meeting the immediate functional needs of the child: a program that is more limited in its goals, and focuses on nonverbal communication and receptive language.

Wetherby and Prizant (1992) describe several guidelines, which they identified in the behavioral and developmental literatures, to assist in language program development. One guideline emphasizes that the goals of intervention should be based on both developmental and functional criteria. Although acknowledging the importance of developmental programs, the authors point out that a priority should be placed on helping participants communicate verbally and/or nonverbally so that they can be more effective in their social interactions. For example, they suggest that early program goals should focus on helping children to make requests and on eliciting joint attention, so that they are less inclined to use inappropriate and immature behaviors to regulate their social environment. Relatedly, the authors stress that particular attention should be given to understanding the communication functions of problem behaviors so that children can be taught alternative ways of expressing frustration, controlling their emotions, and getting their needs satisfied. Wetherby and Prizant (1992) also recommend that the natural environment should be used to teach important language responses and that emphasis should be placed on helping family, peers, and significant others to interact more effectively with persons with autism. This guideline was developed in recognition of the fact that communication is a transactional event in which two or more people are involved, each of whom must be able to understand and respond to the words/gestures and intent of the other's communication.

It is beyond the scope of this chapter to review specifically the wide variety of speech and language training programs employed with children with autism. However, a number are particularly worthy of mention. Ogletree (1998) separates treatment approaches into four general categories: consultation, discrete trial training, natural training paradigms, and nontraditional.

Traditionally, speech therapists focused on the person with autism and provided only general support to parents and significant others. However, as caretakers became more actively involved in the children's educational programs, therapists expanded their role. A consultation approach involves establishing a partnership between a professional therapist and individuals who are in close contact with children with autism, including parents, teachers, and peers. This partnership is directed at establishing speech and communication goals and best treatment practices. How this partnership proceeds varies considerably depending on the therapist and those who seek consultation. The consultation approach is typically employed in conjunction with a program administered in a clinic setting by a speech therapist.

A second approach to speech therapy is discrete trial training. As mentioned earlier in this chapter, discrete trial training is a highly structured approach that employs a variety of behavioral techniques, including the active use of prompts (verbal, imitation, and physical) and reinforcement. In this approach the structure of the speech program is established by the speech therapist; however, the parents are trained by the therapist to implement the speech program. This approach differs from the consultation model in the nature of therapist involvement, the specificity of parent training, and the highly intensive nature of the actual child therapy. Sometimes the parent trainer is not a formally trained speech therapist, but a person skilled in the use of the discrete trial training approach.

In contrast to discrete trial training, the natural training approach is implemented in a daily living environment. Frequently, this approach is used in conjunction with discrete trial training. In one variation of natural language training, the structure of the program is dictated by the child's response and interests. In other variations, trainers arrange the environment in order to increase the probability of specific child language responses. For example, stimuli, used as part of discrete trial training, are introduced into the natural environment and speech behaviors are actively modeled by the trainer. In this approach, like discrete trial training, prompts and reinforcements are employed.

In addition to these three approaches to developing speech, Ogletree (1998) mentions several nontraditional approaches, including auditory integration training (AIT) (discussed earlier in this chapter) and facilitated communication. AIT is typically utilized with individuals who display hypersensitivity to sound, in order to improve listening and speech skills. The facilitated communication approach is employed with individuals who have limited or no verbal abilities. The facilitator provides the trainee support in using an augmentative communication device, such as a communication board. Critics of this approach contend that the facilitator is dictating the communication response, not the trainee; that is, the trainee does not actually learn to communicate independently. Reviews of existing research examining this therapy offer little evidence for its efficacy (Mostert, 2001). Facilitated communication, however, is similar to a wide array of more accepted procedures that are directed at either augmenting or providing a client an alternative means of communication.

Augmentative and alternative communication training

Typically augmentative and alternative communication programs use some type of device or aid when children are unable or have difficulty acquiring speech. A wide range of specific materials and technologies exist for assisting persons with autism, including cards with pictures and words on them and language devices with prerecorded messages that can be activated through a variety of responses. Considerations that influence the choice of a specific communication system include: the sensory and motor capabilities of the client, the system's potential for expansion into more complex language forms, the client's motivation to use the system, the system's portability, and the ability of recipients to understand the communication.

The technology for assisting communication has become increasingly sophisticated as computer software has evolved and been interfaced with sound/speech synthesizers. For example, computers can be used to convert pictures, printed words, and other symbols into a speech format. Less technology-driven alternative communication approaches include the Picture Exchange Communication System (PECS) and sign language. These approaches, which are widely employed, are popular choices for historical, pragmatic, and economic reasons, as well as because of their established utility. The PECS and sign language approaches are briefly described here.

Picture Exchange Communication System (PECS)

Visual systems utilize pictures, printed words, objects, or combinations thereof for communication purposes. They often involve the use of some type of physical aid, such as a communication board, a notebook, or other devices to carry and/or display the visual materials. Portability and convenience of use are especially important in selecting a particular system. The PECS program, developed by Bondy and Frost (1993), is the most widely known of these visual systems.

During PECS training, objects or activities are chosen that serve as reinforcers for the trainee. Early stages of training involve prompting the trainee to put a picture of a desired object/activity (e.g., cookie) in the hand of the trainer, who in turn verbalizes what the child wants ("You want a cookie!") and then gives the child the object (the actual cookie). As training proceeds, prompts are gradually withdrawn to encourage the trainee to initiate spontaneously the request for what he/she desires through the use of the proper picture card. Subsequent training focuses on teaching the trainee to request other objects or desired activities, thus allowing the trainee to choose from a range of objects/activities the one most preferred at a particular time and to express that choice by giving the picture of the preferred object/activity to the trainer. This step requires that the child learn to discriminate between objects/activities. Later stages of training focus on teaching the trainee to respond to questions by using single and multiple picture responses. The basic approach to training falls under the rubric of behavior education described previously. For more complete information on PECS, the reader is referred to Bondy and Frost (1994)

Sign language

When children with autism have difficulty acquiring oral speech, sign language may become a treatment of choice, depending on the child's sensory, motor, and cognitive capabilities. For some children, signs are easier to teach than oral speech responses. Because no physical aids are required, signing is easily exportable to any communication situation. Moreover, sign language systems can be employed to express or receive messages of a highly complex nature. Sign language can be taught using an array of prompting and reinforcement procedures, using formats similar to those of discrete trial training discussed previously.

The major drawback of a signing approach is that signing is often not understood by those with whom the child interacts. Thus, in order to be useful, training programs need to teach not only the child but also significant others in the child's life to sign. Signing programs, although typically employed when traditional communication training programs fail, may aid in the acquisition of oral speech. Unless extensive hearing and/or motor impairments exist, signing procedures for children with autism can be conjoined with speech as part of a total communication package. One signing program commonly employed with speech-delayed children is American Sign Language. For a concise review of signing and other alternative communication systems, the reader is referred to Scheuermann and Webber (2002).

Play therapy

Play is generally viewed as an activity vital to a young child's development. It is through play, often referred to as a child's work, that children practice and develop their sensorimotor skills, early on through repetition of simple motor responses and subsequently through the complex coordination of different motor and verbal behaviors. Play behaviors are initially reflexive and simple, but become increasingly intentional, that is, under the child's voluntary control. As this process proceeds, it influences the wiring of the sensory, motor, and other parts of the brain.

Through play, children explore and learn about their environment and how it operates, including what it looks, sounds, feels, smells, and tastes like, as well as how it responds. Through play children learn about permanence and change in the structure of the environment, cause and effect relationships, and how objects can be used. From these experiences children form internal representations of objects in the environment and thinking processes evolve that allow the child to organize, plan, and even to transform reality through symbolic and imaginary play actions.

Children with autism often find their environment to be more disorganized, confusing, and frightening than other children; probably because of their motor deficiencies, hypersensitivities, attention problems, cognitive limitations, and communication problems. As a consequence, their interactions with the environment frequently become restricted. They cope with a challenging environment through ritualistically ordering the environment, or they may cognitively or behaviorally withdraw from their surroundings. When this occurs, play often becomes stereotyped and less complex. It also becomes asocial in nature; specifically because people are a large part of the confusing environment with which they have to contend. Whereas ordinary play is invigorating and pleasurable for typical children, for children with autism it is often a source of frustration and anxiety.

Historically, play therapy, influenced by psychoanalytic theory, was seen as a vehicle for helping children to express fears and reenact social conflicts. Through observing play, therapists attempted to gain insights into children's problems. Play therapy provided a structure to facilitate emotional catharsis. More recently, through the contributions of fields like psychology and occupational therapy, play has become a major vehicle for understanding and evaluating children's sensorimotor, cognitive, linguistic, social, and emotional development.

Although play can be particularly challenging and frustrating for children with autism, it is also an invaluable tool for helping them develop. Through assessment of children in play situations, a profile of their strengths and limitations can be developed to guide the structure of the play therapy. Through play programs, children with autism can be taught object play, imaginary play, and social play skills. From a basic process perspective, they can be taught attentional, imitation, motor-planning, and language responses. Moreover, play can be employed to help them tolerate and process sensory stimuli as well as to regulate their emotions. It can also be used as a vehicle for generalizing skills taught in more structured situations.

In establishing a play program, a variety of therapeutic/educational strategies and structures have been employed. At one end of a continuum, the structure is quite flexible and child-based, in the sense that the child's own actions become the critical components upon which therapy is built. In contrast, other programs are more structured; children, after an assessment of their strengths and limitations, are taught specific skills. Some programs have both unstructured and structured components. Less structured approaches to play therapy tend to be more an art form and for that reason are more difficult to transfer to parents and volunteers. In contrast, structured approaches can be readily taught. Both types of programs focus on creating a positive motivational environment for the children. Unstructured programs try to keep children motivated by letting them engage in activities of their choice. Structured programs also provide choices to children, but direct them toward activities designed to build specific skills. The children are further motivated through active use of reinforcers and incentives.

Most play programs use a variety of prompts to promote development. Structured programs, however, are often more specific in their designation of the prompts to be employed, how these prompts are sequenced, and how they are faded out. Such prompts include physical assistance, modeling, and verbal instruction. Most structured programs try to provide enough support to maintain the children's motivation and performance. They also pay special attention to the play space and play materials, arranging these spaces and materials in order to achieve specific program goals. Many structured programs create play spaces that are smaller, less distracting, and orderly. For example, the TEACCH model, discussed earlier in this chapter, emphasizes well-defined and less cluttered spaces for play activities, along with routines for proceeding through spaces in order to promote a feeling of security and learning.

In programs designed to promote social play, choice of partners is critical. Often adults are initially employed as partners; specifically because of their ability to be more sensitive responders, initiators, and supporters of play. Peers are subsequently introduced in a gradual fashion, after they are given training on how to interact with the child with autism. Optimally, all play programs should be designed to allow growth in the complexity of the skills taught and to promote generalization of play routines into natural environments. For further information on play programs, the reader is referred to Greenspan (1992), Schuler and Wolfberg (2000), Baranek, Reinhartsen, and Wannamaker (2001), and especially Scheuermann and Webber (2002).

Holding therapy

This controversial therapy is based on the assumption that social withdrawal in children, including those with autism, develops as a consequence of conflictual relationships with people around them, particularly the child's mother. As a consequence of this conflict, anxiety is produced and transferred to other social situations, which then leads the child to withdraw from social interactions. This view of autistic withdrawal has been espoused by Bettleheim (1967), Tinbergen and Tinbergen (1983), and seems also to be suggested by Kanner and Eisenberg (1956). From a developmental theoretical perspective, these authors appear to be suggesting that children with autism form avoidant attachments to their mothers and other primary care-takers which in turn are generalized to other social relationships. Support for this position is minimal; research suggests that the rate of secure attachment among children with autism is similar to that of children with other developmental disorders (Rogers, Ozonoff & Maslin-Cole, 1993).

Developed by Welch (1988), holding therapy attempts to correct the faulty bond between mother and child by having a parent hold, forcibly if necessary, their child in a face-to-face manner while making eye contact. The child is held until he/she no longer struggles, whereupon the child is released. When viewed within a learning theoretical perspective, it appears that social proximity, in the absence of struggle, is negatively reinforced through the termination of an aversive holding restraint. Thus, it appears what the child learns is not to struggle, a passive response: that is, not struggling leads to the withdrawal of forcible holding. From a classical conditioning learning perspective, it could be argued that the person holding the child is likely to become associated with the experience of being forcibly held, and thus elicit, not reduce, social anxiety. From both a developmental and learning perspective, the rationale underlying holding therapy does not seem to make good theoretical or educational sense. No research evaluating the efficacy of this approach could be found. For these reasons, this therapy is not recommended.

Nevertheless, the idea of a therapy that focuses on helping parents form a secure emotional bond with their children has merit. Because the experience of raising a child with autism can create considerable anxiety and stress for the parents, as well as for the child, it is possible that the parent–child relationship will be adversely affected. For this reason, it is important that parents learn to cope with the challenges associated with having an autistic child so that they can enjoy and nurture them. They need to learn how to relate to their children, who have sensory, motor, cognitive, and communication problems, and who often perceive the world as threatening. With professional support parents can come to understand the characteristics of their children, what types of physical and social situations are fear-evoking for them, and how to relate to them in a sensitive fashion. As a consequence, the positive bond between parents and children should become strengthened. This focus on developing a positive parent–child bond is emphasized by the Option Institute.

The Option Method

This method was developed by the parents of a child who was autistic (Kaufman & Kaufman, 1976). Based on their experience with their son, the Kaufmans developed the Option Institute to help parents with children similar to their own. More specifically, the program was designed to help parents understand and accept their children, as well as to reduce their guilt by bringing them to the realization that they have been doing the best they could to help their children. Parents are shown a new way of relating to their children. This treatment emphasizes the importance of creating a therapy environment free of distraction. The parents are taught to enter into their children's world, not making demands on them, but rather enjoying the children they have and creating a pleasurable social experience for them. Moreover, parents are shown the value of starting where their children are and how to gradually extend their children's behavior in order to facilitate growth.

The Option approach has many positive features with its focus on: reducing parent anxiety, fostering positive parental attitudes about themselves and their children, and creating a therapy that is nonthreatening to the child. The general approach is reminiscent of humanistically oriented therapies and child-rearing philosophies that were prevalent in psychology and education in the middle of the twentieth century. Specifically, children and adults were viewed as having an inner capacity for development and growth that could be actualized through their experiences with an environment that is permissive and accepting. Although the Option program is structured in a general sense, it does not appear to be based on any established educational principles or curriculum and seems to ignore or de-emphasize the use of structured techniques that have been developed to help children with delays to learn. At present there is no empirical support for the utility of this method.

Music, dance, and art therapy

Although the efficacy of music, dance, and art therapies have not been subjected to empirical examination, there is testimonial evidence suggesting their potential utility. There are many reasons to consider these therapies. They can be designed to take advantage of and build on the special abilities and interests of individuals with autism as well as to help them to develop in areas in which they are deficient. For example, art therapy may assist children with good visual–spatial skills to become more adept at drawing and to express themselves through their art. Dance and music therapy provides proprioceptive, vestibular, and auditory stimulation sought after by some children. At an emotional level, music, dance, and art have the capacity to reduce tension and evoke pleasure. Trevarthen, Aitken, Papoudi, and Robarts (1996) point out that the tones and rhythms that accompany activities, such as walking, breathing, and the heart beating, are captured in music. At a behavioral level, these therapies can serve as a vehicle for promoting skills, a means of self-regulating emotions, and an outlet for pent-up energy. From a social perspective, music, dance, and art can provide a nonthreatening and pleasurable forum for social engagement. Finally, from a professional standpoint, the development of these various activities as therapies for children with autism provides a unique interdisciplinary and creative oppor-tunity for people in the humanities and social sciences to work together. It is important, however, that such therapies, as they are developed, be empirically evaluated to determine their effectiveness.

L'Arche communities

L'Arche is described here, not because it is a formal treatment for autism per se, but because it represents a type of approach that can profoundly affect the lives of people with autism and other developmental problems as well as those who care for them. L'Arche is a community made up of people, with and without handicaps, who live and grow together through their relationship with each other. L'Arche was founded in 1964 by Jean Vanier, a theologian, in France. Vanier, with a friend, Thomas Philippe, opened the first L'Arche home, where they lived with two mentally handicapped men. Although guided by Christian principles, L'Arche is ecumenical. Dozens of L'Arche homes now exist worldwide, serving people of all races, creeds, and capabilities. The International Federation of L'Arche was created in 1972 to advise the network of L'Arche communities, although it retains no authority over them. L'Arche communities bring together people "who are talented and strong with people who are poor and marginalized" (Vanier, 1995, p.55). The communities are encouraged to grow in their own unique ways.

The mission of L'Arche is threefold: to provide love, security, and satisfying work to people with developmental disabilities so they can have a fulfilling life, within both a home setting and society; to foster family-like relationships where each person's gifts can be celebrated in the context of community living; and to reveal to the world the value and talents of people who are otherwise often rejected or ignored. L'Arche is based on the belief that each person with or without a disability has a special and unique value.

L'Arche communities live as families. The goal of L'Arche is to create a home where relationships can grow between persons with handicaps and those members who assist and live in community with them. The members of L'Arche have a wide range of handicaps and talents. Assistants come from various backgrounds: some are young and take a year off from studies, others have established themselves professionally but want a new way of life. Members live on the same level in complementary relationships. Distinctions between those who are helped and those who are helping are minimized. There are no prearranged plans for the members' development nor a set time for their leaving. L'Arche differs from many other types of group living arrangements in its emphasis on quality of life, spiritual development, the permanency of the home, an association with other homes, a live-in policy for assistants, and a concern for the "care-givers" as well as those who receive care. The L'Arche homes bear similarities to other group arrangements where people with handicaps live and work in agrarian communities. For further information about L'Arche the reader is referred to Coppersmith (1984), Downey (1986), Harris (1987), Nouwen (1988), Shearer (1997), and Vanier (1997).

Other intervention directions

Examination of the interventions discussed thus far in this chapter reveals that most have been directed at addressing the needs of individuals with autism in the sensory, motor, language/communication, and social areas. Some of the programs, like behavior education and TEACCH, also focus on promoting adaptive behavior in self-help academic and vocational areas. In contrast, considerably less emphasis has been placed on developing interventions that explicitly address the emotional and cognitive needs of persons with autism. As suggested in Chapters 2, 3, and 4, the emotion and cognitive systems may play an important role in the development of autism.

Several programs, however, have focused either directly or indirectly on anxiety reduction. For example, a number of the sensory integration training programs previously described are directed at decreasing the anxiety experienced by individuals as they encounter challenging auditory, tactual, and other sensory stimuli. Moreover, TEACCH uses program structuring to help students for whom change is upsetting. In addition to these programs, other attempts to reduce anxiety and control emotions are mentioned in the autism literature, including the use of exercise and deep muscle massage. For example, Escalona, Field, Singer-Strunck, Cullen, and Hartshorn (2001) point out how massage therapy has been employed to enhance parasympathetic activity and reduce problems in areas like sleep. At present, however, more systematic attention needs to be given to addressing the emotional needs of individuals with autism, for example, by using procedures that have been successfully employed with persons with anxiety disorders, such as systematic desensitization and reciprocal inhibition.

Similarly, there has been little emphasis on addressing the cognitive needs and deficiencies of individuals with autism. Given the unique cognitive characteristics displayed by these individuals (see Chapter 2), the importance of cognitive processes in theories of autism (see Chapter 3), and the considerable research that has been conducted in this area, it is surprising that more attention has not been given by professionals to the utilization of cognitive therapies, in particular cognitive behavior therapy (CBT) with this population. CBT emerged in the 1960s as an outgrowth of applied and basic research in the areas of learning and cognition (Bandura, 1969). This approach differs from behavior education programs, such as applied behavior analysis, in that the cognitive antecedents of behavior are focused on during intervention rather than behavior per se. Cognitions, such as attitudes, beliefs, attributions, and strategies, are recognized as having causal influence on behavior and emotions, as well being influenced by behavior, emotions, and the surrounding environment. Although cognitions are covert responses, they are viewed as being subject to the same environmental influences as overt behaviors.

From an educational and treatment perspective, CBT focuses on developing or modifying a person's cognitive responses. A variety of interventions have emerged that can be classified under the rubric of CBT, including rational-emotive therapy, cognitive therapy, metacognitive training, self-instruction, and visual imaging. These approaches have been employed both to modify distorted thinking and to correct cognitive deficiencies and defects. More specifically these approaches have been used to reduce anxiety, depression, aggression, anger, impulsivity, and pain as well to develop social understanding, reading comprehension, mathematics performance, and problem-solving (Kendall, 1991). Cognitive behavior therapy teaches individuals new ways of processing, remembering, and utilizing information. Although CBT has been effectively applied with a variety of clinical populations and in academic settings, its development as a treatment for developmental disorders like mental retardation and autism has only begun to emerge.

Whitman (1987, 1990) suggested that CBT procedures, such as self-instructional training, are useful for children with developmental disorders who have developed some language proficiency, and are particularly beneficial for children who have difficulty processing information given them by socialization agents and/or using such information to regulate their behavior and emotions. For example, some children in academic situations cannot articulate how they should go about solving a simple math problem or in a social situation what to do when a peer comes up and greets them. Other children can state what they should do in such situations but cannot use this knowledge to guide their actions. Self-instruction and a companion procedure, correspondence training, have been used to increase attention, promote math problem-solving, improve classroom behavior, and develop vocational skills in children with mental retardation and autism. Self-instruction teaches children to process information through having them verbalize what they should do in specific performance situations, and then to use these verbalizations to guide their behavior; thus it promotes both knowledge acquisition and knowledge utilization. Currently cognitively oriented programs which incorporate procedures such as self-instruction are starting to evolve to address the social and academic needs of persons with Asperger's and higher functioning autism (Myles & Simpson, 1998). In Chapter 7, the use of self-instruction is further discussed as an important approach for helping individuals with autism self-regulate their behavior and act independently.

Strategies for dealing with challenging behaviors

In establishing and implementing any educational or therapeutic program for persons with autism, the cooperation of the individual is critical to its success. Behaviors like noncompliance, hyperactivity, inattention, avoidance, stereotypy, self-injury, and aggression can interfere with the successful implementation of a program. If such behavior problems are not effectively addressed, they tend to become habitual, often escalating in frequency and intensity. Moreover, as children with behavioral problems get older, they may be increasingly defined by these problems, rather than their positive characteristics and educational needs; as a consequence they are sometimes excluded from educational/therapeutic programs.

Behavior educators emphasize that all behaviors, whether adaptive or maladaptive, serve a function for the individual. Before implementing a behavior reduction program for individuals with autism, it is important to determine what function inappropriate behavior serves for them. Does it provide access to objects, activities, social outcomes, or situations that are positively reinforcing? Does it allow the individual to escape from an unpleasant situation? Is the individual trying to communicate his/her needs through the behavior? The answers to these questions can be quite useful when making program decisions.

In developing a behavior reduction program, behavior educators as a matter of general principle try to use procedures that are positive rather than punitive in nature, and where possible enhance individual choice rather than restrict it. One of the common misconceptions about behavior reduction programs is that punishment is the procedure of choice when misbehavior occurs. In fact, it is the procedure of last choice. In this section, behavior deceleration procedures are outlined, generally in order from those that are more positive to those that are more restrictive in nature. These procedures include: extinction, differential reinforcement, time-out, response cost, and aversive stimulation. Although differential reinforcement is the most desirable option for dealing with problem behaviors, extinction is discussed first because it is one component of the differential reinforcement technique. All of these techniques have been widely employed and extensively evaluated.

Extinction

To appreciate the rationale for use of extinction procedures, the process by which behavior is learned needs to be understood. Learning theory emphasizes that most inappropriate (as well as appropriate) behaviors are developed and maintained through positive and/or negative reinforcement. Positive reinforcement involves the application of a "valued" stimulus/event or "reward" after a response occurs that in turn leads to a subsequent increase in that response. For example, many misbehaviors occur because an individual wants and receives attention from significant others. Negative reinforcement involves the withdrawal of an "aversive" stimulus after a behavior occurs that results in a subsequent increase in that behavior. An example of negative re-inforcement is a teacher allowing a child to leave an educational situation that the child finds unpleasant after the child engages in an undesirable behavior (e.g., self-stimulatory behavior, aggression, inattention, or running away). Allowing the child to leave the unpleasant situation after a "misbehavior" occurs often serves to negatively reinforce or increase that behavior.

During extinction the developmental process that leads to misbehavior is reversed by discontinuing the process of positive or negative reinforcement that historically has been in place. For example, children would not be given "positive" attention or allowed to escape from an undesirable to a more desirable situation when they are noncompliant. Although conceptually easy to understand, extinction can be difficult to apply. For an extinction program to be successful, it must be consistently applied. If it is not and the misbe-havior is occasionally reinforced, that is, intermittently reinforced, the behavior is likely to increase in frequency and be even more difficult to remediate. The use of extinction typically results in a temporary increase in the misbehavior (an extinction burst) before it decreases; this increase is probably due to the child's frustration because the misbehavior is no longer reinforced. Although this temporary increase routinely occurs during the extinction process, it is sometimes misinterpreted as a failure of the procedure and the procedure is discontinued or applied inconsistently. Such actions often result in the misbehavior becoming more firmly entrenched.

A number of factors must be considered in deciding whether to use extinction to reduce problem behavior. These factors include how firmly the behavior is established and the specific nature of the misbehavior. Behaviors that have become strong habits, that is, have a long history of occurrence and have been intermittently reinforced, are difficult to modify through the use of an extinction procedure. In contrast, misbehaviors that have developed more recently are easier to extinguish. A second consideration in determining whether to use extinction relates to the nature of the behavior to be reduced. If the behavior produces adverse consequences that cannot be socially tolerated, even temporarily, such as self-injury or injury to other people, then extinction is not the procedure of choice. When the misbehavior has serious consequences or has a long history of occurrence, a procedure other than extinction should be considered, such as differential reinforcement, response cost, or time-out.

Differential reinforcement

Differential reinforcement refers to a technique in which one or more desirable behaviors are reinforced, while other "undesirable" behaviors are placed on extinction. Thus, differential reinforcement consists of two procedures, reinforcement and extinction. For example, in a teaching situation a child's nonattending responses are ignored, that is, placed on extinction, and attending responses are positively reinforced. Another example of a differential reinforcement program is ignoring stereotyped behavior, such as hand-flapping behavior, and reinforcing more socially desirable hand movements, such as playing with a toy. The main objective of a differential reinforcement program can be to increase desirable behaviors, to decrease undesirable behaviors, or more typically to accomplish both of these goals. Differential reinforcement can also be employed to teach a child when or in what situation a particular response is desirable and when it is not. For example, in an expressive language training program a child is reinforced for saying "circle" when shown a circle, whereas this same response (saying "circle") is put on extinction when a square is presented.

Response cost and time-out

In addition to reinforcement procedures, a variety of techniques falling under the general rubric of punishment can be employed. Punishment can involve either the withdrawal or presentation of a stimulus event following a response; in either case, by definition the procedure results in a reduction in the frequency of the response. Punishment by withdrawal techniques is typically preferred over punishment by presentation techniques, for reasons to be developed in the next section.

Two commonly employed procedures, which bear some similarity to extinction techniques, are classified under punishment by withdrawal. They are response cost and time-out. Response cost involves the loss of a reinforcer that is in the possession of the individual. The reinforcer taken away either has a tangible quality (e.g., food, money, or some other desirable object) or involves an activity like watching television. Sometimes response cost procedures are used in conjunction with token economies; misbehavior results in the loss of tokens which could have been exchanged for desirable objects or activities important to the individual.

In contrast to response cost, which involves removal of reinforcers, time-out involves removal of the individual from a situation in which positive reinforcers are available. For example, if a child enjoys playing in a room full of toys, a misbehavior, such as hitting another child, results in the offending child being removed from the room or being placed in a time-out chair away from the toys for a short period of time.

Application of aversive stimuli

In contrast to response cost and time-out, some punishment procedures involve the administration of aversive stimuli. Examples of this type of punishment are: social disapproval (such as "no!"), negative feedback "that is wrong", or the delivery of a physical stimulus, such as restraint or a spanking.

Punishment, especially physical punishment, is not recommended. If it is employed, it needs to be administered under very controlled circumstances, and only when previously discussed procedures do not work. Moreover, physical punishment should not even be considered for misbehaviors unless they harm or place at risk for harm the misbehaving individual or others. The problem with punishment, particularly when the punitive stimulus is very aversive, is that it generates negative emotions (anxiety, fear) which can become associated with specific situations, activities, and the punishing agent (e.g., teacher or parent). After being punished, a child is likely to become upset, an emotion that can interfere with learning and can lead to physical or psychological attempts by the child to escape or avoid the situation in which punishment occurs, as well as the agent who administers the punishment. Moreover, punishment, if used frequently, can have a long-term impact on the individual, resulting in inhibition, lack of initiative, giving up easily, and dependency. Because children with autism tend to be socially avoidant and inhibited, the use of punishment with this population is even more problematic.

Another problem with punishment is that it often reinforces the individual (teacher, parent) for using it; specifically because it often works, reducing behavior at least in the short term. If punishment is successfully employed, there is a temptation to use it again and again; sometimes its use increases to a point that it becomes a favored "educational" technique. Finally, if punishment involving physical aversive stimulation is used when the "teacher/parent" is in a state of frustration, it can inadvertently be intensified to the point of abuse. In this regard, because punishment often loses its effectiveness when repeatedly employed, it typically needs to be intensified to have a desired effect. For these reasons, and many more, punishment, particularly procedures using physical aversive stimulation, is not recommended for use except in extraordinary, highly controlled, and well-monitored situations. Creative educators find ways to deal with misbehaviors that do not involve the use of punishment procedures. For a review of deceleration procedures, the reader is referred to Scheuermann and Webber (2002).

Other deceleration procedures

There are numerous other strategies that can be used to decrease undesirable behavior. A few of these will be mentioned here, including environmental control, self-regulation, and anxiety reduction. When environmental control is employed, the environmental situations in which undesirable behavior occurs is analyzed in order to determine those aspects of the environment that precipitate or are associated with the occasion of the undesirable behavior. Then those critical aspects of the environment are altered or removed. For example, in designing a program to promote sustained attention in an academic task situation, it may be established that certain environmental stimuli, such as noise or an open window, lead to inattention. To reduce inattention and increase attention, distracters are removed, at least until sustained attention is developed.

A second deceleration procedure involves teaching children responses that help them self-regulate their undesirable behavior. As children develop, language becomes an increasingly critical tool for controlling their behavior. There are a wide range of self-regulatory responses, involving language, which children can be taught to employ. For example, they can be taught to communicate their needs rather than acting out in order to get what they want. Another self-regulatory procedure that can be used with children who have good verbal and cognitive skills is problem-solving. This procedure involves teaching children to analyze situations associated with misbehavior and to generate, evaluate, and select appropriate strategies for reducing that misbehavior.

A final deceleration strategy involves assessing the anxiety level of an individual and examining the relationship between his/her emotional state and misbehavior. To the extent that anxiety is associated with misbehavior, strategies can be developed to reduce this anxiety. For example, if anxiety and distractibility are associated, anxiety reduction procedures, such as vigorous physical exercise, massage, music, or engaging in a relaxing enjoyable activity, can be introduced either before, during, or after a demanding task.

General comments on behavior reduction programs

Whenever possible, interventions should be focused on promoting adaptive behaviors. Maladaptive behaviors often disappear when children are taught new skills and ways of obtaining things that are important to them. When behavioral deceleration programs are employed, they should be used in conjunction with positive reinforcement programs. If the sole focus of a program is on reducing misbehavior, the program is probably destined for failure. When deceleration programs are employed, they should involve the least restrictive procedure possible. Procedures such as differential reinforcement and extinction should ideally be used. Procedures such as response cost, time-out, and social punishment should be utilized only when these less restrictive techniques do not work. If children have language skills, emphasis should be placed on teaching them how to verbally self-regulate their behavior. Finally, it is critical for all procedures to be applied in a correct and consistent fashion. Behavioral educational interventions frequently fail, not because they are ineffective, but because the interventions are inappropriately or inconsistently employed.

Summary

A variety of claims have been made regarding the effectiveness of educational and therapeutic interventions for children with autism. Such claims are often based on anecdotal evidence and personal testimonies. The majority of interventions reviewed thus far in the chapter have not been subjected to rigorous empirical scrutiny. The only intervention that has been extensively evaluated is the behavior education (or applied behavior analysis) approach. Support for the efficacy of this approach comes from a large body of basic research with humans and animals, as well as applied research with a wide variety of nonclinical and clinical populations, including individuals who display developmental delays and autistic behaviors. It is important to note that many other therapies, such as speech, occupational, and play therapy, often use behavior education techniques as their main teaching tool. Although claims have been made by some proponents of the ABA approach that the children treated recovered from their autism, no real evidence is available to support this conclusion. Some critics of the behavior education approach suggest that there is limited or no evidence indicating that the ABA approach is more effective than other approaches (Prizant & Rubin, 1999). However, it makes little sense to conduct such comparative research until there is solid evidence that the treatments to be compared with ABA are effective in the first place.

Other than the behavior education approach, TEACCH is probably the most widely recognized intervention for individuals with autism. Like ABA, TEACCH incorporates a clinical evaluation component as a part of their intervention. Clinical evaluations, while useful, provide only information about whether a program recipient is showing positive gains during the intervention. They do not systematically examine, using appropriate experimental controls, whether the gains are actually a function of the intervention or some other uncontrolled factor. TEACCH is difficult to evaluate in its entirety because it has so many different educational components; because new components are periodically introduced; and because this program is applied across the life span. Although there is only minimal research evidence indicating the efficacy of TEACCH, this approach is generally to be commended for its attempt to include components that have been empirically validated, such as ABA, as part of its total program.

For reviews evaluating educational interventions that have been employed with autistic individuals, the reader is referred to a clinical guideline report put out by the Autism Society of America, Mudford et al. (2000), Mostert (2001), and the New York State Department of Health Early Intervention Program (1999). The clinical practice guideline, put out by the New York State Department of Health, is a particularly comprehensive review of behavioral and educational approaches. This report was written by an independent multidisciplinary panel convened by the New York State Department of Health. This panel systematically reviewed scientific research evaluating a wide variety of interventions and used this evidence, combined with expert clinical judgment, to develop the guidelines. Only one approach was recommended with enthusiasm by the panel. Specifically, it recommended that "principles of applied behavior analysis (ABA) and behavioral intervention strategies be included as important elements in any intervention program for young children with autism" (p. 15). A number of approaches were not recommended because of lack of research evidence indicating their efficacy, including the developmental relationship model (informally referred to as "floor time"), sensory integration therapy, music therapy, touch therapy, auditory integration training, and facilitated communication.

Biomedical treatments

In the aforementioned technical report published by the New York State Department of Health Early Intervention Program (1999), which presented clinical practice guidelines for children with autism, a variety of medication and diet therapies were evaluated. Many of these therapies, as well as several other treatments, will be briefly described and evaluated here, including pharmacological, hormone, anti-yeast, homeopathic, immunologic, vitamin and diet, and craniosacral manipulation.

Pharmacological treatment for children with autism

In this section, most of the major pharmacological treatments that have been used with children with autism will be examined. Although no pharmaceutical has been found to be a "cure" for autism, many medications are used to control specific autistic and co-morbid symptoms, as well as to manage problem behaviors. Psychotropic medications exert their effects on mental and behavioral symptoms through influencing central nervous system chemistry. Studies evaluating these medications typically look at their impact on target symptoms as well as unintended adverse effects. In the New York technical report (1999), 99 articles were reviewed that examined the efficacy of several psychotropic medications, including haloperidol (a neuroleptic or antipsychotic medication), naltrexone (an opiate antagonist), clonidine (an alpha adrenergic agonist), and fenfluramine (a stimulant medication). The report concluded that although "some medications have been shown to be effective in reducing maladaptive behaviors in children with autism", most have been associated "with relatively high rates of side effects", such as dyskinesia (a condition involving involuntary muscle movements), agitation, increased stereotypy, and toxic impact on organs (p. IV–86). The report points out that psychotropic medications are seldom administered to children under three years of age because of the potential for adverse side effects and because behavioral and other problems in this group are often manageable through other types of intervention. The American Academy of Pediatrics notes that drug therapies should be used in conjunction with, not as a substitute for, developmental, educational, behavioral, and habilitative therapies (AAP, 2000).

Research evaluating drugs that have been proposed to treat autism is on the increase. For example, one organization, the RUPP (Research Units on Pediatric Pharmacology) Autism Network, has organized multicenter trials at Indiana University Medical School, Ohio State University, Johns Hopkins University Kennedy Krieger Institute, UCLA, and Yale University. With this accelerated emphasis on drug testing, better information on treatments should be available more quickly than in the past. In this section, the following classes of drugs will be discussed: neuroleptics, serotonin re-uptake inhibitors, opioid antagonists, stimulants, adrenergic agonists, anticonvulsants, and possible future drug treatments, such as oxytocin and ampakines.

A number of methodologies have been used in evaluating the safety and efficacy of pharmacological treatments. Two study parameters are particularly important; these are blinding and control groups. Blinding parameters can include blinded, double-blinded, and open label studies. "Blinding" refers to not knowing whether a treatment given is experimental or control; in single-blinded studies the subject does not know the condition to which they have been assigned; in double-blinded studies neither the subject nor the therapist knows the condition. Open label studies are not blinded and all participants knows what treatment is used. Double-blinded studies most effectively avoid problems of experimental bias. Experimental treatments are generally compared against some type of control condition; often a placebo control group is employed. Control can be managed by the classic control group design, in which subjects are randomly assigned to an experimental or control condition, or a crossover design, in which subjects go through both control and experimental conditions. The highest quality studies utilize both blinding and control procedures, are performed at multiple sites, and have large numbers of subjects. These studies are resource-intensive and generally occur after smaller, less controlled studies have suggested that a treatment is effective.

NEUROLEPTICS

Neuroleptics are a class of drugs that bind to and inactivate receptors in the brain, such as those for dopamine, histamine, and serotonin. Neuroleptics are commonly used as anti-psychotic treatments for delusions, hostility, and hallucinations in schizophrenic patients. These drugs were considered good early candidates for the treatment of autism; specifically because older children and adults with autism were found to have high levels of serotonin in their blood and cerebrospinal fluid. Early studies using older neuroleptics, such as haloperidol and thioridazine, were found to decrease maladaptive behaviors, but had very troubling side effects. The side effects included: sedation, irritability, weight gain, and abnormal motor movements (rigidity, tremors, restlessness), also known as "extra-pyramidal dyskinesia". Some of these side effects were reported to continue long after the withdrawal of the drug (see a review by Tsai, 1999).

Risperidone is a newer neuroleptic that appears to produce less severe side effects. It binds to both dopamine and serotonin receptors and blocks their action. Several double-blind and open label studies evaluating this drug found that children diagnosed with autism showed improvements in social relatedness and reductions in hostility, aggression, irritability, agitation, and hyperactivity (Malone, Maislin, Choudhury, Gifford & Delaney, 2002; McDougle, Holmes, Carlson, Pelton, Cohen & Price, 1998; Turgay, Binder, Snyder & Fisman, 2002). Several side effects of risperidone treatment were reported, including weight gain, sedation, increased appetite, and some abnormal movements; though these movement problems were milder and shorter in duration than those seen with haloperidol and thioridazine.

The RUPP Autism Network has a multicenter, double-blinded, three-phase study of risperidone underway. These phases involve: an eight-week double-blinded trial (Phase 1); a four-month open label trial for those who showed improvement in Phase 1 (Phase 2); and a randomized, double-blind, placebo discontinuation of treatment (to examine discontinuation effects, some children will get a placebo, while others will continue to get risperidone) (Phase 3) (McCracken et al., 2002; McDougle et al., 2000). Phase 1 is complete; Phases 2 and 3 are still in progress. Phase 1 results included data from 82 boys and 19 girls with autism at five sites. A variety of clinical rating scales and checklists were used to evaluate behavioral effects. The children given risperidone showed a significant decrease in a number of target behaviors (including tantrums, aggression, and self-injury) compared to children on placebo (69% versus 12%). Irritability scores also decreased by 56.9% in the treatment group versus 14% in the placebo group. These positive effects, which were shown by two-thirds of the children at the end of the eight-week trial, were maintained for up to six months. Side effects included weight gain, increased appetite, drowsiness, dizziness, drooling, mild tremor, and mild dyskinesia (McCracken *et al.*, 2002).

SEROTONIN RE-UPTAKE INHIBITORS

Fluoxetine (trade name Prozac) has been found to be useful in treating some symptoms of autism in both children and adults, especially in patients with co-morbid conditions of depression and anxiety. Improvements in language, cognition, and social relatedness, as well as reductions in ritualistic and obsessive behaviors, have also been documented in several studies. Positive responses have been observed more often in participants whose families had a history of affective disorders. Side effects that have been noted with fluoxetine include: insomnia, restlessness, decreased appetite, hyperactivity, and agitation (Cook, Rowlett, Jaselskis & Leventhal, 1992; Ghaziuddin, Tsai & Ghaziuddin, 1991; Koshes, 1997). A more recent placebo-controlled crossover study of fluoxetine by Buchsbaum, *et al.* (2001) also showed reduction in participant obsessions and anxiety. PET scan information revealed that fluoxetine increased metabolic activity in the right frontal lobe, particularly in the anterior cingulate gyrus and orbitofrontal cortex. The cingulate gyrus is a deep frontal lobe structure that plays an important role in attentional processes. This area of the brain communicates with the limbic system (primitive emotions) and the prefrontal cortex (assessment of threat, pleasure, and goal-oriented activity). Low activity in these areas has been associated with autistic symptoms.

Other drugs that inhibit serotonin re-uptake, such as fluvoxamine and clomipramine, have been examined and found to relieve some symptoms of autism. Fluvoxamine was tested in adults with autism in a 12-week, double-blind, placebo-controlled trial and was found to reduce repetitive thoughts and behaviors, aggression, and other maladaptive behaviors, and also to improve social relatedness and language usage (McDougle, Naylor, Cohen, Volkmar, Heninger & Price, 1996). Pediatric effectiveness still needs to be determined (Tsai, 1999). Finally, clomipramine, a serotonin re-uptake inhibitor, was compared to desipramine, one of its metabolites and a weak inhibitor of norepinephrine re-uptake. Clomipramine was more effective than either placebo or desipramine in reducing stereotypic behaviors, anger, and compulsive behaviors. Both drugs were more effective than a placebo in reducing hyperactivity (Gordon, State, Nelson, Hamburger & Rapoport, 1993).

OPIOID ANTAGONISTS

High levels of opioids have been found in the cerebrospinal fluid of some autistic children. Opioids reduce pain perception and can induce feelings of euphoria. Opioid antagonists bind to the opioid receptors in the brain and block the action of naturally occurring opioids. Children who perform self-injurious behaviors often have elevated levels of endogenous opioids. It appears that opioids inhibit the feeling of pain associated with self-injurious behaviors. The release of opioids through self-injury may possibly serve as a reward for the behaviors. Kolmen and coworkers found in two well-designed studies that Naltrexone, an opioid antagonist, reduced hyperactivity and restlessness in about one-half of the participants (Kolmen, Feldman, Handen & Janosky, 1995, 1997).

STIMULANTS AND ADRENERGIC AGONISTS

Stimulant drugs, such as Ritalin (methylphenidate), have been prescribed for autistic children to reduce hyperactivity and attention difficulties. Research evaluating the efficacy of these drugs indicated greater improvements for higher functioning children; however, results have been inconsistent. Side effects observed include increased aggression and stereotypic behaviors. In general, stimulants are not widely prescribed for autism per se, but rather to control behavior problems (Quintana, Birmaher, Stedge, Lennon, Freed, Bridge & Greenhill, 1995; see also review by Tsai, 1999).

Alpha adrenergic agonists, such as clonidine, attach to the central and peripheral nervous system receptors for norepinephrine and other catecholamines and behave like those chemicals. Jaselskis and coworkers performed a double-blind, placebo-controlled trial of clonidine with hyperactive children with autism. The children receiving clonidine showed a modest reduction in irritability and hyperactivity on parent and teacher ratings. Sedation and reduced blood pressure were side effects. Participants also developed a tolerance to the medication (Jaselskis, Cook, Fletcher & Leventhal, 1992).

ANTICONVULSANTS

Several anticonvulsant medications are used to control seizures which occur in almost one-third of individuals with autistic spectrum disorders. These drugs include valproic acid, divalproex sodium, lamotrigine, topiramate, carbamazepine, and vigabatrine. Research suggests that anticonvulsant medications are effective in controlling seizures and may be useful in improving emotional stability and reducing aggression, even in patients without a history of epilepsy (Di Martino & Tuchman, 2001; Hollander, Dolgoff-Kaspar, Cartwright, Rawitt & Novotny, 2001; McDougle, Stigler & Posey, 2003).

Possible future treatments

Oxytocin is a small (nine amino acid) peptide hormone, normally secreted during nursing and childbirth. In animal studies, oxytocin has been found to be associated with pro-social behaviors, especially those involved in nurturing. It is sometimes called the "cuddling hormone". Animals injected with oxytocin increase their social behaviors. Animals injected with oxytocin blockers reduce their social behaviors and avoid social interaction (Insel & Winslow, 1991). In a study by Winslow and Insel (2002), a strain of mice without endogenous oxytocin (oxytocin knockout mice) showed fewer social behaviors than control mice. For example, they did not recognize familiar mice; subsequently injections of oxytocin led to increased sociability, including recognition of familiars.

Human data suggest a possible role for oxytocin in the treatment of autistic symptoms. A recent study examined the midday levels of oxytocin in 29 autistic and 30 age-matched, nonautistic children. The autistic children had lower levels of oxytocin. Nonautistic children showed increased oxytocin levels with age, while the autistic children did not (Modahl et al., 1998). Hollander, et al. (2003) performed a double-blind, placebo-controlled trial of oxytocin infusions for adults who were diagnosed as having either autism or Asperger's disorders. A reduction in number of repetitive behaviors (e.g., need to know, repeating, ordering, needing to tell, self-injury, and touching) was observed for 13 of the 15 subjects following oxytocin perfusion; in contrast only 6 of the 15 participants in the placebo group showed a decrease in repetitive behaviors, while 6 showed an increase. No differences in side effects between placebo and oxytocin groups were found (Hollander et al., 2003). Although not specifically measured in this pilot study, the authors suggested that social behaviors may also have improved with oxytocin treatment.

R-BH4 is another drug that has been investigated as treatment for autism. It is a chemical required for the synthesis of neurotransmitters, such as serotonin and other catecholamines. In an open label pilot study, six preschool children with autism were treated with R-BH4. Parents reported improvement in eye contact, desire to interact, and the number of words and sounds. A small improvement on the Griffith Developmental Scale was also seen. PET scans showed a 10% increase in the binding of the Dopamine D2 receptor in the caudate and putamen, approaching a level close to the normal (Fernell et al., 1997). The caudate and the putamen (components of the basal ganglia system) are areas deep within the brain which receive a wide variety of inputs from the cerebral cortex, process this input, and feed it back to the motor cortex. The caudate influences motivational processes and the putamen is associated with subconscious coordination of simple sensorimotor behaviors. Because only one study has been conducted on this drug, more research is obviously needed to assess its safety and efficacy.

Ampakines are a relatively new class of drugs that enhance AMPA receptor activity. These receptors aid in the transmission of glutamate signals in the brain. Studies show that areas of the brain normally high in glutamate receptors are less active in autistic patients and have lower densities of AMPA receptors. These drugs have been found to improve memory in patients with Alzheimer's disease. CX516, an ampakine, is currently being evaluated in Phase II clinical trials for its effects on cognitive and behavioral symptoms in individuals with Fragile X and autism (ClinicalTrials.gov, 2003; Danysz, 2002).

Alternative medicine

Before clinically utilizing a treatment, its effectiveness and safety should be evaluated. Some medical treatments employed with children with autism fall into the categories of experimental and alternative medicine. Experimental treatments are treatments that are being studied by researchers; typically, preliminary evidence for their effectiveness has been reported. Researchers sometimes, in addition to examining treatment efficacy, also search for the mechanisms or biological processes through which a treatment produces its effects. Such knowledge can sometimes be used to identify good candidates for a treatment, to avoid interactions with other treatments, and to identify other possible new treatments. Once treatments initially classified as experimental have been extensively evaluated, and adequate proof of efficacy and safety are provided, they become part of conventional medicine. Alternative medicine is a term given to nonconventional medical practices. In contrast to experimental treatments, alternative treatments have either not been empirically evaluated or evidence for their effectiveness has not been found in research that has been conducted. Currently, despite lack of empirical evidence, alternative medical procedures are frequently employed as treatments for autism or for medical conditions associated with autism. Among the most widely marketed of the alternative therapies are hormone therapy, anti-yeast therapy, immunologic therapy, homeopathy, vitamin therapy, dietary therapy, and craniosacral manipulation.

HORMONE THERAPIES

Hormones, secreted by the endocrine glands in the body, help regulate a number of physiological functions, including growth, metabolism, digestion, temperature, and immune function. In the New York technical report (1999) the use of adrenocorticotropin (ACTH), a hormone regulating growth and metabolic processes, and secretin, a hormone that plays a role in digestion, were examined as potential treatments for autism. Neither was found to be an effective therapy. Moreover, concern was expressed about adverse health effects associated with using hormones as a treatment for children who do not have a documented hormone deficiency. Because of publicity surrounding secretin, and its possible "miraculous" effects on autism, this therapy is examined in greater detail.

Secretin is a 27 amino acid polypeptide that is secreted by the small intestine in response to hydrochloric acid from the stomach. It is in turn absorbed into the blood and causes the pancreas to secrete copious amounts of bicarbonate, which in turn neutralizes the acid in the gut; thus secretin serves a vital protective process. Secretin also decreases the circulation to the gut and mildly inhibits intestinal motility, slowing the passage of intestinal contents. Because of its protective and calming effects on the gut, secretin is used as a part of diagnostic tests that are conducted to evaluate the causes of gastrointestinal disorders like chronic diarrhea and irritable bowel syndrome.

Autistic children, as well as other children, who have gastrointestinal problems may receive secretin during diagnostic testing. One patient with autism, Peter Beck, at age four, received secretin during laboratory tests that were being conducted to evaluate the causes of his chronic diarrhea. During a three-week period following the secretin infusion his behavior markedly changed. Peter picked up over a hundred words, said short sentences, answered questions, and increased eye contact. His diarrhea also improved. These effects reportedly lasted for six months. Other case studies also reported similar types of improvement, sparking interest in secretin as a possible therapy for autism (Beck, Beck & Rimland, 1998). Beck *et al.* (1998) suggested that secretin may have improved the children's autistic condition through restoring normal intestinal mucosa, thereby reducing the absorption of large proteins or toxins from the gut into the bloodstream, thus preventing leaky gut syndrome (see Chapter 3).

When employed "therapeutically" (as opposed to diagnostically), secretin has been administered intravenously. Lower dosages are usually given when doses are spaced six weeks apart, while higher dosages are employed for single dose treatments. Although a number of early case studies suggested that secretin may have been responsible for a reduction in autistic symptoms (Kaminska, Czaja, Kozielska, Mazur & Korzon, 2002), recent multicenter trials have not supported this hypothesis (Coniglio *et al.*, 2001; Corbett *et al.*, 2001; Dunn-Geier *et al.*, 2000; Lightdale *et al.*, 2001; Owley *et al.*, 2001; Roberts *et al.*, 2001). Most of these studies included children both with and without gastrointestinal complaints. Reports of side effects of secretin treatment are mixed, with some studies reporting no side effects and others studies reporting rash, generalized flushing of head, neck, and chest immediately after infusion, fever, tachycardia, vomiting, and sustained irritability and crying for two weeks after treatment. Thus, based on these and other multicenter controlled trials, secretin does not appear to show promise as a therapy for autism.

ANTI-YEAST THERAPIES

Yeast, such as candida, is a type of fungus that is found in human beings. A problem occurs if there is an overgrowth of yeast, as sometimes occurs when antibiotics or steroids are used for an extended period. Advocates of anti-yeast therapies suggest the use of oral antifungal medications, or special diets that purportedly have antifungal characteristics, as a treatment for autism. The rationale underlying the use of anti-yeast therapies as a treatment for autism appears to be based on a questionable premise: that autistic symptomatology is due to an overgrowth of yeast in the intestinal track. The New York technical report (1999) does not recommend the use of these types of therapies and expresses concern about a range of potential adverse side effects associated with them.

HOMEOPATHY

An Internet search for autism treatment will yield over 10,000 sites on homeopathy and autism. Numerous testimonials are presented concerning the efficacy of this approach and web pages assert that almost all children with autism can be cured or improved through homeopathic treatment.

Homeopathy is also mentioned in some books on autism (Waltz, 1999). Homeopathy utilizes as remedies in treating medical conditions agents that produce the same or similar medical conditions in healthy subjects; for example, treating fatigue with a substance that causes fatigue in a healthy subject (Stehlin, 1996). Substances that have been recommended for the homeopathic treatment of autism include arsenic, mercury, and various amphibian toxins. These compounds are diluted to homeopathic concentrations.[2]

The use of extreme dilution distinguishes homeopathy from the field of immunology, which uses vaccines as treatments. Vaccines contain a small, but measurable, amount of a critical substance (usually in the form of protein or dead viruses). The body responds to this substance by forming cells that produce large amounts of antibodies. These cells can subsequently be activated when the subject is exposed again. The body's immune system response to the substance contained in vaccines can be easily measured. In contrast, homeopathic remedies contain no measurable active ingredient because of the extreme dilution procedure; moreover, available evidence indicates such remedies do not exert any influence on the immune system.

Large meta-analytic studies have been performed to examine the overall effects of homeopathy as treatment for a variety of disorders. Meta-analysis typically examines groups of studies that have very similar methods. A meta-analysis by Cucherat, Haugh, Gooch, and Boissel (2000) initially examined 150 homeopathic treatment studies; only five of these studies were judged to be of high scientific quality. When these five studies were examined, no significant difference was found between placebo treatment and the homeopathic treatment. Cucherat *et al.* (2000) concluded that "the strength of evidence is insufficient to conclude that homeopathy is clinically effective" (p. 32). Meta-analytic studies by both Cucherat *et al.* (2000) and Linde, Scholz, Ramirez, Clausius, Melchart, and Jonas (1999) have also shown that as the quality of the research studies included in the analysis increases, the differences between homeopathic remedies and the placebo treatments decrease.

IMMUNOLOGIC THERAPIES

Because of findings suggesting that a subset of autistic patients have unusual immune system activity and speculation that this activity may somehow cause autistic symptoms, immunological therapies have been proposed and employed as a treatment for autism. These therapies involve the use of transfer factor, pentoxifylline, or intravenous immunoglobulin. Transfer factor is a small molecule produced by leukocytes (immune cells). An open label pilot study by Fudenberg (1996) reported an improvement in food sensitivities and autistic behaviors after treatment with transfer factor. Although this finding is provocative, treatment efficacy needs to be studied using a double-blind procedure and a placebo-controlled crossover design.

Pentoxifylline is a drug that inhibits the enzyme phosphodiesterase, and has several effects on the immune system. Pentoxifylline inhibits tumor necrosis factor (TNF) production by macrophages, lymphocytes (immune cells), astrocytes, and microglia cells of the brain. Pentoxifylline increases blood flow, reduces blood platelets, and inhibits the re-uptake of serotonin, norepinephrine, and dopamine. Although four open label pilot studies of pentoxifylline have shown a reduction in autistic symptoms in children (Gupta, Rimland & Schilling, 1996), double-blind, placebo-controlled crossover studies are also needed to adequately evaluate the efficacy of this drug.

Intravenous immunoglobulin therapy (IVIG) uses soluble antibodies from multiple donors (2000–10,000 donors per batch) as a therapeutic agent. This therapy has been employed to treat immune deficiency states, autoimmune disorders, and inflammatory disease, as well as autism. Gupta, Aggarwal, and Heads (1996) performed an open label pilot study of IVIG with ten children with autism, aged 3–12 years, and found significant improvement in eye contact, calmness, and decreased echolalia after treatment. Other studies have not found significant improvement (DelGiudice-Asch, Simon, Schmeidler, Cunningham-Rundles & Hollander, 1999; Plioplys, 1998).

In their review of medical treatments, the New State Department of Health technical report (1999) evaluated the use of IVIG, the major immuno-logical therapy described in the autism research literature. The report indicates that the efficacy of IVIG has not been scientifically demonstrated as a treatment for autism and should not be used. It also points out that IVIG therapy is associated with a number of risks, including infections from immune globulin prepared from blood containing pathogens such as HIV and hepatitis.

VITAMIN THERAPY

Proponents of orthomolecular psychiatry propose that large doses of vitamins can relieve symptoms or cure a variety of psychiatric disorders, such as schizo-phrenia, mental retardation, and autism. The efficacy of a number of vitamin treatments for autism have been evaluated, including vitamin C and vitamin

B_6. The use of supplemental ascorbic acid (vitamin C) was examined by Dolske, Spollen, McKay, Lancashire, and Tolbert (1993) in a small double-blind, placebo-controlled, crossover trial and found to reduce symptoms in schoolchildren with autism. The authors hypothesize this effect is due to the proposed dopaminergic effects of vitamin C. However, the results of this study have not been replicated (Dolske *et al.* 1993).

Vitamin B_6 and magnesium, used in combination, is the most common vitamin treatment for autism. This treatment, which is typically employed for individuals with documented vitamin B_6 or magnesium deficiencies, has also been proposed as a treatment for children with autism who do not have these deficiencies. Rimland, Callaway, and Dreyfus (1978), in a double-blind crossover study, found improvement in behavior in 16 autistic children during vitamin B_6 and magnesium treatment, and regression during vitamin withdrawal. Other studies, however, do not support the efficacy of this treatment. For example, Findling *et al.*, (1997) performed a ten-week double-blind, placebo-controlled trial of ten children with a high dose vitamin B_6 and magnesium treatment and found no effect on autistic behaviors. The Cochrane Review, which uses an independent panel of scientists to review published medical reports, did not recommend the vitamin B_6–magnesium treatment because of the questionable methodological quality of those studies that reported benefits (Nye & Brice, 2003). The New York technical report (1999) also examined the use of vitamin B_6 (pyridoxine) combined with magnesium as a treatment for autism. Based on their review of the research literature, it also did not recommend the use of this therapy and expressed concern about unknown side effects as well as the cost of this therapy.

DIET THERAPIES

A number of diet therapies, involving the elimination of products such as milk or wheat, have been suggested as a treatment for autism. The theory behind this type of therapy suggests that food allergies contribute to autism; for example, that children who are allergic to certain food products may develop an excess of morphine-like chemicals which in turn produce or increase autistic behavior. The New York technical report (1999) reviewed a range of studies using various dietary interventions, the majority of which involved eliminating either milk products, which contain casein, or wheat products, which contain gluten. Based on this review, it was concluded that there are no known advantages associated with the use of special elimination diets for children with autism. Although no adverse effects of such diets were found, the importance of proper nutrition was emphasized in their report. Concern about possible costs of therapy were also expressed, as well as about the methods employed in testing for food allergies. The report suggests the use of generally accepted methods, such as interdermal and skin prick testing. Other evaluation methods, such as blood tests for antibodies to specific foods or elimination/add back of specific foods, were considered to be controversial and of questionable validity.

Two other food additives/diet supplements, dimethylglycine and colloidal silver, have been mentioned as treatments for autism. Dimethylglycine is not technically a vitamin, as no deficiency syndrome has been identified. It is classified as a food additive. In the alternative medicine and vitamin literature, it has been purported since 1965 to reduce autistic symptoms. Recently Kern, Miller, Cauller, Kendall, Mehta, and Dodd (2001) examined 37 autistic children in a double-blind study and found no significant difference in autistic symptomatology between placebo and dimethylglycine treatment groups. Similarly, Bolman and Richmond (1999), studying eight male autistic children in a double-blind, crossover trial, found no significant differences on behavior and symptom scales between dimethylglycine treatment and placebo groups. Thus, at present, there is no convincing evidence in the medical literature for the efficacy of this treatment.

Colloidal silver, a suspension of very fine silver particles in liquid (sometimes water), has been advertised through health food sites on the Internet as helpful in treating autistic symptoms and diarrhea in autistic children. There is a risk associated with taking colloidal silver. It can cause agyria, a permanent grayish discoloration of the skin and other organs from silver deposits in the tissue. The FDA declared in 1999 that no nonprescription drug containing colloidal silver or silver salts could be legally marketed for the treatment or prevention of disease. The FDA strongly discourages the use of colloidal silver (FDA, 1999).

CRANIOSACRAL MANIPULATION

Craniosacral manipulation has been proposed, mostly through the Internet, as an alternative treatment for autism. It involves the manual manipulation of the bones of the skull and the spine. Practitioners view this procedure as both diagnostic, since the practitioner can apparently judge the "tightness of cranial membranes", and therapeutic, as the manipulation is purported to relieve the tight condition of the connective tissue around the brain. It is sometimes used by chiropractors and some osteopaths. The Upledger Institute website reported that autistic children showed increases in their interactive and language skills after craniosacral adjustment and that the improvement lasted about three to six months. There are no reports available in Pub Med evaluating the efficacy of this procedure for children with autism. Greenman and McPartland found that about 5% of adult patients receiving craniosacral therapy were injured by the treatment (Greenman & McPartland, 1995). Because of a lack of research, this treatment is not recommended for children with autism.

Summary

Based on research conducted thus far, only a few medical interventions have shown promise as treatments for autistic symptomatology. These interventions involve the use of psychotropic medications for symptoms such as stereotypy, social withdrawal, and anxiety. Some symptoms that accompany autism, such as hyperactivity and inattention, have been treated through the use of medications such as clonidine, imipramine, and naltrexone. The psychotropic medication that currently shows the most promise for tantrums, aggression, and self-injury is risperidone for children. Several new drugs, such as oxytocin or ampakines, show promise but need to be evaluated further. In general, psychotropic interventions are recommended for children only when educational and behavioral interventions have not proved successful and/or when the children have serious behavioral problems. When employed, psychotropic medications should be used in conjunction with educational interventions and should be discontinued as soon as possible. Often when children progress in the development of their social, language, and cognitive skills, the need for the use of medications to control symptoms is reduced. Before using psychotropic medications, potential side effects must be scrutinized and factored into the decision-making process. Medications do not currently cure autism; rather they control, at least in the short term, symptoms such as anxiety, mood disorders, hyperactivity, attention problems, and sleep disorders. As a consequence of controlling these types of symptoms children may be more receptive to educational programs that focus on improving adaptive behavior.

Although there is some empirical support for the use of several psychotropic medications, this is not the case for a variety of other medical interventions that have been employed with children with autism, including most hormone treatments, secretin therapy, immunological treatments, anti-yeast therapies, vitamin therapies, and diet therapies. These treatments are not recommended at the present time, because there is either minimal or no evidence of their effectiveness, there are potentially serious side effects associated with the use of some of them, and/or the treatments are costly.

With the exception of some symptom-specific medications, most medical treatments for autism are probably best characterized as either experimental or alternative. Several of the medical treatments in this section are experimental (e.g., risperidone, oxytocin, and ampakine) because there is preliminary evidence suggesting that they may be useful in treating some autistic symptoms. Many of the other procedures, such as homeopathy, immunologic therapy, diet therapy, and vitamin therapy, are best characterized under the rubric of alternative medicine. They are being employed, and sometimes heavily promoted, as treatments for autism without any well-developed theoretical rationale for their usage and in the absence of methodologically sound research indicating their effectiveness. These interventions have basically developed outside the framework of science.

Alternative treatments for autism are often adopted by consumers because they have gained notoriety either based on the testimonial evidence of satisfied customers, and/or based on the charismatic presentations of those who developed the treatments and financially profit from their employment. Many of the consumers of such therapies are looking for a magic bullet for their children's autism and adopt alternative procedures out of hope and sometimes desperation, not always considering the costs and potentially serious side effects. Perhaps the greatest problem associated with the use of alternative therapies occurs when they are used in place of procedures that have been empirically established as effective.

Making prudent treatment decisions for individuals with autism is a difficult enterprise at best. The following questions and guidelines may be helpful in guiding parents and therapists in their decision-making. Has the treatment been developed within the framework of a formal discipline like education, psychology, occupational therapy, physical therapy, or medicine? Has the treatment been empirically shown to be useful with individuals with autism and/or a similar disability? Is there a standardized treatment protocol? Is the process by which the treatment exerts its effect understood and does it make theoretical sense? Is there any evidence of undesirable side effects associated with the delivery of the treatment? In general, parents and therapists should feel more secure in their choice of a treatment to the extent that it makes theoretical (and common) sense; has been developed within the framework of a formal discipline; is standardized; has been empirically evaluated as effective when employed with individuals with autism; and has been shown to have no, or manageable, undesirable side effects. Unfortunately, only a few of the therapies/educational programs discussed in this chapter meet these criteria.

Final thoughts

Although only a limited number of educational and medical interventions for autism were recommended in this chapter, it is critical for research to continue to evaluate those procedures that show promise but have not yet been proven to be effective. As the protocols for these treatments are standardized and examined, it may be that empirical evidence of effectiveness will be found for some of them. Because of the high interest shown by therapists and researchers in developing new interventions, it seems likely that new and successful treatments will emerge. Larger clinical trials evaluating promising interventions may find that some interventions, while not generally effective, are useful for a certain subpopulation of individuals with autism or for certain types of symptoms. It is critical that as new, and perhaps improved, variations of existing interventions are developed, they be evaluated and compared with already validated interventions. In the future it is hoped that those who advocate different approaches to treating autism will try to seek, where possible, common ground. They might find that a hybrid of their different treatments is superior to their separate treatments.

Notes

1   Growing emphasis has been placed by autism educators and therapists on developing intervention approaches that treat the primary characteristics of children with autism spectrum disorder; that is, those characteristics that appear to play a central role in the early development of this disorder. It should be clear, however, from examination of Chapters 2, 3, and 4 in this book, and from a general reading of the literature, that there is little consensus on what constitutes these primary characteristics. Common candidates include anxiety/arousal, sensory, and imitation problems, as well as deficiencies in the areas of joint attention, executive functioning, and theory of mind processes. Until more theoretically based research takes place which examines the mechanisms underlying development of autism, firm conclusions about the primary characteristics of autism are not likely to be reached.

2   The dilutions called for in homeopathic remedies are commonly referred to as 24X, 30X, or 200C. In X series, this means that the original "mother tincture" is diluted serially, 1 ml in 9 ml of water or alcohol, repeating this procedure for the number of times stated. For example, a 30X dilution is diluted 1 in 10^{30} or 1 with

30 zeroes. A patient would have to drink over 7000 gallons to get one molecule of the original substance. In contrast to the X series, the C series starts with a base dilution of 1 ml of mother tincture in 99 mls of water or alcohol, and is repeated the number of times stated. Homeopathic practitioners believe a water matrix is created through dilution and shaking; the original mother tincture changes the shape or configuration of the water molecules around it. This water matrix is postulated to be transmitted to the water inside the body, changing the body to produce its effect. The matrix can presumably be transmitted into solids in tablet form. Independent researchers, however, have not been able to confirm any differences between deionized water and homeopathic remedies of high dilution, thus strongly suggesting that homeopathic medications are inert (Aabel, Fossheim & Rise, 2001; Hirst, Hayes, Burridge, Pearce & Foreman, 1993).

References

Aabel, S., Fossheim, S. & Rise, F. (2001) "Nuclear magnetic resonance (NMR) studies of homeopathic solutions." *The British Homeopathic Journal 90*, 14–20.

AAP (American Academy of Pediatrics) (2000) "Practice Parameter: Screening and diagnosis of autism." *Neurology 55*, 468–479.

Ayres, A. J. (1979) *Sensory integration and the child.* Los Angeles: Western Psychological Services.

Bandura, A. (1969) *Principles of behavior modification.* New York: Holt, Rinehardt and Winston.

Baranek, G., Reinhartsen, D. & Wannamaker, S. (2001) "Play: Engaging young children with autism." In R. Huebner (ed) *Autism: A sensorimotor approach to management* (pp. 313–352). Gaithersburg, MD: Aspen.

Beck, G., Beck, V. & Rimland, B. (1998) *Unlocking the potential of secretin.* San Diego: The Autism Research Institute.

Berard, G. (1993) *Hearing equals behavior.* New Caanan, CT: Keats.

Bettleheim, B. (1967) *The empty fortress: Infantile autism and the birth of self.* New York: The Free Press.

Bolman, W. M. & Richmond, J. A. (1999) "A double-blind, placebo-controlled crossover pilot trial of low dose dimethylglycine in patients with autistic disorder." *Journal of Autism and Developmental Disorders 29*, 191–194.

Bondy, A. & Frost, L. (1993) "Mands across the water: A report on the application of the picture-exchange communication system in Peru." *The Behavior Analyst 16*, 123–128.

Bondy, A. & Frost, L. (1994) "The picture exchange communication system." *Focus on Autistic Behavior 9*, 1–17.

Buchsbaum, M. S., Hollander, E., Haznedar, M. M., Tang, C., Speigel-Cohen, J., Wei, T. C., Solimando, A., Buchsbaum, B. R., Robins, D., Bienstock, C., Cartwright, C. & Mosovich, S. (2001) "Effect of fluoxetine on regional cerebral metabolism in autistic spectrum disorders: a pilot study." *International Journal of Neuropsychopharmacology 4*, 119–125.

ClinicalTrials.gov (2003) Effects of CX-516 on functioning in Fragile X and autism: Study ID Number CORX-CX516-013.

Coniglio, S. J., Lewis, J. D., Lang, C., Burns, T. G., Subhani-Siddique, R., Weintraub, A., Schub, H. & Holden, E. W. (2001) "A randomized double-blind, placebo-controlled trial of single-dose intravenous secretin as treatment for children with autism." *Journal of Pediatrics 138*, 649–655.

Cook, D. & Dunn, W. (1998) "Sensory integration for students with autism." In R. Simpson & B. Myles (eds) *Educating children and youth with autism* (pp. 191–240). Austin, TX: Pro-Ed.

Cook, E. H., Rowlett, R., Jaselskis, C. & Leventhal, B. L. (1992) "Fluoxetine treatment of children and adults with autistic disorder and mental retardation." *Journal of the American Academy of Child and Adolescent Psychiatry 31,* 739–745.

Coppersmith, E. (1984) "A special 'family' with handicapped members: One family therapist's learnings from the L'Arche community." In C. Hansen & E. Coppersmith (eds) *Families with handicapped members* (pp. 150–158). Rockville, MD: Aspen Systems Corporation.

Corbett, B., Khan, K., Czapansky-Beilman, D., Brady, N., Dropik, P., Goldman, D. Z., Delaney, K., Sharp, H., Mueller, I., Shapiro, E. & Ziegler, R. (2001) "A double-blind, placebo-controlled crossover study investigating the effect of porcine secretin in children with autism." *Clinical Pediatrics (Phila) 40,* 327–331.

Cucherat, M., Haugh, M. C., Gooch, M. & Boissel, J. P. (2000) "Evidence of clinical efficacy of homeopathy: A meta-analysis of clinical trials." *European Journal of Clinical Pharmacology 56,* 27–33.

Danysz, W. (2002) "CX-516 Cortex pharmaceuticals." *Current Opinion in Investigational Drugs 3*(7), 1081–1088.

DelGiudice-Asch, G., Simon, L., Schmeidler, J., Cunningham-Rundles, C. & Hollander, E. (1999) "Brief report: A pilot open clinical trial of intravenous immunoglobulin in childhood autism." *Journal of Autism and Developmental Disorders 29,* 157–160.

Di Martino, A. & Tuchman, R. F. (2001) "Antiepileptic drugs: affective use in autism spectrum disorders." *Pediatric Neurology 25*(3), 199–207.

Dolske, M. C., Spollen, J., McKay, S., Lancashire, E. & Tolbert, L. (1993) "A preliminary trial of ascorbic acid as supplemental therapy for autism." *Progress in Neuropsychopharmacology & Biological Psychiatry 17,* 765–774.

Downey, M. (1986) *A blessed weakness.* San Francisco: Harper & Row Publishers.

Dunn-Geier, J., Ho, H. H., Auersperg, E., Doyle, D., Eaves, L., Matsuba, C., Orrbine, E., Pham, B. & Whiting, S. (2000) "Effect of secretin on children with autism: A randomized control trial." *Developmental Medicine and Child Neurology 42,* 796–802.

Escalona, A., Field, T., Singer-Strunck, R., Cullen, C. & Hartshorn, K. (2001) "Brief report: Improvements in the behavior of children with autism following massage therapy." *Journal of Autism and Developmental Disorders 31,* 513–516.

FDA (US Food and Drug Administration) (1999) "FDA talk paper: FDA issues final ruling on OTC products containing colloidal silver." www.fda.gov/bbs/topics/ANSWERS/ANS00971.html.

Fernell, E., Watanabe, Y., Adolfsson, I., Tani, Y., Bergstrom, M., Hartvig, P., Lilja, A., von Knorring, A. L., Gillberg, C. & Langstrom, B. (1997) "Possible effects of tetrahydrobiopterin treatment in six children with autism – clinical and positron emission tomography data: A pilot study." *Developmental Medicine and Child Neurology 39,* 313–318.

Findling, R. L., Maxwell, K., Scotese-Wojtila, L., Huang, J., Yamashita, T. & Wiznitzer, M. (1997) "High-dose pyridoxine and magnesium administration in children with autistic disorder: an absence of salutary effects in a double-blind, placebo-controlled study." *Journal of Autism and Developmental Disorders 27*(4), 467–478.

Fudenberg, H. H. (1996) "Dialysable lymphocyte extract (DLyE) in infantile onset autism: A pilot study." *Biotherapy 9,* 143–147.

Furnham, A. & Bond, C. (2000) "The perceived efficacy of homeopathy and orthodox medicine: A vignette-based study." *Complementary Therapies in Medicine 8*, 193–201.

Ghaziuddin, M., Tsai, L. Y. & Ghaziuddin, N. (1991) "Fluoxetine and autism: more useful in the presence of depression." *Journal of the American Academy of Child and Adolescent Psychiatry 30*, 508–509.

Goldstein, H. (2000) "Commentary: Interventions to facilitate auditory, visual and motor integration: Show me the data." *Journal of Autism and Developmental Disabilities 30*, 423–425.

Gordon, C. T., State, R. C., Nelson, J. E., Hamburger, S. D. & Rapoport, J. L. (1993) "A double-blinded comparison of clomipramine, desipramine and placebo in the treatment of autistic disorders." *Archives of General Psychiatry 50*, 441–448.

Grandin, T. (1995) *Thinking in pictures.* New York: Vintage.

Greenman, P. E. & McPartland, J. M. (1995) "Cranial findings and iatrogenesis from craniosacral manipulation in patients with traumatic brain syndrome." *Journal of the American Osteopathic Association 95*, 182–188.

Greenspan, S. I. (1992) *Infancy and early childhood.* Madison, CT: International Universities Press, Inc.

Gupta, S., Aggarwal, S. & Heads, C. (1996) "Disregulated immune system in children with autism: Beneficial effects of intravenous immune globulin on autistic characteristics." *Journal of Autism and Developmental Disorders 26*, 439–452.

Gupta, S., Rimland, B. & Schilling, P. D. (1996) "Pentoxifylline: A brief review and rationale for its possible use in the treatment of autism." *Journal of Child Neurology 11*, 501–504.

Harris, G. (1987) "L'Arche: Homes for people who are mentally retarded." *Journal of Counseling and Development 65*, 322–324.

Hirst, S. J., Hayes, N. A., Burridge, J., Pearce, F. L. & Foreman, J. C. (1993) "Human basophil degranulation is not triggered by very dilute antiserum against human IgE." *Nature 366*(6455), 525–527.

Hollander, E., Dolgoff-Kaspar, R., Cartwright, C., Rawitt, R. & Novotny, S. (2001) "An open trial of divalproex sodium in autism spectrum disorders." *Journal of Clinical Psychiatry 62*(7), 530–534.

Hollander, E., Novotny, S., Hanratty, M., Yaffe, R., DeCaria, C. M., Aronowitz, B. R. & Mosovich, S. (2003) "Oxytocin infusion reduces repetitive behavior in adults with autistic and Asperger's disorders." *Neuropsychopharmacology 28*, 193–198.

Insel, T. R. & Winslow, J. T. (1991) "Central administration of oxytocin modulates the infant rat's response to social isolation." *European Journal of Pharmacology 203*, 149–152.

Jaselskis, C. A., Cook, E. H., Fletcher, K. E. & Leventhal, B. L. (1992) "Clonidine treatment of hyperactive and impulsive children with autistic disorder." *Journal of Clinical Psychopharmacology 12*, 322–327.

Kaminska, B., Czaja, M., Kozielska, E., Mazur, E. & Korzon, M. (2002) "Use of secretin in the treatment of childhood autism." *Medical Science Monitor 8*, BR22–26.

Kanner, L. & Eisenberg, L. (1956) "Early infantile autism." *American Journal of Orthopsychiatry 26*, 556–566.

Kaufman, B. & Kaufman, S. (1976) *To love is to be happy with.* London: Souvenir Press.

Kazdin, A. (2001) *Behavior Modification in applied settings* (Sixth edition). Belmont, CA: Wadsworth/Thomson Learning.

Kendall, P. C. (1991) *Child and adolescent therapy: Cognitive-behavioral procedures.* New York: Guilford Press.

Kern, J. K., Miller, V. S., Cauller, P. L., Kendall, P. R., Mehta, P. J. & Dodd, M. (2001) "Effectiveness of N,N-dimethylglycine in autism and pervasive developmental disorder." *Journal of Child Neurology 16,* 169–173.

Kitahara, K. (1983/84) *Daily life therapy* (Vols 1, 2 & 3). Tokyo: Musashino, Higashi, Gakuen School.

Kolmen, B. K., Feldman, H. M., Handen, B. L. & Janosky, J. E. (1995) "Naltrexone in young autistic children: a double-blind placebo-controlled crossover study." *Journal of the American Academy of Child and Adolescent Psychiatry 34,* 223–231.

Kolmen, B. K., Feldman, H. M., Handen, B. L. & Janosky, J. E. (1997) "Naltrexone in young autistic children: replication study and learning measures." *Journal of the American Academy of Child and Adolescent Psychiatry 36,* 1570–1578.

Koshes, R. J. (1997) "Use of fluoxetine for obsessive-compulsive behavior in adults with autism." *American Journal of Psychiatry 154,* 578.

Lightdale, J. R., Hayer, C., Duer, A., Lind-White, C., Jenkins, S., Siegel, B., Elliot, G. R. & Heyman, M. B. (2001) "Effects of intravenous secreting on language and behavior of children with autism and gastrointestinal symptoms: a single-blinded, open label pilot study." *Pediatrics 108,* E90.

Linde, K., Scholz, M., Ramirez, G., Clausius, N., Melchart, D. & Jonas, W. B. (1999) "Impact of study quality on outcome in placebo-controlled trials of homeopathy." *Journal of Clinical Epidemiology 52,* 631–636.

Lovaas, O. I. (2003) *Teaching individuals with developmental delays: Basic interventional techniques.* Austin, TX: Pro-Ed.

Malone, R. P., Maislin, G., Choudhury, M. S., Gifford, C. & Delaney, M. A. (2002) "Risperidone treatment in children and adolescents with autism: short- and long-term safety and effectiveness." *Journal of the American Academy of Child and Adolescent Psychiatry 41,* 140–147.

McCracken, J. T., McGough, J., Shah, B., Cronin, P., Hong, D., Aman, M. G., Arnold, L. E., Lindsay, R., Nash, P., Hollway, J., McDougle, C. J., Posey, D., Swiezy, N., Kohn, A., Scahill, L., Martin, A., Koenig, K., Volkmar, F., Carroll, D., Lancor, A., Tierney, E., Ghuman, J., Gonzalez, N. M., Grados, M., Vitiello, B., Ritz, L., Davies, M., Robinson, J. & McMahon, D., Research Units on Pediatric Psychopharmacology (RUPP) Autism Network (2002) "Risperidone in children with autism and serious behavioral problems." *New England Journal of Medicine 347*(5), 314–321.

McDougle, C. J., Holmes, J. P., Carlson, D. C., Pelton, G. H., Cohen, D. J. & Price, L. H. (1998) "A double-blind, placebo-controlled study of risperidone in adults with autistic disorder and other pervasive developmental disorders." *Archives of General Psychiatry 55,* 633–641.

McDougle, C. J., Naylor, S. T., Cohen, D. J, Volkmar, F. R., Heninger, G. R. & Price, L. H. (1996) "A double-blind, placebo-controlled study of fluvoxamine in adults with autistic disorder." *Archives of General Psychiatry 53,* 1001–1008.

McDougle, C. J., Scahill, L., McCracken, J. T., Aman, M. G., Tierney, E., Arnold, L. E., Freeman, B. J., Martin, A., McGough, J. J., Cronin, P., Posey, D. J., Riddle, M. A., Ritz, L., Swiezy, N. B., Vitiello, B., Volkmar, F. R., Votolato, N. A. & Walson, P. Research Units on Pediatric Psychopharmacology (RUPP) Autism Network. (2000) "Background and rationale for an initial controlled study of risperidone." *Child and Adolescent Psychiatric Clinics of North America 9*(1), 201–224.

McDougle, C. J., Stigler, K. A. & Posey, D. (2003) "Treatment of aggression in children and adolescents with autism and conduct disorder." *Journal of Clinical Psychiatry 64* (Suppl. 4), 16–25.

Modahl, C., Green, L., Fein, D., Morris, M., Waterhouse, L., Feinstein, C. & Levin, H. (1998) "Plasma oxytocin levels in autistic children." *Biological Psychiatry 43*, 270–277.

Mostert, M. (2001) "Facilitated communication since 1995: A review of published studies." *Journal of Autism and Developmental Disorders 31*, 287–313.

Mudford, O., Cross, B., Breen, S., Cullen, C., Reeves, D., Gould, J. & Douglas, J. (2000) "Auditory integration training for children with autism: No behavioral benefits detected." *American Journal on Mental Retardation 105*, 118–129.

Myles, B. & Simpson, R. (1998) *Asperger syndrome: A guide for educators and parents.* Austin, TX: Pro-Ed.

New York State Department of Health Early Intervention Program (1999) *Clinical practice guideline: The guideline technical report – Autism/pervasive developmental disorders assessment and intervention for young children (0–3 years).* Albany: New York State Department of Health Early Intervention Program.

Nouwen, H. (1988) *The road to daybreak.* New York: Doubleday.

Nye, C. & Brice, A. (2003) "Combined vitamin B6-magnesium treatment in autism spectrum disorder (Cochrane Review)." *Cochrane Library*, Issue 2. Oxford: Update Software.

Ogletree, B. (1998) "The communicative context of autism." In R. Simpson & B. Myles (eds) *Educating children and youth with autism: Srategies for effective practice* (pp. 141–172). Austin, TX: Pro-Ed.

Owley, T., McMahon, W., Cook, E. H., Laulhere, T., South, M., Mays, L. Z., Shernoff, E. S., Lainhart, J., Modahl, C. B., Corsello, C., Ozonoff, S., Risi, S., Lord, C., Leventhal, B. & Filipek, P. A. (2001) "Multisite, double-blind, placebo-controlled trial of porcine secretin in autism." *Journal of the American Academy of Child and Adolescent Psychiatry 40*, 1293–1299.

Plaud, J. & Eifert, G. (1998) *From behavior theory to behavior therapy.* Boston: Allyn & Bacon.

Plioplys, A. V. (1998) "Intravenous immunoglobulin treatment of children with autism." *Journal of Child Neurology 13*, 79–82.

Prizant, B. & Rubin, E. (1999) "Contemporary issues in interventions for autism spectrum disorders: A commentary." *Journal of the Association for the Severely Handicapped 24*, 199–208.

Quintana, H., Birmaher, B., Stedge, D., Lennon, S., Freed, J., Bridge, J. & Greenhill, L. (1995) "Use of methylphenidate in the treatment of children with autistic disorder." *Journal of Autism and Developmental Disorders 25*, 283–294.

Rimland, B., Callaway, E. & Dreyfus, P. (1978) "The effect of high doses of vitamin B_6 on autistic children: a double-blind crossover study." *American Journal of Psychiatry 135*(4), 472–475.

Roberts, W., Weaver, L., Brian, J., Bryson, S., Emelianova, S., Griffiths, A. M., MacKinnon, B., Yim, C., Wolpin, J. & Koren, G. (2001) "Repeated doses of porcine secretin in the treatment of autism: a randomized, placebo-controlled trial." *Pediatrics 107*, E71.

Rogers, S., Ozonoff, S. & Maslin-Cole, C. (1993) "Developmental aspects of attachment behavior in young children with pervasive developmental disorders." *Journal of the American Academy of Child and Adolescent Psychiatry 32*, 1274–1282.

Rydeen, K. (2001) "Integration of sensorimotor and neurodevelopmental approaches." In R. Huebner (ed) *Autism: A sensorimotor approach to management* (pp. 209–244). Gaithersburg, MD: Aspen.

Scheuermann, B. & Webber, J. (2002) *Autism: Teaching does make a difference.* Belmont, CA: Wadsworth.

Schneck, C. (2001) "The efficacy of a sensorimotor treatment approach by occupational therapists." In R. Huebner (ed) *Autism: A sensorimotor approach to management* (pp. 139–178). Gaithersburg, MD: Aspen.

Schopler, E., Mesibov, G. & Hearsey, K. (1995) "Structured teaching in the TEACCH system." In E. Schopler & G. Mesibov (eds) *Learning and cognition in autism* (pp. 243–267). New York: Plenum Press.

Schuler, A. & Wolfberg, P. (2000) "Promoting play and socialization." In A. Wetherby & B. Prizant (eds) *Autism spectrum disorders: A transactional developmental perspective* (pp. 251–277). Baltimore, MD: Brookes.

Shearer, A. (1997) *L'Arche.* Washington, DC: President's Committee on Mental Retardation.

Stehli, A. (1990) *The sound of a muscle.* New York: Doubleday.

Stehli, A. (ed) (1995) *Dancing in the rain.* Westport, CT: The Georgiana Organization.

Stehlin, I. (1996) "Homeopathy: real medicine or empty promises." *FDA Consumer Magazine 30* (10) e-copy at www.fda.gov/fdac/features/096_home.html.

Stokes, T. & Baer, D. (1977) "An implicit technology of generalization." *Journal of Applied Behavior Analysis 10*, 349–367.

Sulzer-Azaroff, B. & Mayer, G. R. (1991) *Behavior analysis for lasting change.* Fort Worth: Holt, Rinehardt & Winston, Inc.

Thompson, B. & Andrews, S. (2000) "An historical commentary on the physiological effects of music: Tomatis, Mozart and neurophysiology." *Integrative Physiological and Behavioral Sciences 35*, 174–188.

Tinbergen, A. N. & Tinbergen, E. (1983) *Autistic children: New hope for a cure.* London: George Allen and Unwin.

Trevarthen, C., Aitken, K., Papoudi, D. & Robarts, J. (1996) *Children with autism: Diagnosis and interventions to meet their needs.* London: Jessica Kingsley Publishers.

Tsai, L. Y. (1999) "Psychopharmacology in autism." *Psychosomatic Medicine 61*, 651–665.

Turgay, A., Binder, C., Snyder, R. & Fisman, R. (2002) "Long-term safety and efficacy of risperidone for the treatment of disruptive behavior disorders in children with subaverage IQs." *Pediatrics 110*(3), e34.

Vanier, J. (1995) *The heart of L'Arche.* Toronto: Novalis.

Vanier, T. (1997) *One bread, one body.* Toronto: Novalis.

Waltz, M. (1999) *Pervasive developmental disorders: Finding a diagnosis and getting help.* Sebastopol, CA: O'Reilly & Associates.

Waterhouse, S. (2000) *A positive approach to autism.* London: Jessica Kingsley Publishers.

Welch, M. (1988) *Holding time.* London: Century.

Wetherby, A. & Prizant, B. (1992) "Facilitating language and communication development in autism: Assessment and intervention guidelines." In D. Berkell (ed) *Autism: Identification, education and treatment* (pp. 107–134). Hillsdale, NJ: Lawrence Erlbaum.

Whitman, T. L. (1987) "Self-instruction, individual differences, and mental retardation." *American Journal of Mental Deficiency 92*, 213–223.

Whitman, T. L. (1990) "Self-regulation and mental retardation." *American Journal on Mental Retardation 94*, 347–362.

Whitman, T. L., Scibak, J. W. & Reid, D. H. (1983) *Behavior modification with the severely and profoundly retarded.* New York: Academic Press.

Wilbarger, P. & Wilbarger, J. L. (1991) *Sensory defensiveness in children aged 2–12.* Denver, CO: Avanti Educational Programs.

Williams, D. S. (1992) *Nobody nowhere.* New York: Doubleday (Republished, 1999, London: Jessica Kingsley Publishers).

Williams, D. (1996) *Like color to the blind.* New York: Times Books–Random House (Republished, 1999, London: Jessica Kingsley Publishers).

Williams, M. & Shellenberger, S. (1996) *How does your engine run? A teacher's guide to the Alert Program for self-regulation.* Albuquerque, NM: Therapy Works.

Winslow, J. T. & Insel, T. R. (2002) "The social deficits of the oxytocin knockout mouse." *Neuropeptides 36*, 221–229.

CHAPTER 6

Family Stress and Coping

with Julie Lounds

Families who have a child with autism are faced with a challenge unlike that confronted by most families. The challenge occurs early, is lifelong, and is associated with a variety of other problems (personal, vocational, marital, financial, etc.). These problems are encountered within a broader social context that has its own pattern of unique stressors. Some social scientists contend that modern families are under greater stress than their predecessors, in part because the historical prototype of the family as a nuclear social system consisting of two parents, one working and the other remaining at home to care for the children, has changed. Even today this prototype of a nuclear family is often perceived as an ideal against which all other family forms are evaluated and often found deficient.

It is difficult to characterize the typical modern family of today because it takes so many forms. In addition to the nuclear family, there are families with single parents, adolescent parents, divorced parents, remarried parents, same-sex parents, blended families, adoptive families, two-working-parent families, and welfare families. Although most, if not all, of these families existed in earlier years, they have increased in prevalence and are more readily acknowledged. Just as the social structure of the family has changed, so too has its function, which once promoted interdependence, togetherness, child-centeredness, and domesticity (Elkind, 1995). Today additional and often contradictory functions have been added that encourage individualism, member autonomy, community involvement in child rearing, and personal growth. Current families live in social environments that are rapidly changing, more technological, more intrusive, and often less safe. Whichever form families take and whichever functions are emphasized, the dynamic and changing nature of modern families and the environments in which they live have created an array of new stressors.

As the structure and functions of families have changed, politicians, clinicians, educators, and researchers have raised questions about how today's families can best be supported. Special attention has been given to families who are under greater stress and in need of support, including families with children who have been diagnosed as having a developmental disability such as autism. Researchers have increasingly focused their efforts on understanding the nature of the stressors facing challenged families, the effects of stress on family members, the types of coping resources available and utilized by these families, and more generally at discovering why some families are more successful than others in facing challenges. Even though families vary considerably in the stressors they face, they also share many similarities in the types of problems confronted and the methods of coping they employ.

In the present chapter, stress and coping will be examined in families with autistic children. This literature is closely related to and informed by a broader literature on childhood disabilities and family adaptation. Estimates of the number of children in the United States in this broader category, although varying considerably, easily exceed two million, and are much higher, depending on what disabilities are considered (see Thompson & Gustafson, 1996). There is often considerable discussion in this literature concerning what is stress and what constitutes a stressor. Although there are many meanings of stress, the following definition will be used in this chapter: stress is a "mental or emotional tension or strain characterized by feelings of anxiety, fear, etc." (Webster's New World College Dictionary, 1999). In and of itself stress is neither good nor bad. On one hand stress and its accompanying physiological effects can help mobilize the body for action. On the other hand stress can sometimes incapacitate a person, leaving them disoriented and even helpless.

For the purposes of the present discussion a stressor will be defined as something which produces stress. The term "challenge" will be used interchangeably with "stressor" to refer to events that are typically stressful for most persons as well as to events that are potentially stressful, that is, stressful for some and not others. What impact a stressor has on a person or a family unit depends on other factors, such as how a person perceives the stressor and how one copes with the stressor. Stressors, although defined by their effects, typically refer to events or stimuli that occur in the environment, such as the birth of a child who is later diagnosed with autism, or within the body of an individual, such as a disease. What constitutes a stressor for one individual is not necessarily the same as what constitutes a stressor for another individual. Because the effects of a stressor or challenge vary considerably across individuals, the reasons for these individual differences will be discussed at some length.

This chapter will describe the broad variety of stressors that confront families with autistic children and then examine the impact, both positive and negative, of these stressors on different members of the family and the general family structure. Next the characteristics of families who most successfully confront the challenges associated with raising a child with autism will be reviewed. In a final section, strategies for promoting family coping and resiliency will be discussed. This analysis will be supplemented by the discussion of both theory and research. In order to get a more dynamic feeling for the challenges confronted by families with autistic children, and how they cope, this discussion will begin with the story of a family with a child with autism as told by the mother. For the sake of privacy, the mother's name is not presented.

A Mother's Story

I couldn't believe how easy my labor and delivery was. It was nothing like the horror stories I'd heard during pregnancy. After a short five and a half hours, Spencer was born, and he was perfect. Ten fingers, ten toes, and all. Forty-eight hours later, my husband Greg and I were headed home from the hospital, ready to embrace our new role as parents.

Being first-time parents, this was all new to Greg and me; so we didn't know quite what to expect out of our child. But by the time Spencer was seven or eight months old, we were noticing that he seemed to be doing things a little slower than "normal". We didn't worry, though. Babies develop at different rates, right? Then at ten months we started to worry a little. We had finally taught him to sit pretty well, but he was completely immobile—making no attempts to crawl. Everyone told us not to worry, and we were given all sorts of opinions about why he wasn't crawling and plenty of advice on how to get him to crawl. The problem was, crawling wasn't the only area he was behind in. That was the most obvious one and therefore got the most attention. But there were other things, like limited toy play, and a lack of language development, and so when he was 11 months old, we took him to a pediatric neurologist. At this point, we weren't worried that anything serious was wrong. In fact, I was planning on the neurologist just confirming that children develop at different rates, and that Spencer was a little behind but would catch up. So I was stunned when I heard him say, "Spencer is significantly developmentally delayed to the point of concern." He ordered tests and referred us to other doctors and therapists, and my life took a turn that day that I never would have expected.

The next two years were a whirlwind of doctor appointments, tests, early intervention programs, and prayer. We spent that time ruling out one thing after another, and doing everything we could to help Spencer progress. He did progress physically. We were thrilled when at 14 months he learned to crawl and at 20 months started walking. We got such a kick out of his "turbo crawl" as we would call it. He always crawled with his hands fisted, and he would crawl very fast, often crawling as fast as he could in circles. When he started to walk, he walked completely on his toes. Other than physically, though, things weren't progressing. He wasn't "catching up" like we hoped he might.

The word "autism" first came up from Spencer's speech therapist when he was 26 months old. She had noticed some "red flags" after having worked with him for 13 months. She recommended a behavioral pediatrician who specialized in pervasive developmental disorders, and suggested it might be worth seeing her. Although I hardly knew anything about autism, I felt like this was the right direction. We had ruled out so many other things. Despite receiving some opposition from extended family members and friends, we decided to look into this.

We saw the doctor and then went in again for a follow-up three months later. After these two visits she had all but diagnosed him with autism. Although he didn't "officially" get diagnosed as autistic until five months later by another doctor, the diagnosis made sense to us. At the age of two and a half, Spencer was making no attempts at any sort of communication, and he didn't seem to understand anything either. His fine motor skills were very limited. He didn't feed himself at all, and he was very picky about food textures. He also didn't chew. He didn't really play with toys, and he definitely didn't play with them in a normal way; rather he would turn them over and over again, or bang on them endlessly. He loved taking the couch cushions off the couch and pushing them around the room, and he could climb stairs forever. He was also very fascinated with his hand, and would hold his left hand in front of his face and open and shut it, open and shut it. He showed no interest in other children; in fact he seemed to not even notice them. And his relationship and interactions with us, his family, were far from typical. He did have two things, though, that he did show interest in. The first was lights and the second was music. Although he had no words, he had been humming since he was 15 months old. And shortly after he turned two, he started humming actual tunes. First "I Love You" from Barney, and then "Twinkle, Twinkle, Little Star". He still hums both of these tunes in perfect pitch, and music is a huge part of his life.

Spencer's diagnosis brought mixed emotions, and it produced different emotions in different people involved in his life. For some it brought grief and denial, others sympathy and sadness, others more love and understanding. Some people fully embraced and accepted it and just wanted to learn more, others closed up and didn't know how to deal with the situation. For me, the diagnosis first brought relief. After a year and a half of searching, I finally had an answer. It also brought a lot of stress for Greg and me. Because although we had one answer, we now had many new questions. Autism? What does that mean?

Autism has meant a whole new life that we never dreamed of. I never even thought about having a child with a disability. That was the kind of thing I saw on "20/20", that happened to other people, not me. Every aspect of our life changed. Our social life greatly diminished as it was very difficult to either take Spencer places or leave him with a babysitter. Anytime we did take Spencer in public, it was very difficult. We dealt with a lot of hurtful comments from people who didn't have a clue as to what we were dealing with. And it often just felt too hard to explain. Our home had to change to deal with Spencer's innocently destructive behaviors and his lack of understanding of danger. Our life became much more rigid and routine. And we gave up much of our privacy as we opened up our home to therapists, day in and day out. My schedule was filled with therapy, doctor appointments, and autism, autism, autism. At times I went full speed ahead, and at times I felt completely over-whelmed, and I didn't want one more person telling me about one more "miracle cure" for autism. And yet, I did long for suggestions for helping Spencer; there were so many different ideas out there. It got very frustrating trying to figure out which method, medicine, or theory was best for Spencer. People disagreed and had very strong opinions. And since autism is a spectrum disorder, and there is so much variation, what works for one person doesn't necessarily work for another. Then there was the money issue. Each "solution" cost a lot of money, creating quite a financial burden. Especially because we would try one thing, like vitamin therapy, and when it didn't work, try something else.

After Spencer was initially diagnosed with autism, we also discovered that he had a seizure disorder, which is quite common with autism. He was having "silent" seizures 24 hours a day, almost nonstop. Soon after discovering this, he also started having grand mal seizures. This has brought on a whole new set of challenges, as we have had to deal not only with the seizures, but trying to stop them. It was a constant struggle getting Spencer to take his medicine. Moreover, he had side effects from the medicine that affect every part of his life.

It feels almost impossible to fully express the impact of this life experience of ours. It has been exhausting—physically, mentally, and emotionally. For Greg, it has brought an enormous amount of stress to an already very stressful time in his life when he was in medical school and residency.

When Spencer was three years old, our second son, Nicholas, was born. What an impact Spencer has had on him. Being the second child, Nick has had to compete for our attention with another child; especially so because he is the sibling of a child who requires so much attention. And yet, he has very much been like a first child to us because our experience with Spencer was so different. Like any younger sibling, he looks up to his older brother and often imitates what he does. Unfortunately, these aren't always appropriate behaviors. At times he has been confused and upset as he wonders why we don't discipline Spencer in the same way we do him. And yet now at the age of three, he has long been assuming the role of older brother. He is very protective of Spencer. He is very independent and helpful. Even though he doesn't fully understand Spencer's differences, Nick treats him differently than he treats other children. He doesn't try to play with him; rather he will bring him his favorite toys, help feed him, and wash his hair in the bath. And yet Nick still gets mad at him like any other sibling when Spencer does things he doesn't like. It has been an interesting experience to raise both a "typical" child and a child with special needs. It has been a challenge to try to meet their individual needs, and have as "normal" a family life as possible. Nick has done an excellent job so far dealing with the challenges of having a sibling with autism, and I know it will prove to be a great experience for him in his life.

This has been, by far, the biggest challenge of either Greg's or my life. It has been a struggle and a sacrifice. It has been the biggest test of our marriage. And yet, it has brought us closer than we could have ever imagined, because the two of us are the only two people in the world who really know what we have gone through. Because of that, we have leaned on each other so many times when we would otherwise have felt completely alone. We have cried together, worried together, complained together, and felt sorry for ourselves together. We have stayed up nights with Spencer together, made many decisions together, and wondered, together, if we could face one more day. We have prayed together, and prayed together, and prayed together. And we have laughed together, and smiled together, and felt joy together. And that's the most important thing, because besides being the biggest challenge of our lives, it has also been the biggest blessing of our lives.

We have learned and grown so much. We have learned to appreciate more, to take less for granted, to judge less, and to love more. We have learned patience, understanding, and compassion. We have learned to rely on God and others for help, because we can't do this alone. And we have learned that God often knows better than we do the experiences we need in life. We have learned to set priorities, and we have discovered what really matters. We have met wonderful people we never would have met, and had wonderful experiences we never would have had. When we find one thing that works with Spencer, it makes up for the ten things we tried before that didn't. We cheer at every little success. We have learned to find joy in simple things and, by doing so, we have found so much joy; because there is so much joy in raising a child with special needs. There is so much to smile and laugh at. And there is so much more to Spencer than his special needs. He is a darling, fun, unique little boy who loves the beach, music, going in the car, and going through the line at the grocery store. He laughs hysterically when the clerk scans our items. He just loves the sound of the beep. And so we're laughing at him laughing, and everyone's staring and no one knows why we're laughing and none of us care.

And so you see, six and a half years into this journey, we can't imagine life without Spencer and his big wide grin.

A model of family adjustment

From a developmental perspective, the challenges confronting families with children with autism, such as those described in "A Mother's Story", are quite varied and changing as their children mature. Moreover, the ways these challenges affect families differ considerably. Guralnick (2000) proposed a model attempting to represent this diversity. In his model, the stressors faced by families are related to:

- seeking and making sense out of an enormous amount of information
- receiving a diagnosis
- time and money resources
- maintaining a sense of control.

The stressors are described in terms of their impact on the families, including the parent–child interaction, how parents monitor and organize their child's physical and social environments, and how they provide for their child's health and safety. These family patterns of interactions are not only influenced by the aforementioned stressors, but in turn influence the subsequent development of the child with the disability.

A similar, but more articulated, model of family adjustment is presented in Table 6.1. This model lists common challenges that confront families who have a child with autism, the types of effects that having a child with autism can have on a family, and most importantly, describes protective factors that can serve to increase family resiliency and to reduce the potential adverse effects of the challenges on the family. The challenges confronting the family include:

- searching for a diagnosis
- confronting the diagnosis
- learning about autism
- searching for services
- financial burdens

- social stigmatization
- family role changes
- advocacy demands
- child-specific challenges.

The effects of these challenges on the family are many. They influence spousal, marital, parental, and sibling adjustment. The protective factors, which can potentially moderate or reduce the impact of these challenges on family adjustment, include:

- historical factors
- family coping characteristics
- interfamilial and extended family social supports
- community/professional supports.

Finally, the model indicates that the development of the child with autism is influenced by how the family adjusts to the challenges. As will be discussed, the model acknowledges that family factors provide only one source of influence on the child's development; other critical factors include the child's genetic/biological characteristics and community supports.

Challenges confronting families of children with autism

The challenges listed in Table 6.1 will be described in this section, first examining those that are general to most if not all families and then exploring those which vary more across families, such as the specific characteristics of children with autism.

Early developmental problems: The search for a diagnosis

The parents of a child with autism are usually the first to realize that something is wrong with their child. If they are first-time parents, they may come to this realization later than experienced parents, but often before the professionals, typically medical doctors, with whom they initially consult. Early developmental assessments employed by physicians are often crude and rely heavily on parental report. Medical concern about the child is not usually expressed unless the child is far behind in achieving major developmental landmarks; for example, if extensive delays in sitting, crawling, and walking are manifested. The social, communication, and other unique behavioral

Table 6.1 A family adjustment model			
Family challenges	Family protective factors	Family adjustment	Child effects
Searching for a diagnosis Confronting the diagnosis Learning about autism Searching for services Financial burdens Community response and stigmatization Family role changes Advocacy demands Child-specific challenges	Historical factors Family coping resources: • parenting readiness • emotional competence • problem-solving skills • optimism • organizational abilities • religiosity and spirituality Family social supports (includes supports from immediate family members, relatives, friends, and the community)	Parental adjustment Marital adjustment Parenting behavior Sibling adjustment	Development of the autistic child

Note: The impact that family challenges have on family adjustment depends on family protective factors. Family protective factors serve to buffer or moderate the potentially adverse influences that these challenges can have on family adjustment. In turn family adjustment influences child development and adjustment.

characteristics associated with autism are difficult for inexperienced professionals to detect and interpret before the child is three years of age. Because of the considerable variability that exists in the developmental trajectories of typical infants and toddlers, the task of assessing early atypical development is extremely challenging and requires an extensive evaluation performed by an experienced diagnostician familiar with autism and other developmental disorders.

During this early prediagnostic period of uncertainty, parents oscillate between feelings of relief that accompany reassurances from the family physician, and anxiety as they are increasingly convinced that all is not right. As their concern increases, parents often engage in patterns of fact-finding, seeking information from relatives, other parents, books, the Internet, and eventually an array of other professionals in medical and educational service communities. As pointed out in "A Mother's Story", the stress associated with this period of uncertainty sometimes becomes so great that a diagnosis of autism is accompanied by a feeling of relief, specifically because their child's problem now finally has a name.

Confronting the diagnosis of autism

Because the literature on autism is replete with discussion of the various stages that parents are thought to go through after receiving a diagnosis, only brief mention of them will be made here. The stages have both emotional and cognitive components, the latter relating to parents' perceptions about the meaning of the diagnosis and its family implications. Although the specific stages described in the literature vary, they often include mention of denial, anger, guilt, helplessness, grief, acceptance, and hope (see, for example, Tommasone & Tommasone, 2000; Ziolko, 1993). However, parents likely differ in which stages they go through as well as the order that these stages occur. Some individuals fluctuate back and forth from one stage to another. All of the stages represent a way of reacting to and/or dealing with the pain associated with receiving the diagnosis. These strategies are not unique, however, to parents of children with autism (Kübler-Ross, 1969). The coping mechanisms employed during this process are sometimes primitive, but understandable, and often serve a protective function, at least in the short term.

DENIAL

Because many parents know that something is wrong with their child, a diagnosis that confirms their expectation may not come as a surprise. Despite this awareness on the part of the parents, a specific diagnosis of autism is never fully anticipated, and often leaves them confused and searching for information. Once the seriousness of the disorder is understood, a sense of unreality may creep in, accompanied by the feeling that this cannot be happening to them. Denial may manifest itself in many forms, including not talking about the diagnosis with anyone, going on as if nothing happened, distrusting the diagnosis, and searching for another diagnosis. Although seeking a second and third opinion is not unreasonable, and even advisable, at some point the reality of the diagnosis and its implications must be confronted. Denial is also sometimes reflected in the overly optimistic attitude of parents about their children's abilities, skills, and future capabilities. Denial serves in the short term, however, to insulate parents from the full intensity of pain until they can deal more directly with what is an unpleasant reality. Although some parents remain in denial for longer periods of time, parents gradually begin the process of confrontation because of the need to help their child. Both informal and formal social supports can greatly assist parents through this, as well as the other stages.

ANGER

Anger is a common way of dealing with pain. Anger temporarily redirects the parents' focus from their pain and also represents an initial attempt to understand what has occurred. Anger may be directed at God, professional personnel, a wife or husband, or at oneself. The anger, even if it is in a sense warranted, seldom serves to improve the way the parent feels; perhaps in the short term, but not in the long term. Anger is a primitive instinctual response that, while generally unproductive, is completely understandable and sometimes cathartic.

GUILT

Guilt involves the feeling that one is somehow responsible for what has occurred. Parents can feel guilty because they think they are responsible for their child's autism; they could have done more earlier to help their child; and/or they should be doing more currently. Guilt springs, at least in part, from a sense of helplessness and not knowing what to do. Psychodynamic theorists often talk about guilt as anger turned inward. Although feelings of guilt may motivate the parent to search for information and utilize resources at their disposal, this emotion is often unproductive and if chronic will eventually lead to depression and inaction.

GRIEF AND ACCEPTANCE

The experience of grief and grieving begins the process of acknowledging what has occurred and accepting what has been lost. Grief is an emotional response precipitated by the realization that the child the parents have is not the one they thought they had, expected to have, or wished to have. Their expectations have been violated. In addition, grief also accompanies the parents' increasing awareness that the life they thought they would have is likely to be significantly altered and that the task and experience of parenting is going to be more challenging than they thought. For example, they begin to realize that their own expectations for a certain type of career and career advancement may need to be significantly modified; that their marital relationship will be altered in various ways; that their lifestyle, recreational pursuits, and their visions of a distant future, including grandchildren and retirement, may need some adjustment; and that their pride in their child's accomplishments will be based on different standards. One parent eloquently compared having a child with a disability to an expected journey in which you thought you signed up for Italy, but instead ended up in Holland. Holland is fine, just different from Italy (source unknown).

As a process, parental grieving takes place to a large extent early in a child's life. However, as the child develops and the parents become more fully aware of what autism is and its implication for the family, grieving often continues, albeit in a more moderated fashion. Although grief work may be sustained over a long period, the emotional intensity is typically moderated as parents come to accept, love, and enjoy the child they have. Full acceptance involves an understanding of their child and the nature of autism, a diminution of anxiety and grief, and the development of realistic expectations on the part of the parents regarding what the future holds for their family and their child.

Learning about autism

Once a diagnosis is given and parents begin to confront their feelings of loss, they are in a better position to help their child. The healing process is facilitated through gaining knowledge. This educational process for some parents comes mainly through what professionals tell them. Other parents, however, actively search for information through reading, the Internet, talking with other parents, and going to conferences and workshops. It is not unusual to meet parents who seem to know as much or more than the professionals to whom they go for assistance. For such parents, professionals play less the role of expert and more a person whom the parents use to test and seek validation for their ideas about autism and its treatment. Such parents start out as students and end up as teachers, but like all good teachers these parents continue to study and learn.

This type of role reversal requires a change of attitude and behavior on the part of both parents and professionals. Parents learn to assume more responsibility for their children's welfare by increasing their knowledge about autism and by learning to approach professionals with less awe and deference and more realistic perceptions of what they know and can do for their family. They learn that even an "expert's" knowledge is finite, and in some cases quite limited, and that it is not prudent to accept in an uncritical fashion what they are told. Conversely, professionals working with parents need to approach these parents with some humility, recognizing both the limits of their own knowledge, as well as appreciating the wisdom that many parents accumulate through experience and active self-education.

The search for services

The search for services can be very time-consuming and frustrating because children often require many different types of interventions, such as those offered by speech, occupational, physical, and developmental therapists, dieticians, neurologists, and educators. Unfortunately, some of the services required by children with autism may not be readily available in the immediate community. For parents who have financial resources to go beyond the community to purchase services, a different dilemma presents itself. Because of the multiplicity of services available at a national level, they wonder which would be most appropriate for their child.

As they approach various service providers, parents often go through a rather elaborate process of information giving and seeking. Because some professionals have limited expertise in the area of autism, the parents may have to educate the professionals about autism and their children's needs, and even be prepared to make suggestions about how therapies and educational services might be best structured to serve their child. In order to avoid program redundancy, to create continuity of program delivery, and to integrate various program efforts, parents are sometimes cast into the role of program coordinator. As program coordinators, they must share with professionals information about programs that have already been put in place. Although some service agencies help coordinate a child's programs, a dynamic and unified service delivery system often occurs only as a consequence of the efforts of parents.

Financial issues

A major problem encountered by almost all families, even those with a greater income, is finding the money to pay for services required by their child. The costs of services are often considerable. Guralnick (2000) points out that changes in the family structure may place further financial burdens on the family once a child has been diagnosed with autism; specifically because one of the parents needs to or feels compelled to stay home to assist in child-rearing. As families put programs in place for their children, the children's and families' futures are continually reevaluated. Decisions often have to be made within families regarding what they need most, what they can do without, and how to prioritize their spending. Considerable sacrifices may occur as decisions are made about family housing; educational, transportation, and recreational need; as well as the types of services they can afford for their child with autism. Although financial support from governmental and community sources can be obtained, this support is not always immediately available when early interventions need to be put in place.

Community response and stigmatization

Virtually all parents discuss the challenges and problems associated with engaging their social network and entering into the broader community. They describe the stares, unkind comments, and active avoidance that sometimes occur. Such problems particularly come to the forefront as their children have difficulty adapting to new settings, like a supermarket. Parents mention that the adverse community response is exacerbated by the fact their children "look normal". Sometimes parents use these awkward and difficult social encounters as an opportunity to educate the public about autism; at other times, parents decide to save their energy for other "battles".

As indicated in "A Mother's Story", parents frequently comment on how the patterns of their social relationships change after having a child with autism. Donenberg and Baker (1993) point out that as demands on family time increase, socialization with friends and even extended family becomes increasingly restricted. Occasionally, friends have difficulty adapting to and dealing with autism and become avoidant, which in turn leads to increasing feelings of isolation by parents. Wolf, Noh, Fisman, and Speechley (1989), examining the relationship between social support and the well-being of mothers of autistic children, found, not surprisingly, an overall positive correlation between stress and depression. Results indicated, however, that mothers who had more support were less likely to be depressed, regardless of the amount of parenting stress they experienced.

Siblings may also have difficulties as they introduce their brother/sister with autism to their friends. Roeyers and Mycke (1995) examined the sibling relationships of 60 children between the ages of 8 and 15; 20 had a sibling with autism, 20 had a sibling with mental retardation, and 20 had a nondisabled sibling. They found that siblings of children with autism reported more embarrassment about their sibling relationships than children in the other two groups. Relationships with relatives may also be altered in negative ways. More often, many families comment on how their children's autism has helped them to appreciate the generosity and love of their family and friends, as well as to become aware of a wonderful new community of caring and supportive people.

Family role changes

One of the most difficult challenges that families confront is the unanticipated role changes that inevitably occur when their child is diagnosed with autism. In many families, parents make the decision that one of them, often the mother, needs to remain at home to care for their child. Although this parent might have stayed at home with their child under more typical circumstances, she or he often feels compelled to delay or abandon personal, educational, and career goals. The stay-at-home parent often assumes the roles of service coordinator, teacher, and advocate. Working parents similarly may change the way they enter into and pursue their careers; for example, they may restrict the time they dedicate to their paying job. Family adjustment is influenced by how satisfactorily parents negotiate these role changes.

Bristol, Gallagher, and Schopler (1988) assessed family roles and adaptation in two groups of families: a group with nondisabled boys and a group with developmentally disabled boys, about half of whom were autistic. They found that a discrepancy between parental perceptions of actual and perceived appropriate support from a spouse was associated with negative adaptation for parents of children with a disability. For example, mothers who perceived that fathers were not helping around the house as much as the mothers thought they should be were more likely to be depressed, regardless of the actual time the fathers spent completing household tasks. They also found that fathers who had a child with a developmental disability appeared to be less involved in the care of that child than fathers who did not have a child with a disability. Interestingly, this relationship held even when examining families in which mothers as well as the fathers worked outside of the home.

Milgram and Atzil (1988) conducted a similar study, in which they examined stress and the division of labor between parents of autistic children. Parenting problems were related to the number of parenting tasks performed by each parent, the division of the overall parenting responsibility, and parental satisfaction with that division of responsibility. For fathers greater parenting responsibilities were related to lower life satisfaction. In contrast, it was not the absolute care-taking burden that the mothers assumed that most affected their well-being, but how equally they felt the care-giving was divided between them and their spouse. Both of these aforementioned studies suggest the importance of communication and negotiation between parents regarding the distribution of responsibilities related to the care of their child with autism. Specifically, it is important for parents to discuss the roles each parent thinks are appropriate for both themselves and their spouse, and how much of the care-taking burden each parent perceives he/she is currently carrying and should carry.

In addition to parental role changes, siblings can be cast into unexpected roles. For example, they are sometimes given child-care and supervision responsibilities for their brother or sister with autism. Moreover, the siblings may find that their personal time with their parents is reduced. In families with typically developing children, older siblings often assume some responsibilities for the care of their younger siblings. Negotiation of this sibling care-taking role may become more difficult, however, if the child has a sibling with autism, particularly one who is older. Roeyers and Mycke (1995) evaluated the relationships between birth order and the sibling relationship when one of the siblings had a developmental disability. They found that sibling relationships between developmentally disabled and nondisabled sibling pairs were most problematic when the sibling with a disability was zero to three years older than the nondisabled child.

In a review of research, Stoneman (2001), examining the care-taking roles of siblings when there is an autistic child in the family, concluded that the assumption of a care-taking role is often accompanied by sibling conflict and anxiety, particularly while this role relationship is being negotiated and formed. Roeyers and Mycke (1995) found, however, that children with autistic siblings (both older and younger) who were knowledgeable about autism had more positive sibling relationships than children with less knowledge. However difficult these sibling relationships are, Stoneman

(2001) concluded in her review that there is no evidence that a younger sibling caring for an older sibling is harmful to the siblings or to their relationship in the long term. In "A Mother's Story" it was suggested that a younger child may actually benefit from growing up with a sibling with autism.

Advocacy

One of the role changes assumed by many families involves becoming an advocate for one's child and for autism. Historically, in the area of mental and physical health services, the development of new services has often occurred through parental advocacy. Advocacy is a way of coping with the demands associated with raising a child with autism; it is both a protective factor against stress as well as a process that can be stress-inducing. Advocacy is a complex process, involving an individual or group of individuals, which is directed at creating awareness in the broader community concerning what autism is, its prevalence, and the need for new and specialized services. Advocacy often begins through discussions with professionals in charge of community service-delivery systems. It often involves creating community supports through the recruitment of like-minded people and the media. Advocacy can also involve talking to, educating, and challenging politicians and legislators. Occasionally, when change is difficult to initiate through such dialogues, advocacy may lead to the use of the legal system to establish the rights of children with developmental problems, such as the right to equal treatment and freedom from harm.

Child-specific challenges

The challenges faced by families can vary considerably depending upon the characteristics of their children with autism. Because autism is a spectrum disorder, these characteristics vary greatly. Children with autism can be severely retarded, intellectually normal, or have superior abilities. They can be nonverbal or linguistically quite competent. They may have motor deficiencies, sensory issues, and medical problems, or they may not display any of these problems. They may or may not manifest signs of hyperactivity, hearing impairments, epileptic seizures, immune system deficiencies, and various behavior problems, such as self-injury and aggression. The number and extent of these problems will influence the types and number of adjustments families need to make. Families whose children require extensive professional services face a bigger challenge.

Learning how to relate to and rear a child with autism is a difficult task. New ways of parenting must be acquired. Parents with children who develop slowly in one or more areas often need to acquire a new way of thinking about development and achievement. In order to address their children's emerging needs, parents often seek professional consultation. They may need to learn new skills to assist their children if they display:

- delayed language and social development
- cognitive deficiencies
- restrictive eating patterns
- hyposensitivities and hypersensitivities
- poor emotion-regulation
- toilet-training problems
- gross and fine motor deficiencies
- stereotyped behaviors
- obsessions and noncompliance
- other previously described problems.

A number of researchers have found the amount of stress parents experience is directly related to the severity of symptoms their children present. Tobing and Glenwick (2002) examined the relationship between the severity of functional impairment and parenting stress for mothers of children with autism and mothers of children with Pervasive Developmental Disorder – Not Otherwise Specified (PDD-NOS). Not surprisingly, children with autism were found to have more severe symptoms than children with PDD-NOS. Mothers of children with autism also reported greater parenting stress than mothers of children with PDD-NOS. More generally, the authors found that, regardless of whether children were classified with autism or PDD-NOS, more severe impairments were related to higher levels of parenting stress.

Konstantareas and Homatidis (1989) further explored the child impairment–stress relationship by examining which symptoms cause the greatest stress for mothers and fathers. They interviewed mothers and fathers separately, asking them about the characteristics of their autistic child that they found most challenging. Interestingly, somewhat different answers to the questions were found for mothers and fathers. Fathers reported feeling most stressed by their autistic child's lack of verbal communication and anxiety reactions. Mothers, on the other hand, were most stressed by their children's stereotypical behaviors, visual preoccupations, and inappropriate emotional responses to situations. Mother and fathers agreed, however, on the characteristic that produced the most stress when raising an autistic child: self-injurious behavior.

Summary

The impact of the challenges described in this section on family functioning varies considerably depending upon the nature of the specific challenges. For example, families who have fewer financial resources will probably experience greater stress than families who have a high income. However, the degree of stress actually experienced by a family relates not only to the level of a particular challenge, but also to the total number of challenges confronted. Families who have little money, a child with multiple handicaps in addition to autism (e.g., epilepsy, deafness, severe motor difficulties, and mental retardation) and difficulty finding appropriate community services will be stressed to a greater extent than families who do not have to cope with this many problems. The ultimate impact of the challenges described in this section depends on factors that serve to protect the family. These factors will be discussed in a later section. In the next section, the types of effects these challenges can have on a family will be examined.

Autism and its impact on the family

As families encounter the challenges mentioned in the last section, they have to make a variety of adaptations. The impact of these challenges on family functioning is individualized and quite diverse. When the adjustment of families of children with autism is studied, the negative effects are often focused upon, while the positive effects, such as those pointed out in "A Mother's Story", are ignored. In a subsequent section, family resiliency will be examined, including possible reasons why some families are insulated from the more adverse effects of stress and experience unanticipated positive effects as their families grow and become empowered. In this section, the potential negative and positive effects on families with children with autism will be examined. From a prevention and intervention perspective, it is important to understand what the negative effects are in order to do something about them. Family adaptation will be examined in four areas: parental socioemotional adjustment, marital adjustment, parenting behavior, and sibling adjustment.

Parental socioemotional adjustment

Because of the extensive challenges confronting parents of children with autism, it should come as no surprise that some experience stress-related disorders. For example, Olsson and Hwang (2001) conducted a large-scale study in which they examined depression in three groups of mothers: mothers of children with autism, mothers of children with an intellectual disorder, and mothers of typically developing children. They found that mothers of autistic children were more depressed than mothers of children with intellectual disabilities who were not autistic; this latter group in turn was more depressed than mothers of typically developing children. More specifically, 50% of mothers who had an autistic child, 45% of mothers who had a child with an intellectual disability, and 15–21% of mothers of control children had elevated depression scores. The results suggest that mothers of children who have any type of disability are at greater risk for depression. Thompson and Gustafson (1996) indicate in a review of research that mothers and fathers of children with chronic illnesses are also at greater risk for a variety of socioemotional problems including anxiety, depression, and unhappiness.

A review of research by Moes (1995) indicates a general pattern of stress in mothers who are primary care takers of autistic children. Koegel *et al.* (1992) explored this pattern by examining the stress profiles of mothers living in different geographical and cultural environments who had autistic children of different ages and different functioning levels. Mothers were from urban California, rural West Virginia, and Germany. They found, regardless of environment, child age, and functioning level, that mothers of autistic children had very similar stress profiles and that those profiles were markedly different from those of a sample of mothers who did not have children with autism. Mothers of children with autism were worried about their children's level of cognitive impairment, their ability to function independently, their acceptance in the community, and more generally about the future life of their children.

To what extent the primary wage earner in these families, typically the father, experiences similar stress is not as clear. Moes, Koegel, Schreibman, and Loos (1992) examined the stress patterns of mothers and fathers who had a child with autism and found that mothers reported higher levels of parenting stress than fathers. In contrast, Konstantareas and Homatidis (1989), who evaluated the amount of symptom-related stress for mothers and fathers of autistic children, found that parents reported similar amounts of stress. Moes (1995) suggests that fathers' sources of stress may be different than mothers and more related to financial concerns. Thus, it is possible that studies that find lower levels of stress in fathers compared to mothers of autistic children may not be evaluating the types of stressors that are most salient for fathers.

Although it is not clear whether fathers generally experience less absolute stress compared to mothers, a study by Noh, Dumas, Wolf, and Fisman (1989) indicates that fathers of autistic children are at significant risk for stress problems. Their sample included parents of children with autism, Down's Syndrome, Conduct Disorder, and parents of typically developing children. While these researchers did not directly compare the parenting stress of mothers and fathers with autistic children, they found that fathers of autistic children were 12 times more likely to experience clinical levels of stress than fathers of typically developing children. In contrast, mothers of children with autism were six times more likely to experience clinical levels of stress than mothers of typically developing children. In summary, research indicates that both mothers and fathers of children with autism are at a risk for developing stress-related problems.

Although parents of children with autism and other developmental disabilities seem to be at greater risk for experiencing stress-related disorders, they also report a variety of positive outcomes including: increased happiness, personal growth, stronger family ties, greater tolerance for diversity, and appreciation of life's gifts (Summers, Behr & Turnbull, 1989). In "A Mother's Story" presented in the beginning of this chapter, it was noted that as a consequence of raising a child with autism, the family learned "patience, understanding, and compassion". While such anecdotal reports are common, it is clear that more research is needed to examine the specific types of positive outcomes in families who have children with autism and why some families seem to experience these outcomes more than others. In general, most research suggests that there are large individual differences in the personal adjustment of parents of children with autism and other disabilities, with some parents doing very well and others having serious problems.

Marital adjustment

The extensive challenges faced by families of children with autism not only place individual members of the family at risk for maladjustment, but also threaten personal relationships between family members, including the marital relationship. Although Siegel (1996) suggests that the rate of separation and divorce among parents of autistic and PDD children is higher than in the general population, definitive data on this issue is not readily available. Existing data suggest that marital problems and divorce among parents of autistic children are not uncommon. It must be remembered, however, that the divorce rate in the general population is high; for example, in the United States it is around 50%. In one of the few studies examining the marital relationship, Bristol *et al.* (1988) found that parents of boys with developmental disabilities (55% of whom were diagnosed with autism) reported more marital adjustment problems than a matched sample of parents with typically developing children. A review of literature by Norton and Drew (1994), discussing possible reasons for marital difficulties, suggests that the diagnosis of autism produces powerful emotions and may represent for some parents a symbol of shared failure. They also point out that the reshaping of family roles, which typically occurs after a diagnosis, can be a very stressful process.

One of the major predictors of divorce among married people with children is the strength and stability of the couple's relationship before their children were born. Marriages that are more stable prior to the onset of a major stressor are more likely to endure when the family is significantly challenged. Anecdotal reports from married couples, as well as a review of the literature by Norton and Drew (1994), suggest that many parents of children with autism feel that their relationship was strengthened after the birth of their child. Konstantareas and Homatidis (1989) reported that even though over half of a group of mothers of autistic children expressed the need for additional support from their spouses, both spouses in these families gave the maximum possible rating of closeness with their spouse in 92% of the cases: a finding that, if reliable, is astounding. Clearly, more research examining the nature and reasons for marital conflict, and how the marital relationship changes over time in families who have children with autism, is needed.

Parenting behavior

Adapting to their new role, parents of autistic children must learn about what autism is and the specific ways that their children are different from other children. They need to develop new parenting strategies to address their children's hypersensitivities, motor delays, attentional difficulties, language and communication problems, conceptual deficiencies, anxieties and fears, obsessions, rigidity, and other behavioral problems. They need to learn about what their children find challenging and how to structure their children's environments to best support development and learning. In a study by Kasari,

Sigman, Mundy, and Yirmiya (1988), the interactions of parents with their young children with autism were videotaped during a play session and compared to those of care-givers of mentally retarded and typically developing children. They found that parents of autistic and mentally retarded children used specific strategies to control the play sessions. For example, parents of children with mental retardation were more likely to point to objects during play, while parents of autistic children spent more time keeping their children on task by utilizing behaviors such as holding their children on their laps. Furthermore, parents of autistic children used more positive feedback with their children than did parents of mentally retarded or typically developing children. This study suggests that parents of children with special needs specifically tailor their behaviors and interactional styles to compensate for their children's cognitive and behavioral limitations.

Many parents do an exceptional job in this regard. They become experts in autism. They learn how to do physical, occupational, speech, and sensory integration therapies. They learn about play therapies, TEACCH, and applied behavior analysis. Some mothers like Catherine Maurice even write books about how to teach children with autism (Maurice, 1993). Although Maurice is exceptional in that she wrote a book, she is but one of an army of mothers and fathers who have acquired great expertise. Unfortunately, there are other parents who have a problem assuming new roles as care-taker and teacher of their children.

Parenting children with autism is not an easy task and may result in relationship problems. One particular difficulty parents sometimes experience is trouble bonding with their autistic child. A study by Hoppes and Harris (1990) explored this issue through questionnaires and interviews with mothers of children with autism and mothers of children with Down's Syndrome; specifically they examined the mothers' perceptions of their children's attachment to them and the satisfaction they experienced in their relationship with their children. They found that mothers of autistic children reported feeling that their children were less attached to them than did mothers of children with Down's Syndrome; they also appeared to derive less gratification and pleasure from their relationships with their children. The authors conducted in-depth interviews with a subgroup of mothers with autistic children in order to more fully explore the mothers' feelings about their relationships with them. Ninety per cent of mothers said that they wished their children were more attentive to them, and 70% indicated that they sometimes felt their children treated them more as a physical object than as a person who was important to them. Some mothers went on to say it seemed that the only reason their autistic child treated them preferentially was because they were the ones providing for their child's needs. Future research should address the prevalence of such perceptions in this population of mothers, as well as examine how such perceptions influence parenting behavior and the parent–child bonding process.

The challenges confronting parents of children with autism sometimes seem overwhelming. When this occurs, parenting likely suffers. It is difficult for parents to learn about and deal with autism when their own life and emotions are not under control. It is not easy to be sensitive to a child's needs when experiencing severe stress. In extreme circumstances, children may even be neglected or abused. As a population, children with autism are likely at greater risk for abuse and neglect than the general population (Siegel, 1996). In an effort to determine the actual scope of maltreatment among children with disabilities, a study by the National Center on Child Abuse and Neglect indicated that the incidence of maltreatment was 1.7 times higher for children with disabilities than for children without disabilities (National Center on Child Abuse and Neglect, 1993). The causes of abuse and neglect of children with autism and other developmental disabilities seem to be the same as for other children. Parents who neglect or abuse their children typically are under greater stress, lack coping resources, have limited financial resources, and often have not been parented well themselves. Moreover, parents who do not have adequate family, friend, or community supports are at particular risk for developing parenting problems.

Sibling adjustment

Siblings of children with autism often have very different childhood experiences than siblings of typically developing children. Sometimes they are expected to assume considerable responsibility for the care and supervision of their autistic sibling. Because of the overall demands required in caring for an autistic child, parents often worry that they are spending too much time with their children who have autism and too little time with their other children. However, this impression is not supported by existing research. A review of the literature on sibling and family relationships where one sibling has a developmental disability, revealed that older siblings of children with a disability get the same amount of attention from their parents as older siblings of typically developing children (Stoneman, 2001). In addition to wondering if they are giving their nonhandicapped children too little attention and too many responsibilities for the care of their handicapped siblings, parents worry more generally about whether their own level of stress might adversely affect their children.

The existing literature has been inconclusive about whether siblings of autistic children experience more stress or adjustment problems. A study by Kaminsky and Dewey (2002) explored one mechanism that could help explain why different studies have come to different conclusions. They examined the relationships between social support, loneliness, and adjustment in siblings of children with autism. Although their study included both older and younger siblings in their sample, the majority (80%) of the siblings were older than their brother or sister with autism. Siblings who reported experiencing greater social support from friends and classmates were less likely to have problems with loneliness and academic achievement. Although adjustment problems in some siblings of children with autism may be related to how they are parented, this study emphasizes the importance of the peer network and its effects on sibling adjustment. Whether supportive peer networks develop in the first place may depend in part on how autism is introduced to these peers by the siblings and parents of a child with autism.

Siegel (1996) suggests that there are different prototypical ways that siblings learn to cope with a brother or sister with autism. These coping mechanisms include becoming parentified, a superachiever, or withdrawing. The parentified child assumes a parent-like role, taking on more and more of the responsibilities for caring for their handicapped sibling and maintaining the household. Their sense of worth and being valued is tied up with these activities. Although it seems reasonable for siblings to acquire a helping role to some extent, a problem develops when this becomes their predominant way of acting, particularly if it prevents the development of the sibling in other areas. Because children can be very helpful, parents have to be careful to restrict the responsibilities they place on them.

A second coping mechanism mentioned by Siegel (1996) is that children become superachievers; specifically they try to compensate for their handicapped sibling's deficiencies by dedicating themselves to getting their parents' attention by being exceptional in areas such as academics and/or athletics. Again this method of coping only becomes problematic when the children's whole identity and self-esteem is so tied in to these endeavors that any failure is devastating and results in the children feeling like they are letting their parents down. Siegel (1996) suggests that siblings who cannot achieve in socially desirable ways sometimes try to get their parents' attention in other ways, such as by being a clown or through acting out and becoming oppositional.

A third way of coping cited by Siegel (1996) is for the sibling to withdraw, essentially giving up in their attempt to gain their parents' attention. As a consequence, parents' ability to help and influence their nonhandicapped child is reduced. Ultimately, such children are likely to be subject to influences outside of the home, which may not be favorable. Moreover, such children are likely at risk for becoming depressed, specifically because withdrawal as a coping mechanism is in essence a way of expressing helplessness and giving up.

In order to prevent the development of these types of problems, it is important for parents to be aware of and responsive to their nondisabled children's needs. Parents should try to be sensitive to their children's overtures and create exclusive time for them—time that is not utilized for prob-lem-solving, but for enjoyable activities. As their children mature, parents can help them understand in age-appropriate ways what autism is, how it influences their sibling's development, and how it affects the family. Parents can explore their children's thoughts and feelings about having a brother or sister with autism. They can help them interpret and manage their reactions to their peers and adults outside the family, especially in situations that are embarrassing and stressful. They can help them understand why some indi-viduals stereotype others and act in prejudicial ways. Finally, parents can help their children to be aware of the great diversity that exists around them and how enriching this diversity can be. The research literature suggests that parents often do a good job in this regard, because children with siblings who are handicapped frequently grow up to be empathetic and caring adults.

Summary

The ultimate impact that the challenges listed in Table 6.1 have on the family likely depends on the number of family members adversely affected. Stress escalates exponentially as more family members have difficulty coping. However, even if only one member of the family is adversely affected, problems can occur. Because the family is a dynamic system of interdependent members, any time one member is adversely impacted, the probability of a spread of effects cascading to other members is increased, particularly if the family member has problems of a more severe and chronic nature.

Resiliency in families: The role of protective factors

In the previous section, the intent was to show that families of children with autism have a variety of adjustment problems, but that such problems are not at all inevitable. In fact, many families cope very well. Some parents increase in self-esteem while others experience depression; some marriages are strengthened while others fall apart; some parents become empowered in their role as teachers and advocates for their children while others feel helpless as they try to address their children's needs; and some siblings grow into caring and productive human beings while others have adjustment problems. Thus, some families demonstrate considerable resiliency under stress whereas others do not.

In order to be resilient, an individual, family, group of people, nation, or culture has to be challenged in some significant way. Families with children with autism certainly experience a significant challenge. Resiliency can be demonstrated in a variety of ways. One way is for an individual or family, after showing signs of initial distress, to recover and function well. Some parents, who are initially depressed after learning their child has autism, recover and cope effectively with their problems. Such individuals and families learn how to deal with their problems. Problems are viewed as challenges that can be overcome and opportunities for learning.

A second way of demonstrating resiliency is for an individual, or family, to face a challenge without ever developing any significant problems, such as the boxer who gets hit hard but does not falter. Some theorists refer to this phenomenon as a display of invulnerability. There is discussion in the literature about the invulnerable individual, who even though severely traumatized, continues to function well. True invulnerability may be the exception rather then the rule. When major trauma occurs, "wounds" may occur even though they are not apparent. Such "wounds" may remain initially hidden, only to surface later. It is also possible that invulnerability develops in some people as a consequence of a history of being challenged and learning over time how to cope successfully with such challenges.

A third way of being resilient is for families or individuals to display, temporarily, symptoms of distress and then not only to recover, but to become even stronger than they were before as a consequence of meeting and overcoming the challenges. Examples of this sort of resilience are numerous. Lance Armstrong, a world-class bicycle racer, developed testicular cancer. Despite a poor prognosis he overcame the disease, returned to racing, and went on to win the Tour de France numerous times. Christopher Reeve,

"Superman" in the movies, had his spinal cord severed. Although he has not fully recovered from his physical injury, he has become a real-life superman, an articulate and passionate advocate for those who have suffered from such an injury. In the autism literature examples abound, they include Catherine Maurice, a parent of a child with autism who overcame her emotional struggles to become a successful mother, author, and a powerful role model for many parents (see Maurice, 1993), and Temple Grandin and Donna Williams, who through their writing and examples have helped us all to understand what being autistic means and to celebrate the richness that diversity can bring. Some theorists describe individuals like Lance Armstrong, Christopher Reeve, Catherine Maurice, Temple Grandin, and Donna Williams as thriving in the face of challenge.

To understand these different types of resiliency and how many families of children with autism succeed despite the challenges they face, the concepts of risk and protective factors are introduced here. Risk factors, such as single parenting, poverty, or having a child with a severe developmental disability, increase the probability of undesirable outcomes and maladjustment in families. In contrast, protective factors, such as a good marriage and community social supports, increase the probability of desirable outcomes when families are challenged. Protective factors can buffer or neutralize the effects of risk factors. To gain insights into why some families of children with autism are resilient in the face of a challenge and others are not, their profile of risk and protective factors must be evaluated. When the lives of these families are closely examined, it is clear that resiliency is not a one-time phenomenon or a simple process. These families are repeatedly challenged as their children grow and their circumstances change. They may show uniform resiliency across time when meeting all challenges; however, it is also possible that they will show greater resiliency in the face of some challenges than others.

In this section, the family adjustment model introduced earlier is further discussed in order to provide insights into how protective factors influence family resiliency (see Table 6.1). The protective factors described in this model bear similarities to those contained in various parenting conceptualizations in the developmental literature, such as those put forth by Belsky (1984) and Whitman, Borkowski, Keogh, and Weed (2001). More specifically, the family adjustment model proposes that three groups of factors exert important influences on family functioning: historical factors, family coping resources, and family social supports. Although not depicted, the model in Table 6.1 assumes that historical factors influence the development of family coping resources and, in turn, that family coping resources and family social supports influence each other in a reciprocal fashion. Families who have more coping resources are more likely to develop a more extensive social support network. In turn, social supports can assist in strengthening family resources. In combination, these three sets of protective factors can serve to buffer or moderate the adverse influences of stressors that confront families who have children with autism, thereby enhancing family adjustment. Each of these protective factors and their respective roles will be examined in this section.

Historical factors

The coping resources, parenting skills, and attitudes that mothers and fathers manifest in the family setting are influenced by the social environments in which they were reared. The ways parents interact with each other and their children are affected by their prior familial and extrafamilial relationships (see Belsky, 1984). For example, it is known that abused and neglected children are at a greater risk for abusing and neglecting their own children as adults (Kaufman & Zigler, 1987). Conversely, children who were parented in a sensitive and responsive fashion are likely to become empathetic and attentive parents as adults. Moreover, many other personal traits and socioemotional characteristics, such as optimism and depression, have, at least in part, social origins.

This construct, historical factors, was not included in the family adjustment model to suggest that parenting and family relationships are pre-determined by the past, but rather to indicate that historical factors play a role in the development of social habits and attitudes and more specifically influence how family members cope with challenges. Adjustment in families is a dynamic process that continues to evolve over time. Family members can learn from experience and through reflective analysis of their personal histories. Parents who examine and try to understand their history are in a much better position to adapt to new life environments and challenges and to learn from their own and others' experiences as well as from formal intervention programs. Thus, while personal histories influence personal action, individuals are constantly in the process of reconstructing themselves as new challenges are encountered. In the last section of this chapter and in Chapter 7, interventions to assist in this reconstruction process will be discussed.

Family coping resources

The resources and characteristics of parents may influence their relationships with each other and their interactions with their children, as well as their own personal well-being. In this section some of the more important resources of parents and their children that influence family adjustment and resiliency will be examined. These resources include parenting knowledge and skills, emotional intelligence, problem-solving skills, optimism, organizational skills, and religiosity/spirituality.

PARENTING KNOWLEDGE AND SKILLS

Whitman *et al.* (2001) present and review research relating to a model of parenting that emphasizes the critical influence of cognitive readiness to parent on parenting effectiveness and child development. Parents who are cognitively prepared to parent know more about how children develop, possess positive attitudes about their parenting role, and have an understanding of appropriate parenting practices. Such parents are more sensitive to their children's needs and are better teachers. As a consequence they are also better able to facilitate the development of their children.

Because of the nature of autism, the task confronting parents of children with this disorder is very challenging. Parents who know more about autism and its treatment, as well as how to parent a child with autism, will be better able to address the needs of their children. These parents need to know not only how typical children develop, but also how children with autism deviate from a normal developmental trajectory. For example, they need to learn why their child with autism becomes upset when encountering new environments and why he or she has difficulties acquiring new skills. These parents need to adjust their expectations about how quickly their children will learn. They have to acquire a variety of new skills in order to teach their child more effectively. The knowledge that parents possess, along with their perceptions of their parenting role and their parenting skills, affects the quality of their parent-child interaction, their own feelings of well-being and competency, as well as their level of stress (see Whitman *et al.*, 2001).

Results of a study by Tunali and Power (2002) suggest that mothers of children with autism realign their priorities and place more emphasis on the importance of their parenting role. Interviewing mothers of autistic children and mothers of typically developing children, they asked questions about their attitudes toward home, career, and their marital relationship. Mothers of children with autism placed less emphasis on career success and were more likely to believe that mothers with young children should not work outside the home. These mothers reported spending more of their leisure time on home-centered activities. These attitudes and behaviors likely evolved, at least in part, from a conviction that their talents and energies had to be directed to helping their child with autism.

EMOTIONAL COMPETENCE AND ADJUSTMENT

Goleman (1994) and Sarni (1999) emphasize the importance of emotional competence in the lives of both adults and children. Emotional competence refers to an array of skills that facilitate personal adjustment and the quality of interpersonal relationships. For example, emotionally competent people are able to identify, label, and discuss the wide array of emotions they are experiencing. They can read the emotional states of other people. They understand that there may be an incongruity between what people say about their feelings and their actual feelings. They are aware of the ways emotions can influence a person's actions. They understand how people can maintain simultaneously conflicting feelings such as sadness and joy, and love and hate. Most importantly, they are able to control and manage in effective ways strong negative emotions such as hostility and fear. As adults and parents they are able to teach others, including their children, how to develop these competencies.

Individuals with emotional competence are more likely to be able to cope successfully with life's challenges and disappointments and are less likely to develop serious emotional problems like depression. They are more able to develop satisfactory relationships with others and to achieve occupational success. Goleman (1994) contends that emotional competence, or what he refers to as "emotional intelligence", is a more accurate predictor of personal and vocational success than cognitive intelligence. Emotional competence is felt to be such an important life skill that many professional people, including psychologists and educators, are suggesting that it be taught as part of the regular school curriculum. Despite its importance, individuals vary widely in the skills that compose emotional intelligence. Goleman suggests that as a population, Americans are not very emotionally literate. Similarly, John Gottman in his book *The Heart of Parenting* emphasizes the need for parents to become better emotion coaches for their children (Gottman, 1997).

The development of emotional competence takes on added importance when examining adjustment in the families with children who have autism. Parents who have developed skills in emotion management will be better able to manage their own emotions, address the emotional needs of their partners, and resolve conflicts that arise within the family. These skills are also useful in helping parents understand the emotional states of their children without autism and assisting them in clarifying and managing their feelings about their siblings with autism. Finally, these skills are useful in helping parents develop emotional competence in their children with autism. As discussed in Chapters 2 and 3, one of the major deficiencies of children with high functioning autism and with Asperger's Syndrome is their inability to understand their own emotional states as well as those of other people. Moreover, all children on the autism spectrum have great difficulty regulating strong emotions, particularly their feelings of anxiety and fear, in social situations (Attwood, 1998). Increasingly, it is being realized that parents can help their children with autism understand their own as well as others' emotions. For examples of such emotion management programs, the reader is referred to McAfee (2002), Moyes (2001), and Myles and Adreon (2001).

PROBLEM-SOLVING SKILLS

Because of the multiplicity of challenges confronting parents of children with autism, problem-solving skills are invaluable aids in helping them cope with major crises and daily hassles. More generally, the ability to solve problems in a prompt and efficient manner is important for personal adjustment. A typical paradigm used in teaching problem-solving is fairly straightforward. The first step involves clearly defining the nature of the problem that is being confronted. Next, brainstorming is encouraged to generate a variety of possible solutions. Then each of the solutions are evaluated and the one judged most likely to solve the problem is selected for execution. After the strategy is executed, the results of its implementation are monitored to see if the problem is solved. If it is not, the entire sequence is gone through again.

In order to become a good problem-solver, however, practice is needed. Supervision from experienced problem-solvers is helpful, in particular if it supports the development of this skill, rather than simply providing solutions to the individual with the problem. Clinical psychologists and counselors often teach this skill to their clients. A family approach to problem-solving can also be very useful in dealing with family relationship problems and in opening up communication. Because a group is involved, broader information is generated to assist in defining and solving problems. Moreover, involvement of the whole family in this process helps empower each of the members, thereby creating a closer bond between them.

OPTIMISM

Because of the extensive adjustment that families of children with autism have to make, it is not usual for family members to experience emotional turmoil. In the short term most of these families feel acute anxiety, and even panic. After a period of time most family members are able to work through this phase, gradually calming their emotions and looking at things more rationally. If they cannot achieve this, outside help may be necessary. Chronic stress often leads to depression. Depression in this type of situation typically occurs because family members do not know how to cope with the many uncertainties that follow a diagnosis of autism and end up fearing the worst. They feel helpless. They view not only the present but also their future as bleak. They focus mostly on the negative aspects of a situation, imagine catastrophes that are unlikely to occur, and magnify the importance of even small problems. This type of reaction is certainly understandable and even, in the short term, to be expected. Families and parents are not sure what the future will hold, what they need to do as a family to help their child, and whether they will be able to do what is necessary. They wonder whether they will be able to cope financially, emotionally, and cognitively with the demands placed on them.

Families that are able to weather the storm that comes with the discovery that their child is autistic learn to look at the world differently. They see a future where their children will learn and grow and be more actively engaged in the world. They come to appreciate the children they have, including the characteristics that make them unique. They discover a community of caring and generous people who help them on a journey they did not expect to make. They find that some of the values they once held about what is important have changed and that their children are helping them find new and important meanings in life. They become empowered, discovering new sources of strengths and abilities they did not know they possessed. In the process they develop new, more optimistic attitudes about their life and their children with autism.

As Seligman (1998) points out, attitudes are learned, including the attitudes that lead to depression as well as the attitudes that lead to happiness. Whereas pessimistic attitudes lead to inactivity, helplessness, and sadness, positive and more optimistic attitudes lead to hope, engagement, and a variety of positive emotions, including pride and joy. Resilient families learn how to be optimistic and that optimism pays rich dividends. From this perspective, the actual challenges that a family faces are less important than the attitudes family members have about these challenges. Dunn, Burbine, Bowers, and Tantleff-Dunn (2001) examined coping mechanisms in families that included an autistic child. They found that parents who viewed their life as being out of their control and coped with their problems by escaping from them or distancing themselves were more likely to suffer from depression, and were more likely to be socially isolated. Moreover, this tendency to cope with problems by escaping was associated with more spousal relationship problems. In contrast, Hastings and Johnson (2001) found that parents of children with autism who were able to positively reframe events that were challenging were less likely to report being depressed.

ORGANIZATIONAL ABILITIES AND TIME MANAGEMENT

Families who take care of the needs of all their members are more likely to function well and experience less conflict and stress. Because a child with autism places many demands on the family, families sometimes feel they need to focus almost exclusively on meeting that child's needs while ignoring the rest of the family. Sanders and Morgan (1997) have found that mothers and fathers of autistic children reported less family participation in recreational activities and lower family involvement in political, social, intellectual, and cultural activities than parents of typically developing children. Although reducing participation in such activities may often be necessary to help families cope, this strategy, if carried to an extreme, is a recipe for disaster. Parents need to take care of themselves, each other, and their other children. They require time for sleep, recreation, and work. They must take care of their health and take time to heal when they are sick. Completely ignoring these types of needs leads to a gradual increase in family stress, depletion of resources, and ultimately to an inability to help their autistic child.

Because modern family life is busy and sometimes chaotic, families cope by developing structures and routines that help them deal with the demands of the day. Families with children with autism are not unique in this regard; however, the demands placed on these families are often greater. Because many families with children with autism have extensive therapies and educational programs to fit into their schedules, organizational and time management skills are invaluable. In order to address the needs of all its members, the establishment of priorities and routines is critical to family survival. For example, many of these families have volunteers coming into their homes on a daily basis to help them with the therapies. Schedules need to be developed and goals established to guide volunteer activities. The volunteers need to be trained, coordinated, and supervised. Despite the fact that many families do not have well-developed organizational skills, they can acquire them with training and practice.

Although studies have not examined the effects of time management programs in families that have a child with autism, Lang (1992) found reduced anxiety among college students who were taught to use simple time management techniques, such as scheduling and making written lists of things to do. Similarly, Macan (1996), examining the effects of time management training on employees from a social service agency, found that participants reported feeling more in control of their time, not only after training, but four to five months after the completion of the intervention. Using a broader sample of employees, Macan (1994) similarly found that setting goals and establishing priorities, and more generally appreciating the importance of being organized, was critical in establishing control of one's life. For information on time management programs the reader is referred to Covey, Merrill, and Merrill (1996), Loehr and Schwartz (2003), and Morgenstern (2000).

RELIGIOSITY AND SPIRITUALITY

For many families, religion and spirituality provide comfort, support, and encouragement. A few recent studies have examined the role that religion plays in the lives of parents with autistic children. Tarakeshwar and Pargament (2001) found that the role religion plays varies considerably. For example, some individuals rely exclusively on themselves as they cope, other individuals rely exclusively on God for assistance in time of need, and still other individuals see themselves in an active partnership with God as they cope with life's challenges. In their study the authors examined the role of what they portrayed as positive and negative religious coping in families with autistic children. Examples of positive religious coping included: seeking spiritual support, perceiving illness as an opportunity for spiritual growth, and the use of collaborative religious coping, such as group prayer. In contrast, negative religious coping included expressions of religious discontent with one's congregation and God. They found that use of positive religious coping techniques was related to stronger feelings of well-being, whereas the use of negative religious coping practices was related to higher levels of depression. The researchers also found that the sharing of religious beliefs between partners was a source of support for them. The authors suggested that shared faith decreased marital distress and enhanced the support that parents offered each other. More generally, the authors suggested that religion could be a source of strength, but also was sometimes a source of distress when coping with the challenges related to raising a child with autism.

In examining the influence of religion and religiosity on coping, a distinction is sometimes made between organized religion and personal religious beliefs. A study by Coulthard and Fitzgerald (1999) explored the role of organized religion and personal beliefs as sources of support for parents of children with autism, and then further investigated the relationship between support from organized religion, personal beliefs, and the parents' health status. The participants consisted mainly of mothers who were asked to fill out questionnaires related to their children's symptomatology, their own general health, and the support they received from religious organizations as well as from their personal beliefs. As defined in this study, personal beliefs could, but did not have to, have a religious component; however, such beliefs helped parents give meaning to their life and put into perspective their child's disability. Prayer was viewed as part of the personal belief system. Overall, parents reported receiving more support from their personal beliefs than from organized religion, and those parents who reported more support from their personal beliefs had better health than those who reported little or no support from such beliefs. Parents who sought comfort in prayer had the fewest health problems. In contrast, most parents felt that churches and organized religion did not provide them as much support as other community agencies. It is important to note that these findings could be a function of the particular groups of mothers who filled out the questionnaires, and not representative of all mothers who have an autistic child.

Family social supports

The last protective factor to be discussed is family social supports. Social supports can serve many functions, including the provision of financial, emotional, and practical resources. Most of the family characteristics just summarized influence the number and quality of social supports available to the family. For example, parents who are more knowledgeable, optimistic, and organized are more likely to seek out, find, and maintain social supports that are helpful to the family.

In many families with children with autism, one of the parents, typically the mother, takes over the role of primary care-taker for the child while the other parent works. Although role differentiation is necessary for the survival of the family, role sharing is also important. The mother or primary care-taker needs active assistance from her spouse and, if age-appropriate, her other children. Mothers who feel that their partners are actively sharing in the care-giving roles and helping with household responsibilities report feeling less depression and a greater sense of well-being (see Milgram & Atzil, 1988). This assistance not only relieves the mother of part of her responsibility, but can also be very useful in that it provides the child with autism with a broader range of experiences and relationships. The challenge is to develop this family role-sharing in a way that is equitable and allows each member some autonomy to pursue personal agendas that are important to him or her.

Although the first and most critical source of social supports comes from within the immediate family, grandparents, aunts, uncles, and cousins can, however, provide invaluable financial, emotional, or instrumental help. For example, grandparents, if they are in the same geographical area, may act as babysitters, companions, and even teachers, extending the child's therapies. Katz and Kessel (2002) explored the role of grandparents of children with a developmental disability and found that the amount of grandparent involvement was directly determined by the parents. Grandmothers were generally more involved than grandfathers. Many grandparents reported, however, wanting to be more involved with their developmentally disabled grandchild than they were. From a resiliency perspective, families that have more of these informal supports from the extended family, as well as friends, are less stressed and better able to cope. Access to such supports for child care has been associated with lower levels of parental anxiety, depression, and stress as well as greater parental confidence in handling the challenges associated with raising a child with autism (Sharpley & Bitsika, 1997).

Because of the nature of autism, a wide variety of community and professional supports for the family and the child are also necessary. These supports vary widely depending on the needs of the child, but often include occupational, physical, and speech therapy, developmental and educational programs, and medical and dietary services. The impact of these services on the family also varies depending on their accessibility and quality. Sometimes even though services are available, accessibility may be restricted because of excessive demand for services by the community and/or lack of money to purchase such services. Quality of the services is related to the therapeutic expertise of the staff and their experience in working with children with autism, how early in the life of the child these services are available, and the frequency with which these services can be offered. Programs that are offered only occasionally and are available only when the child is older may have limited impact. The quality of the services is also related to how the service agencies interface with the family, for example, whether the services contain a parent-training component that allows an educational or therapeutic program to be extended into the home setting.

For many parents, respite care and daycare are important when coping with the challenges associated with raising a child with autism. Although these services may be available, they are not always easily accessible. The most common "respite" from parenting is provided through members of the immediate and extended family. In general, respite care has been associated with lower stress and a better quality of life, particularly for mothers (Chan & Sigafoos, 2001). The quality of respite care is an important concern for families raising a child with autism. Sharpley and Bitsika (1997) asked parents of autistic children about their perceptions of respite care arrangements as well as their levels of stress. They found that the level of stress experienced by the parents was directly related to the quality of respite care: parents reported less stress when the care-givers had better understanding of their autistic child's difficulties and needs. Chan and Sigafoos (2001) came to a similar conclusion when reviewing studies on the effects of respite care services for families who have a child with a developmental disability. In the next section, some of the major types of services needed by families who have children with autism will be briefly described. Such services play an important role in enhancing family resiliency.

Specific community supports

In Chapter 5, interventions focused on treating and educating the child with autism were summarized. To the extent that such interventions are successful, family stress should be reduced and family resiliency enhanced. However, not all of the family needs outlined earlier in this chapter are addressed by such child-focused programs. In this section a number of family-based interventions and services will be described. These services include:

- diagnostic assistance and developmental planning
- case management
- parenting interventions
- counseling and medical programs
- financial assistance
- volunteer assistance
- parent/sibling support groups.

To the extent that such services are available and of good quality, family stress should be reduced and family resiliency enhanced.

DIAGNOSTIC CONSULTATION AND DEVELOPMENTAL PLANNING

As mentioned in Chapter 1, diagnostic evaluation can be obtained in a variety of settings. Although most medical doctors are not trained to give such diagnoses, they make referrals if they feel that a developmental problem exists and/or the family requests further evaluation. Within most medium-to-large-size cities, diagnostic evaluation can be obtained through school systems, child-clinical psychologists, developmental pediatricians, and developmental assessment clinics. If financial resources allow, it is a good idea for families to search for an autism clinic, which are typically found in larger cities, often within a university setting. Such autism clinics can be located through an Internet search.

Most diagnostic clinics also conduct developmental assessments and assist families in formulating a developmental plan to guide intervention over the short and longer term. Developmental assessments evaluate the children's strengths and limitations in multiple areas, including fine and gross motor skills, self-help, receptive and expressive language, social and preacademic skills. An assessment of sensory functioning, particularly vision and hearing, is also advisable. If these latter evaluations are not available at an assessment clinic, they can be obtained in most communities at a speech and hearing clinic and from ophthalmologists specializing in child vision assessment. The evaluation process sometimes includes an assessment of the child's intellectual abilities. However, this type of assessment, particularly during early childhood, may be inaccurate and is of minimal use in establishing a developmental intervention plan.

A good developmental assessment will not only let parents know how their child is functioning but also provide a detailed plan regarding the types of intervention needed and specific intervention goals. After such an assessment, parents should know not only what their child's diagnosis is, but also how to proceed from an intervention perspective.

CASE MANAGEMENT

Because children with autism typically are in need of and receive a wide array of services from different professional personnel, parents can be overwhelmed as they try to locate specific services, provide case history information to the various therapists/educators, and coordinate communication between professionals about assessments that have been conducted and the status of ongoing interventions. Ideally, a person within an agency, such as a social worker, helps parents perform these tasks, a service that is an invaluable aid both to parents as well as to professionals who are in need of this information. If a case manager is not available, parents need to keep updated assessment and therapy files and periodically send or carry these files to each of the respective therapists who work with their child. Current therapy and educational reports help reduce unnecessary redundancy in services, ensure consistency in services where overlap is needed, and alert professionals concerning current program goals and emerging problems that need to be addressed.

PARENTING INTERVENTIONS

Parenting is one of the most important activities that adults perform in their life. Despite its importance most parents receive little or no formal training concerning how to parent. Based on the extensive concerns that parents report about their children and the growing number of cases of children with socioemotional, behavior, and learning problems, it is clear that parent education programs can provide invaluable assistance for all families (Gottman, 1997). Parent education programs are particularly useful for parents with children with special needs and developmental/learning problems. Some counseling and psychological clinics provide parenting clinics and workshops. Families with children with autism might well benefit from such a program, if their goal is to develop general parenting skills. A more specialized parent-training program that helps parents address all of their children's needs is typically not available and indeed would be difficult to structure unless coordinated by an autism clinic that provides a wide range of services.

However, families can be given the assistance that they need through consultants who help parents establish home programs, or through therapists at clinics who are willing to export their programs into the home. Many speech, occupational, and physical therapists will provide such services during clinic visits or upon request will sometimes make home visits to assist families. Consultants who help families set up applied behavior analysis programs can be particularly helpful in establishing educational goals for the child with autism, providing parents techniques for assisting their children in reaching these goals, dealing with behavioral problems, and helping parents establish a team of paid and volunteer teachers. Educators who use the TEACCH approach also are committed to coordinating school and home programs.

COUNSELING AND MEDICAL SERVICES

Many families are reluctant to seek out counseling and psychological services because they associate such services with having a mental illness or some sort of serious maladjustment. However, these services can provide general assistance to most families with children with autism, as well as specialized assistance to family members who are experiencing sadness and depression, acute anxiety and panic attacks, marital distress, problems with siblings, and other problems related to managing stressors associated with rearing a child with autism. For example, family-oriented counseling and psychological services can assist families through the grieving process, provide anxiety management techniques, help families negotiate role conflicts, clarify dynamics underlying marital problems, promote effective family communication, teach problem-solving and time-management skills, and help siblings deal with conflicts and feelings of anxiety and anger. Counseling services are typically focused on helping family members grow and on preventing the development of serious problems.

In addition to counseling services, specialized medical services can often enhance family functioning. All children with autism should also receive routine physical examinations and, if appropriate, neurological examination to assess brain functioning and possible seizure activity. Even though children do not show overt behavior signs of seizures, they may be experiencing microseizures that are detectable only via a full neurological assessment. Such seizures, which are often quite treatable, may be related to a child's attentional and learning problems. In addition, parents need to make sure they look after their own health. Parents who are suffering from acute anxiety and/or depression probably should consider consulting a doctor regarding the appropriateness of medication. However, if a medication approach is pursued, the problems producing anxiety and depression should still be addressed in counseling and stress management programs.

FINANCIAL ASSISTANCE

Because of the cost of all these interventions, families of children with autism will require financial assistance. Such assistance can come from a variety of private, local, state, and federal sources. Parents can typically locate these sources by talking with other parents of special needs children, and agencies providing services. This process should begin as soon as possible after the diagnosis of autism is received. It is also a good idea for parents to contact political representatives at all government levels regarding their need for assistance. This type of contact not only serves to alert politicians of family needs, but also provides an opportunity for parents to advocate on behalf of their children for more extensive services and supports.

VOLUNTEER SUPPORTS

Most communities have numerous agencies that provide volunteer assistance. Some of these agencies recruit volunteers for the specific purpose of helping families with special needs children. In addition to community agencies, many colleges and universities have volunteer organizations and practicum courses that place students in home programs. Families who have children with autism need to actively consider this option. Volunteers can provide assistance through babysitting and respite care, as well as by helping with home-based educational and therapeutic programs. Parents who have a home-based applied behavioral analysis program often need a team of four or more volunteers to help with its implementation. Volunteers can also serve more informal roles as a friend or big sister/brother for siblings in the family.

PARENT AND SIBLING SUPPORT GROUPS

In many communities, families with children with autism band together to establish informal and formal support groups. These groups can serve different functions. Most groups provide emotional support, opportunities for exchanging information, and problem-solving assistance. Sometimes they serve an advocacy role, helping to catalyze new services. Because many of the parents in these groups have extensive experience with and information about autism, they can serve as mentors to parents whose children have been recently diagnosed as autistic. Because members of support groups vary considerably in their needs and expertise, those groups that arrange their agendas to serve specific member needs are more likely to be successful. In a series of studies, Bitsika and Sharpley (1999, 2000) evaluated a support group for parents of autistic children. In the first study, the support group focused on information-sharing and discussion of problems. The researchers found only minimal improvements in the general well-being of parents who participated. At the end of the support group, parents indicated that they would prefer more specific assistance to help them cope with the daily hassles and crises. In a second study, situation-specific stress management techniques were taught to group members, resulting in a marked improvement in parents' well-being.

Volunteer programs in some communities are specifically designed to help the siblings of children with autism. One program, Super Sibs, that was developed at the University of Notre Dame in Indiana, matches up college students who have siblings with disabilities, as volunteers to work with nonhandicapped children who also have a brother or sister with a disability. This unique program provides nonhandicapped children an informal forum for discussing and reflecting on what it is like to have a brother or sister with a disability and how this disability is affecting them and their family.

Summary

Family members who cope successfully with the challenges of having a child with autism often serve as a source of inspiration for others and become role models because of their strength, compassion, and willingness to help those in need. Family researchers are only beginning to understand the individual and social factors that produce such resiliency. The protective factors described in the last section provide a preliminary answer to the question of why some families seem to thrive in the face of challenge. As the challenges confronting families with children with autism are better articulated and the factors that underlie family resiliency are better understood, it is likely that more effective intervention programs will be developed to help these families. What is already abundantly clear is that these families are in need of quality services from the community.

In the next chapter a variety of recommendations will be made that have direct implications for assisting and supporting families who have children with autism. Some of these recommendations are directed at empowering parents to more effectively help themselves. Other recommendations are directed toward professionals who provide services; researchers who are involved in systematic efforts to expand our knowledge about the nature of autism and how best to treat it; and politicians and program administrators who help formulate new social policies that affect the lives of families and their children with autism. More generally, the recommendations are designed to enhance family resiliency and protect families who are severely challenged.

References

Attwood, T. (1998) *Asperger Syndrome: A guide for parents and professionals.* London: Jessica Kingsley Publishers.

Belsky, J. (1984) "The determinants of parenting: A process model." *Child Development 55,* 83–96.

Bitsika, V. & Sharpley, C. (1999) "An exploratory examination of the effects of support groups on the well-being of parents of children with autism-I: General counseling." *Journal of Applied Health Behaviour 1*, 16–22.

Bitsika, V. & Sharpley, C. (2000) "Development and testing of the effects of support groups on the well-being of parents of children with autism-II: Specific stress management techniques." *Journal of Applied Health Behaviour 2*, 8–15.

Bristol, M. M., Gallagher, J. J. & Schopler, E. (1988) "Mothers and fathers of young developmentally disabled and nondisabled boys: Adaptation and spousal support." *Developmental Psychology 24*, 441–451.

Chan, J. B. & Sigafoos, J. (2001) "Does respite care reduce parental stress in families with developmentally disabled children?" *Child & Youth Care Forum 30*, 253–263.

Coulthard, P. & Fitzgerald, M. (1999) "In God we trust? Organized religion and personal beliefs as resources and coping strategies, and their implications for health in parents with a child on the autistic spectrum." *Mental Health, Religion & Culture 2*, 19–33.

Covey, S. R., Merrill, R. A. & Merrill, R. R. (1996) *First things first: To live, to love, to learn, to leave a legacy.* New York: Fireside.

Donenberg, G. & Baker, B. L. (1993) "The impact of young children with externalizing behaviors on their families." *Journal of Abnormal Child Psychology 21*, 179–198.

Dunn, M. E., Burbine, T., Bowers, C. A. & Tantleff-Dunn, S. (2001) "Moderators of stress in parents of children with autism." *Community Mental Health Journal 37*, 39–52.

Elkind, D. (1995) "School and family in the postmodern world." *Phi Delta Kappan* (September), 8–14.

Coleman, D. (1994) *Emotional intelligence: Why does it matter more than IQ?* New York: Bantam Books.

Gottman, J. (1997) *The Heart of Parenting: Raising an emotionally intelligent child.* New York: Simon & Schuster.

Guralnick, M. J. (2000) "Early childhood intervention: Evolution of a system." *Focus on Autism and Other Developmental Disabilities 15*, 68–79.

Hastings, R. P. & Johnson, E. (2001) "Stress in UK families conducting intensive home-based behavioral intervention for their young child with autism." *Journal of Autism and Developmental Disorders 31*, 327–336.

Hoppes, K. & Harris, S. L. (1990) "Perceptions of child attachment and maternal gratification in mothers of children with autism and Down syndrome." *Journal of Clinical Child Psychology 19*, 365–370.

Kaminsky, L. & Dewey, D. (2002) "Psychosocial adjustment in siblings of children with autism." *Journal of Child Psychology and Psychiatry 43*, 225–232.

Kasari, C., Sigman, M., Mundy, P. & Yirmiya, N. (1988) "care-giver interactions with autistic children." *Journal of Abnormal Child Psychology 16*, 45–56.

Katz, S. & Kessel, L. (2002) "Grandparents of children with developmental disabilities: Perceptions, beliefs, and involvement in their care." *Issues in Comprehensive Pediatric Nursing 25*, 113–128.

Kaufman, J. & Zigler, E. (1987) "Do abused children become abusive parents?" *American Journal of Orthopsychiatry 57*, 186–192.

Koegel, R. L., Schreibman, L., Loos, L. M., Dirlich-Wilhelm, H., Dunlap, G., Robbins, F. R. & Plienis, A. J. (1992) "Consistent stress profiles in mothers of children with autism." *Journal of Autism and Developmental Disorders 22*, 205–216.

Konstantareas, M. M. & Homatidis, S. (1989) "Assessing child symptom severity and stress in parents of autistic children." *Journal of Child Psychology and Psychiatry 30*, 459–470.

Kübler-Ross, E. (1969) *On death and dying*. New York: Scribner.

Lang, D. (1992) "Preventing short-term strain through time-management coping." *Work and Stress 6*, 169–176.

Loehr, J. & Schwartz, T. (2003) *The power of full engagement: Managing energy, not time, is the key to high performance and personal renewal*. Champagne, Il: Free Press.

Macan, T. H. (1994) "Time management: Test of a process model." *Journal of Applied Psychology 79*, 381–391.

Macan, T. H. (1996) "Time-management training: Effects on time behaviors, attitudes, and job performance." *The Journal of Psychology 130*, 219–236.

Maurice, C. (1993) *Let me hear your voice: A family's triumph over autism*. New York: Fawcett Columbine.

McAfee, J. (2002) *Navigating the social world: A curriculum for individuals with Asperger's Syndrome, high-functioning autism and related disorders*. Arlington, TX: Future Horizons.

Milgram, N. A. & Atzil, M. (1988) "Parenting stress in raising autistic children." *Journal of Autism and Developmental Disorders 18*, 415–424.

Moes, D. (1995) "Parenting education and stress." In R. L. Koegel & L. K. Koegel (eds) *Teaching children with autism: Strategies for initiating positive interaction and improving learning opportunities* (pp. 79–93). Baltimore: Brookes.

Moes, D., Koegel, R. L., Schreibman, L. & Loos, L. M. (1992) "Stress profiles for mothers and fathers of children with autism." *Psychological Reports 71*, 1272–1274.

Morgenstern, J. (2000) *Time management from the inside out: The foolproof system for taking control of your schedule and your life*. New York: Henry Holt.

Moyes, R. A. (2001) *Incorporating social goals in the classroom: A guide for teachers and parents of children with high-functioning autism and Asperger Syndrome*. London: Jessica Kingsley Publishers.

Myles, B. S. & Adreon, D. (2001) *Asperger syndrome & adolescence: Practical solutions for school success*. Shawnee Mission, KS: Autism/Asperger Publishing.

National Center on Child Abuse and Neglect (NCCAN) (1993) *A report on the maltreatment of children with disabilities (DHHS Contract No. 105–89–1630)*. Washington, DC: National Clearinghouse on Child Abuse and Neglect Information.

Noh, S., Dumas, J. E., Wolf, L. C. & Fisman, S. N. (1989) "Delineating sources of stress in parents of exceptional children." *Family Relations 38*, 456–461.

Norton, P. & Drew, C. (1994) "Autism and potential family stressors." *The American Journal of Family Therapy 22*, 67–76.

Olsson, M. B. & Hwang, C. P. (2001) "Depression in mothers and fathers of children with intellectual disability." *Journal of Intellectual Disability Research 45*, 535–543.

Roeyers, H. & Mycke, K. (1995) "Siblings of a child with autism, with mental retardation and with a normal development." *Childcare, Health and Development 21*, 305–319.

Sanders, J. L. & Morgan, S. B. (1997) "Family stress and adjustment as perceived by parents of children with autism or Down Syndrome: Implications for intervention." *Child & Family Behavior Therapy 19*, 15–32.

Sarni, C. (1999) *The development of emotional competence*. New York: Guilford Press.

Seligman, M. (1998) *Learned optimism*. New York: Pocket Books.

Sharpley, C. F. & Bitsika, V. (1997) "Influence of gender, parental health, and perceived expertise of assistance upon stress, anxiety, and depression among parents of children with autism." *Journal of Intellectual and Developmental Disability 22*, 19–28.

Siegel, B. (1996) *The world of the autistic child: Understanding and treating autistic spectrum disorder.* New York: Oxford University Press.

Stoneman, Z. (2001) "Supporting positive sibling relationships during childhood." *Mental Retardation and Developmental Disabilities Research Review 7*, 134–142.

Summers, J. A., Behr, S. K. & Turnbull, A. P. (1989) "Positive adaptations and coping strengths of families who have children with disabilities." In G. Singer & L. Irvin (eds) *Support for care-giving families: Enabling positive adaptation to disability* (pp. 27–40). Baltimore: Brookes.

Tarakeshwar, N. & Pargament, K. I. (2001) "Religious coping in families of children with autism." *Focus on Autism and Other Developmental Disabilities 16*, 247–260.

Thompson, R. J. & Gustafson, K. E. (1996) *Adaptation to chronic illness.* Washington, DC: American Psychological Association.

Tobing, L. E. & Glenwick, D. S. (2002) "Relation of the Childhood Autism Rating Scale – Parent version to diagnosis, stress, and age." *Research in Developmental Disabilities 23*, 211–223.

Tommasone, L. & Tommasone, J. (2000) "Adjusting to your child's diagnosis." In M. Powers (ed) *Children with autism: A parent's guide* (pp. 22–43). Rockville, MD: Woodbine House.

Tunali, B. & Power, T. G. (2002) "Coping by redefinition: Cognitive appraisals in mothers of children with autism and children without autism." *Journal of Autism and Developmental Disorders 32*, 25–34.

Webster's New World College Dictionary (Fourth edition) (1999) New York: Macmillan.

Whitman, T. L., Borkowski, J. G., Keogh, D. A. & Weed, K. (2001) *Interwoven lives: Adolescent mothers and their children.* Mawah, NJ: Erlbaum.

Wolf, L. C., Noh, S., Fisman, S. N. & Speechley, M. (1989) "Brief report: Psychological effects of parenting stress on parents of autistic children." *Journal of Autism and Developmental Disorders 19*, 157–166.

Ziolko, M. (1993) "Counseling parents of children with disabilities: A review of literature and implications for practice." In M. Nagler (ed) *Perspectives on Disability.* Palo Alto, CA: Health Market Research.

CHAPTER 7

Recommendations to Parents, Therapists/Educators, Researchers, and Social Policy-Makers

In this chapter, a series of recommendations will be made to parents, therapists, researchers, and social policy-makers regarding the development, implementation, and evaluation of intervention programs for children with autism. Currently, parents who are raising children with autism are confronted with a mass of information regarding the types of intervention programs they should implement. Because of the complexity, ambiguity, and often conflicting nature of this information, they often have difficulty deciding how to proceed in establishing a program for their children. For this reason a number of recommendations will be made to parents regarding intervention program philosophy and structure, as well as parental roles, attitudes, and responsibilities. In a subsequent section, recommendations will be made to professionals who provide therapeutic and educational supports to children with autism and their families. These recommendations will focus on how professionals can assist in the implementation and evaluation of effective programs for children with autism and support families in the development of home programs. Next, a series of recommendations will be made to researchers regarding areas that are in need of empirical study. Finally, recommendations will be made to persons who are in charge of making social policies as well as those who are in a position to influence social policy, which includes most citizens. These recommendations are directed at creating infrastructures that will allow for the development and delivery of more effective research and intervention programs. Table 7.1 summarizes these recommendations.

Table 7.1 Recommendations to parents, therapists/educators, researchers, and social policy-makers

Parents	Therapists/ Educators	Researchers	Social policy-makers
1) Become a student of autism	1) Develop a partnership with parents	1) Develop early diagnostic assessments	1) Focus on early intervention
2) Begin intervention early	2) Coordinate school and home programs	2) Focus on development	2) Establish local autism centers
3) Develop structured programs	3) Promote self-regulatory behavior	3) Evaluate promising therapies	3) Support public policy research
4) Become an intelligent consumer of services	4) Emphasize evaluation	4) Develop curricula for teaching complex social skills	4) Support basic and applied research
5) Think scientifically	5) Become interdisci plinary		
6) Do not expect cures soon			
7) Consider carefully what is the best educational arrangement			
8) Become an advocate			
9) Take care of yourself and your family			

Recommendations to parents

Become a student of autism

Parents are in a position to help their children with autism in ways that no one else can, because of their extensive knowledge about their children's capabilities and limitations, their ability to interpret the meanings and reasons for their children's actions, and their commitment to helping their children. Although therapists and teachers can provide critical assistance in helping children with autism, their impact is limited because of the brevity and intermittent nature of their contact with the children, and sometimes by their lack of knowledge about autism and expertise in working with this population. For all these reasons, parents are often cast into the role of primary teacher and therapist. Not surprisingly, parents feel ill-prepared to assume this responsibility. To prepare for this role and to better help their children, parents must become students of autism.

Although some parents might question their ability to become good students of autism, they are uniquely qualified because they are motivated learners, driven by the desire to help their children. They also have an intuitive understanding of autism as manifested in their child. Now is a good time to become a student of autism because of the numerous and rapidly increasing resources available to parents. These resources include books written by scholars, researchers, therapists, parents of autistic children, and people with autism. In addition, the Internet is becoming an increasingly excellent source of information, particularly the websites of professional organizations that are directly involved in work with autism. Internet chat rooms can also be of great help to parents with specific questions. Another major source of information comes through the contact parents have with professionals who work with their children. Increasingly, professionals realize that a major part of their job is to act as a resource for the families they serve. Parents need to actively and strategically seek out information from these professionals. An invaluable source of assistance also comes from other parents who have children with autism, particularly those who have been successful in searching out resources and services for their children. In addition, many parents augment their learning by participating in professional workshops on autism and professional conferences held by organizations like the Autism Society of America. Finally, an increasing number of parents are becoming paraprofessional therapists as a consequence of the training they receive at workshops and from consultants who help them establish home-based educational programs.

Begin intervention programs early

The importance of beginning intervention programs as early as possible cannot be overemphasized. Even if a formal diagnosis of autism has not been confirmed, but only suspected, it is appropriate to put interventions in place to address any significant developmental problems that are occurring, whether they be in the motor, sensory, cognitive, language, or social areas. A formal diagnosis of autism often has little impact on the goals of an intervention program, although it should influence how such programs are structured. The rationale for early intervention programs is compelling and based on both basic and applied research, as well as developmental theory.

From a biological perspective, it is known that during early infancy, brain development has already proceeded to the point where billions of neurons, the basic building blocks of the brain, have been formed. The process of inter-connecting these neurons, however, has only begun (Bornstein & Lamb, 1992). During the early years of a child's life, trillions of connections between neurons are formed. Many of the connections are later eliminated with the passage of time. The early experiences of the child play a critical role in deter-mining which connections between neurons are developed and sustained and which ones disappear. Although genes play a vital role in developing the building blocks of the brain, the environment is the vital force determining how these blocks will be specifically organized, or to use another metaphor, how the brain is wired.

Basic processes, including sensory, motor, perceptual, cognitive, and linguistic, are influenced by the environments in which children with autism live. Not only do these separate processes become wired, but the various processes, such as the visual and motor, the visual and auditory, and the language and sensorimotor, become interconnected with each other through experience. Cognitive processes emerge out of this vast pattern of connec-tions. Body and person recognition develop. Thoughts become linked to emotions. Inhibitory pathways are formed which allow emotions to be controlled as social rules are learned.

This extremely complex developmental process is disrupted when autism occurs. What exactly produces this disruption is not well understood, nor are all the specific effects of this disruption on later development. Genes undoubtedly play a role through influencing how basic brain biochemistry and structures evolve, as well as by placing restrictions on the way environ-ments influence the wiring of the brain. Nevertheless, the environment has a profound influence on the development of children with autism.

Phenomenologically, it appears that children with autism do not experience the environment around them in the same way as typically developing children. Based on the writings of individuals with autism, such as Temple Grandin and Donna Williams, it seems that their environments are often chaotic and unpredictable, as well as frightening (Grandin, 1995; Williams, 1992). It also appears that in order to reduce the chaos and fear, children with autism change the ways they interact with their surroundings so as to better control environmental stimulation. Obsessive, ritualistic, and social withdrawal behaviors likely emerge to assist them in managing their environments and to make sensory input more intelligible.

What do early intervention programs do? They are directed at creating environments that are safe and predictable, thus reducing the need for children with autism to develop coping mechanisms that disengage them from their environment. Early intervention programs are directed at facilitating normal development in a context that provides appropriate social and emotional supports. From a neurological perspective, the brain of the child with autism will get wired; it is just a question of how—either by an environment created and controlled by the child or by an environment created by educators and parents to promote learning.

Although the brain, including the brain of children with autism, is extremely malleable, there are limits. There are windows of opportunity for the wiring of emotional, motor, sensory, cognitive, and language processes. If, due to restrictions in the environment, proper stimulation of these processes does not occur within a certain time frame, their development may be inhibited and delays may occur. Although delays may be at least partially remediated through intervention programs, learning becomes more difficult if it occurs outside of these windows of opportunity. More basic processes, including sensory, motor, and emotion, appear to be wired earlier than language and social processes. However, because all of these processes are interwoven in the brain, it is important to address any emerging delays and deficiencies as soon as possible.

From a psychological perspective, learning occurs in whatever environment a child is placed; however, not all learning is equally adaptive. Maladaptive behaviors that are established can become habitual. The more established such habits become, the more difficult they are to break. Maladaptive behaviors, such as social avoidance, stereotypy, and ritualistic behaviors, appear to develop because they serve a purpose for children with autism: they reduce fear and anxiety. Such habits, however, make the learning of adaptive behaviors more difficult. Early intervention programs are directed toward establishing new patterns of adaptive behavior that make unnecessary the maladaptive habits or symptoms of children with autism. To the extent that the initiation of intervention programs are delayed, the establishment of new adaptive habits takes longer, and complex behaviors, like language, become much more difficult to teach. Although it cannot be stated with any precision how soon early intervention programs should begin, a general rule of thumb is to initiate early intervention programs as soon as possible, with the structure of those programs dictated by the child's age and developmental level.

Develop structured programs

In order for any child to learn, an environment must be structured so as to have order and predictability. Environments that are constantly in a state of flux are not only difficult to adapt to and learn in, they are also stressful. Children with autism are particularly in need of structure in their educational programs. Because of their sensory, motor, cognitive, language, and social problems, they tend to have more difficulty coping with typical environments and social interactions. Children with autism become more easily stressed when confronted with change, because they have fewer resources for coping with change than children who do not have their disability. As a consequence, they disengage attentionally from the social environment. Many of the symptoms of autism, including obsessions with certain stimuli and compulsive adherence to certain routines, appear to be ways of coping with and controlling environments that are complex, chaotic and emotionally overwhelming.

For these reasons, structured intervention programs that follow set routines are advantageous to children with autism. Structure helps keep children from getting anxious and frees them up cognitively to benefit from educational and training experiences. Change, when it needs to occur, should be introduced in a slow and orderly fashion. As children with autism acquire new adaptive behaviors and coping skills, they should be able to tolerate change more easily. A critical question that needs to be answered is what exactly constitutes a structured program? Sometimes the answer to this question is given by providing examples of what some individuals construe to be a structured program, such as play therapy. The provision of these types of general examples, however, does not provide specific information about what is meant by structured, and can be very misleading.

Analysis of educational and therapeutic programs suggests that structured programs should have the following characteristics: clearly defined goals, intervention procedures, and educational materials. A well-structured intervention also specifies how a child's newly acquired skills and behaviors will be generalized into everyday living environments. More specifically, educational goals should be defined in a concrete fashion so that intervention programs can be consistently delivered and goal achievement reliably evaluated. Educational interventions should be articulated in enough detail so as to allow a standard treatment protocol to be transferred to and consistently delivered by parents, teachers, volunteers, and professional personnel. Finally, the environment surrounding treatment, including program materials, room arrangements, and program order, should be specified. In formulating structured programs, the child's developmental level, pattern of strengths and limitations, interests, choices, and motivational level should be considered. Insofar as is possible, children should be given information about the exact nature of the program structure as well as changes that might occur in that structure once it is established.

Become an intelligent consumer of services

Parents approaching professionals for services for their children need to become intelligent consumers. Before they meet with service providers, parents should have some ideas about what services they want and have done a thorough enough investigation to determine which professionals can best provide these services. Upon meeting with the service provider, parents should feel free to ask questions about the exact nature of the services the provider can deliver, the rationale for these services, and the experience the provider has had in working with children with autism. If appropriate, the parents should evaluate the provider's willingness to extend the program into the home setting and to teach the parent how to administer it. The parents should be open-minded enough to consider carefully what the provider says, but should not automatically assume "the doctor always knows what is best." If the provider does not listen to the parents, or consider carefully the information parents give to them, parents are well-advised to search out other service providers and second opinions. Because parents only gradually become "experts" in autism, they may be less intelligent consumers of services than they would ideally like to be. However, as they read and learn, their expertise will rapidly grow.

Think scientifically

In an emerging area like autism, where questions are more numerous than good answers, there is considerable speculation by parents about which of the many treatment approaches available are best for their children. Some treatments are quite controversial, and many of them have not been empirically evaluated. Sometimes, a treatment is selected based on the testimonials of either the person who developed the treatment and/or parents who believe that their children were helped by the treatment. Some parents tend to jump on one treatment bandwagon after another, hoping to help their children. Even though some of the treatments are very expensive, parents may feel guilty if they do not give their children every chance to get better. Eventually parents ask themselves the following questions: How should we make decisions concerning what is best for our child? How can we most wisely allocate our financial resources to help our child?

One approach to answering questions like these is to think scientifically. Thinking scientifically involves considering the treatment as objectively and dispassionately as possible. The need for parents to help their children can generate intense emotions, which in turn can endanger the unbiased analysis needed to evaluate a treatment. Earlier, the recommendation was made for parents to learn as much as they could about autism and its treatment. As parents read the treatment literature they should ask themselves a series of questions including: What exactly is the treatment? How does the treatment produce its effects; specifically, is a rationale given for how the treatment works or why it should work? How much empirical evidence is there for the effectiveness of the treatment? Have the side effects of the treatment, particularly the potentially adverse side effects, been systematically investigated? In instances where the precise nature of the treatment is unclear and where reputable empirical research evaluating the treatment is either absent or does not yield convincing evidence of its efficacy, parents should be wary about using the treatment with their children.

Frequently, parents are unduly swayed toward using particular treatments based on the testimonials of other parents or professionals in the absence of empirical evidence. Parents sometimes ask what is wrong with basing their treatment decisions on such testimonials. One answer is that testimonials are often given by people who want to and often need to believe in the treatment's effectiveness, including parents, who spent considerable time and money on the treatment, and professionals, who developed the technique and often profit from people using their treatment. Testimonials are often based on perceptions where people focus on what they want to or expect to see and contradictory evidence is ignored. Testimonials are not usually based on research that evaluates treatment effects and side effects using appropriate experimental protocols. To the untrained observer, treatments sometimes appear to work, but in reality a child is not really changing or is changing for other nontherapeutic reasons. Nevertheless a conclusion is reached that the treatment was effective and responsible for the change, when in fact it was not.

A major problem with testimonial evidence is that it ignores the possibility of placebo effects. Placebo effects are real; persons do improve, however the effects are not due to the treatment administered, but rather a result of other things that accompanied but were not a part of the treatment. For example, placebo effects may be due to the fact that parents or other people treat the child differently after the treatment is given. They expect the children to change and they react to the children as if they have changed, creating a self-fulfilling prophecy. The effect of expectations on behavior can be very powerful. Some researchers have suggested that up to 90% of the medical cures in the last century were due entirely, or in part, to placebo effects. Researchers investigating treatments typically employ designs to control for and/or evaluate placebo effects.

Occasionally, the comment is made, "What does it matter if treatment effects are produced through placebo mechanisms?" In one sense, it is good if it works, but substantial money may be paid for a treatment that in and of itself is not effective. Should parents pay a lot of money for a sugar pill? Research endeavours to understand placebo effects and design effective treatments based on the mechanisms that produce them. Another problem with treatments that capitalize on placebo effects is that these effects are often temporary, that is, they are not maintained over time. Parents who use untested treatments are frequently told when their children show no change or temporary changes that their child needs more treatment, thus further increasing the cost of the treatment.

A final note of caution to parents regarding testimonial evidence: Professional therapists, like parents, can be swayed by this type of evidence. They may recommend treatments based on the anecdotal reports of their clients and their own informal observations. Because many therapists are not well trained in the use of scientific methods, they are subject to the same logical fallacies and emotional influences as parents. Professional therapists are invested, like parents, in wanting to help children and wanting to believe that what they are doing is useful. They may also be ego invested because they know that their reputation as a therapist is in large part based on how successful they are. Relatedly, a therapist's belief in their treatment's efficacy may be influenced by financial considerations; people do not seek out services that do not work.

Do not expect cures soon: There are no magic bullets

Some parents are continually shopping for new treatments that might help their children recover from their autism. They hope that the next treatment that is tried will be the one that will bring their children out of their autistic world. Their hopes may be encouraged by other parents' stories or by times when their own children showed unexpected competencies: brief snapshots of the children they thought they would have before the symptoms of autism became apparent.

What is the likelihood of a miracle treatment being developed that will cure autism? Based on our present state of knowledge, parents are well-advised to temper such hopes. Autism is a complex disorder, most likely caused by deficiencies in a number of genes, perhaps 15 or more. It is likely further triggered by environmental events occurring during early development, probably during the prenatal phase. Although major advances are being made in the search for the causes of autism, the advent of "curative" types of treatment awaits the isolation of these specific genes and environmental triggers, as well as the biochemical processes they control. This search will take time, particularly because of the polygenetic (more than one gene) nature of autism. The likelihood of finding a miracle cure for autism is quite low if the genetic and environmental processes that underlie its development are not first understood. Moreover, because of the diversity of the symptomatology associated with autism, it is quite possible that the causes of autism may not be the same for all individuals with this disorder.

If a miracle cure is not likely to be found soon, what should parents do? Most importantly, they should be optimistic about the future. Currently, there are numerous research programs directed at isolating the genetic, biological, and environmental processes that produce autism. Some of these projects are starting to provide initial insights into the mechanisms underlying autism. In their advocacy role, parents should encourage their political representatives to support funding for basic research on autism. Even though primary prevention, which involves a cure for autism, is not yet possible, researchers are gradually coming to better understand how autism unfolds. With such knowledge, secondary prevention and treatment programs can be designed to alter the developmental trajectory of children with autism and moderate the severity of this disorder.

The "faces" of autism are already changing. Currently, many children with autism do not display all the classical characteristics of this disorder. For example, they frequently form strong bonds with their parents and are affectionate, socially attentive, and quick learners. As new therapeutic and educational programs evolve and are put in place, this positive trend is likely to continue. Until definitive cures for autism are discovered, parents should initiate, as early as possible, intervention programs that have been shown to be effective. Conversely, they should be very cautious about spending their time and money on unproven "quick cure" treatments that have a low probability of success and may even adversely affect their children's development.

Consider carefully what is the best educational arrangement for your child.

In the 1960s and 1970s, there was a major movement in the United States to deinstitutionalize persons with severe developmental disabilities and place them in the mainstream of society. As part of this "normalization" movement, emphasis was put on delivering services to people with disabilities in the same locations that services were given to nondisabled people. Educationally, "normalization" was often translated to mean placing children with disabilities in regular classrooms, sometimes referred to as "mainstreaming". The general rationale for mainstreaming was complex, but reasonable. The major assertion was that traditional educational services for the disabled were inferior to regular educational services and denied individuals with developmental problems their rights to the best possible treatments and educational programs. In addition, it was felt that mainstreaming would reduce discrimination and prejudice and promote better understanding and acceptance of children with disabilities by the general population.

Currently, for these and other reasons, parents often prefer that their children with autism be placed in regular classrooms. They feel that there are higher expectations for children in regular classrooms and that their children will benefit from having greater demands placed on them. They also believe that typically developing children are better role models for their children than children who are developmentally delayed.

In practice, mainstreaming takes many forms; some children are mainstreamed throughout the day, others for certain periods of the day for activities like music and recess. Children with autism spectrum disorders who are mainstreamed throughout the day sometimes, but not necessarily, have the same curriculum as their peers. Frequently, they have classroom aides and/or resource rooms to provide them with extra assistance. How effective mainstreaming is for children with autism spectrum disorders likely depends on the quality of the regular classroom teachers, the classroom aides, and the extra resources available. Typically, regular classroom teachers and aides have little training in the area of autism.

In contrast, some schools have special education programs for children with autism that involve less mainstreaming. The personnel for such programs are teachers who often have some training and experience in the area of autism. Increasingly, as teaching techniques have evolved for working with children with autism, and as this population's needs and learning styles become better understood, the curriculum, as well as its delivery, in these "special" classrooms has diverged from that found in the regular classroom. More specifically, curriculum goals are not based so much on what children of a particular age should be doing as a group, but more on the developmental level, achievements, and strengths of the specific student; in short, the curriculum is more individualized. These modifications can, and sometimes are, introduced into a regular classroom; however, when this occurs, the child with autism is receiving a different curriculum from other children. What cannot be as easily transported into the regular classroom are some of the more structured routines and instructional procedures emphasized in programs like TEACCH and discrete trial training.

Ultimately, what parents need to consider, when selecting or advocating for their children's educational program, is the nature of the curriculum and the quality of teaching in the regular versus special classroom environment. Although mainstreaming children with special needs has many positive features, it may not always be in the child's best interests. Mainstreaming emphasizes the importance of educating, together, students with and without disabilities. However, consideration should also be given to what is the best educational plan that can be put into effect for the student with disabilities. The ideal program is one that is tailored to the educational needs of the child, promotes learning, and takes place in the "least restrictive" and normalized environment that supports these educational objectives. Decisions concerning child placement should be initially based on which type of program best facilitates academic achievement, as well as appropriate social and life skills, and then on integrating the child to the fullest extent possible into the mainstream of society. The best arrangement may well consist of a hybrid program with some mainstreaming in a "regular" classroom and some specialized teaching arrangements in another classroom.

Become an advocate

When appropriate services are not available or readily available to children with autism, parents need to become advocates. Parents are the natural advocates for their children; specifically because they are familiar with their children's needs, the services that have been provided to them, and those that need to be provided. Advocacy is a multifaceted skill which can be learned. Decisions have to be made, however, concerning what battles are most worth fighting. Mutual problem-solving and negotiation with those who have the power to initiate change is always preferable to confrontation. During the advocacy process the rationale for change and the type of service structures parents believe their children need should be articulated as clearly as possible. It is desirable that written proposals for change be shared prior to face-to-face meetings. Whenever possible, groups of individuals with a shared interest in developing new services or modifying existing services should organize and present their ideas together. There is power in numbers. Where satisfaction is not obtained, appeals should be made to a higher authority, for example, in a school to a principal, superintendent, or a school board. When appropriate, politicians who may be in a position to create change should be lobbied. Some advocates help their political representatives draft new bills to be considered for legislation. If all else fails, a legal approach to advocacy may sometimes be appropriate. Many of the rights children with disabilities now enjoy have come about as a consequence of general advocacy, new legislation, and litigation.

In discussing educational advocacy for children with autism, Mulick and Butler (2002) point out that the number of legal suits brought against school systems has risen in recent years. Most of these suits have been initiated by parents and typically focus on obtaining appropriate educational programs for their children. When such suits have been settled in favor of the parents, the presentation of their case has focused on: documenting their child's lack of progress in programs administered by the school system; describing violations of federally mandated guidelines, such as those stipulated in the Individuals with Disabilities Education Act (IDEA); and demonstrating that more appropriate educational plans are available and being successfully implemented elsewhere.

Take care of yourself and your family

Parents, being parents, often place their children's needs ahead of their own. Parents of children with autism often reshape their lives in order to help their children gain every possible advantage. In the process, they may ignore their own needs as well as those of their spouses and other children. Because the family is a system of interconnected members, what affects one member of the family affects the others. Ultimately, if the needs of some of the members are ignored for an extended period of time to meet the needs of another, the whole family may suffer, including the one most obviously in need of help.

Parents and other family members need to learn how to share and rotate responsibilities so that each has some time to pursue their own interests and find moments of respite. Parents, who are naturally self-sacrificing, may have to learn to be a bit selfish. In order to take care of family needs, extra familial supports also need to be developed and fostered, including supports from relatives, friends, church groups, volunteers, and community agencies. If resources allow, paid support personnel can be very helpful if they are properly trained.

Recommendations to therapists, teachers, and other professional personnel

Develop a partnership with parents

Professionals, in part depending on their discipline, vary in their conceptions about the nature of their relationships with those to whom they provide services. Some professionals adhere more to an "expert" model, where the "doctor"/professional knows what is best for the client and the client is expected to adhere to the prescriptions and programs provided. The expert model assumes a large knowledge gap between the professional and client and that clients need professionals to solve their problems. Moreover, clients are expected to trust professionals to do the right thing and certainly should not challenge the professionals' authority. Another aspect of this model is that families are viewed as dysfunctional and lacking the capacity to help themselves (Powell, Hecimovic & Christensen, 1992).

In contrast to this conception is the partnership model. In this model the professional views the family as a rich resource composed of individuals who are often quite knowledgeable about autism, frequently the best judges of the child's needs, and are the child's primary teachers. The professional seeks to empower parents by encouraging them to ask questions, to learn about the therapeutic service to be offered, and to assist in designing and implementing the therapeutic program. The professional becomes more a program designer, a parent trainer, and a consultant rather than primarily being the person who directly provides services to a child client. The child with autism is viewed as embedded in the family and the client becomes the family.

Some professionals fear that they will work themselves out of a job if they give away their discipline by teaching others to conduct therapeutic programs. In reality, what happens is that professionals develop a new and more dynamic role that allows the therapeutic activity to be extended and intensified. The professional essentially develops a cadre of paraprofessionals. Quality control is maintained by the professionals carefully teaching and monitoring the behavior of the paraprofessionals (parents, volunteers, etc.).

Coordinate school and home programs

Feinberg and Vacca (2000) point out that there is an inherent tension between parents and school personnel. Educators wish on one hand for families to be actively involved in decision-making, but on the other hand want families to "advocate something that is consistent with what the school district has to offer" (p. 133). Schools, even though they can be a hallmark of a progressive society, are, as many institutions, frequently more conservative by nature. Families of children with autism are often asking for change in a school's normal manner of operation, thus increasing tension. Tensions may escalate if school personnel point out to families that their teachers are not properly trained to work with children with autism; that they have an obligation to their other children who are typically developing, which should not be compromised; and that available resources are not sufficient to individualize educational programs, particularly when the needs of children with autism are so disparate from those of other children.

If a partnership is to evolve between school personnel and families, both have to view the other as allies, not adversaries. A true partnership requires mutual expression of viewpoints, creation of mutually agreed-on objectives, brainstorming, creative problem-solving, and accommodation. A blueprint needs to be developed that allows educational programs to be individualized to the fullest extent possible and be exportable into the home situation. Moreover, school personnel need to be receptive to extending successful home education programs into the classroom. To help ensure that the blueprint becomes reality, both schools and families have to lobby on each other's behalf for whatever new resources are necessary.

Promote self-regulatory behavior

One of the major problems confronting educators and therapists who work with children with autism relates to behavior maintenance and generalization. Maintenance refers to a process whereby behaviors, once learned by a student, continue to occur across time in the situations in which they were initially taught. For example, a child who learns to label the parts of his/her body, when requested by a teacher, continues to be able to do so at a later date. Generalization refers to a process in which behaviors learned in one situation are transferred to other situations, particularly to situations similar to those in which the behavior was originally learned. For example, a child who learns to label the part of his/her body at home in the presence of their parents, can also do so at school in the presence of a teacher, and can identify the same parts of another person's body. This type of generalization is variously called "situational", "stimulus" and "person generalization".

Many teachers/therapists emphasize initial learning over maintenance and generalization of learning, in part because of the assumption (or hope) that children will maintain and generalize what they have learned without a lot of extra instruction. This assumption is questionable. Most children with autism have difficulty maintaining what they have learned and an even greater problem transferring or generalizing what they have learned to new situations. Because of maintenance and generalization problems, greater educational focus needs to be placed on programming in these areas. A wide variety of techniques for promoting maintenance and generalization have been established and shown empirically to be effective when working with children with developmental disabilities. These techniques include: over-training, systematic review and retraining as necessary, changing reinforcement schedules from continuous to intermittent and from fixed to variable, changing from primary reinforcers like food to secondary reinforcers like praise and affection, utilizing common stimuli across situations, programming in multiple situations and with multiple trainers, and training in natural environments (Whitman, Scibak & Reid, 1983).

Another approach to instruction, less commonly emphasized by teachers and therapists, involves teaching children to self-regulate their own behavior. A survey by Wehmeyer, Agran, and Hughes (2000) suggests the importance of promoting self-determination in educational programs for students with disabilities. Because independent action is valued by society, children with autism who become self-regulatory are more likely to be perceived and reacted to in a positive fashion by others (Whitman, 1990). Although the focus of self-determination programs (or what is referred to here as self-regulation) varies, the objectives of such programs commonly include the promotion of decision-making, problem-solving, choice-making, self-management, self-awareness, self-advocacy, and goal-setting. There are several advantages to teaching self-regulation to children with autism. By exercising self-regulation, children act without external direction and thus become independent. In addition, they are more likely to maintain what they have learned and generalize responses to situations in which they have not been explicitly trained. As a consequence, they are more likely to be able to live in normalized settings where close supervision is not possible.

Two basic approaches have been employed in teaching self-regulation. The first approach involves gradually fading external controls until a child is acting without supervision. For example, a child is taught, initially through teacher prompts and contingent reinforcement, how to solve an arithmetic problem. Subsequently, prompts and reinforcers are gradually removed. A second approach involves the use of a child's language and self-instruction. One of the primary distinctions between behavioral and cognitive-behavioral educational approaches to promoting maintenance and generalization is that the latter approach emphasizes the use of the child's own language to control behavior. Children are taught to verbalize what they must do in a learning situation and then are taught to follow their own verbal directives.

Because of their language deficiencies, there is evidence to suggest that a traditional instructional approach may be less effective than self-instruction with persons with developmental delays (Whitman, 1987). The traditional approach emphasizes control of behavior through verbal direction by significant others, such as teachers and parents. This mode of instruction assumes a certain degree of linguistic control by the person being taught that may not actually exist. Children with autism who possess language often cannot use it to direct their own behavior. This approach also potentially establishes a habit of reliance on others. In contrast to a traditional didactic approach, a self-instructional approach makes particular sense in working with children with autism because they have difficulties using language as a vehicle for monitoring, evaluating, and controlling their own behavior. Because of these limitations, they also likely have difficulty reflecting on and interpreting the actions of others; that is, they seem to lack a theory of mind (see Chapter 3). In order to develop self-regulation, a student with autism must possess a certain level of language proficiency in order to develop verbal regulation skills.

There is reason to believe that children with autism who are verbal can become self-reliant through self-instructional training, specifically because of its systematic emphasis on providing the student relevant verbal cues for self-direction, teaching children appropriate use of these verbal cues, and then ensuring that the student is able to use these verbal cues to regulate his/her behavior. During self-instructional training the instructional burden is initially assumed by the teacher, but, as the student acquires proficiency in following the teacher's verbal direction, teacher support is gradually withdrawn and the student assumes a more active role by verbally regulating his or her behavior. Thus, the self-instructional format provides the general linguistic tools necessary to regulate behavior and then teaches the active use of these tools. The reader is referred to Chapter 4 for further discussion of self-instruction and self-regulation.

It should be noted that the usefulness of a self-instructional approach for teaching self-regulation is also related to the content contained in the instruction. Instructional content is at least as important as the instructional format. In previous research on self-instruction, investigators have utilized an interrogative format and have emphasized the following instructional components: task analysis statements, general and specific strategic statements concerning how to complete a task, self-monitoring and self-evaluation statements, and self-reinforcement (Whitman, 1987). During training, students are taught to pose and then answer specific questions about what they need to do, what they know, and how they should self-monitor in order to ensure task success. Thus, this approach fosters the development of metacognitive and executive processing strategies—skills that children with autism do not normally display in teaching situations (see Chapter 2).

In establishing self-regulation, the value of a self-instructional approach also depends on the range and type of tasks presented as well as the specific analytic skills taught. During instruction, students need to be exposed to a wide variety of tasks requiring either similar or different strategies for solution. They must learn to:

1.   analyze the respective task structures

2.   discriminate differences in task structures, and reach a decision about what kind of task it is

3.   choose the proper strategic approach.

To show generalization, an individual must learn to recognize the similarities between a training and a generalization task and to recognize when a response or strategy utilized in one situation is applicable in another situation. In the process they also learn to discriminate when it is not appropriate to make a particular response to a situation (Whitman, 1987).

Emphasize evaluation

In any rapidly emerging area, such as autism, where many new therapeutic and educational techniques are being introduced, it is critical to evaluate the efficacy of these procedures. All too often, without evaluation, techniques proliferate through the evangelistic efforts of the technique's developers and disciples. Because parents are not typically trained to think scientifically, their selection of therapeutic programs for their children is often guided by emotion and testimonial evidence, rather than solid empirical data. Thus, it is critical for professionals who serve children with autism to use, where feasible, techniques that have been empirically validated. Sometimes, however, because of the unavailability of validated techniques, therapists employ unvalidated but promising techniques, modify existing techniques, or develop their own new intervention programs. In such instances, it is imperative that therapists evaluate the efficacy of these techniques as they employ them with their clients. Clinicians, like business people, are essentially selling a product and should be held accountable for the products they deliver. This evaluation process provides critical information to a therapist about whether their interventions are really helping their clients or need to be discontinued. Such an evaluation also constitutes a first important step in a formal validation process that involves comprehensive and systematic empirical studies.

Most clinicians have an educational background that has provided them at least some training in program evaluation and experimental design. With the advent of single-subject methodologies, clinicians do not need elegant or large-scale group designs to evaluate the efficacy of their programs. Single-subject designs emphasize the gathering of baseline data before the implementation of treatment, as well as data collection during treatment and after treatment, to assess learning, maintenance, and generalization. The use of such methodologies are now routinely encouraged by many consultants who employ behavior education approaches, such as discrete trial training, for teaching children with autism (Lovaas, 2003).

Become interdisciplinary

Because children with autism often receive many different types of services, professionals need to be aware of the programs, in addition to their own, that serve their clients. This awareness is important to the development of an integrated service approach. Proper integration involves insuring that the various programs used with a client complement one another in an appropriate fashion. In some instances, professionals need to consider utilizing not only their own treatment/educational regimens but, where appropriate, extending the treatment regimens established by other therapists/teachers. For example, if a successful program has been established for controlling aggressive behavior, this program might reasonably be used in all therapeutic/educational settings. Similarly, language training procedures might be introduced across training settings. Consistent application is often the key to the success of a program. Although therapists cannot do it all, they can sometimes integrate with minimum effort successful programs established by others into their own.

In order to develop a dynamic multidisciplinary program, professionals need to establish communication with other therapists and talk to parents about the nature of other programs that are in place for their clients. Case conferences, in which the therapeutic team is brought together, should be used, at least intermittently, to establish a coordinated effort. A case manager can also be invaluable in facilitating and coordinating communications between therapists/educators. In the absence of case conferences or a case manager, parents should be encouraged to assume the role of coordinator, specifically through sharing information and formal clinical reports across therapists.

Recommendations to researchers

Develop early diagnostic assessments

Because autism is a developmental disorder, the delays associated with it accumulate over time. For this reason intervention programs need to begin as early as possible in order to change the developmental trajectory of children with autism from one of increasing delays to growth in adaptive behavior. In order to initiate prevention and intervention programs, it is necessary to identify as soon as possible children with autism. Unfortunately, instruments for assessing autism in the first years of life are only beginning to emerge. The task of developing early diagnostic assessments is complicated by the fact that many of the classic symptoms of autism are not manifested or are difficult to detect in their early stages.

For this reason, more attention needs to be given to the study of groups of infants at high risk for becoming autistic, in order to better understand the nature of early development in those children who are eventually diagnosed as autistic. Groups at high risk include: infants who have siblings or close relatives who have autism; children who manifest early signs of autism but cannot yet be diagnosed as autistic; infants with developmental delays that are not clearly associated with some other disorder; and children whose parents have clinical problems, like Obsessive–Compulsive Disorder, that have been found to be associated with autism.

At present, instruments for assessing autism during its initial stages are emerging; however, many of these assessments are composed of items that are suspected to be early versions of later autistic symptoms. To broaden the pool of potential early markers, developmental studies of children at risk for autism are needed to search for other developmental anomalies that are correlates or precursors of later diagnosable symptoms of autism. These early developmental correlates may include behaviors in domains that are not part of the present autism diagnostic system, such as motor, sensory, or emotional markers. Another top research priority is to isolate biological markers of autism that are genetic, neurological, or neurochemical in nature (Bristol-Power & Spinella, 1999). For further discussion of early diagnostic procedures, the reader is referred to Chapter 1.

Focus on development

In addition to studies that are designed to assist in the formulation of better early diagnostic instruments, researchers need to focus more generally on studying children at risk for autism in order to better understand how their development occurs over time, specifically, early development in the emotional, sensory, motor, cognitive, language/communication, and social areas. For example, through studies of early emotional reactivity, emotional regulation, sensory acuity, sensory tracking, hypersensitivities, hyposensitivities, muscle tone, motor coordination, visual-motor skills, orientation behaviors, habituation responses, vocalization patterns, and adult–infant interactions, valuable insights into the individual processes leading to autism are likely to be provided.

Research also needs to examine how development in one area, for example motor functioning, influences development in other areas, such as emotional, sensory, or cognitive functioning and vice versa, in order to better understand the intersystem influences described in the model presented in Figure 4.3 (see Chapter 4, p. 156). Relatedly research needs to study the concurrent and longer-term influences of early developmental anomalies, such as those sometimes observed in the motor and sensory areas, on adult–child social interactions, cognitive functioning, and language development. More also needs to be known about the influences of early adult–child relationships on later child development. Although there is no reason to believe that parents cause autism, it may be that early developmental problems in the children lead to asynchronous and noncontingent styles of parenting, which in turn adversely affect the developmental trajectories of children with autism.

Evaluate promising therapies

The use of unvalidated therapies by therapists and parents is perhaps greater in the area of autism than for any other childhood disorder. The reasons for this situation are likely several. Because autism is symptomatically such a complex disorder, no single treatment approach has emerged, but rather a myriad of therapies directed at different aspects of the disorder. As a consequence, the task of validating so many different therapies has been major, if not daunting. In addition, because a number of therapies were originated by clinicians who were not trained in an experimental tradition, systematic evaluation of the efficacy of these therapies was not part of the developmental process. Finally, until more recently, the area of autism has not been a topic to which applied developmental researchers have been drawn in great numbers. However, because of the precipitous increase in the diagnosis of autism, public and scientific attention has been drawn to this area, and funding for autism research is becoming more readily available.

As suggested in Chapter 5, with the exception of applied behavior analysis and certain pharmacological treatments, most of the therapies used with children with autism have not been empirically validated. Research is needed to examine not only new interventions but also more popular unvalidated therapies, such as those directed at promoting sensory integration, motor functioning, language and communication, play and cognitive functioning, as well as the more controversial treatments, such as those involving diet alteration, vitamin supplements, homeopathic "medicines", hormone administration, and immunological treatments. From a design perspective, such studies should examine not only the direct effects of the therapy, for example the effect of auditory therapy on auditory processing, but also its indirect effects on other processes, such as attention, emotion regulation, and social interaction. Both short-term and long-term effects, as well as positive and negative effects, should be scrutinized. Finally, experimental designs should be employed that include not only a no treatment comparison group, but also some type of placebo or attention-control condition. Because of the evangelical fervor associated with the use of some treatments, it may well be that their effects are at least in part a function of placebo mechanisms, such as therapist and parent expectations.

Develop curricula for teaching complex social skills

One of the major challenges confronting applied researchers is developing and evaluating programs for helping higher functioning children with autism and Asperger's Syndrome to function more effectively in social situations. They need to be taught not only specific behavioral skills but also to understand the thoughts and actions of others. Rudimentary techniques are starting to evolve, such as those described by Carol Gray (1994), but much more needs to be done before a full developmental curriculum for teaching these skills is in place. As these programs evolve, research should evaluate their efficacy. A number of interesting questions are in need of answers in addition to whether different social skills and aspects of emotional intelligence can be taught. For example, if children with Asperger's Syndrome can be taught to understand better their own minds and emotions, do these cognitive skills generalize to helping them better understand the perspectives and emotional states of others, and do these skills improve their social interactions with and acceptance by their peers who do not have an autism spectrum disorder?

It is interesting to note that the recent push by educators to develop socioemotional training programs for children with autism is consistent with a more general emphasis by educators, researchers, and policy-makers on promoting socioemotional adjustment as a means of supporting young children's readiness to learn in school. Raven (2002) summarizes a variety of research findings that indicate children who are more emotionally adjusted are more likely to experience school success. Conversely, she points out that children with emotional difficulties are more difficult to teach and are more often disliked by teachers and classmates, thereby causing them to lose valuable opportunities to learn from both. Raven (2002) suggests that interventions focusing on socioemotional development should be directed at helping not only increase children's emotional knowledge, but also to control their emotions.

Recommendations to social policy-makers

Focus on early intervention

Traditionally in the United States, a disproportionate share of public resources go toward the development and implementation of educational programs for school-age children. Children in primary and secondary schools have enjoyed more diversified, well-developed, and individualized curricula than preschool children. Considerably less emphasis has been placed on early education and intervention programs for infants, toddlers, and preschoolers, with the exception of programs like Head Start that are directed at children living in poverty. Special education programs that exist for young children with disabilities, such as autism, are often confined to half-day programs which begin when children reach three years of age. Programs, both out-of-home and in-home, for children who are in the birth-to-three age range, while emerging, are even less developed and vary considerably in their availability and quality from state to state.

There are a number of compelling social policy arguments for placing greater emphasis on early intervention programs for toddlers and young children who are diagnosed with autism. First, programs that begin early can prevent some of the delays and symptoms commonly associated with autism from ever developing. Programs that begin later are often confronted with children who have more intractable learning styles and behavior problems; as a consequence these intervention programs have to spend considerable time on remediation and breaking maladaptive habits. Moreover, programs that begin at later ages are not nearly as successful as those initiated at an early age. Second and relatedly, from a cost perspective, because early intervention programs prevent many delays, they reduce the amount of money that would otherwise have to be spent later, on extra teaching personnel and specialized programs. The bottom line is: invest now in early prevention and intervention programs or invest much more, later, in intervention programs that will be less successful. Third, because the diagnosed incidence of autism has risen and is now estimated to be about 1 in 250 children, the need for early services has escalated greatly in recent years; however, the development of new specialized programs for children with autism has not kept pace (Schopler, Yirmiya, Shulman & Marcus, 2001).

Special attention needs to be given by social policy-makers to establishing intensive home-based parent training programs. Early intervention programs for young children with autism need to focus more on exporting speech, physical, occupational, and behavior education programs from the clinic into the home environment. Because these children spend the vast majority of their time at home, this is the environment in which systematic prevention and intervention programs are most needed and will likely have the most impact. In order to put proper programs in place, funding is needed for consultants to go into the home and show parents how to administer the programs, to monitor parents' use of the programs, and to make program adjustments as necessary. In addition, funding is needed to bring in trained personnel to help parents directly implement these programs, which is often intensive and time-consuming. Although early intervention programs need to be a fundamental component of any autism education effort, it is also critical for these types of programs to be continued during elementary school. As Brooks-Gunn (2003) points out, "It is magical thinking to expect that if we intervene in the early years, no further help will be needed by children in the elementary schools years and beyond" (p. 3).

Establish local autism centers

At present, most communities, with the exception of large cities, do not have community centers dedicated exclusively to serving children with autism and their families. Typically, children with autism are referred to agencies that coordinate and provide services to children with mental retardation and other developmental delays. The staff in such agencies often do not have well-developed expertise in the area of autism. Children with autism are often placed in programs that are more generic in nature and do not directly address their developmental needs.

Because of increases in the "diagnosed" incidence of autism, it is imperative that centers be developed in every medium to large population area to work with children with autism and their families. At a minimum, such centers should provide information to parents about autism, its diagnosis and treatment, and family financial assistance, as well as make referrals to appropriate social agencies. Information could be dispensed in a variety of ways, via telephone, over the Internet, through face-to-face contact, and through classes. An autism center could and ideally should provide an array of other services. For example, it could provide early diagnostic services and early intervention programs. Early intervention services should consist of both nursery/preschool programs as well as home programs, all of which are closely coordinated to ensure program consistency. Moreover, consultation services could be provided to assist families in developing specialized programs that are not directly provided by the center or other community agencies. Center programs could also focus on helping families deal with the stress of raising children with autism through the coordination or provision of family counseling services, support groups, and respite care services. In addition, a center could help coordinate home-based programs with school programs once children enter kindergarten. Relatedly, centers could play a key role in helping schools and teachers establish appropriate programs for children with autism through conducting workshops and one-to-one consultations with teachers. Finally, autism centers could have a research and program evaluation component that is developed with the assistance of nearby colleges and universities.

Support public policy research

At present, the types of autism education programs administered in various localities differ considerably across communities and countries of the world. Emphasis needs to be placed on evaluating the success of these diverse programs, using uniform and standardized assessments. The outcomes of programs likely vary depending on their philosophy, structure, place of administration, and hours of programming per week. The results of such program evaluation research could be used to inform future social policy concerning the types of interventions that are recommended and publicly supported. Particular attention needs to be given to evaluating programs for three- to five-year-old children that are home-based, specifically because this type of program is now viewed as one of the most effective options for treating autism.

Feinberg and Vacca (2000) point out that the concept of family-centered care has had a critical influence on the delivery and structure of early intervention programs during the birth-to-three period. However, there is often a schism between the delivery system that occurs during this period and the later three- to-five-year delivery system. When children with autism reach age three, programs become more community-based, and supports for intensive home-based programs often dissipate at a time when many professionals are emphasizing the importance of such interventions. Thus, when children reach age three, families often need to rely on their own initiatives and resources to ensure the continuance of a home program. Some families with more resources, particularly financial, are able to purchase the services of consultants to assist with the development of programs like Applied Behavior Analysis (ABA), whereas others have to rely on whatever community services are available. Most of the families with children with autism fall in the second category. In the majority of these families one of the parents does not work, typically the mother, who stays home to care for their child, thus creating financial problems in families that may already be living at or near the poverty level. The impact of economic pressures on these families is often considerable and includes: increased stress, anxiety problems and depression in family members, family discord, and divorce. In turn, these types of problems likely impact parenting availability and quality, and the efficacy of intervention efforts. For these reasons, special attention needs to be given to the development of supports for low income and other needy families.

Rosman, Yoshikawa, and Knitzer (2002) point out that childhood disability is overrepresented in families in poverty and families on welfare. The reasons for this relationship are likely complex and multidirectional. Having a child with a disability increases demands on family resources, thus producing financial pressures and needs. Conversely, restricted finances and poverty can create circumstances that can adversely influence the developmental trajectory of the child with a disability and, in extreme circumstances, produce a disability. From a public policy perspective, Rosman *et al.* (2002) emphasize that more attention needs to be given to evaluating how special populations, including families who have children with autism, are affected by welfare and antipoverty policies. They suggest that welfare policies likely impact such families in significantly different ways than other families living in poverty. Currently, the impact of policies, which are part of the Individuals with Disabilities Education Act (IDEA) and the Personal Responsibility and Work Opportunity Reconciliation Act (PRWORA), on families of children with autism, needs to be carefully evaluated.

Support basic and applied research

At present, considerable increases in funding for basic and applied research are needed. For example, research is needed:

- to isolate the specific biological causes of autism
- to assist in the development of instruments for assessing autism at its earliest stages

- to evaluate unvalidated medical treatments and educational interventions
- to develop new medical treatments and educational interventions.

Such research is not easy to conduct. One of the major problems confronting investigators who conduct these types of projects is finding an adequate number of participants. The number of participants in most autism research studies ranges from 10 to 30. Most investigators find it difficult to gain access to large samples, particularly if their research occurs outside of a major metropolitan area.

From a design perspective, small sample sizes severely restrict the types of research questions that can be asked, as well as limiting the generalizability of the findings. Moreover, many of the important research topics that currently need to be addressed require a large sample size, such as those that:

1. compare the effectiveness of different treatments

2. examine the characteristics of individuals with autism (e.g., age, severity, and specific configurations of symptoms) who most benefit from a particular treatment

3. evaluate the interrelationship of different developmental processes and symptoms (e.g., sensory, motor, cognitive, and socioemotional).

For this reason, a different approach to conducting research needs to be considered by funding agencies, particularly for projects in the social sciences. Rather than concentrating on the funding of smaller projects by single investigators, more emphasis needs to be placed by granting agencies on supporting collaborative multisite and multi-investigator projects that have access to large numbers of participants and that utilize standardized experimental protocols.

Funding agencies also need to consider more actively supporting applied and basic autism research that involves collaboration between investigators from different medical and social science disciplines. Because of the complex nature of autism and its treatment, support of such collaborative research may help to catalyze the development of more comprehensive theories of autism and new effective interventions, as well as more generally reduce the provincialism and adversarial relationships that exist between disciplines currently working in the area of autism. With increased support for research on autism, it is likely that major advances will be made toward understanding the specific causes of this disorder and in developing effective treatments and educational programs.

References

Bornstein, M. & Lamb, M. (1992) *Development in infancy: An introduction.* New York: McGraw-Hill.

Bristol-Power, M. & Spinella, G. (1999) "Research on screening and diagnosis in autism: A work in progress." *Journal of Autism and Developmental Disorders 29,* 435–437.

Brooks-Gunn, J. (2003) "Do you believe in magic? What can we expect from early childhood intervention programs?" *Social Policy Report: Giving Child and Youth Development Knowledge Away 17,* 1–15.

Feinberg, E. & Vacca, J. (2000) "The drama and trauma of creating policies on autism: Critical issues to consider in the new millennium." *Focus on Autism and Other Developmental Disabilities 15,* 130–137.

Grandin, T. (1995) *Thinking in pictures.* New York: Vintage Books.

Gray, C. (1994) *Comic strip conversations.* Arlington, VA: Future Horizons.

Lovaas, O. I. (2003) *Teaching individuals with developmental delays.* Austin, TX: Pro-Ed.

Mulick, J. & Butler, E. (2002) "Educational advocacy for children with autism." *Behavioral Interventions 17,* 57–74.

Powell, T. H., Hecimovic, A. & Christensen, L. (1992) "Meeting the unique needs of families." In D. E. Berkell (ed) *Autism: Identification, education and treatment* (pp. 187–219). Hillsdale, NJ: Erlbaum.

Raven, C. C. (2002) "Emotions matter: Making the case for the role of young children's emotional development for school readiness." *Social Policy Report 16,* 3–19.

Rosman, E., Yoshikawa, H. & Knitzer, J. (2002) "Toward an understanding of the impact of welfare reform on children with disabilities and their families: Setting a research and policy agenda." *Social Policy Report 16,* 3–15.

Schopler, E., Yirmiya, N., Shulman, C. & Marcus, L. (2001) *The research basis for autism intervention.* New York: Kluwer Academic/Plenum Publishers.

Wehmeyer, M., Agran, M. & Hughes, C. (2000) "A national survey of teachers' promotion of self-determination and student directed learning." *Journal of Special Education 34,* 58–68.

Whitman, T. L. (1987) "Self-instruction, individual differences, and mental retardation." *American Journal of Mental Deficiency 92,* 213–223.

Whitman, T. L. (1990) "Self-regulation and mental retardation." *American Journal on Mental Retardation 94,* 347–362.

Whitman, T. L., Scibak, J. & Reid, D. (1983) *Behavior modification with the severely and profoundly retarded: Research and application.* New York: Academic Press.

Williams, T. (1992) *Thinking in Pictures.* New York: Vintage Books

Subject Index

Author Index

DATE DUE